PANIC

THE STORY OF MODERN
FINANCIAL INSANITY

MICHAEL LEWIS

PENGUIN

PENGUIN BOOKS

Published by the Penguin Group
Penguin Books Ltd, 80 Strand, London WC2R 0RL, England
Penguin Group (USA) Inc., 375 Hudson Street, New York, New York 10014, USA
Penguin Group (Canada), 90 Eglinton Avenue East, Suite 700, Toronto, Ontario, Canada M4P 2Y3
(a division of Pearson Penguin Canada Inc.)
Penguin Ireland, 25 St Stephen's Green, Dublin 2, Ireland
(a division of Penguin Books Ltd)
Penguin Group (Australia), 250 Camberwell Road,
Camberwell, Victoria 3124, Australia (a division of Pearson Australia Group Pty Ltd)
Penguin Books India Pvt Ltd, 11 Community Centre,
Panchsheel Park, New Delhi – 110 017, India
Penguin Group (NZ), 67 Apollo Drive, Rosedale, North Shore 0632, New Zealand
(a division of Pearson New Zealand Ltd)
Penguin Books (South Africa) (Pty) Ltd, 24 Sturdee Avenue, Rosebank,
Johannesburg 2196, South Africa

Penguin Books Ltd, Registered Offices: 80 Strand, London WC2R 0RL, England

www.penguin.com

First published in Great Britain by Penguin Books 2008
First published in the United States of America by W. W. Norton & Company, Inc. 2009
4

Copyright © Michael Lewis and McSweeney's, 2008
Introductions copyright © Michael Lewis, 2008
All rights reserved

The moral right of the author has been asserted

Printed in England by Clays Ltd, St Ives plc

978-0-141-04231-2

www.greenpenguin.co.uk

CONTENTS

INTRODUCTION: INSIDE WALL STREET'S BLACK HOLE   3

PART I
A BRAND-NEW KIND OF CRASH

STEPHEN KOEPP, "Riding the Wild Bull"   14

SCOTT MCMURRAY AND ROBERT L. ROSE, "The Crash of '87: Chicago's 'Shadow Markets' Led Free Fall in a Plunge That Began Right at Opening"   20

FROM THE BRADY COMMISSION REPORT   25

TIM METZ, from *Black Monday: The Catastrophe of October 19, 1987 ... and Beyond*   30

MICHAEL LEWIS, from *Liar's Poker: Rising through the Wreckage on Wall Street*   36

STEPHEN LABATON, "The Lonely Feeling of Small Investors" 43

RICHARD J. MEISLIN, "Yuppies' Last Rites Readied" 47

ERIC J. WEINER, from *What Goes Up* 50

LESTER C. THUROW, "Did the Computer Cause the Crash?" 54

TERRI THOMPSON, "Crash-Proofing the Market; A Lot of Expert Opinions, but Few Results" 57

THE ECONOMIST, "Short Circuits" 62

ROBERT J. SHILLER, "Crash Course: Black Monday's Biggest Lesson— Don't Run Scared" 65

FRANKLIN EDWARDS, from *After the Crash* 71

PART II
FOREIGNERS GONE WILD

REED ABELSON, "Mutual Funds Quarterly Report; The Forecast Looks Brighter for Adventure Travel" 79

THE NEW YORK TIMES, "Thailand Warns Currency Speculators" 82

DAVID HOLLEY, "A Thai Business Wonders, Will It All Crumble?" 83

PAUL KRUGMAN, Reporter Associate Jeremy Kahn, "Saving Asia" 86

INTERVIEW WITH ROB JOHNSON, from *Frontline*'s "The Crash" 96

THE ECONOMIST, "Finance and Economics: A Detour or a Derailment?" 106

MICHAEL LEWIS, "Pulling Russia's Chain" 110

INTERVIEW WITH JEFFREY D. SACHS, from *Frontline*'s "The Crash" 113

MICHAEL LEWIS, "How the Eggheads Cracked" 124

JOSEPH STIGLITZ, "10 Years After the Asian Crisis, We're Not Out of the Woods Yet" 145

KEITH BRADSHER, "Asia's Long Road to Recovery" 148

CHOE SANG-HUN, "Tracking an Online Trend, and a Route to Suicide" 153

PART III

THE NEW NEW PANIC

THE NEW YORK TIMES, "Bigger Netscape Offering" 162

THE NEW YORK TIMES, "Underwriters Raise Offer Price for Netscape
Communication" 163

LAURENCE ZUCKERMAN, "With Internet Cachet, Not Profit, a New Stock is Wall
St.'s Darling" 165

CARRICK MOLLENKAMP AND KAREN LUNDEGAARD, "How Net Fever Sent
Shares of a Firm on 3-Day Joy Ride" 169

MICHAEL LEWIS, "New New Money," from *The New New Thing* 176

REBECCA BUCKMAN AND AARON LUCCHETTI, "Cooling It: Wall Street Firms Try
to Keep Internet Mania from Ending Badly" 186

JACK WILLOUGHBY, "Burning Up" 193

JOHN CASSIDY, from *Dot.con: The Greatest Story Ever Sold* 208

ERICK SCHONFELD, "The High Price of Research: Caveat Investor: Stock and
Research Analysts Covering Dot-Coms Aren't as Independent as You Think" 216

KATHARINE MIESZKOWSKI, "Fumble.com: Internet Companies Threw
Millions into the Air at the Super Bowl. They're Still Pretending They Scored
a Touchdown" 219

MARK GIMEIN, "Meet the Dumbest Dot-Com in the World" 228

JAMES SUROWIECKI, "The Financial Page: How Mountebanks Became
Moguls" 231

JERRY USEEM, "Dot Coms: What Have We Learned?" 234

MICHAEL LEWIS, "In Defense of the Boom" 239

PART IV

THE PEOPLE'S PANIC

DAVE BARRY, "How to Get Rich in Real Estate," from *Dave Barry's
Money Secrets* 264

JOHN HECHINGER, "Shaky Foundation: Rising Home Prices Cast Appraisers in a Harsh Light"   276

JOHN CASSIDY, "The Next Crash"   283

ROBERT JULAVITS, "As Bubble Speculation Rises, Industry Sees Little Fear"   294

PETER S. GOODMAN, "This Is the Sound of a Bubble Bursting"   299

CHRISTOPHER DODD, Opening Statement of Chairman Christopher Dodd— Hearing on "Mortgage Market Turmoil: Causes and Consequences"   308

JAMES SUROWIECKI, "Subprime Homesick Blues"   313

ROGER LOWENSTEIN, "Triple-A Failure"   316

LARRY ROBERTS, from "Rudolph the Red-Nosed Reindeer"   330

KATE KELLY, "Bear CEO's Handling of Crisis Raises Issues"   332

MICHAEL LEWIS, "What Wall Street's CEOs Don't Know Can Kill You"   341

DAVID HENRY AND MATTHEW GOLDSTEIN, "The Bear Flu: How It Spread"   345

MICHAEL LEWIS, "A Wall Street Trader Draws Some Subprime Lessons"   350

PAUL KRUGMAN, "After the Money's Gone"   353

MATTHEW LYNN, "Hedge Funds Come Unstuck on Truth-Twisting, Lies"   356

GREGORY ZUCKERMAN, "Trader Made Billions on Subprime"   359

ACKNOWLEDGMENTS   367

GLOSSARY   369

CONTRIBUTORS' BIOGRAPHIES   379

CREDITS   387

PANIC

Inside Wall Street's
Black Hole

T he striking thing about the seemingly endless collapse of the subprime-mortgage market is how egalitarian it has been. It's nearly impossible to draw a demographic line between the victims and the perps. Millions of ordinary people ignorant of high finance have lost billions of dollars, but so have the biggest names on Wall Street, and both groups made exactly the same bet: that real estate values would never fall. Stan O'Neal, the former CEO of Merrill Lynch, was fired for the same reason the lower-middle-class family in the suburban wasteland between Los Angeles and San Diego may have lost its surprisingly nice home. Both underestimated the likelihood of an unlikely event: a financial panic. In retrospect, the small army of Wall Street traders who lost tens of billions of dollars in subprime-mortgage investments looks as naïve and foolish as the man on the street. But there's another way of viewing this crisis. The man on the street, for the first time, acted on the same foolish principles that have guided the behavior of sophisticated Wall Street traders for the past few decades.

If you had to pick a moment when those principles first appeared a bit shaky, you could do worse than the 1987 stock market crash—the event that opens this anthology of financial writing done immediately before, during, and after the panics that have punctuated, often, the most recent financial era. Black Monday was the first of a breed: a crash that suggested disastrous economic and social consequences but in the end had no serious effects at all. The bursting of the Internet bubble, the Asian currency crisis, the Russian government bond default that triggered the failure of the hedge fund Long-Term Capital Management—all of these extreme events have been compressed into a fantastically short space of financial history. And all seemed, in the heat of the moment, to have the power to change the world as we know it. None of them, it turned out, was that big a deal for the U.S. economy or for ordinary citizens.

But the 1987 crash marked the beginning of something else too—a collapse brought about not by real or even perceived economic problems but by the new complexity of financial markets. A new strategy known as portfolio insurance, invented by a pair of finance professors at the University of California at Berkeley, had been taken ''p in a big way by supposedly savvy investors. Portfolio insurance evolved from the most influential idea on Wall Street, an options-pricing model called Black-Scholes. The model is based on the assumption that a trader can suck all the risk out of the market by taking a short position and increasing that position as the market falls, thus protecting against losses, no matter how steep. Nearly every employee stock-ownership plan uses Black-Scholes as its guiding principle. A pension-fund manager sitting on billions of U.S. equities and fearful of a crash needn't call a Wall Street broker and buy a put option—an option to sell at a set price, limiting potential losses—on the S&P 500. Managers can create put options for themselves, cheaply, by selling short the S&P as it falls, and thus, in theory, be free of all market risk.*

Good theory. The glitch was discovered only after the fact: When a market is crashing and no one is willing to buy, it's impossible to sell short. If too many investors are trying to unload stocks as a market falls, they create the very disaster they are seeking to avoid. Their desire to

---

* Some of Wall Street's private language is necessary and useful, but a lot of it seems designed to mystify outsiders. For the reader unfamiliar with the language there is a glossary at the end of the book.

sell drives the market lower, triggering an even greater desire to sell and, ultimately, sending the market into a bottomless free fall. That's what happened on October 19, 1987, when the sweet logic of Black-Scholes was shown to be irrelevant in the real world of crashes and panics. Even the biggest portfolio insurance firm, Leland O'Brien Rubinstein Associates (cofounded and run by the same finance professors who invented portfolio insurance), tried to sell as the market crashed and couldn't.

Oddly, this failure of financial theory didn't lead Wall Street to question Black-Scholes in general. "If you try to attack it," says one longtime trader of abstruse financial options, "you're making a case for your own unintelligence." The math was too advanced, the theorists too smart; the debate, for anyone without a degree in mathematics, was bound to end badly. But after the crash of 1987, individual traders at big Wall Street firms who sold financial disaster insurance must have smelled a rat. Across markets—in stocks, currencies, bonds—the price of insuring yourself against financial disaster rose. This rise in prices and the break with Black-Scholes reflected two new beliefs: one, that huge price jumps were more probable and likely to be more extreme than the Black-Scholes model assumed; and two, that you can't manufacture an option on the stock market by selling and buying the market itself, because that market will never allow it. When you most need to sell—or to buy—is exactly when everyone else is selling or buying, in effect canceling out any advantage you once might have had.

"No one believes the original assumptions anymore," says John Seo, who comanages Fermat Capital, a $2 billion-plus hedge fund that invests in catastrophe bonds—essentially bonds with put options that are triggered by such natural catastrophes as hurricanes and earthquakes. "It's hard to believe that anyone—yes, including me—ever believed it. It's like trying to replicate a fire-insurance policy by dynamically increasing or decreasing your coverage as fire conditions wax and wane. One day, bam, your house is on fire, and you call for more coverage?"

This is interesting: The very theory underlying all insurance against financial panic falls apart in the face of an actual panic. A few smart traders may have abandoned the theory, but the market itself hasn't; in fact, its influence has mushroomed in the most fantastic ways. At the end of 2006, according to the Bank for International Settlements, there was $415 trillion in derivatives—that is, $415 trillion in securities for which there is no completely satisfactory pricing model. Added to this are trillions more in exchange-traded options, employee stock options, mortgage bonds, and God knows what else—most of which, presumably, are still priced using some version of Black-Scholes. Investors need to believe that there's a rational price for what they buy, even if it requires a leap of faith. "The model created markets," Seo says. "Markets follows models. So these markets spring up, and the people in them figure out that, at least for some of it, Black-Scholes doesn't work. For certain kinds of risk—the risk of rare, extreme events—the model is not just wrong. It's very wrong. But the only reason these markets sprang up in the first place was the supposition that Black-Scholes could price these things fairly."

Black-Scholes didn't work; trillions of dollars' worth of securities may have been priced without regard to the possibility of crashes and panics. But until very recently, no one has bitched and moaned about this problem too loudly. Lay folk might harbor private misgivings about the clergy, but as lay folk, they are reluctant to express them. Now, however, as the subprime market unravels, a revolt against the church seems to be taking shape.

One of the revolt's leaders is Nassim Nicholas Taleb, the best-selling author of *The Black Swan* and *Fooled by Randomness* and a former trader of currency options for a big French bank. Taleb can precisely date the origin of his own personal gripe with Black-Scholes: September 22, 1985. On that day, central bankers from Japan, France, Germany, Britain, and the United States announced their intention to torpedo the U.S. dollar—to reduce its value in relation to the other countries' currencies. Every day, Taleb received a list of his trading positions from his firm, and a matrix telling him how much money he stood to make or lose, given various currency fluctuations. That September 22, when the central bankers announced their plan to lower the dollar's value, he made money but didn't know it. "I didn't know what my position was," he says, "because the movement was outside the matrix they'd given me." The French bank's risk-analysis program assumed that a currency crash of this magnitude would occur once in several million years and therefore wasn't worth considering.

Taleb made a killing that day, but it wasn't thanks to a grand plan and it wasn't happy money. "People in dark suits started coming from Paris," he says. "They said that the only way I could have made that much was to have taken far too much risk." But he hadn't. They had simply failed to account for the true nature of risk in financial markets. "Then I started looking at the history of markets," he says. "And I saw that these sorts of things happened all the time." Taleb became obsessed with the way prices in the options market, based on the famous Black-Scholes model, underestimated the risk of extreme and rare events. He set up trading to profit from events by buying up disaster insurance that would, according to Black-Scholes, be considered overpriced. When October 19, 1987, arrived, he was prepared. "Ninety-seven percent of all the returns I ever made as a trader, I made on that day," he says.

In the past two years, Taleb has coauthored a pair of papers that have appeared in the sort of academic journals that originally published the Black-Scholes model. He and his coauthor attack the model head-on in its own language (math), and as much as call for a retraction of the Nobel Prize awarded to Myron Scholes and Robert Merton for their work in creating the model. "This is what I'm saying to Merton and Scholes," Taleb says. "You guys are just parasites. You're not bringing anything useful to the market. You are lecturing birds on how to fly. You're watching them fly. And then you're taking credit for it."

He's saying more than that, actually. He's saying that the academics, in lecturing the birds, have made flying more difficult. Like John Seo—like a lot of traders who understand both the math of Black-Scholes and the reality of the marketplace—Taleb believes that the model has a pernicious effect: By leading investors to think they understand complicated financial risk when they actually do not, and by mispricing that risk, Black-Scholes encourages them to take more chances than they rationally should. In a post–Black-Scholes world, these companies, more than anyone else, would be compelled to reduce their exposure to financial catastrophe and to raise the prices at which they sell financial insurance to others. Indeed, if no one has made too much of a stink about mispriced risk until now, it may be because the chief victims have been the big Wall Street firms that typically wind up owning that risk. "The main reason there isn't a fundamental public outcry about Black-Scholes," says Seo, "is that the main losers from its mispricing are broker-dealers." The crashes happened, yet only Wall Street traders—rather than living and breathing human beings with whom the world could empathize—suffered.

The collapse of the subprime-mortgage bond market is different from the general run of modern financial panics in this respect: It involves millions of blissfully oblivious people who have never heard of the Black-Scholes options-pricing models. Nevertheless, it was Black-Scholes that gave them—and the rest of the financial system—the excuse to risk the roof over their head. They were followed by the mortgage brokers who lent them money and the banks that funded the brokers. Black-Scholes is no longer just a model; it's a climate of opinion about financial risk. It wasn't only big Wall Street firms but a lot of small real estate speculators—otherwise known as homeowners—who, in effect, sold put options too cheaply against the risk of extreme, rare events. That many of these people literally live inside the investment that they've speculated on sharpens the pain but fails to drive home the point. Financial panics have become almost commonplace; events that are meant to occur once in a millennium now seem to occur every few years. Could this be because the financial system was built on an idea that badly underestimates the risk of catastrophes—and so conspires with human nature to create them?

But I get ahead of myself, and the story this anthology seeks to tell. Let's go back and begin at the beginning.

PART I

A BRAND-NEW KIND

OF CRASH

There's a simple idea behind this anthology: to re-create the more recent financial panics, in an attempt to show how financial markets now operate. Since the early 1980s, when financial markets embraced the new complexity, there's been an extraordinary amount of turmoil, invisible to all but the handful of dealers in the relevant markets. This book describes only the most obvious panics, the ones covered as they happened in the newspapers, and analyzed ad nauseam after the fact. Each section opens with a piece or two that captures the feeling in the air immediately before things went wrong. It then moves on to the many attempts to come to grips with the strange and unexpected seeming disaster that just occurred. After the 1987 stock market crash the U.S. government convened a commission to produce a report, but there were a lot of other less formal attempts that, taken together, describe something new: the seemingly causeless panic.

To get at the nature of this first of the new panics, and the others that follow, this anthology draws on the accounts of the moment, along with the slew of literature, magazine pieces, books, economic papers, government reports—that attempts to explain what newspapers can only describe. While the daily journalists tend to have the events to themselves, these postmortems are all-you-can-eat buffets to which the guests are allowed to bring not only their wisdom but their neuroses. The author Eric Weiner, whose work follows, had the bright idea, after the crash of 1987, of calling up all the most important financial people and asking them what they were thinking and doing before it. So many were just waiting for a crash! (Then why didn't they get rich?) On the other hand, the economist Franklin Edwards, in his introduction to a nearly 3,000-page compendium of economic papers on the causes of the crash, admits, "the bottom line is that no one knows."

Reading the accounts of the day, and the days after the panics, you realize that there are two financial markets. There's the real-time Wall Street, where the risk takers are anxious and greedy and fearful and devious, and people with the most sensational psychological disorders that render them unsuited for ordinary social life get rich. Then there's the other, theoretical after-the-fact Wall Street, in which all these odd human beings, and the chaotic events they create, are made to seem more or less rational and easily explainable. Never is this contrast more clear than during, and immediately after, a panic. Just before a panic all is well—usually more than well. Then the panic strikes, chaos ensues, and a dramatic status upheaval commences. People who were on top of the financial order plummet to the bottom. People whose opinion was most valued are now ridiculed. Others who were on the sidelines race onto the field of play. The guy out in the wilderness who had been saying for the past four years that the good times were an illusion and a sham is wheeled in to take a bow and then hustled off stage, so that everyone else can regroup, and the whole process can start over again.

And so it does, but with enough of the details changed that, up close, the new madness looks entirely different from any madness that has ever before happened. The crash of October 1987 is a case in point: the world's first seemingly traumatic financial event without obvious economic causes or consequences. It took a while even for putative crash experts to get their minds around the idea. Panic historian and economist John Kenneth Galbraith said he was just hoping the ensuing economic collapse wouldn't prove as painful as the Great Depression. A lot of people assumed something big had changed: the end of capitalism, or, at the very least, the death of the yuppie. The day after the crash—to take an example from these pages—Wall Street analyst turned sociologist Eliot Janeway told Richard Meislin of the *New York Times* that "these yuppies are unprepared and unconditioned" for the hard times to come. But as it turned out, those yuppies were so well prepared that they survived to create many more crashes.

The crash of 1987 marks the beginning of the Age of Financial Unreason, when panic became just another, quotidian aspect of financial life. At the time, to a lot of people, it felt like the end of something. In retrospect it appears to be more of a beginning.

And it had, in the end, consequences. For instance, it caused a shift, across financial markets, in the price of the crash insurance sold by the more sophisticated Wall Street traders. It also caused, I believe, a shift in the commentary in and around financial markets. Comb the financial press before the crash and you find the sort of innocent accounts that you never find again, at least in American newspapers. One of the leading stock gurus of that time, for instance, was a fellow named Robert Prechter, whose ability to see the future was explored, seriously, in a number of news reports. (Interestingly, the author of the best of these didn't want to see his work reprinted.) I can still remember, as a young man on a trading desk, being told that in order to understand the stock market I had first to understand something called Elliott Wave Theory. Then the stock market crashed, Robert Prechter failed to predict it, and I was allowed to go on ignoring wave theory. Other wave theorists later swore they had used their waves to predict the crash but somehow, after October 19, 1987, you didn't hear as much about Eliott Waves as you did before it. But every moment has its wave theory, just as every wave theory seems to have its moment.

Readers will notice another thing these panics share: the characters. The 1987 crash kicked off Alan Greenspan's tenure as chairman of the Federal Reserve, for instance, and the subprime-mortgage market collapse, with which this anthology ends, ended it. The 1987 crash also marked the debut of several other people, who are never very far away from market turmoil of the next two decades. One is the mania scholar Robert Schiller—whose warnings and autopsies appear in this collection. Another is John Meriwether, the manager of traders who specialize in abstruse quantitative strategies. My former boss has exhibited an amazing ability to make and lose money, and to be present on the scene of panics, staring with the crash of 1987.

Finally, the 1987 stock market crash was also my own introduction to the bizarre turmoil of modern financial markets. When the market went into its free fall I was still working on Wall Street, and thinking of leaving to write a book about the place. I was already taking notes. I spent most of October 19, 1987, standing beside one of Wall Street's biggest stock trading businesses, watching it come unglued. I included a description of that moment in my first book, and I also include one here. But crashes and panics make for interesting stories and, once I'd become a full-time journalist, I found myself pulled back to write about them. I've included one of these in each section, for old times' sake. It's my hope that the reader finds them as interesting as I have found the rest of this collection.

Riding the Wild Bull

STEPHEN KOEPP

Time, *July 27, 1987*

K atherine Bonner, stock-market player, is not afraid of those brainy, brawny institutional investors who routinely turn Wall Street upside down with their 100,000-share transactions. Nor is she intimidated by those high-tech program traders who can send the Dow Jones averages reeling with their computer-powered stampedes. In fact, Bonner is not only making what she modestly calls a "good living" in the market but is earning enough to help out her grandchildren and great-grandchildren too. A highly active investor, Bonner, an 80-year-old Houstonian, has built up a handsome portfolio by studying financial news assiduously, visiting her discount broker every morning and afternoon to keep tabs on the market and making her picks ahead of the professional pack. "I am not all that smart, I've just got some common sense," says Bonner, a former artist and pharmacist. Institutional investors take note: right now Bonner likes oil and pharmaceutical stocks.

Bonner is among millions of individual Americans who are making a private killing in the wild bull market of the 1980s, which will turn five years old on Aug. 13. They have come back with growing confidence to the stock market they fled during the bearish 1970s. "The longer the bull market goes on, the more believers there are," says Charles Neuhaus, a broker for Houston's Underwood, Neuhaus. During the first half of this decade, the number of Americans who own shares in individual companies or stock-market mutual funds increased from 30.2 million to more than 47 million, according to a study by the New York Stock Exchange. While half those shareholders own stock in only one company or fund, the other 23 million or so include many investors who have turned stock picking into a serious pursuit.

These individuals are reaping lucrative profits during an era in which the big institutional players would seem to have all the advantages: research, resources and speed. While individuals control nearly two-thirds of all stocks, or about $2 trillion worth, institutional investors turn over the remaining third at such a rapid pace that they account for 80% of all stock transactions. Private investors are much more likely to sit tight with chosen stocks. But the more active individuals are finding their own tools and tricks. They now cut the cost of commissions by ordering through discount brokers, follow obscure companies through a growing number of newsletters, keep their holdings in convenient cash-management accounts and even get stock quotations through hand-held radio receivers.

The biggest boon, however, is the seemingly relentless bullishness of the market. The remarkable run of the Dow Jones industrial average began in August 1982 at the lowly level of 776.92. The Dow, having more than tripled in value since then, is now so high that investors sometimes get a kind of queasy altitude sickness that requires a retreat. That is what happened this spring, when a sizable sell-off sent the Dow tumbling 190 points from a record 2405.54 on April 6 to a low of 2215.87 on May 20. But then the Dow began a summer surge to new heights. Last Friday the Dow closed over 2500 for the first time ever, ending the day at 2510.04, up 54.05 points for the week. Since the beginning of the year the Dow has risen fully 614.09 points, or more than 30%, a bounteous half-year return by any standard. One reason for the latest rally is a huge improvement in company profits, thanks to corporate streamlining and a declining U.S. dollar, which has boosted export sales.

Yet the volatility of the market is inspiring a mixture of excitement and fear, since the Dow's stratospheric level gives it a tendency to sweep

up and down from time to time by 50 points or more a day. When individuals reap an overnight windfall, they can become manic and even a
little careless about where to put the money next. "Clients are calling
about speculative stocks that they've heard about at cocktail parties over
the weekend. I'm worried about this," says Jerry Tisserand, a broker for
Thomson McKinnon Securities at a branch in Evansville, Ind. At the
same time, many investors realize that a bear market could hit at any
moment. Some become spooked by sudden downdrafts and sell too
soon. "It's hard to keep people in the volatile blue chips. They're getting
whipsawed," says Richard Geier, a broker for Reynolds DeWitt Securities
in Cincinnati.

The disconcerting gyrations of the mainstream stocks, which are heavily played by institutional investors, have inspired many private investors
to march to a different ticker. They prefer to find lesser-known companies whose stocks are undervalued or potential earnings overlooked.
But to arrive at a hot property before Wall Street professionals is a feat
that requires lots of homework, constant vigilance and a cool head. Says
Investor Jeffrey Solomon, a hardware-sales representative based in Great
Neck, N.Y., who carries a hand-held stock monitor at all times and studies charts and newsletters every night: "The astute investor can beat
money managers. They are human. They panic, become euphoric or get
emotional just like all of us." At 32, Solomon has accumulated a five-
figure profit pile.

Nearly every investor develops a personal method or specialty. Investor Tedd Determan of Chicago, who puts most of his $1.4 million port-
folio into small, fast-growing stocks, often invests in companies whose
products he appreciates as a consumer. A confessed "popcorn freak," he
savored the brand made by Golden Valley Microwave Foods, and so he
bought the company's stock. It has gone up nearly 70% in value during
the past year. In another instance, Determan was so impressed with the
service at Jiffy Lube International, a franchised auto-service chain, that
he bought 3,000 shares at 9 1/2. Current price: 15 5/8.

Determan studies annual reports and other documents before taking
the plunge, but if he has any remaining questions, he simply calls the
company president. That opportunity, he points out, is one of the lesser-
noted benefits of investing in small ventures. When he became concerned
about an earnings downturn at Innovative Software, Determan called the

chief financial officer there, who reassured the investor that the profit slump was "just a glitch." So Determan held on to the stock, which proceeded to zoom from about 10 last November to 22 now, even after a 3-for-2 split.

In line with Determan's principle, many private investors like to put their money into ventures they understand or industries in which they have unusual chances to spot a breakthrough product. Says Hugo Quackenbush, senior vice president of the Charles Schwab discount-brokerage firm: "Airline pilots, for example, may know some kind of gadget that is being made by a company that may escape the attention of the big guys on Wall Street."

Some investors succeed by shunning glamour. Russell Faucett, a Los Angeles financial adviser who spends about half his time managing his personal portfolio, looks for solid, small Rust Belt companies with lackluster earnings and low profiles. Says he: "Well, my stocks are kind of boring actually, and of course they are of no interest to the big investment firms, because the brokers can't tell a good story about them to their clients."

The stock-picking bug has even bitten people who would ordinarily take no pleasure in studying price-earnings ratios and balance sheets. "It's so simple, it's insane. If you do this carefully, it's like picking money off trees," declares Michael Petryni, a Los Angeles screenwriter, sounding more like a TV pitchman. But behind the scenes, Petryni spends at least two hours a day studying financial papers like *Investor's Daily* and following stock quotes using the same computer terminal on which he writes his scripts.

Many investors are surprisingly daring at an early stage. Fairfax Randall, a Houston homemaker and sometime interior decorator, boosted her portfolio from $250,000 to $2 million in just three years by leveraging, or borrowing money to increase her stock-market wagers. But she ventured naively into risky stock options and lost $1.5 million during the 1981–82 recession. Then, through cautious decisions and hard work, she built her portfolio back to $2 million. Says she: "The stock market is my absolute love. I don't buy pretty clothes, and I never spend much money on myself. I put it all in the market."

Not everyone is willing to risk such setbacks, especially if the savings in question are earmarked for retirement or education. J. H. Freeman, a

70-year-old former financial manager of a Houston law firm, is primarily interested in steady-dividend income rather than a zooming but precarious stock price. Thus he prefers companies with reliable profits, like power utilities. Though his taste is conservative, Freeman has doubled the value of his portfolio in five years.

For all the variety of their methods, private investors have many common guidelines. For example, many small investors avoid buying individual foreign stocks, since they may have trouble getting timely information about the securities. Small-time investors generally shun stock options, futures and other risky instruments unless they have carefully constructed a way to use them as a hedge against losses in their common-stock portfolio. Finally, they frequently establish predetermined selling points at which they will dump a stock to cut their losses or capture their gains. Says Melissa Lamb, 28, a Manhattan real-estate broker who is learning the hard way: "I have picked some good ones, but I just wait and wait in the hope of a bigger profit, until all the profit evaporates."

The desire of so many investors to make their own decisions has become a boon for discount stock brokerages. These firms charge smaller commissions than full-service investment firms because, unlike the traditional houses, the discounters provide no advice or portfolio management. For example, on a sale of 100 shares of a $60 stock, a discounter's commission would be about $50, in contrast to nearly $100 at a full-service brokerage. As a result, the percentage of retail stock transactions placed with discounters has increased from 8% in 1982 to an estimated 22% this year. Most successful is San Francisco–based Charles Schwab, the largest U.S. discounter, whose revenues have gone up from $42.7 million in 1981 to $308.3 million in 1986. Schwab notes that the typical size of the accounts held by its 1.5 million customers is between $50,000 and $100,000.

Both discounters and full-service brokerages have produced a wealth of tools to help individual investors keep up with the technical capabilities of the professionals. Schwab sells its customers a personal-computer program called The Equalizer (price: $99.95), which enables an investor to keep track of a portfolio, place an order and call up stock-price quotes, research reports and financial news. Telemet America, one of the several firms offering hand-held devices for monitoring stock quotes, now serves 16 cities and 10,000 customers, 90% of whom are private investors.

For those who want to play the market but lack the time or inclination to gamble on specific stocks, mutual funds have been the answer. Stock funds grew by $41.7 billion during 1986, a 33.4% increase, to reach total assets of $166.4 billion. But the number of stock funds, now in the hundreds, has mushroomed so fast that selecting one can be almost as tricky as picking individual issues. Even so, it is hard to go wrong in such a strong bull market. During the first half of the year, the average stock fund rose some 22%.

All told, the growth of individual participation in the market should come as a welcome trend for corporate America. The tendency of private investors to put their money on the line for relatively long periods of time is a desirable counterweight to the fickleness of Wall Street money managers, whose what-have-you-done-for-me-lately attitude has long bedeviled corporate managers. Average investors tend to be more patient in waiting for results. Fortunately, their patience is not exactly being put to a test these days.

The Crash of '87: Chicago's "Shadow Markets" Led Free Fall in a Plunge That Began Right at Opening

SCOTT MCMURRAY AND ROBERT L. ROSE

The Wall Street Journal, *October 20, 1987*

T he panic began here.

An eerie quiet settled over the teeming stock-index futures pit at the Chicago Mercantile Exchange early yesterday as traders watched the beginning of the worst washout in stock-market history.

With trading delayed in many major New York Stock Exchange issues because of order imbalances, Chicago's controversial "shadow markets"— the highly leveraged, liquid futures on the Standard & Poor's 500 stock index—were, for just a few minutes, the leading indicator for the Western world's equity markets.

And the stock-index markets were leading the way down—fast. In a nightmarish fulfillment of some traders' and academicians' worst fears, the five-year-old index futures for the first time plunged into a panicky, unlimited free fall, fostering a sense of crisis throughout U.S. capital markets.

The day posed an unprecedented test for the nation's financial futures markets. Many traders long have wondered how index futures and options would function if stocks were in a free fall, and yesterday these new markets clearly hit their limits. First, stock-index futures speeded stock price declines, nearly quintupling previous record one-day drops. Then, as buyers fled the market in alarm, trading nearly dried up, temporarily preventing the markets from functioning as a hedging mechanism—their principal reason for existence.

The situation was "unique in the history of the futures markets," said Thomas Russo, a New York futures and securities lawyer. "This is a day we will long remember."

Within seconds of the open, S&P 500 stock-index futures prices sank 18 points—surpassing the nerve-racking record declines scored in an entire day on Friday. Salomon Brothers Inc. began unloading contracts at an unheard-of rate of 1,000 at a time, dumping more than $600 million in stock-index futures in the first hour of trading alone, one pit trader estimated. Salomon officials couldn't be reached for comment on the estimate.

With no limits on futures prices and regulators in disagreement over the advisability of a trading halt, there was nothing to stop the 80-point free fall in the S&P 500 that ensued.

"Everybody's awe-struck," said John Gustafson, a futures analyst with Discount Corp. of New York Futures, who stood just a few feet off the S&P pit. In the offices of the city's three major futures and options exchanges, officials began preparing to make more than a record $2 billion in intraday margin calls. Up the street at the Chicago Board Options Exchange, a market maker wept softly in the men's room.

Gradually, of course, the focus of attention shifted yesterday from the futures markets to the Big Board as activity in major issues there gathered momentum. By midday, the plunge in the Dow Jones Industrial Average nearly matched the tumble in futures, focusing attention again on the stock market itself.

But by the close, the futures markets were signaling the possibility of further carnage today. S&P 500 futures for December settlement dropped nearly 30%, or 80.75 points, outstripping the 23% drop in the Dow Jones Industrial Average. The futures also closed at more than a 20-point discount to the index itself, a bearish signal. Unless that relationship changes radically when trading begins today, arbitrage traders are likely to buy the relatively cheap futures and sell the stocks in the index, further depressing the stock market.

"This is just what many people had feared," said Merton Miller, a professor of finance at the University of Chicago. Like a ride on a frighteningly efficient financial roller coaster, the breakneck pace of futures trading can foster panic and eliminate time for buyers to assess the situation and enter the market.

"It's somewhat analogous to a bank run," Mr. Miller added. "Everybody thinks, 'If only I can get first in the queue, I'll be all right.' Once it starts, it builds on you."

Traders applauded the futures markets for sustaining yesterday's wild price moves and staying open throughout the day, despite trading delays in stocks and options. Officials of Chicago's big exchanges said late yesterday that all their members had met margin calls so far.

Index futures are contracts for future delivery of cash based on the value of such broad market indicators as the S&P 500 stock index. Traders use them to hedge against risk on their stock portfolios, as well as to speculate on the future direction of the stock market as a whole.

Nevertheless, the wild action raised anew some longstanding issues. Analysts, traders and academicians have long fretted about the price-battering potential of portfolio insurers, big institutional investors who use a hedging technique that requires them to keep selling futures the more the stock market falls. Portfolio insurers did indeed help touch off yesterday's steep declines, but their initial wave of selling soon expanded to an avalanche that encompassed all kinds of traders, from arbitragers to mutual funds.

Also, many traders wished for even a brief respite from yesterday's frenzied selling. Unlike other futures markets, stock-index futures trade without price limits. In the past, such limits have tended to halt price moves, at least temporarily, and slow major trends. In a silver-market crisis in 1979, for instance, price limits slowed extreme volatility and stretched major market trends over a period of months.

In other instances, regulators have temporarily halted futures trading to permit government officials and traders to adjust to sudden changes in the market outlook. When President Jimmy Carter stopped $2 billion in grain shipments to the Soviet Union in 1980, for instance, the Commodity Futures Trading Commission suspended grain futures trading for two days while the government indemnified grain exporters and made other price-propping moves.

But in stock-index futures, regulators are sharply divided over whether trading halts should be imposed. Securities and Exchange Commission Chairman David Ruder has advocated trading halts as a response to chaotic trading. But the current acting chairman of the CFTC, Kalo A. Hineman, has said he opposes such moves.

Yesterday, as institutions and investors scrambled to lay off at least some of their risk in futures, trading in the index markets virtually dried up at several points, threatening a liquidity crisis on the Merc's trading floor. At mid-morning, the S&P prices were moving up two points, then back down, in less than a minute, as sellers scrambled to fill orders at any price they could get.

On the Chicago Board Options Exchange, which offers trading in an option on the S&P 100 stock index, a rotational system for opening trading kept the market orderly. "Operationally, we're doing great," said CBOE President Charles Henry. But delays of as much as 45 minutes in filling orders were common. "Bache, Merrill and Shearson have orders like this," a CBOE floor official told CBOE executives, holding up his two hands with a six-inch gap in between.

The liquidity squeeze also posed an extraordinary threat to the clearinghouses on the major exchanges, which guarantees futures trades. Although the Chicago Merc has raised various stock-index margin requirements recently, yesterday's 20-point move in S&P 500 futures at the open alone would have effectively wiped out, on paper, the minimum $10,000-per-contract margin deposit the exchange demands of speculators.

The Merc demanded additional margin deposits of $1.6 billion from its 92 clearing members yesterday, exchange officials said. A Chicago Merc official said total margin deposits against positions in S&P 500 are about $2 billion. Exchange officials also denied rumors that any Merc clearing members were in financial trouble as a result of yesterday's washout. The Merc had a special order-matching session scheduled for midnight last night.

An official of Board of Trade Clearing Corp., which clears trades for the Chicago Board of Trade, said the exchange had issued three intraday margin calls totaling about $400 million yesterday. Late yesterday, the Board of Trade raised initial margins for speculators in its Major Market Index futures.

Separately, Options Clearing Corp., the Chicago organization that clears options trades for U.S. securities exchanges, said it had made intraday margin calls totaling $180 million early yesterday to about two-thirds of its 190 member firms.

Nevertheless, the sell-off sparked a fire sale on exchange seats as traders scrambled to cover their losses. The price on an index- and option-trading membership on the Chicago Merc tumbled 19% to $118,000 yesterday, with seven seats changing hands and eight more offered for lease. Five full Chicago Board of Trade memberships were sold, with the price tumbling to $375,000 from the previous sale at $530,000 last Oct. 6, then recovering late in the day to $400,000.

And the streets of Chicago were uncharacteristically quiet after the market closed. On LaSalle Street in the heart of the city's financial district, a lighted brokerage sign that usually radiates the Dow Jones Industrial Average blinked incomprehensibly when the drop passed the two-digit mark, then simply flashed zero.

From the
Brady Commission Report

At 8:05 A.M. New York time, sources reported that U.S. forces had responded to Friday's attack by the Iranians on a U.S.-flagged Kuwaiti tanker by bombing Iranian oil platforms in the Persian Gulf. Though a flight by investors to dollar securities in the wake of Gulf tensions might have been expected, fears of the demise of the Louvre currency accord proved stronger, causing the dollar to weaken substantially as foreign currency trading began in New York. The Treasury bond market opened with yields higher—the 30-year bond rose to 10.50 percent—and orders to sell shares of stock flooded the floor of the New York Stock Exchange.

By 9 A.M., large sell-order imbalances were reported on the New York Stock Exchange. Prior to 9:30 A.M., there was approximately $500 million, or 14 million shares, waiting to be sold through the direct order turnaround system, or D.O.T. Between 9:30 A.M. and 10 A.M., another $475 million to sell was loaded into D.O.T. This represented approximately 25 percent of the first half-hour's record volume of 51 million shares. Over the next hour, new orders to sell another $1.1 billion of shares were entered into D.O.T. This massive selling pressure was accumulated while many major stocks remained closed for trading due to the order imbalances.

In Chicago, the Major Market Index opened at a price of 430, dropping 11 points, or 2.5 percent, from Friday afternoon's weak close. On the Chicago Mercantile Exchange, the portfolio insurers who had fallen behind in their selling programs on Friday reacted quickly, selling in excess of 3,000 contracts in the first half hour. This activity was 18 percent of the total volume traded in the time period and 24 percent of the nonlocal volume.

9:45 A.M., the Dow Jones industrial average was off 21 points. Because most of the D.J.I.A. stocks did not open on time, the average was based in part on Friday's closing prices. Selling pressure was intense from mutual funds and index-arbitrage-trading-oriented investors. One mutual fund complex sold $500 million in the first half-hour, representing 25 percent of the volume. At least 6.2 million shares, or 12 percent of total volume, were sold by index arbitragers in the first half-hour.

At this point on Monday, the apparent discount between the contract and the index varied between 10 and 17 points. For the day, a premium of 1 point would have represented fair value. The size of the discount, or premium, had become one of the most widely followed indicators of the direction of the stock market, even by investors who do not use the futures exchanges as a trading vehicle. The potential arbitrage profits which could be earned by selling the index and simultaneously buying the contract amounted to an annualized return of 47 percent at these price levels.

Ironically, the large discount on Monday morning was illusory. Since many of the stocks in the index had not yet opened, the index was calculated from the Friday closing prices. Although the index arbitragers clearly knew that many stocks had not yet opened, they nevertheless believed that a large discount existed. This belief led the index arbitragers to conclude that the market was headed much lower, and instead of simultaneously selling the index and buying the contract, many merely sold the index and waited to buy what they believed would be a cheaper contract. Aside from encouraging the index arbitragers to hold back on buying the futures half of the arbitrages, the apparent discount also discouraged buyers of stock from entering what appeared to be a relatively overpriced, weak stock market.

By 10:30 A.M., the D.J.I.A. was down 104 points. In the next half-hour, it dropped another 104 points, to 2,080. Volume at 11 A.M. had already reached 154 million shares, a record pace. At 10:33 A.M., a portfolio insurer with the ability to sell either stock or futures for its clients sold the first of thirteen $100 million baskets of stock it would unload that day. This institution sold stock rather than futures because the size of the discount in the futures market made selling stocks seem relatively more attractive. This alternative of selling stock was not available to most of the other larger portfolio insurers because they do not have the authority to sell clients' stocks. Therefore, they continued to sell futures throughout the morning and early afternoon at tremendous discounts to the prices in the stock market.

By approximately 11 A.M., most stocks had finally opened sharply lower on the New York Stock Exchange and the index arbitragers who had not yet completed their arbitrage by buying futures suddenly realized that the spread between the contract and the index was virtually nonexistent. Caught in a short squeeze, they rushed into the market to buy the contract, and it rallied from 254 at 10:50 A.M. to 265.5 at 11:40 A.M. During this period, portfolio-insurance selling temporarily abated, and short coverings by one large foreign investor—which bought $218 million in futures—caused the contract to trade at a premium to the index for the only time of the day. Between 11 A.M. and 11:40 A.M., index arbitragers bought approximately $110 million of stocks while selling futures. Non-trading-oriented investors, believing that the market might have reached a support level, also began to purchase stocks.

The market, however, began a dramatic reversal at 11:40 A.M., with the contract plunging from 265.5 to 251.5 by 12:40 P.M., while the D.J.I.A. fell from 2,140 at 11:46 A.M. to 2,053 at 12:55 P.M., as 36 million shares, or $1.3 billion, were routed through the D.O.T. system. The price declines were caused by the lack of significant buyers and the resumption of large selling by the portfolio-insurance providers. Between 11:30 A.M. and 1:30 P.M., the portfolio insurers sold over 10,000 futures contracts, the equivalent of $1.3 billion. These contracts amounted to 28 percent of the total futures volume traded and 41 percent of public volume. Index arbitragers during this period sold approximately $350 million in stock. More significantly, straight program selling of stocks totaled $560 million, of which one portfolio insurer alone sold $400 million of stock.

1:09 P.M., the Dow Jones news wire reported that the chairman of the Securities and Exchange commission said that he had not discussed halting trading on the N.Y.S.E. with the exchange or President Reagan, although "anything is possible." He continued, ". . . there is some point, and I don't know what that point is, that I would be interested in talking to the N.Y.S.E. about a temporary, very temporary halt in trading." Between 1:15 P.M. and 2:05 P.M., the contract plunged from 255 to 227; the index fell from 258 to 246, and the D.J.I.A. dropped from 2,081 to 1,969, breaking through the 2,000 level for the first time since Jan. 7, 1987.

By 1:25 P.M., the Dow Jones news wire quoted the S.E.C. as stating that it was not discussing closing the stock markets. However, the uncertainty created by the possible inability to sell may have exacerbated the dramatic selling pressure.

In fact, between 1:30 P.M. and 2:00 P.M., one portfolio insurer sold 1,762 contracts worth $200 million, which represented 20 percent of the total volume during the half-hour. In addition, during this same period, this portfolio insurer sold $500 million of stock. Between 1 P.M. and 1:30 P.M., index arbitragers sold $216 million of stocks, and straight program selling totaled $305 million of stocks. Together these two selling interests accounted for 39 percent of total share volume during this period.

A short-lived rally, the last one of the day, began at 2:05 P.M. and was led by the futures market. The contract rallied from 227 to 239 at 2:35 P.M. The buying interest was concentrated in the futures market and the index rallied only 4 points. The D.J.I.A. rose approximately 50 points to the 2,000 level.

By about 2 P.M., many index arbitragers had discontinued their activity because they could not be assured timely execution of their order. This removed a significant buyer in the futures market and, combined with the continued selling by portfolio insurers, caused the spread between the contract and the index to widen to a huge discount.

Trading-oriented accounts that were not fully invested and were active in both the futures and stock markets chose to buy futures because of their belief that this discount represented a good trading opportunity.

Most of the buying in the stock market by trading-oriented investors was short covering. Most nontrading-oriented investors who were fully invested sold stocks throughout the day to lighten their exposure to the equity market. The only nontrading-oriented accounts that were significant buyers were pension funds and financial institutions, such as bank departments, that perceived bargain prices to exist on many blue-chip stocks.

By 4 P.M. the contract had declined to 200 and the D.J.I.A. had fallen from 2,000 to 1,738, a closing level last reached on April 7, 1986.

From *Black Monday: The Catastrophe of October 19, 1987 ... and Beyond*

TIM METZ

October 20, 1987. New York Stock Exchange, chairman's dining room, 8:30 A.M.: "This market is gonna go up," John Phelan tells the six men sharing breakfast with him. "It's got to bounce back after falling so far yesterday."

The men agree. Absolutely. Must go up.

Four of Phelan's guests are the NYSE's floor directors, in charge of enforcing the exchange's rules and representing the exchange leadership in operating the trading floor. Three of the floor directors are specialists—Donny Stone, John Lyden, the managing partner of Nick, Lyden & Company, and James Jacobson, a partner at Benjamin Jacobson & Sons. The fourth, David Shields, the managing director at Shields & Company, is a floor trader.

The remaining two men in the room are the quietly proficient exchange president, Bob Birnbaum, and Dick Grasso, the executive vice-president, who will succeed Birnbaum in mid-1988. No one needs to be told how important a market recovery today would be. They discuss how Black Monday had put huge strains on the exchange's trading facilities and left several specialists in a deep financial hole. Dozens more will join them if the market collapses today, all seven men know. Banks have been howling since yesterday afternoon about the sharp decline in the value of the securities they hold as collateral on their loans to the specialists and other Wall Street firms.

Yes, there must be buyers today; real buyers, the kind who deserted the market entirely yesterday afternoon as the Dow plunged 200 points in the final hour of trading. The kind that will have to be convinced that the bottom of this market was yesterday. And the NYSE officials know that nothing short of a thumping good rally today will convince them.

But how likely is that after yesterday's numbing disaster?

Well, there are plenty of buy orders for some stocks already streaming into the DOT system from bargain-hunting institutional investors. At this point, the odds of that don't seem great, a chart in the Brady Commission report will show. DOT, the automated order system, started accepting trades at eight o'clock. Now, after a half hour, there are about $25 million of sell orders and $15 million buy orders entered in the system that will handle more than two thirds of today's record trading volume. About a half hour from now, around the time this meeting breaks, it will be a lot worse—about $140 million of sell orders, nearly double approximately $75 million of buy orders. The ratio will improve by the 9:30 opening of the market ($335 million of sell orders against about $315 million of buy orders), but today's trading will get under way with an imbalance of sell orders in the DOT system.

The buy orders will be highly concentrated. For instance, the amount of money to be paid in this morning's opening trades for just four big stocks—IBM, GM, Exxon, and Atlantic Richfield—will total $276 million.*

Altogether, this is not the kind of climate one usually associates with thunderous rallies. It's clear that the rally so desperately needed now won't come about unless something is done to encourage buying and discourage selling, too. Both are within the power of the men in this room.

Program traders relied on the DOT system to dump billions of dollars' worth of stocks onto the market yesterday. After the George Anders piece in Monday morning's *Journal* that explained how program trading

* Arrived at by multiplying the opening price of each stock by the share volume of the opening trade, then totaling these four results.

would act to fuel a market meltdown, this morning the press is full of accusations that program trading caused the crash. Phelan knows he can ask all member firms to refrain voluntarily from using the DOT system for program trading today, and no one will dare refuse. And this is precisely what he will do ahead of today's opening.

Meanwhile, the floor directors can help stimulate the needed buying— just by doing their jobs and conveying the consensus of this morning's meeting to all the specialist traders on the floor well ahead of the opening. The specialists will take it from there. After all, one of their principal tasks is to determine stock prices at each morning's opening.

Supply and demand and market forces and all those technical factors may ultimately determine stock prices, the men in this room know. But it is the specialist who decides where they start trading each day, and today they will start higher. Much higher. "We had two goals Tuesday morning," Phelan will recall. "One, get rid of [the specialists'] inventory; two, but don't go too high [with the prices] or you won't get rid of it."

Of course, that is a matter far easier to say than to do. Phelan knows that it won't just be a matter of the specialists' setting high opening prices, selling their excess inventories into the opening, and living happily ever after, not in this stunned and wobbly market. Today the wrong opening price could be disastrous, and a price too temptingly high could easily attract more sellers than buyers.

The higher opening prices Phelan and the others have in mind are a double boon. They'll allow the specialists who are selling into the opening to both trim their losses and the inventory sales and raise more capital to help cope with the still-powerful army of sellers that Phelan and his colleagues know is lurking out there.

Thanks in part to yesterday's chaos, specialists will have greater than usual latitude at today's opening. Many investors yesterday who made their orders contingent on specific prices—the usual practice among institutional traders—saw prices fall so fast that they were obsolete in the market before the orders could be executed. Chastened, they will enter today with orders to be executed "at the market"—essentially, at whatever price the specialist determines the market to be. The Brady Commission will find that "the vast majority of orders to buy at the market's open were 'market orders,' enabling the NYSE specialists to open stocks significantly higher than Monday's close."

The Brady Commission's report will cite order imbalances in the delayed openings of 92 stocks (compared with 187 on Monday). Again, specialists will operate under crisis procedures that allow them to hold back any indications of the bid and asking price spreads on the delayed stocks for a half hour after the trading day begins. Yet even the relaxed rule will be widely ignored as some specialists delay their indications for hours, and as "many specialists" begin trading at prices far above yesterday's closes without putting out any preopening indications at all.

One explanation could be the "Bambi" theory—if you can't say something nice, don't say anything at all. It's clear that "something nice" this morning would be an indication that suggests an opening price sharply higher than yesterday's close. But alas, more than a few specialists will be staring at imbalances of sell orders, not buy orders. Howard Kramer, the SEC staffer who will analyze specialist trading in a sample of sixty-seven blue-chip stocks, will find that twenty-six of them have had delayed openings today. Among that group "most of the imbalances—certainly the biggest ones—are on the buy side." But, in a look at the data six months from now, he will see many sell-side imbalances in the group too. "Looking at the data here in front of me, I estimate about sixty percent have buy-side imbalances and forty sell imbalances," he will say.

Many of the indications that are posted on the ninety-two stocks where trading is delayed at the opening will be of limited value. The SEC's report will note that many of the preopening indications have such wide price spreads that they will offer no real guidance to potential buyers or sellers. For example, General Electric, which closed at 41⅞ yesterday, will have an initial opening indication of 45 bid, 65 asked, at 9:52 A.M. and another of 40-55 at 10:30 before it opens at 46½ just before 11 o'clock. The GE specialist will be telling the world that more than twenty minutes after the day's session has begun, would-be buyers and sellers are still as much as $20 apart, and that an hour into the trading day they'll still be at least $15 apart in one of the most heavily traded stocks on earth. To a professional trader, such indications amount to a KEEP OUT sign.

Other specialists will open their stocks sharply higher in spite of seemingly small buy-order imbalances. For example, Atlantic Richfield, one of the thirty Dow Jones industrials, will open at 75, up 10 on opening volume of 267,000 shares, and a buy-order surplus of just 13,000 shares.

Shortly before ten o'clock, as the SEC will report, a Lasker, Stone &

Stern specialist will open Coca-Cola stock, another thirty Dow industrial, up 10, or 33%, Donny Stone's Johnson & Johnson stock, not one of
the thirty industrials, but an important S&P 500 component included in
nearly every program trader's market basket, also will open late and up
10 points.

The trader specialist for Spear, Leeds & Kellog will list indications of
35-45, then of 40-50 on shares of J. P. Morgan & Company, the bank
holding company, which closed yesterday at 27¾. Trading will begin
shortly after ten o'clock—at 47, up 69%. J. P. Morgan will be one of
seven NYSE stocks to be reallocated to other specialists over the next
six months because of improper or inadequate specialist performance
during the crash.

Close observers will see the disciplinary moves as ironic in light of
the clear pattern of opening that will follow Phelan's breakfast meeting
with the floor directors this morning. The punishments will seem perfunctory and in response to pressure from the SEC, whose report will cite
"several instances of specialist performance in opening their stocks that
raise questions about the specialist's maintenance of a fair and orderly
market."*

Phelan, the floor directors, and other officials realize that to achieve
today's goals, the exchange must keep the program traders on the sideline;
which is now being arranged. At the opening, the NYSE will announce
that it has asked members to refrain from using the DOT system to execute program trades today.†

* The SEC report discloses that the NYSE had begun "several investigations of specialist
performance during the week of October 19" and that the specialists in two issues (to early
February) had agreed to withdraw them and allow their reassignment. Spear Leeds will be one
of the two. Yet the loss of Morgan stocks is hardly a disaster. Even after it loses Morgan, Spear
Leeds, the exchange's largest specialist firm, will still be making markets in 153 Big Board
stocks.

† The exchange will allow program orders loaded into DOT ahead of the opening to be
executed. The SEC will find that a few members apparently ignored the request and that still
others completed program trades manually, by carrying orders around to the specialists' posts.
However, overall, program selling of all types totaled only 24.4 million shares, or 4% of volume
on Tuesday, October 20, down from 89 million shares, or just under 15% of the trading on
Black Monday. At tomorrow's opening the NYSE will announce an indefinite extension of the
ban, but will partly lift it on November 3 to allow use of DOT for programs loaded into the
system ahead of the opening. All restrictions on the use of the system for program trades will

The Dow will soar 127 points in this morning's first thirty minutes of trading and 196 points in the first hour. The specialists will be "very heavy sellers on the opening transaction and during the first 30 minutes of trading," the SEC will report, "as many used the opportunity to liquidate their large positions from the previous day."

"You can make a case that what they did was entirely fair and reasonable," Brandon Becker, the SEC official in charge of dealing with self-regulatory agencies, will say six months hence. "You can't really make a judgment one way or the other without examining a whole lot of individual openings." Yet the massive report he and his colleagues at the SEC's Division of Market Regulation produce will be less charitable: "As with October 19, the Division believes the openings on October 20 deserve scrutiny by both the Commission and the NYSE."

Even as Phelan and the floor directors complete plans to avert another disaster on the stock exchange floor today, the electronic media have arrived to watch and wait for one. Cable News Network, which beams newscasts via satellite to fifty-eight European and Asian nations, was the only TV network camped here yesterday. Now trucks and cables from NBC, CBS, and ABC have joined CNN's outside the exchange building. Throughout the day camera crews will peer down on the trading-floor chaos from the press gallery catwalk up near the ceiling, waiting for the story—the market—to break: "Live from New York, the collapse of the stock market!"

---

be dropped on November 9. Then, early in 1988, the exchange will adopt a measure prohibiting the use of DOT for program trading at any time during a trading day after the Dow Jones Industrial Average has moved more than 50 points from the prior day's close.

From *Liar's Poker: Rising Through the Wreckage on Wall Street*

MICHAEL LEWIS

Monday, October 19, 1987

The stock market fell, of course. It fell as it had never fallen before in history, paused, then fell some more. I rushed back and forth between my seat on 41 and the equity department on 40. The stock market crash had huge and arbitrary wealth redistributionary effects, and the two floors had entirely different reactions to it. A lucky man in the equity department had gone short S&P stock index futures (meaning he made a large bet that the market would fall) on Friday, and by the time he had a chance to close out his bet on Monday the futures were sixty-three points lower, and he had cleared twenty-seven million dollars. His joy was unique. The rest of the equity department was tossed between despair and confusion. Early in the day there was trading. I heard the Brooklyn screams of a dozen men at once. "Yo, Joey!" "Hey, Alfy!" "Whaddya doin', Mel!" "George Balducci, youse can buy twenty-five thousand Phones [AT&T shares] at a half." Later, however, trading dried up, a harbinger of the coming torpor in the stock market. Investors froze like deer in the headlights. Time and time again someone stood up and shouted, "Jeeee-*Sas Christ!*" They were helpless as they watched their beloved market die.

Of course, my customers in Europe were losing their shirts, but there was nothing I could do for them. I thanked Mammon for the umpteenth time for making me a middleman. To a man my customers chose to hunker down and wait out the storm. Meanwhile, the bond market was shooting through the roof, and more than a few bond traders failed to conceal their glee. Once the stock market had fallen a few hundred points, investors began to consider the macroeconomic effects of an honest-to-God crash. The prevailing reasoning in the bond market went like this; Stock prices were lower; therefore, people were less wealthy; therefore, people would consume less; therefore, the economy would slow down; therefore, inflation would fall (maybe there'd even be depression and deflation); therefore, interest rates would fall; therefore, bond prices should rise. So they did.

One bond trader who had bet against the bond market stood up and screamed in the direction of the Statue of Liberty, "Fuck! Fuck! Fuck! Fuck! I bad-mouth the U.S. government, I short their debt, and they fuck me. That's what I do for a living. Why fucking bother?" But most everyone else was long and getting longer. The bond traders were making a fortune. This one day made up for much of the year. As the stock market crashed, the forty-first floor of Salomon Brothers cheered.

And many of us asked our first questions about the wisdom of the firings of the previous week. The world of money was in upheaval. Funds were rushing out of the stock market and into safe havens. The conventional safe haven for money is gold, but this was not a conventional moment. The price of gold was falling fast. Two creative theories made their happy way around the trading floor, both explaining the fall in gold. The first was that investors were being forced to sell their gold to meet margin calls in the stock market. The second was that in the depression that followed the crash, investors would have no need to fear inflation, and since for many gold was protection against inflation, it was less in demand. Whatever the case, money was pouring not into gold but into money markets—i.e., short-term deposits. Had we had a money market department, we could have made a killing presiding over this movement, but we did not and could not. The decline in business after the crash occurred mainly in the equity markets. And which was the one and only department not to cut a single employee? Equities. So the area most directly overstaffed was the one that had made no cuts.

Many of us also asked our first questions about the wisdom of entering the junk bond market. With the stock market crash the market in junk bonds, inextricably linked to the asset values of corporations, temporarily ceased to function altogether. The fickle stock market was saying that one day corporate America was worth $1.2 trillion, and the next only $800 billion. Junk bond investors dumped their holdings when they saw the wild behavior of their collateral. Our Southland junk bond deal collapsed on October 19. When the stock market crashed, the value of 7-Eleven stores and, therefore, junk bonds backed by 7-Eleven stores, crashed, too. From my seat on the trading floor I called my customers in Europe. When I reached my Frenchman, he thanked me for never having sold him junk.*

Most of what happened to a big firm like ours during the crash was largely invisible to the outside world. But one important event was not. Along with other Wall Street firms, Salomon Brothers had agreed to purchase from the British government, and distribute worldwide, 31.5 percent of the shares in British Petroleum. We owned a chunk of the company at the time of the crash. We had lost more than a hundred million dollars on our stake. Who'd have imagined that our largest single equity underwriting would coincide with the largest drop in history in the stock market? Then who'd have imagined that our first big junk bond deal would coincide with the crash of the junk bond market? It was striking how little control we had of events, particularly in view of how assiduously we cultivated the appearance of being in charge by smoking big cigars and saying fuck all the time.

Throughout the crash John Gutfreund seemed in his element. He was, for the first time in ages, making trading decisions. It was a joy to see a

---

* Ironically, Southland, I later learned, should have been a smashing success and was eventually revived. But my skepticism of our skills in junk bonds was not unjustified. In the middle of 1988 the first multibillion-dollar leveraged take-over in America sponsored by Wall Street went bankrupt. The drugstore chain Revco, which had been purchased by its management with junk bond money, supplied by Salomon Brothers, filed for Chapter 11.

man rediscover his youth. He spent little time at his desk. He sprinted back and forth across the floor and held brief strategy sessions with his head traders. At one point his attention drifted to his net worth, and he bought three hundred thousand shares in Salomon Brothers for his personal account. When I overheard him do this, my first reaction was that he was trading on inside information.

My second reaction was that as long as it was legal, I should do it too. Pretty greedy, huh? But also pretty smart. Salomon's stock was crashing faster than the market as a whole; all brokerage stocks were getting hit because investors, who had no way to gauge the internal damage we had suffered, assumed the worst. We were losing small fortunes on both British Petroleum and Southland, our two visible risks. Gutfreund knew, however, that our losses were not what they seemed. We had lucked into twenty-seven million dollars in the equity department, and the bond departments were rolling in dough. A quick calculation showed that Salomon's share price implied a value for the company less than its liquidation value. (If we had been a take-over play three weeks before at thirty bucks a share, we were a bargain now at eighteen. A false rumor spread that Lewie Ranieri had raised money and was returning to buy Salomon Brothers.)

After checking with our legal department to make sure I wasn't following Boesky's footsteps, I followed Gutfreund's and bought a bunch of Salomon shares with the bonus I was busy lobbying for. Many, many others on our trading floor were doing the same. Gutfreund would later say that it bespoke of a faith in the firm when employees bought Salomon shares and that he personally found it encouraging. Perhaps. But I for one wasn't making a statement of faith when I made my purchase. *My* investment was raw self-interest, coupled with a certain abstract pleasure in having found a smart bet. Within a few months Salomon shares had bounced back, from a low of sixteen dollars to twenty-six dollars.

Tuesday, October 20, 1987

The postmortem began. The credit committees convened in an emergency session in New York. Its stated purpose was to assess Salomon's credit exposure to institutions that appeared bankrupted by the events of yesterday, such as E. F. Hutton and the entire community (if you can call it that) of equity arbitrageurs. Instead, for the first half hour the committee members squabbled. All but one man on the committee were American. The exception was a Brit, who flew in from London especially for the meeting. He became a punching bag for the Americans, who pinned blame for the crash squarely on the British government. Why were the limeys insisting on continuing their sale of the state-owned British Petroleum? The traders, who thought pretty much exclusively in terms of short-term market forces, felt that the multibillion-dollar sale of BP shares imposed on the market a weight it could not bear. The whole stock-buying world was panicking at the thought of a new sup-ply of stock. Never mind that the United States was running a trillion dollars' budget deficit, or that the dollar was unstable, or that busts, like their better halves, booms, usually have a logic all their own. A few of the Americans were jumping all over the Brit for the behavior of his country-men. One said, sneeringly, "You guys did just this sort of thing after the war too, you know."

You would think that the battle lines on this day would be drawn along the borders of financial interest instead of the borders of nations. Every-one around the table at the credit meeting was on the same team, but people didn't behave like it. The xenophobia was by no means limited to Salomon Brothers. An American partner of Goldman Sachs, a firm also stuck with a hundred-million-dollar loss on its shares in BP, called a senior Brit at Salomon and blamed him for the problem. But why? It turned out the Goldman partner wasn't thinking of his Salomon counter-part as a representative of Salomon but as a Brit. "Your people damn well better pull it [the BP issue]," he shouted. "If it wasn't for us, you'd all be speaking German."

The shrewder players in our shop weren't looking to affix blame but to find a way out: How could we avoid losing a hundred million dollars on our stake in British Petroleum? Or, to put a finer point on it, how could we persuade the British government to take back its shares at the price it had sold them to us? One of the managing directors from London, who happened to be in New York, actually took me aside to practice an argu-ment he planned to put to the Bank of England. He had calculated the sum of the losses of the banks underwriting BP to be seven hundred mil-lion dollars. He said that the world financial system might not withstand this drain of capital from the system. Another panic could ensue. Right?

Amazing. He was so desperate to avoid the loss that I think he actually believed his lie. Sure, why not? I said. It's worth a try. Basically, it was an old ploy. My boss wanted to threaten the British government with another stock market crash if it didn't take back its oil company.* (Note to members of all governments: Be wary of Wall Streeters threatening crashes. They are tempted to do this whenever you encroach on their turf. But they can't cause a crash any more than they can prevent one.)

Later that day, the last day I clearly recall of my time at Salomon Brothers, I spent an uneasy hour in the training class talking to 250 blank stares. The trainees had reached that state of high despair that resembles accounts I have read of the Black Death of the fourteenth century. They had lost all hope and decided that since they were going to be fired anyway, they might as well do whatever they please. So they all became back-row people. I dodged a paper wad as I entered the room and an impressive amount of apathy as I spoke. It was an audience only Rodney Dangerfield could have appreciated. They didn't care what I had to say on my assigned topic: "Selling to Europeans." But they were vaguely curious if there were any job opportunities in the London office and if I knew when they would be fired. They were sure that they were alone in not knowing what was happening to our company. How blissfully naïve! They were, in particular, angry and frustrated that Jim Massey (who had made the same gung ho speech to them as he had to us) hadn't made at least a token appearance before them. Did they still work for the Brothers, or what?

They were left to wonder for only two hours more. The speaker who followed me was interrupted by the entrance of Jim Massey, flanked by two men who looked like bodyguards, but were only traders. He bore the fate of 250 trainees. Before making it known, however, he explained in merciless detail how difficult the firings had been on senior management, how ultimately they would make the firm stronger, and how these sorts of decisions were always painful to make. And then: "We have made our decision regarding the training program . . . and we have decided . . .

---

* It didn't work. As John Gutfreund explained to our beleaguered shareholders in our 1987 annual report, "By honoring our commitment to our client and proceeding with our underwriting of British Petroleum in the wake of the crash, the firm incurred a $79 million pre-tax loss."

[long pause] . . . to maintain our commitment." You can stay! A handful of people scrambled back into the front row as soon as Massey had left. But the news wasn't as cheery as it sounded. There were no vacancies on the trading floor. At the end of the program most of the trainees became clerks in the back office.

The Lonely Feeling of Small Investors

STEPHEN LABATON

The New York Times, *October 21, 1987*

Vincent H. Bacon, like many people, owns stocks. But yesterday, following the worst decline in stock market history, he did not know what to do about them.

"I haven't sold anything, and I haven't bought anything," said Mr. Bacon, a retired farm machinery dealer from Berkeley, Calif. "I guess if you're neither a bull nor a bear, you're a chicken."

All across America, millions of small investors like Mr. Bacon tried to figure out what to do next, spending much of yesterday puzzled over whether to invest or divest following Monday's historic plunge.

Was it finally time to cash in or to shop for what might be bargain basement stocks? Or would the market continue to slide, making investments in, say, stock options an attractive alternative?

"Everybody Has an Opinion"

"The more I read, the more confused I get," said Dales Y. Foster, a retired architect from Dallas, who has more than $300,000 in stocks and bonds.

"Everybody has an opinion, and everybody sounds like an authority, and nobody gets it right. It's kind of a lonely feeling."

Public fascination with where the market was heading, as it spent most of yesterday zigging and zagging, spawned more than its share of prognosticators. And it nearly led to at least one casualty.

In Chicago, at the corner of Dearborn and Monroe Streets, a large electric sign was flashing the latest figure for the Dow Jones industrial average, courtesy of Paine Webber.

"There was one guy who was crossing the street," said James Sherman, whose office overlooks the corner. "He glanced up at the sign, stopped dead in the middle of traffic and then nearly got run over trying to scramble back to the curb."

"What Am I Doing Here?"

For many people, the problem was not how to cross the street but what to do about Wall Street.

"I-yi-yi-yi-yi," moaned one woman, looking at the electronic ticker at Fidelity Investments on Park Avenue in New York. Her stock had dropped from 65 to 39 3/4 in less than a week, she explained. Then she cried out to no one in particular: "What am I doing here? I've got to go back to the office and make a living."

Other investors, however, viewed yesterday as a chance to do some bargain hunting. Some stocks, they figured, might have reached their nadir.

"I'm nibbling a little bit today at the blue chips—I.B.M., Eastman Kodak, G.M.—the bluest of the blue, with good balance sheets and long-term prospects," said Dhruv D. Sheth, a trader in Berkeley, Calif. "I have an M.B.A. from the Harvard business school, but they don't know anything about this kind of collapse. They don't teach you that in B School."

"We Can't Possibly Compete"

The plunge was a bitter revelation for some investors, such as Eunice Geller, a 61-year-old retiree in Surfside, Fla. After being in the market more than 30 years, she said, "I finally realized that this is a gambling business."

She said: "It was the most stupid thing to get into the market in the 1950's because I know now that it is not a place for small and medium investors. Today large companies loaded with cash are making a killing while we can't possibly compete."

But Elizabeth Rosenberg, a self-proclaimed professional ticker tape analyst in New York, said there was no reason to be selling but good reason to be buying.

"People should buy quality, especially since it is all so cheap," advised Ms. Rosenberg. "I.B.M. was at $103. That's ridiculous. It's a $200 stock. A lot of people are nervous, and that's foolish."

Sellers "Are Going to Be Sorry"

Nearby, Leslie Weinreb was shaking his head. "People who sold Monday are going to be sorry," said Mr. Weinreb, a New Yorker who makes his living writing marriage contracts for Jewish marriages.

Skeptics, meanwhile, were trying to capitalize on the possibility of a further stock decline. They made heavy investments in financial instruments that would go up if the market went down.

"I'm here to buy some put options," said Jim Lichtenberg, a computer programer who ducked into the Charles Schwab office in midtown Manhattan, near his office in Grand Central Station. "I'm expecting panic will take hold for the next couple of days."

For many small investors, panic was fueled by an inability to reach their brokers. By afternoon, lines of people at Manhattan discount brokerage houses snaked outside the doorways, and sometimes it took more than an hour to get inside.

"I Tried to Get Through"

Other people, trying to execute trades by telephone, had to spend many minutes anxiously listening to music while they waited on hold.

"I tried to get through to my broker Monday afternoon, but it was impossible," said Bill Killick, a dance instructor in the New York metropolitan area.

At the First State Pawners, a pawnshop in the heart of Chicago's financial district, a leading—if unofficial—indicator seemed to show that the market had stabilized: The number of Rolex watches, diamond rings and gold necklaces being pawned by nervous commodity traders and stock investors pressed for quick cash fell off sharply from Monday's volume.

"Whenever there is that kind of distress in the markets, our business jumps dramatically," said Steve Greenfield, a partner at the pawnshop. "On Monday we could have used ropes and ushers in here to deal with the crowds."

Many who came in on Monday were traders from the nearby Chicago Board of Trade, easily identifiable by their distinctive work jackets and identification badges.

"What you were seeing were a lot of traders who got caught short on margins and needed quick cash," Mr. Greenfield said.

Yuppies' Last Rites Readied

RICHARD J. MEISLIN

The New York Times, *October 21, 1987*

For the young professionals who have known only a bull market—particularly those who work on Wall Street—the effect of Monday's stock market plunge is likely to go beyond the monetary to the psychological, experts said yesterday.

Marketers, meanwhile, predicted the beginning of the end of yuppies and the free-spending ways that have endeared them to real estate agents, car dealers and fashionable clothiers. And there was gloating among those who have come to associate the word yuppie with a certain type of greed and callousness.

Psychologists and marketers said the market reversal, if it endured, was likely to force a shift in values among people who had seemed to find it difficult to distinguish self worth from net worth.

A "Very Stressful" Time

"People who have had such faith in the stability of those markets are going to be forced to evaluate what they consider stable, predictable and important in life," said Dr. Steven Berglas, a Boston psychologist. "Their sense that the more they made, the more control they had over life is going to be totally ripped from their psyches, and for a lot of people it's going to be very stressful."

Dr. Berglas, who is affiliated with McLean Hospital–Harvard Medical School and is the author of the book *The Success Syndrome*, said he expected a move "toward a reliance on personal relationships, rather than finance, for security."

"You get security from a friend, from a family, from a network, from community," he said. "People are going to be looking around and seeing how vulnerable they are, how they have no one to turn to, that they have no one comforting them over their prize bottle of Margaux. Those are the people who are going to hurt."

Eliot Janeway, the venerable Wall Street analyst, said "these yuppies are unprepared and unconditioned" for a bear market.

A Splintered Dream

"They've greeted every one of these bad days as buying opportunities and as quasi corrections," Mr. Janeway said Monday night. "You listen to all this baloney about corrections—it's a reversal, it's a splintered dream, it's a trauma."

By some counts, the actual number of yuppies is relatively small— 4 million to 5 million, according to the J. Walter Thompson Company, whose surveys define yuppies as mostly younger people earning more than $30,000 and having four or more years of college education. And the number of "super-yuppies, the guys making $200,000 on Wall Street or making partner at 35 in big law firms," is even smaller, said Peter Kim, the advertising agency's vice president of strategic services.

But Mr. Kim said the agency's studies had found a "much more pervasive psychological effect on the entire generation—there was a whole group of people who in many ways emulated the life styles of their yuppie counterparts." It was these "would-be yuppies" who, although less wealthy, had taken such items as $50 running shoes, health club memberships and gourmet ice creams from yuppie fashion to marketing success, he said. A change in consumption patterns among yuppies would have a broad effect on the buying patterns of less affluent young people, he said, and consequently on the fortunes of some businesses as well.

"The collapse of the bull market signifies the reality that the future may not get tremendously better than it currently is, or maybe even get worse," Mr. Kim said. "It will probably force them to make a more realistic appraisal of their financial situation, and spend less on discretionary items."

Spending Cutbacks Seen

Faith Popcorn, chairman of Brain Reserve Inc., a consulting company, also predicted retrenchment by young professionals. "It's like almost drowning—you become a very, very careful swimmer. Yuppies are compulsive. They're compulsive spenders, and I think we're going to find out they're compulsive non-spenders."

She said people had suffered from a "yuppie glut—too much, too soon, too disgusting." And she predicted there would be a lot of young professionals who, after taking a financial beating this week, would trim back on the items they consider to be necessities. "One house, one car, one raincoat—that's what it's going to be," Ms. Popcorn said. Those dealing in luxury items seemed, for the moment, unconcerned, and to varying degrees joined in the broad-scale yuppie-bashing that appeared to be the order of the day.

Tiffany Will Wait and See

An official at Tiffany & Company, Fernanda Gilligan, said she did not expect business to be seriously affected, although she conceded that there might be fewer purchases by those who buy "with opulence in mind," rather than quality.

"We're not making any predictions at this point—holding our breath to see what happens is more to the point," said Mrs. Gilligan, regional vice president for publicity and retail marketing.

"There is still need for the engagement ring. There's still a desire to have a beautiful wedding present. That business will continue," she said. "The tenth $100,000 emerald necklace in your wardrobe may be put off for a bit. But that's not what our business is made of."

From *What Goes Up*

ERIC J. WEINER

JOSEPH GRANO: The weekend before the crash I was at a resort in Vermont giving a seminar on real estate. This doctor from Philadelphia came up to me and started explaining how he had hundreds of options positions all over the place and how he was highly leveraged. I looked at him and said, "You're out of your mind. This market is very tenuous and if I were you I'd deleverage myself now."

Unfortunately, he chose to stay in Vermont for three more days—he got totally wiped out.

HENRY KAUFMAN: On Sunday, October 18, I appeared on *Meet the Press*. Not surprisingly, the journalists pressed me to prognosticate about what the market might do the next day. I tried my best to sidestep such questions by pointing out that there was no analytical way to specifically forecast an extraordinary event such as a crash happening tomorrow. The large setback on Friday already had investors on edge and I had no intention of adding to the turmoil with my remarks. So I sounded more vague and reassuring about the situation than I really felt.

Treasury Secretary James Baker, who was questioned by the panel after me, did not mimic my tactic. When asked about some of the signs that seemed to indicate a deterioration in international monetary and foreign-exchange matters, he said, "We will not sit back and squeeze growth worldwide on the expectation that the United States somehow will follow by raising its interest rates." That remark surprised me and after the program I went up to him and said, "Jim, that was quite a candid statement. The market may not take it the way you may have meant it."

I'll never forget his firm reply. "Henry, some things need to be said."

MICHAEL LABRANCHE: I remember clearly that I was sitting home on the Sunday morning before the crash, and Jim Baker, who was then treasury secretary, was talking on *Meet the Press*. They asked if he was concerned about the stock market sell-off and he said twice, "No, because remember, stocks are already selling off from high levels." Now, I don't think he meant to do this, but he sent the message that he didn't mind if stock prices went down. That's what the perception was. He probably meant to be reassuring, saying the stock market's fine and we just had a sell-off. But I'm sitting there thinking, "Oh, this is not good at all. The market's going to be down another hundred points tomorrow."

LEO MELAMED: That weekend the *New York Times* and every major periodical, whether it was *Barron's*, *Chicago Tribune*, *Los Angeles Times*, all compared what was happening to the 1929 crash. Media analysts on financial markets over the weekend on television all were speaking of comparisons to what happened in 1929. This is October again. Could we go through another Depression? Those comparisons had a great impact on the psychology of investors. If you couple that with the momentum of the week before and the real concerns about the valuation of the dollar versus where interest rates were headed, what you had was a mixture of fear, greed, and concern that was combustible.

PAUL STEIGER: There was a sense of things coming unglued. There was a level of tension in the air that was palpable. We had people working all weekend long just picking up fear and loathing, no question. So when it did hit, the only surprise was how low it went. I mean 500 points—that was awesome.

JOHN PHELAN: At six or seven that night, Corrigan called me and said, "What can I do for you?" And I said, "To begin with, you can provide liquidity to this market." In a position like that everything dries up, everybody pulls back. The financial crises in the eighties, and in the nineties as well, have been liquidity crises. The question is always, how will people react? So Corrigan and I talked about that, and his point was that they'd do whatever they could to help us. He said, "We will provide liquidity to all the markets."

LEO MELAMED: I had a conversation with Alan Greenspan at around eleven on Monday night. By now it was obvious that the collapse in our S&P 500 futures pit in Chicago was accelerating the disaster everywhere else. His question was, "Will you open tomorrow morning?" But Greenspan and I both knew what we were really saying when we talked about whether we would open the market the next day. We actually were discussing whether the longs would be able to pay the shorts.

You see, if the world thought for a minute that some long at the Chicago Mercantile Exchange couldn't pay a short for an S&P 500 futures position, it would mean Morgan Stanley, Goldman Sachs, Salomon Brothers, whoever, couldn't make payment. Think about that for a second. It would set off a chain reaction of gridlock. Nobody would pay anybody if they suspected somebody wouldn't pay them. So the fear was gridlock.

JERRY CORRIGAN: As we got into Monday night I was talking to a lot of people. Greenspan—who was brand-new as chairman, he'd come in August—during the afternoon hours was on a plane to Dallas to give a speech to the American Bankers Association Tuesday morning. When he got off the plane he found out that the market had closed down 508 points. This came as a little bit of an eye-opener to him.

That night, when I was talking to Phelan and everybody else, my primary focus was learning as much as I could as a matter of intelligence from people in the markets. But much more important, I was working with Chairman Greenspan and others as to what we thought the appropriate response of the central bank should be. The immediate question on Monday night was how this was going to play out in other markets around the world. One of the great institutional accidents—and it's not entirely an accident—is that the international community of central bank governors is a very close-knit society. This is still true, but back then we used to meet literally in person, together, every month. We all knew each other. We all trusted each other. So in circumstances like this, the network and the old-fashioned telephone was a remarkably effective device. We were able to monitor what was happening around the world literally as the sun rose in different places. As that occurred, it became quite apparent that the events of Monday in the United States were having profoundly important effects elsewhere.

So over the course of Monday night one of the questions that came up was, should we as the Federal Reserve be prepared to issue a statement, and if so, what should that statement say and when should it be issued? That naturally was a lively topic of conversation. I don't think there was much difference of opinion on whether we were going to have to issue a statement—we were. The real question was, what should it say, and when should it be issued? There's a lot of folklore around this, and maybe it's a bit of an exaggeration, but the original cut of the draft statement was rather technocratic. I, in particular, felt that this was not the environment where you wanted a technocratic statement. You wanted something short, sweet, tight, and to the point, no nuances, no nothing. Fortunately, that's the way it ended up. Then, the next question was, when to issue it? We were all quickly of the mind that the optimal time to issue it would be before the markets opened in the United States Tuesday morning. As I recall, I think it was issued at eight-thirty on Tuesday morning.

Did the Computer Cause the Crash?

LESTER C. THUROW

Technology Review, *February–March 1988*

The fall of the stock market last October has revived an all-purpose lament that seems to be trotted out whenever any of the myriad glitches of modern life occur. What do you blame when your airplane reservation inadvertently gets cancelled or when your phone bill includes a phantom call to Tashkent? Why, computer error, of course. Likewise, not long after the Dow-Jones posted a precipitous 508-point decline last October 19, some observers were blaming computerized "program trading" for the severity and rapidity of the market's decline.

In thinking about this claim, readers would do well to remember a little history. From the Amsterdam tulip mania of 1637 to the bursting of London's South Sea Bubble in 1720 to the Wall Street crash of 1929, the history of capitalism is replete with market panics. What is unusual is not that there was a crash in 1987 but that capital markets functioned for nearly 60 years without one. The role of computerized trading is a minor influence compared with this long-term historical trend.

There are two kinds of program trading, stock-index arbitrage and portfolio insurance. The first depends on discrepancies between the current prices of stocks on the New York Stock Exchange and prices on stock futures—contracts to buy a stock at a certain future date—traded in Chicago. In stock-index arbitrage, a computer program monitors the differential in price between the Standard & Poor's 500-stock index and the "futures index" of the same stocks. The system is programmed so that whenever the differential reaches a certain point, the computer automatically issues orders to buy and sell.

For example, if the price of the futures index is significantly below that of the Standard & Poor's index, then the program will sell stocks and buy futures. In effect, the computer functions just like a human arbitrageur, making money off the gap between the two markets and narrowing the differential in the process.

As the name implies, portfolio insurance is a technique to protect large institutional investors from losses on the stock market. The computer is programmed so that, as stock prices drop, at regular intervals the system sells index futures—contracts to deliver stocks at a later date and at a given price. The price is usually close to the present market value of the stocks. That way, even if the market drops further, the investor will be able to get the agreed-on price of the stocks, rather than the new, lower price. This protects the investor from excessive losses.

Computers make program trading possible because they can monitor more information faster and give the appropriate buy or sell orders long before a human could figure out what to do. However, the techniques of program trading and the software used to practice them are very much human creations. Like all expert systems, they merely mimic the actions of a human expert, in this case a broker. The computer can only respond to events that have already happened and act according to the rules built in to the program by the broker. Thus, to blame the market's rapid fall on the fact the computers are automatically executing decisions that brokers would have made anyway is to make the common mistake of blaming the tool for the actions of the people using it.

If the computer did not cause the crash, what did? It depends on what you mean by the question. If by "cause" you mean the immediate catalyst of the 508-point decline on October 19th, the answer is that nothing or no one in particular caused it. Rather, it was the product of herd panic, not so different from the sudden panic that occurs among herds of antelope on the plains of Africa. To know why the crash took place precisely when it did would require understanding herd psychology, and even the best animal behavior experts don't pretend to know why antelopes (or humans) panic precisely when they do.

However if by "cause" you mean the reason why stock market values had to decline sooner or later, then there is a simple answer. In mid-October interest rates were around 10 percent. This created a price-to-earnings ratio on bonds of ten to one. For every ten dollars of investment in bonds, an individual earned one dollar of interest. At the same time the price-to-earnings ratio in the stock market was twenty to one. In other words, it took twenty dollars to earn on the stock market what it took only ten to earn on the bond market—a clear sign of how overvalued most stocks were.

It makes absolutely no sense to keep buying stocks in such a situation—unless, of course, you think that interest rates are about to come down (lowering earnings on bonds) or that equity earnings on the stock market are about to boom. But last fall, interest rates were on the way up to defend the weak dollar. Since higher interest rates mean constraints on economic growth, it was inevitable that the stock market would fall (whether slowly or quickly) to bring the price of stocks back into equilibrium with that of bonds. Whether stocks were being traded by computers or humans is beside the point.

As to how the two markets were able to get so far out of line without an earlier correction, that is a complicated story. Put simply, it depends upon the age-old willingness to suspend one's critical judgment when lots of money is being made. It happened in the Dutch tulip mania of 1637. It happened again in the computerized stock market of 1987.

Crash-Proofing the Market;
A Lot of Expert Opinions,
but Few Results

U.S. News & World Report, *June 6, 1988*

S ince October, an impressive roster of market experts has huddled, brainstormed and theorized voluminously about just what caused the stock market crash and what sorts of measures, if any, might help prevent another disaster. More than a dozen studies later, agreement is limited: Yes, there were problems related to the economics of the market, to the lack of consistent regulatory supervision and to the way the market goes about its business. But no consensus has emerged on future action. Proponents of increased regulation have bickered with advocates of a hands-off approach, and a stalemate has emerged.

Causes and effects.
All of the reports acknowledge that stocks were critically overvalued by the time the market crashed—the Dow peaked at 2,722 in late August— and that a correction was due. But they diverge on why the October plunge was so sudden and severe. A presidential task force headed by investment banker Nicholas Brady concluded in January that the crash was triggered by a handful of institutional investors using computerized

trading techniques such as portfolio insurance, which can protect investors in falling markets. As prices declined on October 19, the market was flooded with sell orders, many generated by the technique, which pushed prices lower. The heads of the Commodities Futures Trading Commission and the Federal Reserve Board, members of a White House group led by Treasury Secretary James Baker, did not fault computer trading. They blamed, as did Brady, a failure on October 19 of the intricate links between the markets for stocks, stock-index futures and options.

There is dissension, too, about what needs to be done. Reformers' suggestions include unifying the markets under a single regulatory agency, partly because the stock and futures markets have become so interdependent, and stiffening the margin requirements for futures trades so that it becomes more expensive to speculate on the direction of stock prices. Most reformers like the idea of "circuit breakers"—coordinated trading halts on all exchanges when the market rises or falls more than a certain number of points in a day. Also needed, some feel, is better computer communication between the exchanges so trades can be cleared more accurately.

Looking for scapegoats.
The market flaws these solutions address may have helped exacerbate the crash. But most experts feel that singling out one or two malefactors as the cause is an exercise in scapegoating. At nearly 800 points below the market's precrash peak, experts agree, stock prices now are much less overvalued and thus less vulnerable to a sudden sharp decline. That doesn't mean the market may not go much lower; Securities and Exchange Commission Chairman David Ruder told the Senate Banking Committee last week that the October plunge is "a specter that hangs over the system," and a split SEC voted for a series of government actions to avoid a repeat. But Federal Reserve Board Chairman Alan Greenspan argued that "most of the crucial areas are already cured, either by the market levels or by actions already taken" by the stock exchanges. He sees a "very small" chance of another crash.

Investors will have to wait to see who is right. Although some legislation is apt to be introduced in both the House and Senate in coming weeks, most experts give it little chance of passage this late in the current session.

Meanwhile, investors burned last October are salving their wounds on the sidelines, painfully reminded of risks forgotten during the bull-market years and discomfited by the market's aimless gyrations since October. "The pessimism on the part of professionals as well as individuals has everyone in a catatonic state," says Robert Stovall of Stovall/Twenty-First Advisors, a New York money-management firm. And if investors looked to market overseers to act decisively as a signal it is time to venture back onto the playing field, they have so far waited in vain. Political turf wars have hampered any decision about who should regulate what and just how far the reforms should go. Currently, stock trading is regulated by the Securities and Exchange Commission, while the Commodity Futures Trading Commission oversees futures. Because stocks as well as futures are involved in computerized trading, no one agency or exchange is completely in charge of the situation. The SEC would like to regulate both markets, but the Brady bunch recommends putting regulatory authority in the hands of the Federal Reserve. The Fed defers to the established regulators.

One heated part of the debate swirls around the use of computerized-trading techniques that track price discrepancies in the stock and stock-index-futures markets so an investor can benefit by simultaneously buying one and selling the other. Those who oppose such techniques, such as the SEC and the New York Stock Exchange, argue that they steepen the market's routine ups and downs, and they propose raising the margin requirement for buying a futures contract from the current 12 to 15 percent closer to the more than 25 percent required for stocks. Some major brokerage houses, such as Salomon and Goldman, Sachs, have suspended such trading for their own accounts, most of them in mid-May. In April, the New York Stock Exchange imposed a six-month rule prohibiting the use of its electronic order-execution system for program trades if the Dow moves 50 points in one day in either direction.

In the opposition.
Federal Reserve Chairman Greenspan, on the other hand, points up the lack of agreement by arguing in favor of computer-trading techniques. They provide economic value to pension funds and other big institutional investors, says Greenspan, as well as liquidity and stability for the stock market.

The meager White House proposals, which represent a compromise by the SEC, the CFTC, the Fed and the Treasury Department, seem most likely to be enacted, although it could be months before that happens. The study's major suggested reform—a circuit breaker, similar to one Brady proposed, that would halt trading for 1 hour in the stocks, futures and options markets if any one market fell or rose the equivalent of 250 points on the Dow—has traders concerned, however. Says Stovall: "When the market shuts down, it's an admission of failure and almost guarantees that when it reopens there will be more driving it in the same direction."

Such sensitivity to investor psychology has obviously not been a priority of all the reformers, whose bickering has left investors fearful that no one is in control. Granted, uncertainty about the economy is playing its part in keeping investors at bay, since federal budget and trade deficits and rising interest rates continue to cloud the outlook; inflationary pressures are building, and recession seems inevitable—possibly by 1989. Charles Eaton Ill, investment strategist for Nikko Securities in New York, warns that the Dow could bottom out at the 1,350 level. Many foresee a 100-point drop, to the mid-1,800s, before summer's end.

Even if they are right, a 100-point drop is a far cry from the 800 points the Dow has lost since last August. Ironically, the wheel spinning by reformers who had hoped to rebuild investors' confidence in the stock market is giving them one more reason to stay away.

Four Would-Be Reformers

Below are four of the principal players charged with studying the stock-market crash, and how they propose to ward off a repeat of Black Monday:

BAKER: The Treasury Secretary's group would have a "circuit breaker" halt all trading for 1 hour if a market moved the equivalent of 250 points on the Dow.

RUDER: The SEC chairman wants to raise margin requirements in stock-index futures and to let the SEC regulate the futures as well as stocks.

BOWSHER: Charles Bowsher of the General Accounting Office wants better communications and contingency plans among federal authorities and exchanges.

BRADY: His task force calls for coordinating markets under one regulatory agency, circuit breakers, upgraded information systems to monitor transactions in related markets, consistent margins across markets and a unified clearing system.

PROSPECTS: The debate will continue for several months, with tough new laws unlikely. Most probable outcome: Improved computer communications among the markets and smoother operation of the credit, clearing and settlement systems. Some kind of circuit breaker is possible.

Short Circuits

The Economist, *October 21, 1989*

I ntroduced in the wake of the October 1987 crash, circuit-breakers were justified by the dubious proposition that it is wise to halt trading when panic sweeps markets. Breakers suspend trading on particular instruments when prices rise or fall by a pre-set limit, or when imbalances of orders exceed a set figure. Never mind that the surest way to feed panic is to deny speculators access to these same markets. Whatever their merits, circuit-breakers had their first big test on October 13th. They failed.

So-called index arbitrage (the proper name for program trading) took part of the blame for the October 1987 crash, and helped to inspire the circuit-breakers. The worry then was that index futures and the prices of the stocks making up the index had chased each other down in a vicious circle of trading. With circuit-breakers, there may have been less arbitrage, but there was certainly more confusion because each exchange adopted different rules about when to stop trading.

The stockmarket never stopped trading because the Dow Jones industrial average did not fall 250 points, the trigger to stop trading.

By contrast the Chicago Mercantile Exchange (CME) stopped trading in stock-index futures twice on October 13th, each time when the S&P 500 contract fell by the pre-arranged limit. The Chicago Board Options Exchange (CBOE) also stopped trading, though, unlike the CME, it never resumed that day.

Investors therefore faced the worst of both worlds. Faced with lousy liquidity in the stockmarket, they rushed to hedge their positions by selling stock-index contracts in the futures market. When the futures market closed they turned back to dump shares in the cash market.

It was even worse to have the futures market open, but not the options market. For when the CME decided to restart trading in S&P 500 stock-index futures, the CBOE did not follow suit with its S&P option-index contract. With the options market closed, exposed option-traders rushed to the futures pit to cover their frozen positions. Likewise, locked-in traders who had sold put options were forced to cover themselves at the market's lowest point when trading on the CBOE reopened on Monday, October 16th.

The closure of the Chicago options market also frustrated those who wanted to protect the value of their shares by buying put options on a stockmarket index, a technique called portfolio insurance. Instead, some will no doubt have tried to create their own "synthetic" puts with a combination of loans and share- or short-sales—thus adding to the downward pressures. Such synthetic options provide the same profit or loss as the traded kind, but without resorting to options markets.

Indeed, the use of synthetic options in portfolio insurance may increase market volatility. When portfolio-insurers buy options, the rising price of options signals their worry to fellow investors. Since option prices are composed of three elements—strike price, time before expiry and volatility of the underlying stock or bond—a rise in prices indicates that assumptions about volatility are changing. This should enable them to prepare for what might be a wave of heavy trading ahead. Synthetic options provide no such price signals. Markets can then be left short of liquidity when investors begin to act on their fears.

One obvious lesson from Friday the 13th is that circuit-breakers need to be coordinated if they are to have any chance of being effective. Otherwise they cause only confusion, encouraging panic, not preventing it. Coordination means that, if trading is to be halted, it must be halted in every market—cash, futures and options—for the obvious reason that all these markets are linked. Denying access to one part of this connected market, while allowing it in another, is both capricious and unfair. This was obvious directly after the October 1987 crash, but the obviousness was ignored because of turf wars in Washington between the different agencies that oversee American financial markets.

Crash Course: Black Monday's Biggest Lesson—Don't Run Scared

ROBERT J. SHILLER

The Washington Post, *April 10, 1988*

D espite a few aftershocks, such as the 108-point drop of three weeks ago followed by last week's sharp rebound, the stock market seems to be calming down after last October's debacle. Could another crash still lie ahead?

My investigation of the causes of the Oct. 19 market upheaval suggests that another panic, which I'm not predicting, would be far less likely to be ignited by external economic factors than by psychological factors, specifically a self-feeding cycle of investor fear that a day of economic reckoning is at hand. We may, indeed, have nothing to fear but fear itself.

It is not surprising that memory of the October crash lives on. Monday, Oct. 19, 1987, was the most unusual day in stock market history. The percentage decline in the Dow was nearly twice as big as on the day of the next biggest decline, October 28, 1929.

What was ultimately different on October 19, 1987, that accounts for the unusual market behavior? Obviously, a lot of investors decided to sell then. But why on that day? Why so much? With these questions running through my head even as the market plummeted on Black Monday, it occurred to me that the basic causal factors behind an event so big, one that involved decisions by so many people, should be relatively obvious to the participants. Perhaps a direct and straightforward research method was called for. Why not ask investors why they caused such market drops?

Most economists, I should point out, rarely use such surveys; they are skeptical of explanations people give for their behavior, often with good reason. However, my colleague at the Investor Behavior Project at Yale University, John Pound, and I had done previous surveys of investor behavior and found that well-posed open-ended questions can be very helpful along with other research methods.

Since respondents would rely on memory, and since that memory might be altered by hindsight or exposure to media reporting or analysis of the event, I realized it was important to send out questionnaires almost immediately after the crash. I even managed to get over a hundred sent out that very day (a record performance for a university project?) just as the market closed. The rest were sent out later that week to a total of 2000 wealthy individuals who are active investors and 1000 institutional investors. Of these, 605 individual and 284 institutional investors responded.

The survey explored both objective and psychological factors that could explain the market's behavior on Black Monday. These included news events in the week leading up to the crash, investor reactions to stock price movements and to each others' behavior as well as technical analysis and the use of "portfolio insurance" techniques. Obviously all of these played some role, but the survey findings indicate that the market does have a certain "life of its own," and that in explaining Oct. 19, the dynamics of investor thinking and behavior were more important than economic fundamentals.

Looking first at the impact of external events, the survey asked respondents to rate on a one to seven scale the importance of each of 10 then current news stories, judging the importance "to you personally on Oct. 19, 1987, in your evaluation of stock market prospects."

Of the listed news items, the most important for both individual and institutional investors was early news of the crash itself—the 200-point drop in the Dow the morning of Monday, Oct. 19. The second most important story for both was the drop in U.S. stock prices the week earlier, specifically on October 14–16. Though other news stories were also granted some importance (for institutional investors the recent rise in interest rates and Treasury Secretary James Baker's threat to push the dollar lower in response to German interest rate boosts were important), the biggest factor in the crash seems to be a reaction to price declines themselves.

The questionnaire also provided a space to write in another news story, beyond those listed. Ninety individual investors and 55 institutional investors wrote something, usually a list of concerns rather than a news story per se. The most common concern listed was the excessive federal or personal debt. However, hardly anyone wrote in an event that could account for the specific timing of the crash. Only 3 respondents even mentioned an Oct. 14 report that the House Ways and Means Committee had agreed on tax changes that would make corporate takeovers less attractive—an event that many analysts later pointed to as a likely triggering event. Moreover, sellers on Oct. 19 voiced no different concerns from those who bought on that day.

The survey findings thus suggest that Black Monday is best explained as a vicious circle—price decline feeding on previous price declines. There appear to be no other forcing events, other than previous price declines themselves, which large numbers of investors were focusing on that day, that might have prompted so many to sell at the same time.

Of course, the precipitating event might conceivably have been a news story breaking still earlier which engendered the price drop of Oct. 14, which engendered the price drop Oct. 15, which engendered the price drop Oct. 16, which triggered the crash on Black Monday. But if so, then by Oct. 19, the people most involved seem to have forgotten what the supposedly crucial story was. For that matter, it's just as likely that the triggering events were the still earlier price declines in the week of October 5–9. Alternatively, the trigger might have been the accumulation of a lot of small shocks, none of them an interesting story in itself.

This suggests that in seeking to explain the Oct. 19 phenomenon we should focus less on a triggering event than on the mechanics of the vicious circle itself.

In this regard the survey revealed a remarkable amount of concern about the stock market—and relatively little action as a result. Almost everyone heard of the crash as it was unfolding. The average individual investor checked market prices 3.2 times that day—and talked to more than 7 people about it. The average institutional investor checked prices 35 times and talked to 20 other people. Most were emotionally concerned—43 percent of institutional investors admitted suffering physical anxiety symptoms such as rapid pulse, sweaty palms or tightness in chest. Moreover 23 percent of individuals—and 40 percent of institutional investors—reported experiencing a contagion of fear from other investors. Among those investors who actually traded stocks on the 19th (and only about 5 percent of individuals and 31 percent of institutional investors did), the symptoms of panic were considerably higher.

The idea that the severity of the crash is due to a vicious circle is not a new one. The Brady Commission, appointed by the president to investigate the crash, told such a story. But the commission's story put a lot of emphasis on a purely "mechanical price insensitive selling," due to the existence of "portfolio insurance" in financial markets.

The term "portfolio insurance" was chosen by its inventors to be provocative. It is not insurance in the ordinary use of the word but rather "dynamic hedging strategies" under which a vendor of portfolio insurance provides his clients with a program of selling (on the stock index futures markets) after price declines, and of buying after price increases. Portfolio insurance serves much the same function that stop-loss orders have long served.

Portfolio insurance is a relatively new idea, and the amount of funds under portfolio insurance had grown rapidly in the couple of years before the crash. Moreover, the Brady Commission documented that a substantial amount of selling October 19, 1987, was due to portfolio insurance: at least $6 billion in sales out of about $40 billion in total sales on the New York Stock Exchange and S&P 500 stock index futures markets. However, the fact that development of the concept employed abstract mathematical models, and its application involves computers, does not mean that it is so revolutionary an innovation as to account for the severity of the 1987 crash.

The same investors might very well have done approximately the same amount of selling on their own in the absence of portfolio insurance. In other words, the advent of portfolio insurance may simply have led to the professionalization of stop-loss behavior which would have occurred in any case. My survey suggests that may be so. Few institutional investors (only 5.5%) and no individuals reported having portfolio insurance per se. But 40 percent of individuals and 20 percent of institutional investors who actually sold stock on Oct. 19 said they followed a stop-loss policy. In any event, if all—or most—of what was happening October 19 was the mechanical price insensitive selling by portfolio insurers of a relatively small amount of stocks, then stock prices should have rebounded quickly as other investors stepped in to take advantage of the profit opportunity afforded by the depression of prices—which didn't happen.

It is, of course, conceivable that a few crucial decisions by a few important market players were major factors in the crash. If that's the case, there's a good chance that I missed these people in my survey. But neither the Brady Commission nor the Securities and Exchange Commission report on the October market break gave any indication that was so. Indeed, we know that some of the big institutional selling was due to decisions made by individuals such as redemptions of mutual funds shares.

Technical analysis, at least of a sort, did play a role in investor predictions and hence in the decline of demand on Black Monday. Many investors thought that they could time the market to their advantage. But respondents often wrote "gut feeling" as their primary forecasting method and many seemed to be guessing about the psychology of other investors, trying to figure out when others might start selling. In fact this belief that psychological factors are of great importance in explaining market movements explains why so many investors were holding stocks while they also thought the market was overpriced.

Certainly the evidence suggests that there was in 1987 increased investor awareness of the possibility of a crash. This is not to say that people actually expected a crash; for the most part they certainly did not. But the mental association with events of the past was certainly there: People frequently mentioned on the questionnaire that the bull market had gone on with little interruption since 1982; the market was widely viewed as overpriced; there was a perception that computerized trading strategies made markets more vulnerable; there was a feeling that the national debt created dangers for the market. On my questionnaire I asked, "Do you remember thinking or talking about events of 1929 on the few days before October 19, 1987?" Of individual investors, 35% said yes; of institutional investors, 53% said yes.

This strain in investor attitudes helps explain why a tendency towards a vicious circle was in evidence in 1987 and not before. A changed investor attitude may cause investors to interpret big price drops as the beginning of a crash—and hence a signal to sell—rather than an indication of an underpriced market, and hence a signal to bargain-hunt. A changed investor attitude may also cause investors to call their friends' and colleagues' attention to a price decline.

One should bear in mind that most investors, whether individual or professional, do not have clearly formulated forecasts for the future, especially on a day like Oct. 19, when the market began to behave so erratically as to be beyond the bounds of historical experience. There was in fact no expert who had any concrete basis to predict what would happen next. In this situation, simple associations and habits of thought will tend to decide how forecasts come out.

In fact, portfolio insurance may well be a side-effect rather than a causative factor in the crash, its surge in popularity just before the decline arising from the increasing awareness of the possibility of a crash. This same awareness is certainly with us today, and if the market creeps up in value back towards where it was before the crash, so that it appears as overvalued—as the Tokyo but not the New York market again seems to be—this awareness may be even more acute. Big market moves like some of those we saw last year might well be seen again.

From *After the Crash*

FRANKLIN EDWARDS

I want to step back a bit and try to put the various studies in perspective. Each was originally commissioned to determine what caused the crash. After some 2,000 or 3,000 pages the answer is, we still do not know what caused the crash. Much has been said about speculative euphoria, excessive price-earnings ratios, and the like. But the bottom line is that no one knows. Federal Reserve Chairman Alan Greenspan put it well when he said it was an accident waiting to happen. If it had not happened now, it would have happened later.

Did futures cause the crash? All the studies basically agree that the answer is no. The possible exception is the SEC staff study, which says that although futures did not cause the crash, it may have been sharper and gone further than it would have without future markets. No evidence is presented on this point, but the suggestion is there that the futures markets played a role. But even the SEC study begins by noting that it does not address the question of what caused the crash.

Are future markets available? All the studies say yes. I do not think that there is any quarrel about that. These markets provide valuable financial services—hedging and price discovery.

Given those conclusions, how do we make sense of the fact that the studies go on for pages and make recommendation after recommendation to change things? The explanation might be that it takes a brave commission to study a subject for two or three months and say, we do not have any recommendations.

What do they do? They focus on two problems illuminated by the crash: one, the disorderly conditions that existed in the markets and two, something that did not happen but could have happened—a 1930s kind of collapse.

By disorderly markets, I mean conditions under which orders were submitted but not executed and were sometimes returned for no reason at all; prices that were fictitious or wildly out of line; and opening prices on the New York Stock Exchange that had no relation to reality. No one likes to see disorderly conditions. What followed, therefore, were in-depth studies of what caused them.

The second issue was the potential for financial collapse—the fear that clearing associations might have collapsed and that we might have had an economic catastrophe. This is the basis for the recommendations to unify or coordinate clearing mechanisms.

My reaction to these studies is a little bit like being transported back in time. Suppose it is 1910 and the modern automobile drops out of the sky, landing right in front of us. Just to be on the safe side, let us suppose it is a Mercedes. It does everything well. It is fast and very safe; it has a powerful engine and good brakes. But of course in 1910 we do not have the roads to handle that kind of automobile.

We have a dilemma. The Mercedes is much better than the Model T, but what are we going to do about it? One thing we could do is to ban all modern automobiles. Fortunately, none of the studies went so far as to suggest banning futures markets.

The other thing we could do is restrict the use of the modern automobile, on the grounds that it is dangerous. If we did not have adequate roads, all those modern automobiles might crash into one another. We could say, for example, that only certain people can use the modern automobile. By analogy, we could restrict the use of futures markets by imposing high margins or possibly even requiring physical delivery. In other words, we could find ways to make the costs of using this product so high that it would only be available to a few people.

Another way to limit the use of the modern automobile is to restrict speed. For futures markets, we could say, by analogy, that you cannot use the DOT system to trade baskets of stocks; it is too fast. Or we could impose the uptick rule on futures, so that when prices are declining, futures cannot be sold. In other words, slow it down—impose a speed limit. Or we could say that every hour on the hour, cars have to stop moving for fifteen minutes. Similarly, we could impose circuit breakers on markets.

The other thing we could do, of course, is to build better roads (or market-making systems) to take full advantage of the capabilities of the modern automobile (and of futures markets and other derivative markets). What surprises me about many of these studies is that this is the one option that they do not explore.

The emphasis of these studies is on how to curb this new invention "futures," which we all agree is good but which cannot be handled with our present road system. We should not be thinking that way. We should be thinking about improving the roads so that we can use the modern automobile to its fullest capacity.

We need better market-making systems. The time has come to say that quite possibly the specialist system is out of date and not capable of handling portfolio trades.

I do not mean to restrict this criticism to the specialist systems. All our market-making systems should be carefully examined to see whether they are capable of handling the kind of modern trading we have. If they are not, how can they be changed? How can we have better information about the potential buy-and-sell orders and limit orders on the books so that new buyers and sellers can come into the market as they are needed?

Much of the disorder on October 19 and 20 was in SEC-regulated markets—the New York Stock Exchange and the options exchanges. This suggests that there may be something in the SEC rules or in the market-making systems being used by these exchanges that can be improved.

In the rush to make recommendations, each of the studies fails to distinguish clearly between self-correcting problems and problems that might not be self-correcting. If we are going to impose new government regulations, they should be limited to cases where the self-interests of private market participants are not correctly aligned with the social interests—in other words, where there are externalities of some kind. The studies do not distinguish between recommendations to institute physical delivery instead of cash delivery, raising margins, tampering with the clearing associations, and curbing portfolio insurance.

But many of the problems revealed during the crash are quite clearly self-correcting. Mistakes were made. Sometimes you need a crash to illuminate weaknesses. The first ones who ought to know about the weaknesses and who have a stake in fixing them are those who have something to lose by their continued existence. Many of the problems identified will be automatically corrected.

There are also problems that may not be self-correcting, such as the market-making system. It seems to me that strong interests are involved in preserving the specialist systems in general. If there is an area of potential public policy interest, it may be in prodding exchanges to take a close look at their market-making systems to determine whether they are capable of handling the trading we have today.

PART II

FOREIGNERS GONE WILD

t would be interesting to know how many people on Wall Street could have defined the word "baht" before Thailand devalued it, on July 2, 1997. But that event—the decision by the Thai government to quit spending dollars to buy its own currency, in a quixotic attempt to maintain the baht's dollar value on the open market—triggered our next panic. By the time it was over, everyone on Wall Street could define "baht," along with "won" and "rupiah" and maybe even "ringgit."

To summarize, briefly: The collapse of the Thai baht in July 1997 caused the people who had invested in places that reminded them a bit of Thailand (South Korea, the Philippines, Indonesia, Malaysia) to take their money and go home. The next few months resembled a run on a bank, only the bank was all of Southeast Asia. Looking for someone to blame, Malaysian Prime Minister Mahathir Mohamad fingered the hedge fund manager George Soros, who was, he pointed out, by way of explanation, Jewish. This was usefully idiotic. Soros had given up trading (temporarily, as it turned out), but a lot of people who hoped to become the next George Soros were indeed selling Malaysia short in various ways—and making a fortune from the misery of others. By September 1998 the economist Paul Krugman could write, in *Fortune* magazine, that "never in the course of economic events—not even the early years of Depression—has so large a part of the world economy experienced so devastating a fall from grace."

At that point the panic had spread from Southeast Asia to the rest of Asia, including Russia. With the International Monetary Fund pumping in billions of dollars, the Russian government tried and failed to prop up the ruble, the Russian stock market crashed, and finally, on August 19, 1998,

Russia defaulted on its own Treasury bills. A putatively free Russia had a power over the U.S. financial markets that would have been the envy of the old Soviet Union: On August 31, the Dow fell 512 points, its second biggest point loss in history. Less than four weeks later the New York Federal Reserve was bailing out the world's most influential hedge fund, Long Term Capital Management, created and run by John Meriwether. By October the IMF and the World Bank were staging conferences to discuss the global economic crisis, and the U.S. Federal Reserve was following interest rate cuts with even more rate cuts. Like so many of these panics, the Great Asian Collapse was, from the point of view of Wall Street, a tragedy with a happy ending. The stock market boomed. People who managed money for a living raised their fees, by quitting their old firms and opening hedge funds.

This section includes a handful of other real-time newspaper accounts, to give the flavor of various moments, and also some longer after-the-fact testimony by several people intimate with the crisis, either as speculators (Rob Johnson, who worked for Soros) or economists (Jeffrey Sachs and Paul Krugman), advising governments how best to cope with the mess on their hands. I've also thrown in a long piece I wrote for the *New York Times Magazine*, about the collapse of Long-Term Capital Management.

When I went back to visit my former Salomon Brothers colleagues, now working at Long-Term Capital Management, I assumed that the jig was up, not just for them but also for hedge funds. Here was the world's leading hedge fund, in ruins. The effect of the Asian panic, I assumed, would be to discredit hedge funds more generally. They'd been blamed for triggering the crisis, and then for accelerating it to the speed where it threatened to end capitalism as we know it. But the panic—like all these panics—did nothing but strengthen the booming hedge fund industry. Instead of rebelling against the LTCM model, the markets simply rebelled against LTCM—and weakly. (John Meriwether was soon up and running under a different name, JMW partners.)

And so this section, as much as anything else, describes not the fall but the rise of the ever more highly mobile financier, running ever more highly mobile money, as allocator of capital and driver of prices and behavior. Obviously the poor guy in Thailand who lost his company doesn't think of his crisis as a Wall Street subplot. But on Wall Street, that's what it was. Capital was fast. It was about to become even faster.

Mutual Funds Quarterly Report; The Forecast Looks Brighter for Adventure Travel

REED ABELSON

The New York Times, *January 7, 1996*

This could be the year that funds venturing into investor-forsaken places like Mexico, the Philippines and other emerging markets are amply rewarded for their daring.

"We're very optimistic about the year ahead, given what we've had for the last two years," said J. Mark Mobius, the manager of the Templeton Developing Markets Trust, who has been scouting opportunities across the globe for the Franklin Templeton Group since 1987.

Many investors still have a bitter taste in their mouths from their last foray into emerging markets. Salivating after spectacular gains in 1993, when the average stock fund devoted to emerging markets gained 72 percent, investors rushed into such funds just before Mexico unexpectedly devalued its peso in 1994. Markets from Argentina to Hong Kong suffered the aftershocks, and the investors lost money. The average diversified emerging-markets fund lost 10 percent in 1994 and 7 percent in 1995.

But it pays to forgive, if not forget. The emerging markets still represent fast-growing economies where returns are expected to be significantly greater than in developed countries over several years. The declines in many of these markets have made prices attractive and created good candidates for a rebound.

While no one knows when emerging markets will recover, the last two long and grisly years make many analysts and portfolio managers optimistic. "It's easy to say it's going to be better," said Grace Pineda, the manager of the Merrill Lynch Developing Capital Markets fund. Although many countries continue to push for economic change, and their companies report big earnings gains, many stock prices do not yet reflect such improvements.

Some managers, like Mr. Mobius, are looking at the markets that have suffered the most. In Latin America, Mexico, Argentina and Brazil are among the countries most attractive to Mr. Mobius, while Hong Kong tops his list in Asia. "None of the other markets in Asia really excite us," he said. More adventurous than some of his colleagues, Mr. Mobius is making selected investments in Russia and India, despite those countries' reputations as difficult places for foreigners to make money.

To be sure, investors should not count their gains before they arrive. This may not be the recovery year for these markets, warned A. Michael Lipper, the president of Lipper Analytical Services, the mutual fund research firm in Summit, N.J. "The odds favor it," he said. "Let's not give it some Newtonian law."

But the fundamental case for emerging markets still looks convincing. While the domestic stock market is expected to have difficulty maintaining its torrid pace over the next year or two, the emerging markets are expected to pick up speed. The reason is that their economies are expected to grow much more rapidly than those of developed countries. Over the next decade, the World Bank expects Asia, excluding Japan, to have G.N.P. growth of nearly 8 percent, compared with about 3 percent for developed countries like the United States.

"The reason for investing in emerging markets is the return," said Ken Gregory, the editor of the No-Load Fund Analyst, a newsletter based in San Francisco. "Higher growth makes for a compelling argument to invest there."

Asia has already proved to be a fast grower. "We think its long-term record of superior growth will continue through 1996 and 1997 and 1998," said Richard Bruce, a portfolio manager with Rowe Price-Fleming, which manages T. Rowe Price's international funds. Although he does not expect some of these markets, like Thailand and Malaysia, to be spectacular performers in 1996, he sees them as attractive over the next several years.

Most investments in the emerging markets, including Asia's, are also available at much lower prices than just two years ago. The average price-earnings multiple has dropped sharply. And many companies offering their shares to investors for the first time are expected to find much lower prices than comparable concerns did in 1993 and early 1994, according to Mr. Mobius.

Thailand Warns
Currency Speculators

The New York Times, *December 17, 1997*

The Bank of Thailand said yesterday that it would take action against companies that it believes are speculating in dollars. "The central bank will monitor who is buying dollars in a speculative way and will take measures to stop that," said Chaiyawat Wibulswasdi, the governor of the central bank. He did not say what measures would be taken.

The bank called in 15 Thai companies two weeks ago to ask them to sell dollars that they were holding to make future payments on their foreign loans. Yesterday morning, Finance Minister Tarrin Nimmanahaeminda renewed his plea that companies sell dollars to ease the pressure driving the baht to record lows.

A Thai Business Wonders, Will It All Crumble?

DAVID HOLLEY

The Los Angeles Times, *September 10, 1997*

Vorachan Vinyarath's wallpaper-importing business got off to a roaring start when she launched it early last year, while Thailand was still enjoying its decade-long economic boom.

The firm jumped from 30 employees up to 50 in five months, and switched from moderately priced Taiwanese wallpaper to a focus on a luxury Italian brand, supplemented by high-quality imports from the United States and New Zealand.

"When Thailand was in a good economic situation, I think people were overspending," said Vorachan, 55. "That's why we started importing Italian and American wallpaper. People would buy the best things: the best wallpaper, the best this, the best that. They could afford it."

Now, with Thailand's economy suddenly stumbling into a period of near-zero growth or outright contraction, Vorachan, president and main owner of Phoenix Interhome Co., worries about her firm's survival. With the Thai currency at about 35 baht to the dollar—down some 30% since it was floated on July 2—import businesses are taking a terrible beating.

"For the past two months, we can make sales, but we have no profits,"

Vorachan said. "As long as we don't lose money, we are very lucky. I don't know how long the situation will go on like this, but if the baht goes to 40, maybe we'll go bankrupt—not just us, the whole country."

Vorachan does have a plan for survival. She is switching the firm's focus once again, this time to South Korean wallpaper.

South Korean products "are as good quality, but maybe the designs are not so modern or the colors are not so subtle," explained Vorachan's daughter Ploenchan Vinyarath, 25, a graduate of a London art and design college who helps manage the firm.

But even if imports from South Korea—where a falling won holds export prices down—help Phoenix Interhome survive, they won't bring back the good old days, when contractors raced to build condominiums, luxury hotels and huge housing developments.

Indeed, the wallpaper import business says a lot about Thailand's recent, overheated past.

It took off a decade ago, when builders sped up their work in response to rising demand but often let workmanship standards fall. Walls "usually had bad finishes," so "to cover up their mistakes, they had to use wallpaper," Ploenchan said. "Now people are running out of money, so they go for similar ones but not as good quality."

And the bind faced by firms like Phoenix Interhome reflects the myriad difficulties afflicting Thailand's economy today.

The cost of imports, in baht terms, is up sharply. But with the economy slowing, many firms are trying desperately to sell their stock, so it is nearly impossible to raise prices of luxury goods to cover costs—even as the price of food, utilities and other daily necessities rises, Vorachan said.

Meanwhile, a liquidity crunch is rippling through the financial and real estate sectors, affecting any businesses, such as Vorachan's, that depend on them.

"What we are suffering from is that housing is dead," Vorachan said.

The problem is exacerbated because wallpaper is usually "the last job" when homes are built, Ploenchan said. "That's usually when the money runs out," she explained. "That's why we're facing a problem in collecting the money."

Vorachan clings to her natural optimism.

"That's to keep myself happy too," she admitted. "I don't want to think too much. If I see the bad points, I think too much and I can't sleep at night."

The Thai people are also sustained by a widespread belief that there is a "sacred" force that protects the nation, and by deep respect for the royal family, she said.

"We have our king, who is really concerned about the well-being of his people," she said. "Even though we are a democratic country, we still listen a lot to our monarchy. With these two together, we feel we won't go down to the real bottom that other countries suffer. I think this is the lowest we can go. I think we may suffer for a couple of years, and then things will start to get better again."

She adds, "We need an economist with a talented tongue to persuade those foreign investors to come back."

Saving Asia

PAUL KRUGMAN,
REPORTER ASSOCIATE JEREMY KAHN

Fortune, *September 7, 1998*

Whatever happens next, the Great Asian Slump is already one for the record books. Never in the course of economic events—not even in the early years of the Depression—has so large a part of the world economy experienced so devastating a fall from grace. Latin America, once the world champion when it came to economic instability, has lost the title. Compared with Asia's debacle, the tequila crisis of 1995 now looks like a minor wobble; and the once terrifying debt crisis of the 1980s, a positively placid affair.

Moreover, Asia is nowhere near having hit bottom: While the region's currencies seem to have stopped plunging for the moment, its real economies are getting weaker, not stronger. Hong Kong just announced that its economy shrank 2.8% in the first quarter of 1998, its worst recession since World War II. Economists predict that Indonesia's GDP will fall an astonishing 15.1% this year. Compare that with America's worst postwar recession year—1982—when the economy shrank 2.1%. And it turns out that Japan's bad bank debt is not $550 billion, as previously reported, but a whopping $1 trillion. The repercussions from all this bad news are just now being felt, not the least of which is a case of the jitters for the U.S. stock markets.

There have already been many recriminations over whom to blame for this catastrophe. Was it punishment for Asian sins or the nefarious work of evil speculators? Did the IMF make the best of a bad situation or did it simply pour fuel on the fire? There is some point to these arguments: Figuring out who lost Asia may help the world keep this crisis, or the next one, from spreading. But the really important question is, Now what? Do we—meaning the IMF, the U.S. Treasury, and the afflicted countries— stick with Plan A, the strategy we've been following so far? Or is it time to try Plan B? And what is Plan B, anyway?

The short answer is that it is time to think seriously about Plan B. And Plan B is fairly obvious—except that nobody, not even Plan A's harshest critics, has been willing to talk about it openly. But before we get to that, let's remind ourselves of how we got here.

Asia: What Went Wrong

By now the outline of how Asia fell apart is pretty familiar. At least in part, the region's downfall was a punishment for its sins. We all know now what we should have known even during the boom years: that there was a dark underside to "Asian values," that the success of too many Asian businessmen depended less on what they knew than on whom they knew. Crony capitalism meant, in particular, that dubious investments— unneeded office blocks outside Bangkok, ego-driven diversification by South Korean chaebol [large, family-operated conglomerates]—were cheerfully funded by local banks, as long as the borrower had the right government connections. Sooner or later there had to be a reckoning. Even before the crisis, at a time when foreign banks were still lending and Indonesia's debt was rated Baa [for average creditworthiness], the facade was beginning to crumble: Big Korean companies were going belly-up; Thai finance companies were folding.

But financial excess, abetted by undue political influence, and a morning-after hangover are not particular to Asia—remember those Texas thrifts? The unique aspect of Asia's comeuppance is not the awful-ness of the crime but the severity of the punishment. What turned a bad financial situation into a catastrophe was the way a loss of confidence turned into self-reinforcing panic. In 1996 capital was flowing into emerging Asia at the rate of about $100 billion a year; by the second half of 1997 it was flowing out at about the same rate. Inevitably, with that kind of reversal Asia's asset markets plunged, its economies went into recession, and it only got worse from there. The upshot—well, let's quote from the June report of the Bank for International Settlements, an organization based in Basel, Switzerland, that is not usually given to purple prose: "The effects of economic slowdowns, asset price collapses, and banking crises tend to be mutually reinforcing as the curtailment of bank credit depresses asset prices and further deepens recessions. This in turn creates additional problems for banks that are forced to retrench still further. 'Vicious circle' has been an overworked term, but it describes Asia's crisis all too well."

So What Do You Do?

In the early days of the Asian crisis, Stanley Fischer—the economist's economist who is also the second-highest-ranking official at the IMF—warned a Hong Kong audience of "the possibility that [speculative] attacks become self-fulfilling prophecies." He worried, for instance, that any attack that forces a devaluation and higher interest rates would also weaken the banking system. In other words, you can't accuse the IMF of being naive: Officials there understood right from the beginning that the vicious circle the BIS so eloquently describes was a possibility, and they tried their best to prevent it.

Working closely with the U.S. Treasury (whose own No. 2 is, of course, Lawrence Summers, another major economics heavyweight), the IMF came up with a strategy that went like this:

1. Lend the afflicted countries money to help tide them over the crisis.
2. As a condition for the loan, demand that they reform their economies, eliminating the worst excesses of crony capitalism.
3. Require them to maintain high interest rates to entice capital into staying in the country.
4. Wait for confidence to return and for the vicious circle to turn into a virtuous circle.

Even in retrospect, this was by no means a stupid strategy. Imagine for a moment that the U.S. had no deposit insurance, and that doubts about a major bank's management had caused a run by the bank's depositors. What would the Federal Reserve do? Well, it would probably lend the bank some cash to meet its immediate needs; as a condition for the loan, demand that the bank president fire his nephew; and tell the bank to try to hold on to its depositors by offering them high interest rates. Then everyone would cross his fingers and hope for the best.

What's more, this strategy worked the last time around. In 1995, Mexico experienced a crisis that, in its early months, seemed worse than the Asian debacle. Robert Rubin and company rode to Mexico's rescue with a large line of credit; the Mexicans moved to shore up their shaky banks; interest rates in Mexico were pushed sky-high; and then all held their breath. It was a terrible year for the Mexican economy, but in the end everything worked out: Money started flowing in again, interest rates fell, and after slumping 6.2% the first year, Mexico staged an impressively rapid recovery.

In other words, Plan A was the natural thing to try. You might even say that it was inevitable: Given not just the economic but the political logic of the situation, and given the success of a similar strategy in Mexico just two years before, how could the IMF and the Treasury not try to repeat their earlier triumph?

The Critics

While the IMF's response to the Asian crisis may have been a foregone conclusion, that didn't mean that it went unchallenged. From early on there has been a chorus of disapproval, which has left the IMF's public image badly battered. And some of the critics may have been at least partly right—but only some of them, because the critics disagree more with one another than they do with the IMF. Roughly speaking, half of them are hard-money types: people who think that the IMF brought on the crisis by encouraging countries to devalue when they should have kept their exchange rates fixed. The other half are soft-money types, who think that the IMF placed too much emphasis on currency stability. They can't both be right.

Actually, some of them are wrong for sure. The hard-money attack on Plan A—an attack mainly carried out on the opinion pages of *Forbes* and the *Wall Street Journal*, and by other supply-side conservatives—amounts to saying that Asian countries should have defended their exchange rates at all costs. To have done this in the face of massive capital flight, however, would have meant drastically reducing the quantity of money in circulation—producing extremely high interest rates, far higher than what the countries have had to impose. And a central bank that can't print money because it is required to keep the exchange rate fixed can't act as a lender of last resort, providing cash to local banks threatened with runs. (Argentina, whose "currency board" and one-peso/one-dollar policy are much lauded by conservatives, could only watch helplessly as its banking sector started to implode in 1995; luckily the World Bank came to the rescue.)

If you ask the hard-money types why they think their plans would have worked, why they wouldn't have produced a worse catastrophe, the only answer you get is that if only Thailand hadn't devalued, or if Indonesia had established a currency board, confidence would have returned, and everything would have been all right. Well, maybe—but it's a completely circular argument. After all, any economic plan for Asia would have worked if it had instantly restored confidence. Why not skip the currency board and simply tell people to smile more often?

And for those who think that this crisis wouldn't have happened if only we had been on the gold standard, remember that the last time most major currencies were tied to gold was in 1929 . . .

The soft-money critics of the IMF, like Harvard's Jeffrey Sachs—who think less emphasis should have been placed on currency stability—had a better case. They argued—correctly—that the high interest rates the IMF was demanding of countries would cause severe recessions and financial distress, and that as a result even healthy banks and companies would eventually collapse. So instead of insisting that countries raise interest rates to defend their currencies, they thought the IMF should have told countries to keep interest rates low and try to keep their real economies growing.

That advice sounds pretty good, so it's important to understand why smart people like Fischer and Summers didn't take it. For starters, the way the advice was given—wrapped in vitriolic accusations that the IMF was both secretive and incompetent—didn't help. More important, however, the soft-money critics never explained what was supposed to happen to exchange rates. In late 1997 the Korean won lost half its value in a matter of weeks. Wouldn't it have plunged even further, perhaps even gone into free fall, if Korea hadn't raised interest rates? And wouldn't that have risked spurring a hyperinflation—not to mention instantly bankrupting all those banks and companies that had large dollar debts?

These questions never got a clear answer. Jeff Sachs has at times seemed to suggest that lowering interest rates would have strengthened rather than weakened Asian currencies—that even though investors would have received lower rewards for holding won or bahts, the prospective improvement in the state of the real economy would have—you guessed it—restored confidence. At other times he has simply seemed to argue that while the currencies would fall, they wouldn't fall all that much, and little harm would be done. Well, maybe—but as of last autumn that didn't seem as good a bet as Plan A.

And so Plan A it was. But things have not gone too well.

Why the Plan Hasn't Worked

Last autumn nobody imagined that Year One of the Asian crisis could be worse than 1995 in Mexico. But it was: Indonesia is a wreck, and there are few rays of sunshine even in the IMF's obedient client states. What went wrong? Here's a partial list:

IMF mistakes. The IMF clearly got some of the details wrong—and some of those details were pretty big. It insisted that countries cut spending and raise taxes, a gratuitous deflationary policy that worsened the recession and the situation.

Too much leverage. Mexico was able to go through a year of interest rates that ran as high as 75% and survive. Asia's economies, it turned out, were more vulnerable because their corporations were much more highly leveraged. When your debt is four or five times your equity—an unheard-of ratio in the West but standard practice in South Korea—it doesn't take very long for recession plus high interest rates to wipe you out.

Japan. The world's second-largest economy—a country with a stable government, no foreign debt, and no inflation—should have been a locomotive for its neighbors, the way the U.S. was for Mexico. Instead, Japan has been very much part of the problem.

For all these factors, and maybe for other reasons we still don't understand, the past year has been almost unimaginably bad. It is true that the wild currency swings of last year have subsided and that currencies have stabilized enough for some Asian governments to try to cut interest rates a bit, but those rates remain far too high to jump-start their devastated economies. At the same time, the double squeeze of high interest rates and depressed economies is steadily driving even the best-managed companies into bankruptcy.

So what's left of Plan A? Well, Korea and Thailand are proceeding with bank cleanups along the lines of America's savings-and-loan rescue. That is definitely a good thing—but it is not at all clear why it should help promote short-term recovery. (Unless—you guessed it again—it restores confidence.) Anyway, given the deeply depressed state of their economies, bank reform is chasing a moving target: Good loans are turning into bad as you read this. Otherwise, the plan seems to have degenerated into one of waiting for Godot: buying time in the hope that something good will eventually happen.

And it might. Maybe Japan's new Prime Minister will astonish the world by devising a massive stimulus plan that pulls not only Japan but also the whole region out of its slump. Maybe there will be a spontaneous shift in investor sentiment, and money will move from Internet stocks to Asian bonds. Maybe—well, maybe the time has come to think seriously about Plan B.

What Is Plan B?

The hard-money types have been surprisingly quiet about Asia's predicament: They make occasional declarations that none of this would have happened if their advice had been taken, but they don't seem to be making any suggestions about what to do now. The soft-money types are more forthcoming: As always, they insist that Asian countries must cut interest rates in order to have a chance at recovery. And they're probably right. The problem is that the original objection to interest-rate reductions still stands. As Stan Fischer recently put it, "I can't believe that serious people believe that without temporarily increasing interest rates, we could have contained the problems" of plunging currencies. In late June,

Bob Rubin toured Asia urging countries to stick to their tight-money policies, presumably fearing that if they didn't, the region's currencies would again go into free fall.

In short, Asia is stuck: Its economies are dead in the water, but trying to do anything major to get them moving risks provoking another wave of capital flight and a worse crisis. In effect, the region's economic policy has become hostage to skittish investors. Is there any way out? Yes, there is, but it is a solution so unfashionable, so stigmatized, that hardly anyone has dared suggest it. The unsayable words are "exchange controls."

Exchange controls used to be the standard response of countries with balance-of-payments crises. The details varied, but usually they worked something like this: Exporters were required to sell their foreign-currency earnings to the government at a fixed exchange rate; that currency would in turn be sold at the same rate for approved payments to foreigners, basically for imports and debt service. While some countries tried to make other foreign-exchange transactions illegal, other countries allowed a parallel market. Either way, once the system was in place, a country didn't have to worry that cutting interest rates would cause the currency to plunge. Maybe the parallel exchange rate would sink, but that wouldn't affect the prices of imports or the balance sheets of companies and banks.

If this sounds too easy to you, you're right. Exchange controls present lots of problems in practice. Aside from the burden of paperwork and bureaucracy involved, they are—surprise!—subject to abuse: Exporters have an incentive to hide their foreign-exchange receipts; importers, an incentive to pad their invoices. Every country that has tried to maintain exchange controls for an extended period eventually finds the accumulating distortions intolerable, and there is a virtual consensus among economists that exchange controls work badly.

But when you face the kind of disaster now occurring in Asia, the question has to be: badly compared with what? After Mexico imposed exchange controls during the 1982 debt crisis, it went through five years of stagnation—a dismal result, but when your GDP has contracted by 5%, 10%, or 20%, stagnation looks like a big improvement. And think about China right now: a country whose crony capitalism makes Thailand look like Switzerland and whose bankers make Suharto's son look like J. P. Morgan. Why hasn't China been nearly as badly hit as its neighbors? Because it has been able to cut, not raise, interest rates in this crisis, despite maintaining a fixed exchange rate; and the reason it is able to do that is that it has an inconvertible currency, a.k.a. exchange controls. Those controls are often evaded, and they are the source of lots of corruption, but they still give China a degree of policy leeway that the rest of Asia desperately wishes it had.

In short, Plan B involves giving up for a time the business of trying to regain the confidence of international investors and forcibly breaking the link between domestic interest rates and the exchange rate. The policy freedom that Asia needs to rebuild its economies would clearly come at a price, but as the slump gets ever deeper, that price is starting to look more and more worth paying.

You don't have to agree that the time has come to adopt Plan B—or even that it will ever come—to admit that something like this is the obvious alternative to the current wait-and-hope strategy. And yet it is very hard to find anyone, even among the IMF's critics, talking about it. How come?

The Nonconspiracy of Silence

It's no surprise that the IMF and the U.S. Treasury haven't said anything about alternatives to the current Asian strategy. The key players are neither stupid nor doctrinaire, but as a political matter they must of course always express complete confidence in whatever harsh medicine they prescribe. Moreover, even to hint at the possibility of exchange controls might itself cause capital flight and force Asian countries to raise interest rates rather than lower them. In other words, Plan B is like a devaluation: Officials always deny firmly that they would even consider the possibility of such a thing until the moment they do it.

This gag rule applies not only to officials but to anyone who is associated with the strategy: bankers, major institutional investors, and so on. There is even some self-imposed moral pressure on those who have no policy role but are nonetheless broadly sympathetic with the policymakers and their dilemmas. Consider, for example, the situation of an economics professor and sometime journalist who has known Fischer and Summers all his professional life, wishes them well, and understands why they initially tried Plan A. As you might imagine, he would be very reluctant to go public with his doubts—say, to suggest in a major business magazine that the time has come for Plan B—unless he was pretty definitely convinced that Plan A had reached a dead end.

What is surprising is that neither the Western critics of the IMF nor the Asians themselves have talked much about how to cut interest rates without sending currencies into a free fall. Again, some of these people are very smart, and the thought that it might be necessary to resort to temporary exchange controls must have crossed their minds. Why not say so? One suspects that considerations of salesmanship may be playing a role. Cutting interest rates sounds very appealing; imposing exchange controls, with their deservedly unsavory reputation, does not; so maybe the thing is to emphasize the positive and worry about the unpleasant corollaries later.

And for the Asians themselves, the whole reversal of fortune may simply have been too much to take onboard at once. Barely a year ago these were the economies of the future; to admit that they may need to turn back the policy clock, to implement the kinds of emergency measures that the Latin Americans adopted during the 1980s, may be more humiliation than they can stand just yet.

Can you really blame them? If Asian nations did adopt currency controls, they'd have to brace themselves for an even rougher ride. Any chance of attracting new foreign investment would disappear. The financial markets would probably go into another swoon. But the damage, though painful, would be only temporary. As interest rates fell, local economies would eventually recover, confidence would return (for real!), and those nasty currency controls could be dropped—one hopes forever.

But if Asia does not act quickly, we could be looking at a true Depression scenario—the kind of slump that 60 years ago devastated societies, destabilized governments, and eventually led to war. Extreme situations demand extreme measures; it's time to talk about Plan B.

Interview with
Rob Johnson

from Frontline's *"The Crash," Spring 1999*

> *Johnson was a top portfolio manager for George Soros's Quantum Fund, a private investment fund, from 1992 to 1995. He left the money management business in 1996. (Interview conducted in the spring of 1999.)*

Can you explain the importance of exchange rates? . . .

Sure. The exchange rate is essentially the price at which you exchange goods between one society and another. . . . The way in which it tends to affect you . . . [is] your life as an employee. People all around the world are producing. They receive a wage rate in their domestic currency. How that competes with your wage in your own domestic currency, say, Indonesian rupiah vs. U.S. dollars, depends on the exchange rate. The exchange rate's, say, at 2,000, which it was before the crisis, then you have a relative sense of wages and wages adjusted for differences in productivity in the labor force.

It's almost as if the market is a religious icon. I see that mirrored in the very, very high valuation of the U.S. stock market and the tremendous conviction that citizens have that the United States is good, is right. The free market is great, and the stock market is where you put your money. When the exchange rate goes to 16,000, the relative cost of labor of any given quality type in the two societies changes. That sets in motion pressures to relocate employment to where things are cheap and to divest or lay off or cut wages in places where things are now relatively expensive. So at the first level, the competition for employment around the world, the terms in some sense, are set by the combination of the domestic labor costs in each place as translated to put on a comparable footing by the exchange rate.

If the rupiah was at 2,000 to a dollar, what does the investor want vis-à-vis the exchange rate, and what happens when the rupiah begins to lose value?
Well, the exchange rate to the investor is integral to how you value his investments. So it's nice to buy a foreign asset when you think the exchange rate is going to strengthen. For instance, a number of years ago, a guy I know bought a timber farm in New Zealand only because he thought the currency relative to the dollar was going to strengthen by 20% and that the timber farm wouldn't lose money. . . . A strengthening currency implies that the plant that you bought will be revalued higher in successive periods . . .

So if you bought into a country . . . and suddenly there are rumors that the currency is going to devalue, what happens?
Well, in the first instance, many of these developing countries institute exchange rate regimes like the peg to the dollar, a peg to a basket of currencies, to inspire confidence that that won't happen; meaning a devaluation will not happen, and therefore, inspire capital to flow in.

So you start the rumors of devaluation after a long period of stability when a lot of people have been inspired to go in. If there's nothing that's gone in, nothing has to come out. But generally when your question starts, a lot has already gone into the markets, so there can be a stampede. The things you think about at a time like that are, number one, other guys will be afraid, too, so even if [you] don't think they need to devalue, if lots of people run on the currency, it may be a self-fulfilling prophesy.

The second dimension is generally domestic interest rates in the economy skyrocket, because there's been a lot of foreign short-term capital that's gone into the country, like a Thailand or a Korea, that when it gets scared it runs. In essence, what you're doing is borrowing in that currency, transferring through the foreign exchange market and landing somewhere else to cover your exposure. Unfortunately, when those interest rates skyrocket, they often weaken the fabric within the economy.

Because?
Construction gets depressed, high interest rates make working capital expensive for businesses, and many, many companies come under stress, consumer durable purchases slow down. . . . Many times, when the economy starts to stagnate investors and speculators say, "Well, now the economy is weakening. They're going to need a weaker exchange rate to stimulate exports and come out of their slump." But if that belief is reinforced, then the currency gets weaker still, which means interest rates go higher still, and the devaluation almost becomes self-fulfilling.

And the smart traders have figured that out ahead of everybody else?
The smart traders and investors will have studied what you might call the vulnerability of the economy, and they will say, "Is this economy in the jaws of the lion?" where the lion is this process we've just discussed. If they feel it is a candidate for that, they may withdraw their investments, so-called removing long positions.

Alternatively, they may take a short position. Now, it's not costless to take a short position because, for instance, in Thailand when people got scared, interest rates might be 40% or 50%. So if you're borrowing at 50%, hypothetically, and lending in the United States at 5% and you wait a year and you don't have a devaluation, you lost 45% of your money, just the difference between the two interest rates.

Who would be borrowing at 40% and investing at 5%?
Anybody that's taking a short position in the currency . . .

What are you betting on? . . .
I'm betting the Thai baht will devalue against the dollar to which it's pegged, and when I make that bet, I need to essentially borrow Thai baht, go to the foreign exchange market, sell my Thai baht and buy U.S. dollars, and then I deposit the U.S. dollars in the bank. The borrowing of

the Thai baht that precedes the foreign exchange transaction, comes at an interest rate and the deposit in the U.S. bank receives an interest rate. If you sit there for a year after putting that transaction on, and you paid 50% to borrow, and you've earned 5% in the U.S. bank, you've lost 45% of your money. If there is no exchange rate devaluation.

But if there is?
. . . let's say you held it for a year, you would net out 45% and then whatever you gained on the other side. But the art of being a good speculator is not to pay 45% for a whole year, it is to pay it for about 72 hours, so that you're just on the train before things go and then you cover the position subsequently, meaning you then take the money out of the U.S. bank, go back through the foreign exchange market, and then buy back the Thai baht and retire the debt that you took out.

So you retire the debt and because the currency has devalued, you've made . . .
Yes. If the Thai baht is at 24 when I sell it and it's 40 when I buy it back, I've made 16 baht in the round trip. Then that offsets . . . that interest rate.

So that's what's called . . . shorting the currency.
Shorting the currency and then covering the short is the retirement of that position. . . . The dynamic is when people sense that an exchange rate is vulnerable. The people who are so-called long in the Thai baht, or have investments that have currency exposure to the Thai baht, are alerted to the potential to lose money, and they do what's sometimes called hedging the currency exposure. It's identical in transaction to shorting by a speculator, but it's shorting against something that's already long. Or the equivalent would be liquidating the position. If you own a plant that produces shoes in Thailand, you could sell the plant, but the other thing you could do is short the currency to insulate yourself from the currency risk while continuing to own the operating business.

A speculator, in addition to thinking about the transaction and the pressure and whether the spike in interest rates will be self-fulfilling is also looking at things like: Did a lot of Thai banks borrow dollars, because dollars had a 5% interest rate, and in tranquil times Thailand had a 12% interest? So the banks were all funding themselves off shore.

Well, you know once they get scared, they've got to cover their positions, too. So, many times what you'll look at as a speculator is, number one, what is the structure of financing in the country? Do corporations and financial institutions have a lot of off-shore borrowing? . . . If you know a lot of domestic institutions have been borrowing abroad to finance domestic business, they're going to get scared and they're going to have to short the baht to cover their exposures, retire their foreign debt, and so forth.

You watch for those kinds of structural situations. You then look at the macro-economic fundamentals: Is this an economy which will come into . . . a realm where it has a policy dilemma, where in order to defend the currency they have to let interest rates go up? If interest rates go up and it weakens the fabric of the economy, which makes it more likely that they will relinquish defense of the currency regime. It makes it more likely that they'll let interest rates and let the currency weaken . . .

A speculator will look for that kind of phenomena. It doesn't mean he created it, but it does mean it's not synthetic. It's a real situation that's going to happen. My own feeling is that most speculative crises are accelerated in time by speculators. Because they see it, they anticipate, and they start to act early, which intensifies the interest rate pressure and causes the thing to play out and rupture. But they don't cause it. It would just take place several months later.

But they do, arguably, make [moves] that can turn it into a stampede . . . there's not time for a government to take moderate steps or figure out what to do.
I think that there is some truth in that. The officials in most countries do what's called intervening in the foreign exchange market. They have foreign exchange reserves at the central bank . . . sometimes they resist the level of the exchange rate or they try to keep it at a certain level. But many in floating rate countries, like the United States and Japan, are not as concerned about the level as they are about the violence of the rate of change. So they will intervene to slow down or give pause or make more orderly the transitions. . . . In essence, the capital market has gotten so large and so forceful that the scale of the capital market relative to the scale of the central bank's tools and reserves has gotten enormous. The markets can gobble up the attempt of the authorities to smooth the transitions, to slow down that velocity of change almost instantly . . .

What was your life like when you were making these trades—hour by hour, minute by minute. Is it possible to explain it?

A little bit. By the time you're active as a portfolio manager in that world, you have read about the data, what election schedules there are, who's strong and who's weak in politics, what potential there is for policy change, government minister speeches, and all the context. It's like an information overload from all around the world.

It's continuously coming at you, but you learn to assess probabilities, probabilities of change, detecting changes in tax policy, interest rate policy, and so forth, and so you get to the point where each day you're watching prices. Prices are either contradicting or they're confirming hypothesis you have about what's happening in the world. Many times, rather than reading something in the newspaper or figuring something out because I've talked to a government minister or what have you, I'll see a price movement. And I know that I don't know that much.

Your entire life is unclear when you're a trader because you're watching, and prices sometimes tell you somebody knows something you don't, you'd better jump on the telephone, talk to people through telecommunications, e-mail, what have you, get over there and find out what's going on that's making those prices change.

Another thing you become very conscious of, this underlying sense of politics is the grid, but a sense of where everybody's positions are. Have people been long and enthusiastic about Internet stocks recently? Well, you know they have. You know there are a lot of people who've bought a lot of it. If you believe there's no more good news, you know that positions are, how we say, vastly accumulated in those Internet stocks. Bad news may cause them to fall very abruptly.

So you're trying to sense, in some sense, the psychology of what people will react to, what positions they have, so the capacity for asset prices to change through volume of changing portfolios, and you're trying to discern what truth is underneath about the world around you. It's not just a question of discerning what's going on, on the political grid or the economic business cycles. It's also understanding how that will inspire action by other people.

John Maynard Keynes once had an analogy that he talked about, and he said, "It's like a beauty contest where you're not judging the pictures of the 10 most beautiful girls; you're judging from the 10 beautiful girls what the other people will think is most beautiful in trying to predict who will win the beauty contest . . . " Some of what you do during the day, then, is talk to other investors and see what they're reacting to in the newspaper, what makes them afraid, what they seem inspired by, what hypotheses they have.

The other thing that's kind of tortuous is when you have a portfolio like this that you're responsible for, you spend almost all your time, even some of your dreaming time, thinking of things that could help you and how you would react. Contingencies—this is called risk management. How am I going to react if this happens or, alternatively, what can I imagine that could happen that could hurt me that I haven't thought of yet? When I sit at the pool on Saturdays with my kids, sometimes they think I'm not there, because in my mind I'm off playing these scenarios through, in my mind. It's very abstract thinking, but it's all about trying to stay a couple of steps and anticipate and understand what's coming up.

You told me that George Soros has a sense or a nose for political instability in the future . . .
Well, in my view, the value of an asset is intermingled with politics. The whole, what I might say, legal regime and sense of trust and how the government sets the rules affects the value of currencies, bonds and equity markets, and if you think if there's going to be a big change in corporate taxes, it's going to affect the stock market. So the government plays a big role in setting expectations of what value will be. . . . A man like Soros, who in his own writing has talked about fleeing Nazi persecution in Hungary and, in the very formative part of his life, understanding political instability, seems to sense when political regimes are gathering strength, under stress, coming unstuck, and that gives him almost like a divining rod to discern when big changes in asset prices are in the offing. I don't think everybody is endowed with that level of sensitivity.

But when somebody like George Soros begins to make a move on a currency, that's not a secret anymore, is it?
Well, there is a very rational process going on in the financial markets. It goes kind of like this, "I know I'm not that smart. But I know Soros is. So I'll watch what he's doing, and I'll go along for the ride." They're drawing inference from his actions that he knows something. Just as I

spoke earlier about detecting from prices that something must be going on, people know that Soros's organization has an extremely sophisticated information-gathering and interpretative capability, and so they draw inference about what's about to change in the world based on the fact that he's got a reputation for early action. Now, in that case, you can go along with the Soros organization or any other fund and be on board for their mistakes, as well as their successes. No one has a perfect batting average.

And I don't think it's just about the scale of money. George Soros has . . . more than $15 to $20 billion under management and that's very large at this day. But it's more important to be smart than to be large. In other words, if I'm choosing who to imitate, I'll imitate a smart guy before I'll imitate a large guy just because, how would I say, you're trying to draw inference about what's happening that you don't know about . . .

If Soros or one of his funds decides to either buy a currency or dump a currency, physically how does that happen. . . .
Let's say the Soros organization, or someone of similar reputation, the Tiger Fund or Moore Capital Management. . . . If they start to transact, what you'll see on the screen is just evidence of change in prices. But it will not be identified with the person who was selling; it will just be a price change. But they're buying and selling vis-à-vis some dealer or broker and that dealer or broker will know. That dealer or broker may also have his own proprietary trading arm and may choose to buy or sell along with the Soros or Tiger, and they may also have other customers, some of whom have been attracted to dealing with them because they know those guys know about Soros.

So it's a bit . . . like your ear to the ground kind of thing. People who are trying to figure out what Soros is doing, try to figure out who he's dealing with. . . . Then you go to those dealers and you promise them your order flow if they'll let you peek under the tent and get a sense—not moment by moment—but just a sense of the transaction . . .

But the Soros organization and the other high reputation funds also think about the strategies of how do you deal with that. In other words, if you know somebody's a real loud mouth and you want to go long $10 million, what you do is you go to the loud mouth and you sell $500 million, let them tell everybody that you're going short, then you step in with a quieter buy, and everybody's selling to you, thinking that you're selling, while you're buying.

Let's talk about the phrase you used that this stuff can be like a "video game" . . .

Well, I think the analog to a video game is that you're looking at electronic screens. When I watch my children playing Nintendo or Sega or Pokemon or whatever the current game is, it's analogous. There's an electronic screen. At some level, the video game is like a virtual reality. You're playing with this game with your imagination. In essence, you're not out in the field experiencing the changes in employment and agricultural harvests and things like that. You're looking at a distillation of all the indicators about that process over an electronic screen. You're removed from the actual economy, all trying to interpret the economy through electronic means. It can take on that video game-like tone because you're sitting in an air conditioned room.

I said that somewhat facetiously because a video game that my son plays, he just plays in the living room and then goes to bed. A video game that international speculators play has a very profound effect of the well being of people through the effect on interest rates, exchange rates, asset prices, commodities prices.

. . . at the time I said that I was hoping to inspire people to be a little bit angry, because at one level, if you view it in that lobotomized fashion, that insensitive way, you say with all of these countries and all of this information and all of these things that you can do, it's a tremendous mental exercise, and it is a tremendous game.

But, at another level, it is not a game, because the consequences of what's happening in the world, and prices and the interaction between investors and the livelihood and well being of people, is much more serious and much more important than just a game. When my son and I played the table 64, it doesn't have any adverse side effects for society. When you're involved in large-scale speculation, there are very real consequences.

It's like we're talking about some chess game in the sky. Most of us don't even have any idea . . . that this game is going on.

Yes, I think that's partially true. The nature of the abstract thinking that's going on in the investment community is sometimes discernible through comments you see in the financial pages. But the way in which all of these prices that affect employment and how goods are bought and sold and what countries experience boom and which countries are in stagnation, I don't think that that connection between how the investor-trader world is setting prices and then the real consequences is well established.

Finance and Economics:
A Detour or a Derailment?

The Economist, *August 22, 1998*

n one respect, at least, the men who drive Russia's economy followed a steady course. A stable, freely convertible rouble brought the inflation rate down and made Russian shares and bonds palatable to foreign investors. Now, by allowing the rouble to fall by up to 34%, forcing borrowers to default on short-term debt and restricting capital-account payments, Russia's government this week managed to undo those achievements literally overnight. Yet it is doubtful whether their dramatic change of direction will be enough to put the troubled economy back on track.

The most immediate danger—the currency panic which was gathering momentum in advance of Monday's devaluation—has receded. Deterred partly by uncertainty, and partly by the huge spreads, of up to 50%, which opened between buying and selling rates, most Russians with rouble savings decided against moving into dollars. The exchange rate on August 20th was 7.9 to the dollar—only a fifth below its rate a week earlier.

The much bigger potential panic concerns the country's 1,600 banks, almost all of which have been made insolvent overnight by the rescheduling of their main asset, short-term government debt. Faced with cashiers who rudely tell them that "money is finished for today," or impose an arbitrary limit on withdrawals, depositors have so far remained remarkably calm. This patience reflects customers' expectations, shaped by the generally patchy standard of service in Russian retail finance, and is unlikely to last indefinitely.

So far as ordinary Russians are concerned, only one bank really matters: Sberbank, the state savings bank, which holds upwards of 80% of Russian households' savings and invests heavily in government debt. Managers maintain that short-term government debt amounts to only a quarter of Sberbank's assets, but they have declined to specify what the remaining three-quarters consist of. If Sberbank's depositors want cash, and if the bank is unable to liquidate enough of its bonds to give it to them, the government will face a serious problem.

The situation facing the privately owned banks is entirely different. Most deserve to fail, and because their business consists more of currency and bond-market speculation than of lending and deposit-taking, the man in the street would hardly notice their demise. On economic grounds, the government should make shareholders bear the loss and intervene only to protect small depositors. But all the important banks operate under the protection of powerful tycoons, who show every sign of expecting the state to bankroll their costly adventures. Poorly connected banks will most likely go under, while the better-connected ones are bailed out by the central bank. The central bank, however, said on August 20th it will guarantee all individual deposits.

The banks have already been allowed to dip into the reserve deposits they are required to keep at the central bank, which practically amounts to printing money to bail them out. The next line of defence will be the central bank's $15 billion of hard-currency reserves, much of it supplied by western taxpayers. Some of this may now be handed over to selected bankers.

Even if the state redeems the mistaken gambles of the past, keeps depositors' confidence alive, and does so without printing huge amounts of money, the future of the Russian banking system remains bleak. Credit ratings for Russian banks have crashed. New restrictions on private-sector capital-account transactions mean that they are unable, for the moment, to pay their foreign creditors. And where will they invest their money? Few have any serious lending skills (as their bad loans testify). Most know no other business than speculating on the debt market.

The second huge casualty of the past days is foreign investors' confidence. The worst outcome, a highly discriminatory treatment of foreign holders of government debt, has been avoided (or at least postponed) thanks to frantic lobbying by, among others, the International Monetary Fund, which threatened to cancel the second tranche of its aid programme to Russia. Details of the debt rescheduling will now be announced on August 24th.

Foreign investors are talking tough. CS First Boston, an investment bank, warned on August 18th that "massive lasting damage is being done to investor sentiment and future willingness to support reform in Russia." But such howls of pain are not entirely convincing. In recent months the rouble debt market has offered huge returns for huge risks, a game strictly for consenting adults. Other countries which have defaulted on their debts have found that foreign investors soon return.

In any case, Russia is not completely cut off from the world financial system. It continues to service the bulk of its debt—that denominated in dollars. For the time being, last month's $22.6 billion IMF-led bailout has not been cancelled (although the World Bank is delaying $400m in aid to the state budget, pending an explanation, due since January, of what has happened to the $900m previously lent).

The third casualty of the government's unexpected moves, and the one least able to bear the pain, is the Russian economy. The rouble's devaluation will not do much to create jobs in industry, because Russia's miserable output of manufactured exports—chiefly clunky cars, vodka and weapons—is not very price-sensitive. Most of Russia's exports are dollar-denominated commodities, which will not benefit from a cheaper rouble. Although imports have become dearer, those relatively affluent consumers who favour French cosmetics and German cars are unlikely to find Russian goods acceptable substitutes.

A bigger tonic to the economy will be the end of three-digit interest rates, which have sucked companies' cash on to the bond market, and away from suppliers and workforces. But that will be counterbalanced by a new squeeze on liquidity: a 90-day freeze on forward foreign exchange contracts, which will leave companies scrambling for hard currency to pay their overseas suppliers. So Russian workers, who will have to save more roubles than before to buy flats (which are priced in dollars) and foreign-made goods, are not likely to see those costs compensated by new jobs, much less higher wages or, for that matter, by wages paid in cash instead of in kind.

So it is not clear that anyone, aside from tycoons, is better off after this new financial package. Although the government can now claim to be running a budget surplus (easy enough, given its debt moratorium), it has yet to crack such fundamental problems as its inability to collect taxes, to enforce property rights and contracts, and to pay workers and pensioners the sums they are due. Even in the current climate of crisis, opposition forces in the Duma, Russia's parliament, are in no great hurry to help the government mend the economy. And, sooner or later, when those postponed debts must finally be paid, Russia will find itself in much the same place it has been until now: out of cash, and desperate for someone to lend it money.

Pulling Russia's Chain

MICHAEL LEWIS

Bloomberg News, August 19, 1998

The global financial system rarely deserves the attention it receives. In theory there is great human drama in the billions of little decisions that rocket capital around our planet, depressing some lives and inflating others. Yet somehow these elemental human passions, heaped into a great pile, become dull and almost meaningless. Still, every now and again, something dramatic and specific happens deep inside global finance that rewards close scrutiny.

In the past few days, such a thing happened in Russia.

There was a time not very long ago, when Russia seemed to be doing fairly well in the global financial news. Not so well as the Czech Republic, perhaps, but not nearly so poorly as South Korea. As recently as last Wednesday, politicians were pretending that everything in Russia was moving in the right direction. The International Monetary Fund had arranged a bailout package of $22.6 billion in loans. Financial confidence in Russia presumably had been restored. Certainly the U.S. Treasury had exhibited little concern; Robert Rubin's alarmist press releases had been directed mainly at Asia. And despite some turmoil in the Russian markets, Russian President Boris Yeltsin was on vacation.

Then, Thursday, the philanthropist George Soros sent a letter to the *Financial Times* of London. "The meltdown in Russia's financial markets has reached the terminal phase," he wrote. "Immediate action is required. . . . Unfortunately, international financial authorities do not appreciate the urgency of the situation."

In a few short paragraphs, Soros picked apart the IMF bailout package and the putative confidence of the world's political class in the Russian economy. He argued, rightly, that the IMF's goal of tight money and fiscal restraint clashed with the immediate need to bail out the Russian financial system. He demanded that Russia devalue its currency 15 percent to 25 percent and then peg the ruble to the dollar. But for the peg to hold, Soros wrote, "the Group of Seven [most industrialized nations] needs to put up another $15 billion."

In another age this sort of letter would have met with derision. A private U.S. citizen writing to a London newspaper demanding that a large country reform itself and that seven others cough up billions of dollars to help it along. Right. But this is not any other age. This is an age in which the levers yanked upon by elected officials no longer effect the direction of the machine. The veneer of official authority is not as important in the global financial system as the power to gain and hold the attention of Bloomberg World—the hundred-thousand or so traders, bankers, investors and analysts attached to Bloomberg terminals. There, official authority seems to be at something of a disadvantage.

Let's go to the tape.

On a normal day, the Bloomberg function that enables traders to call up news about Russia receives about 20,000 hits. The day George Soros published his letter it received 49,000 hits. The Bloomberg function that enables traders to call up news about George Soros normally receives about 140 hits a day. On Thursday it was hit 1,301 times; 1,301 financial people, many of whom no doubt own little pieces of Russia, wanted to know any news about George Soros. Soros' words rippled quickly through Bloomberg World that same day: Analysts up and down Wall Street staged impromptu conference calls to give their new, more pessimistic views on Russia. And on Thursday, the ruble plunged.

On Friday, Official Authority reacted, as it inevitably must. "I say it firmly and clearly," said Boris Yeltsin, from his holiday retreat. "There will be no devaluation. Everything has been worked out." Bloomberg World remained unmoved; the Yeltsin story, to judge from Bloomberg's internal statistics, was poorly read. On Friday, Bill Clinton interrupted his Meditations On the Meaning Of The Word "Sex" to phone Yeltsin. The idea, presumably, was to signal his confidence in Russian reforms. Again, Bloomberg World paid it no attention.

On Monday, George Soros got his way: the Russian central bank devalued the ruble. Previously contained in a narrow range around 6.2 rubles to the dollar, the ruble would now be permitted to float between 6.0 and 9.5 to the dollar. Boris Yeltsin interrupted his vacation and returned to Moscow. Robert Rubin finally leapt in with a press release saying he approved of the devaluation, and that the crisis had passed. But that put only an ersatz, official end to the crisis. The unofficial, authentic climax came Monday afternoon when Soros appeared on Moscow Radio. He said that Russia had "bought itself a little time. The government has stopped the collapse."

What is interesting here is how little markets care about anything elected officials have to say about matters most people assume that elected officials control. It isn't that Bloomberg World has no interest in Bill Clinton or Boris Yeltsin. Traders are glued to their screens whenever stories flash across about Clinton's sex life or Yeltsin's drinking habits. It's just that they have no interest in what Bill Clinton or Boris Yeltsin say about the Russian ruble, or many other financial matters. On finance, they prefer to hear from George Soros. Think of it! If the President of the United States wished to manipulate the world's financial mood, he could do it more effectively by calling Soros and asking him to say a few words.

This is the world we live in.

Interview with
Jeffrey D. Sachs

from Frontline's *"The Crash," Spring 1999*

*Sachs is the Galen L. Stone Professor of International Trade at
Harvard University and the Director of the Center for International Development. He has served as an economic advisor to
governments in Latin American, Eastern Europe, Russia, Asia
and Africa. (Interview conducted in the spring of 1999.)*

*What if a place like Russia is not ready to plunge into the global economy, into
international competition?*
In 1991, a miraculous thing happened, and that's [that] the Soviet Union
ended. . . . So there was an opportunity to build a very healthy and new
world, on the basis of the change that the Russian people themselves
wanted. But for Russia to make that change was going to be one of the
most remarkably difficult and complex passages imaginable. After all,
here was a new country, an empire had ended. . . . Here was a society
which had been dictatorial or authoritarian, for a thousand years, trying
to become a democracy. Here was a centrally planned economy, trying to
become a market economy.

You had great social upheaval. At the same time, the government itself was, literally, financially bankrupt, as a result of what the waning days of the Soviet Union had brought about. They needed massive help. Clever thinking. Lots of ideas. Lots of involvement. What did they get, by and large? They got a seven or eight person mission from the International Monetary Fund, putting up its nose, saying, "Why are you complaining so much? Just pay your debts. Do the reforms. Life will come out fine."

For the first two or three years of this transformation, they heard a lot of lecturing from Washington, but they didn't get any real financial help. I was there as an economic advisor to President Yeltsin. But I could see and said, publicly and privately, that if this has a chance, Russia is going to need a considerable amount of financial assistance. The tragedy is, it never came. What did come, came too late, after the reformers were kicked out. The whole notion that Russia needed some help was more or less scorned in the early years.

Now, we give away tens of billions to Brazil, or to one place or another, without thinking. But in those days, to give even a tiny amount to Russia was viewed almost as anathema by many parts of our own society and our political leadership, whether it was the Bush administration or the Clinton administration. [They] really just didn't want to get deeply involved.

Part of the '90s . . . was also the era of the Washington consensus. Explain that.
As of the late 1980s and early 1990s, a kind of professional consensus arose in Washington. It was called a consensus for the world, but how many people really believed all of it is an open question. A consensus came, at least within Washington, about how countries should change from non-market economies to market economies.

Now, the basic idea was that if a country would put its economy as an integrated piece of the world system, that it would benefit from that with economic growth. I concur with that basic view. The Washington consensus listed 10 or 12 steps—the recipe for economic development. When you look at those, they're all pretty reasonable. But it's a kind of bland list of commandments, rather than a real blueprint of how to get from A to B, much less from A to Z, when you're trying to make an extraordinarily difficult passage from one disaster to hopefully something better. There are so many land mines around that just having the list of the to-do's, the good things that one should do, is not really a strategy or a set of tactics.

So the Washington consensus had a lot of merit in one sense. It did provide some sensible, broad ideas, about how countries that were outside of the international system could become part of the international system. But it became a substitute for real thinking. It became a kind of mantra. It became a substitute for assistance, because the idea was, "You don't need us. You don't need any help. You don't even need a time-out on your debt payments. You just have to follow the magic rules, one through ten, and you'll be just fine."

So, in this sense, everything became over-simplified. The actions of the IMF and the World Bank became very stylized. The U.S. Treasury had its model, and unfortunately, at that level of simplicity, it just doesn't work.

Is the basic mantra, "Open your markets"?
Opening markets is a core part of the idea, because the essential truth for developing countries is, if you try to live by yourself, you will cut yourself off from the amazing progress of world technology. You won't be able to purchase the goods that you need from abroad, because you're not exporting to the rest of the world. You have to be part of the world system.

That's the essential element that's right about the Washington consensus. But how to do it, and what does it mean to open markets, it doesn't mean suddenly to let your banks and your enterprises borrow from New York banks, without any restraint, without any regulation, without any supervision. That's ironically what a lot of countries understood by this. They opened up their financial markets. They took on a huge amount of debt. Then they ended up in a massive amount of trouble down the road.

But that was essentially what we were also proposing, that they open their financial markets, and let capital flow freely.
We were proposing that these countries open their trading systems, which means that goods could flow freely. We were proposing that countries open their financial markets, so that we could lend to them or invest in their shares. We were proposing that these countries open up their economies to our long-term foreign direct investment, where American

firms would build factories abroad. We were proposing, in a sense, that the rest of the world be made safe for American ideas, as they adopted intellectual property rights that gave patent protection to our very innovative economy.

Now, again, there's a lot of truth to a lot of this, but how you do it counts. Just like you don't give a medical diagnosis on one page without seeing the patient, and you don't think that there is one remedy that fits all, the truth of good economic doctoring is to know the general principles, and to really know the specifics. To understand the context, and also, to understand that an economy may need some tender loving care, not just the so-called hard truths, if it's going to get by.

And so-called hot money . . .
To live on hot money, rather than some foreign assistance that may be needed, might work in the short term, and it might absolve the U.S. Congress or the administration of having to do the hard work of asking the American people to lend a hand some place, because after all, the banks will do it. But two or three years down the road, we really regret it. The banks yank their money. The economy collapses. Our foreign policy and economic goals are not met. Of course, the worst losers are the poor people and the poor countries that end up holding the bill.

Who was pushing this?
Globalization was a deep trend pushed by technology and right ideas, as much as anything else. And the failure of dozens of attempts throughout the rest of the world to try to develop in a closed way. So the deep push came from deep forces, but the way that the deep forces were translated into the day-to-day practice came from the U.S. Treasury, the International Monetary Fund, the World Bank. Of course, investment bankers were part of that milieu, as well.

All of this made these emerging market countries quite vulnerable . . .
When countries open up to trade, they generally benefit, because they can sell more, then they can buy more. And trade has two-way gain. When countries open up to financial flows, they can get themselves into a lot of hot water. If our banks are willing to lend to their banks a lot of money at short term, you get into a very vulnerable situation where, for

whatever reason, our banks decide to yank their money, that can bring down the whole economy that's borrowed from the international banks.

So, in the early 1990s, when a lot of the developing world opened up to international capital flows, without the right kind of regulatory environment, and not understanding how vulnerable they would become to panics and euphoric waves of sentiment, coming from London, New York or other money centers, they ended up with a tremendous amount of short-term debt, often invested in very good long-term projects, but projects that weren't going to pay off for five or 10 or 20 years.

If they have short-term debt, that means . . .
If you have a lot of short-term debt, it means that all of that money can be demanded in a very short period of time. Technically, short-term debt means money that's coming due within a year. Typically, it means money that's coming due within 30 to 90 days.

Now, if you have billions and billions of dollars coming due in a country in a short period of time, and if a sense of panic develops among your creditors, so that everybody demands the money out all at once, it's almost inevitable that the debtor economy will collapse, because it won't be able to come up with that amount of money in a short period.

That's what happened in Asia, to start this . . . most recent rolling crisis, in 1997.
In Asia, a lot of successful economies, that had been living on their own saving, decided to open up their financial markets to international capital in the early 1990s. So here were countries doing quite well, but they decided they'd borrow a bit more and do even better. They started borrowing several percentage points of their national income, every year. It added up to about $175 billion of short-term debt, owed by five developing countries in Asia: Indonesia, Korea, Malaysia, the Philippines, and Thailand. That $175 billion could all be yanked quite quickly.

When the creditors, which were mainly international banks, started to have anxieties about Asia in the middle of 1997, and then they started to have anxieties about what the other banks were going to do, because each one thought that the other one was going to get his money out first. Then they realized that the amount of short-term debt that was due was probably about 75% more than the short-term dollar assets that those countries held, a panic developed, in which every bank said, "We don't know and we don't care about the long term of this country. We just want our money out right now."

So, all of a sudden, there was a massive run on Asia, meaning that all the creditors wanted to yank their money out as fast as possible. And Asia didn't have the dollars to pay, so the dollars went into default. The currencies plummeted. Interest rates soared. Working capital disappeared. Production seized up. The whole region went into economic collapse.

Tragically, some of that process was actually aided and abetted in an odd kind of way by the IMF, itself. When the IMF intervened in the Asia crisis, it did it through such provocative steps, like insisting on large scale closures of dozens and dozens of banks, and financial institutions in the region, that the IMF's own actions triggered a large part of the panic, and made everything much worse than it would have been, had the IMF not been there.

Let's skip to Russia. The U.S. Treasury and the IMF were in Russia, standing by, watching a corrupt privatization. Can you talk about that?
The Russian drama began at the end of 1991, when the Soviet Union mercifully ended. Russia and 14 other new countries emerged from the ruins of the Soviet Union. Every one of those 15 new states faced a profound historical, economic, financial, social and political challenge. And for the first year or so, there was almost no-one around.

I had a rare privilege to be watching this from the vantage point of being an advisor to President Yeltsin of Russia. I could see that the IMF was only tangentially involved. Most of the other governments were watching and waiting, but no one was really getting involved in the serious and historic way that the circumstances demanded. By the end of 1992, so many technical mistakes had been made by the IMF, and so little help had come, that most of the reformers had already been pushed aside. Russia was in high inflation, and it was just going off the rails.

In 1993 and '94 most of the rest of the reformers were pushed aside. We ended up, by 1994, ironically with the Clinton administration a little bit more engaged than it had been in 1993. But now engaging with the likes of Viktor Chernomyrdin, an old "apparatchik" who . . . presided over one of the most corrupt privatization practices that one could imagine. Mr. Chernomyrdin emerged from Gasprom. Gasprom was the Russian state monopoly of natural gas. It had almost half of the world's natural gas deposits. Well, under Mr. Chernomyrdin, a lot of that was "privatized," meaning, given away to cronies and friends of the Yeltsin government . . .

Watching this disastrous spectacle was quite horrifying. I approached the IMF, the U.S. government, the Organization for Economic Cooperation and Development in Paris, and I said, "Look, we're watching one of the most corrupt privatizations imaginable. Let's do something. At least blow the whistle. We don't have to stand, and watch, and give aid, and give help at this point. We have to say that this is going to undermine the most fundamental legitimacy of this new society that the Russians are trying to build."

Ah, but we didn't want to have a word. Because, well, the reformers were mostly out. We thought that this government was better than any alternative. So we winked and smiled, turned our head, and ignored what was really a disastrous outcome.

One of the implications of that disaster is that the Russian government not only acted corruptly, not only built up a new oligarchy of billionaires out of nothing, basically, but also gave away its most valuable financial assets—its ownership of the huge natural resource sector in Russia.

Those resources could have been turned into real money, to be used to pay pensions, to close the budget deficit, to keep inflation low, to get the reforms under way. But they gave away those natural resources, and ended up instead relying on borrowing from international speculators and investors, at very high interest rates, on very short-term debts . . .

Talk about the establishment of the GKOs, the short-term government bills. Why were those instruments being set up?
One of the ideas was that the government should be able to borrow cash, both domestically and abroad. In principle and in moderation, there's nothing wrong with that. Every well functioning market economy has a treasury bill market. For the Russian government, if the choice was to always have to go from hand to mouth of what you took in revenue and spending it, versus having some means to borrow domestically and abroad on a market basis, the idea of having a market for treasury bills, which in Russian became called the GKOs. That was all right.

The problem became that the Russian government, without other sources of revenue, without any real "aid" from abroad, facing tremendous political pressures, and I have to add, huge corruption inside, so this is a very mixed picture, went on a borrowing spree, with a lot of it money borrowed from abroad on a very short-term, highly speculative basis.

This, in the end, as in so many other countries, is the immediate factor that did Russia in. But how did Russia get to that point of such dependence on short-term borrowing? First, we being the Western world, wouldn't let Russia off the hook on debt. So there were demands on debt servicing in the early days until they ran out of reserves. Then there was no real aid program, just a fictional aid program. Then, in my way of understanding this, the early reformers were basically pushed away. A lot of the old apparatchiks came back in, and corruption really dramatically increased in '94/'95, particularly around Yeltsin's reelection in 1996, when the government used corrupt practices to give money to business, part of which was returned to the campaign coffers, and helped pay for Yeltsin's reelection.

So by 1996, you had a situation that had a patina of order, a huge amount of corruption. As in so many other foreign policy debacles, the U.S. was saying, "He's our man." We were so happy to be dealing with him, no matter what was really going on. They just don't want to see the reports of the corruption. Rather than using its own natural resources, for example, or the income from them, and rather than getting real assistance with real reform from the outside world, Russia increasingly lived on short-term borrowing. Now, this was an extraordinary merry-go-round. It's what economists call, in essence, a Ponzi scheme. That means, "I'll put money into your scheme, and expect to get a great return, because some greater fool is going to come put in money, the next one." Now, he believes that he'll get out, because there'll be even more money coming in afterwards. The Russian treasury bills were paying 50% returns in dollars. For many months, actually more than a year, in effect, because of this Ponzi game, where each investor believed that there would be a greater fool, or they thought, even more cleverly, in the end, the IMF will come in and give Russia just the money they need, so the last amount can be pulled out. That's how the game was played until August 1998, when Russia ran out of foreign exchange reserves, because it was defending its pegged exchange rate. When the investors stopped lending to Russia, because it looked like the game was up, when they all suddenly said in the press, "If the IMF doesn't quickly lend Russia the money, it's the end of the world." The IMF actually threw in the last $20 billion program, but there was so much desire to get out that the flow that the IMF gave was totally eaten up and Russia simply went into default.

While this Ponzi scheme was building, a lot of investors and then speculators . . . were making a whole lot of money.
Anybody that got the money in and then was smart enough to take it out and go on vacation, make, say, a 50% return in dollars. This was the greatest game in town. What happens with a lot of these guys (mostly it's guys, that's just the truth), is that they get addicted to the easy money. They think they're all super geniuses, masters of the universe. They're going to lend. When they get the money out, they put it back in one more time. That greater fool is going to come, or the IMF is going to come, and get us out.

So a lot of people made money. A lot of . . . clever people that had made a lot of money up to that point, lost a huge amount of money on August 17th when, lo and behold, the IMF couldn't muster another one of these packages. Although even the IMF said, "If only we could do another one of these," because they're addicted to pumping in the money the same way. They like that game. That puts them in the center of attention and center of responsibility. Well, these people lost a lot of money in the end. So some made a lot of money. Everybody made large paper profits for a while. This was a great game.

I was horrified by it and was saying repeatedly in the press, in speeches, in articles, in books, "What's going on? The underlying policies aren't working. The corruption is rampant. The exchange rate is overvalued. The possibility of panic is huge." Yet, the money kept going in, until finally this massive withdrawal. The IMF made one last attempt. It was not enough and the system was finally overwhelmed by its own internal illogic.

Through 1997, this Ponzi scheme and the addiction to debt is building. Then the Asian crisis starts in the middle of '97. How does that affect Russia?
Around October 1997, with the Asia crisis getting worse, a lot of currencies in other parts of the world came under speculative attack. This means that international investors began to believe that those currencies would lose value, so they started withdrawing money. Therefore, the cur-

rencies would have lost value, unless the central banks put in the dollars to keep the currencies stable. Two cases were particularly hard hit. Russia being one; Brazil being the other. Eventually, both of them collapsed.

But in the short term, the U.S. told both of them, "Don't give up. Use your reserves. Defend the currency. Raise interest rates even higher," which I think is the kiss of death for employment, for growth and so on, and which Washington is very happy to give, because Wall Street is getting the high interest rates, among other people. "So don't change your currency. By the way, we'll give you some money, in case you need it, to keep that currency stable." So already, in October 1997, both Russia and Brazil were on a collision course with history. . . . It was absolutely clear. I was amazed at just how bad the advice was. I was amazed with the advice in Asia. I was amazed at the advice given to Russia and to Brazil, because it was basically the same everywhere. "Just raise those interest rates and keep paying the foreign investors, because that's what establishes confidence, after all. If need be, we'll give you the money to do it."

So this went on in Russia. But then another thing happened, oil prices collapsed. So here you had a country where the budget hadn't been observed or honored, for seven years of IMF programs. It was all phony. You had a huge deficit. Who was going to pay for that? You had oil prices collapsing. You had an overvalued currency, in the sense that exporters weren't profitable, so that was another factor. You had Washington saying, "Everything's fine. Just raise those interest rates." This was a textbook case where something should have been done. Of course, nothing was done until the race car hit the brick wall at full speed in a direct collision.

Were you surprised on the 17th of August . . . to find out that Russia was not only devaluing its ruble, but was defaulting on its debts?
. . . I was shocked. I'll tell you why. You sometimes default in dollars when you're, say, Russia or Brazil or others, and you've run out of dollars. Then you can't pay. But what Russia did was really amazing. They defaulted in rubles . . . there's no shortage of rubles. They can print them as much as they want, so it's extremely unusual for a country to default on its own currency, on obligations in its own currency.

It's not so unusual to run out of someone else's currency. By force majeure, as it's called, you absolutely have to declare a default, because you just don't have the dollars. But to do it in your own currency is quite extraordinary. There's more to this story than we really understand, because in some peculiar ways, even Washington may have been a little bit behind that, or not against it. It led to a huge international panic afterwards. But I have a feeling the Russians heard that maybe that wouldn't be so bad. If they did, it was extraordinarily wrong-headed advice.

How the Eggheads Cracked

MICHAEL LEWIS

The New York Times Magazine, January 24, 1999

A lot of unusual things have happened in the four months since Long-Term Capital Management announced that it lost more than $4 billion in a bizarre six-week financial panic late last summer, but nothing nearly so unusual as what hasn't happened. None of the 180 employees of the hedge fund have stood up to explain, to fess up or to excuse themselves from the table. Even the two Nobel Laureates on staff, who could very easily have slipped back into their caps and gowns in the dead of night and pretended none of this ever happened, have stayed and worked, quietly. The man in charge, John Meriwether, has shown a genius for lying low. Photographers in helicopters circle his house, and journalists bang on his front door at odd hours and frighten his wife. Yet whenever the question "Who is John Meriwether?" has demanded an answer, it has been supplied not by those who know him and work with him but by a self-appointed cast of casual acquaintances and perfect strangers. They have described Meriwether and his colleagues as reliable Wall Street stereotypes: the overreaching, self-deluded speculators. In doing so they have missed pretty much everything interesting about them.

Not long ago, I visited the hedge fund's offices in Greenwich, Conn., to see if its collapse made any more sense from the inside than it did from the outside. So many different activities take place in enterprises called "hedge funds" that the term is perhaps more confusing than helpful. In general, hedge funds attract money from rich people and big institutions and, as a result, are somewhat less stringently regulated than ordinary money managers. Long-Term Capital was an especially odd case, less a conventional money manager than a sophisticated Wall Street bond-trading firm. The floor it had constructed in Greenwich was a smaller version of a Wall Street trading floor, with subtle differences. The old wall between the trading floor and the research department had been pulled down, for instance. For most of Wall Street the trading floor is a separate room, distinct from research. The people who pick up the phone and place the bets (the traders) are the highly paid risk takers, while the people who analyze and explain the more complicated securities (the researchers) are glorified clerks. Back in 1993, when Meriwether established Long-Term Capital, he also created a new status system. The title "trader" would no longer exist. At Long-Term Capital, anyone who had anything to do with thinking about how to make money in financial markets would be called a "strategist."

The strategists spent several days with me going over the details of their collapse. They began with a six-hour presentation they had just put together for the investors whose money they had lost, because, as one of the fund's partners puts it: "Virtually no one has called and asked us for the facts. They just believe what they read in the papers." Then I was shown the bets that had cost the strategists their fortunes and their reputations as the smartest traders on or off Wall Street. The guided tour of the spectacular ruin concluded with a conversation with John Meriwether. He, and they, offered a neat illustration of the limits of reason in human affairs.

The first time I saw a market panic up close was also the last time I had seen John Meriwether—the stock-market crash of October 19, 1987. I was working at Salomon Brothers, then the leading trading firm on Wall Street. A few yards to one side of me sat Salomon's C.E.O., John Gutfreund; a few yards to the other side sat Meriwether, the firm's most beguiling character. The stock market plummeted and the bond market soared that day as they had never done in anyone's experience, and the two men did extraordinary things.

I didn't appreciate what they had done until much later. You cannot really see a thing unless you know what you are looking for, and I did not know what I was looking for. I was so slow to grasp the importance of the scene that I failed to make use of it later in *Liar's Poker*, the memoir I wrote about my Wall Street experience. But the events of those few hours were in many ways the most important I ever saw on Wall Street.

What happened in the stock-market crash was one of those transfers of authority that seem to occur in the financial marketplace every decade or so. The markets in a panic are like a country during a coup, and seen in retrospect that is how they were that day. One small group of people with its old, established way of looking at the world was hustled from its seat of power. Another small group of people with a new way of looking at the world was rising up to claim the throne. And it was all happening in a few thousand square feet at the top of a tall office building at the bottom of Manhattan.

John Gutfreund moved back and forth between his desk and the long, narrow row of government-bond traders, where he huddled with Craig Coats Jr., Salomon's head of government-bond trading. Together they decided that the world was coming to an end, as it came to an end in the Crash of 1929. The end of the world is good news for the bond market— which is why it was soaring. Gutfreund and Coats decided to buy $2 billion worth of the newly issued 30-year United States Treasury bond. They were marvelous to watch, a pair of lions in their jungle. They did not stop to ask themselves, Why do we of all people on the planet enjoy the privilege of knowing what will happen next? They believed in their instincts. They had the nerve, the guts or whatever it was that distinguished a winner from a loser on a Wall Street trading floor in 1987.

And in truth they had been the winners of the 80's boom. *BusinessWeek* had anointed Gutfreund the King of Wall Street. Coats was believed by many to be the model for the main character in a book then just published called *The Bonfire of the Vanities*. Coats was tall and handsome and charismatic. He was everything that a bond trader in the 80's was supposed to be.

Except that he was wrong. The world was not coming to an end. Bond prices were not about to keep rising. The world would pretty much ignore the stock-market crash. Soon, Coats would arrive at work and find that his $2 billion of Treasury bonds had acquired a new name: the Whale. Traders near Coats started asking him about the Whale. As in, "How's that Whale today, Craig?" Or, "That Whale still beached?" In the end, the gut decision to buy the Whale cost Salomon Brothers $75 million.

Meanwhile, 20 yards away was Meriwether. When I think of people in American life who might have been like him, I think not of financial types but creative ones—Harold Ross of the old *New Yorker*, say, or Quentin Tarantino. Meriwether was like a gifted editor or a brilliant director: he had a nose for unusual people and the ability to persuade them to run with their talents. Right beside him were his first protégés, four young men fresh from graduate schools—Eric Rosenfeld, Larry Hilibrand, Greg Hawkins and Victor Haghani. Meriwether had taken it upon himself to set up a sort of underground railroad that ran from the finest graduate finance and math programs directly onto the Salomon trading floor. Robert Merton, the economist who himself would later become a consultant to Salomon Brothers and, later still, a partner at Long-Term Capital, complained that Meriwether was stealing an entire generation of academic talent.

No one back then really knew what to make of the "young professors." They were nothing like the others on the trading floor. They were physically unintimidating, their bodies merely life-support systems for their brains, which were in turn extensions of their computers. They were polite and mild-mannered and hesitant. When you asked them a simple question, they thought about it for eight months before they answered, and then their answer was so complicated you wished you had never asked. This was especially true if you asked a simple question about their business. Something as straightforward as "Why is this bond cheaper than that bond?" elicited a dissertation. They didn't think the same way about the markets as Craig Coats did or, for that matter, as anyone else on Wall Street did.

It turned out that there was a reason for this. On the surface, American finance was losing its mystique, what with ordinary people leaping into mutual funds, mortgage products and credit-card debt. But below the surface, a new and wider gap was opening between high finance and low finance. The old high finance was merely a bit mysterious; the new high finance was incomprehensible. The financial markets were spawning vastly complicated new instruments—options, futures, swaps, mortgage bonds and more. Their complexity baffled laypeople, and still does, but created opportunities for those who could parse it. At the behest of John Meriwether, the young professors were reinventing finance, and redefining what it meant to be a bond trader. Their presence on the trading floor marked the end of anti-intellectualism in American financial life.

But at that moment of panic, the young professors did not fully appreciate their own powers. All their well-thought-out strategies, which had yielded them profits of perhaps $200 million over the first 10 months of 1987, wilted that October day in the heat of other people's madness. They lost at least $120 million, which was sufficient to ruin the quarterly earnings of the entire firm. Two years before, they were being paid $29,000 to teach Finance 101 to undergraduates. Now they had lost $120 million! And not just anybody's $120 million! One hundred twenty million dollars that belonged in part to some very large, very hairy men. They were unnerved, as you can imagine, until Meriwether convinced them that they should not be unnerved but energized. He told them to pick their two or three most promising trades and triple them.

They did it, of course. They paid special attention to one big trade. They sold short the newly issued 30-year U.S. Treasury bond of which Craig Coats had just purchased $2 billion and bought identical amounts of the 30-year bond the Treasury had issued three months before—that is, a 29-year bond. (To "short" a stock or bond means to bet that its price will fall.) The young professors were not the first to see that the two bonds were nearly identical. But they were the first to have studied so meticulously the relationship between them. Newly issued Treasury bonds change hands more frequently than older ones. They acquire what is called a "liquidity premium," which is to say that professional bond traders pay a bit more for them because they are a bit easier to resell. In the panic, the premium on the 30-year bond became grotesquely large, and the young professors, or at any rate their computers, noticed. They laid a bet that the premium would shrink when the panic subsided.

But there was something else going on that had nothing to do with computers. The young professors weren't happy making money unless they could explain to themselves why they were making money. And if they couldn't find the reason for a market inefficiency they became suspicious and declined to bet on it. But when they stood up on Oct. 19, 1987,

and peered out over their computers, they discovered the reason: everyone else was confused. Salomon's own long-bond trader, the very best in
the business, was lost. Here was the guy who was meant to be the soul of
reason in the government-bond markets, and he looked like a lab rat that
had become lost in a maze. This brute with razor instincts, it turned out,
relied on a cheat sheet that laid out the prices of old long bonds as the
market moved. The move in the bond market during the panic had blown
all these bonds right off his sheet. "He's moved beyond his intuition," one
of the young professors thought. "He doesn't have the tools to cope. And
if he doesn't have the tools, who does?" His confusion was an opportunity
for the young professors to exploit.

Years later it would be difficult for them to recapture the thrill of this
moment, and dozens of others like it. It was as if they had been granted a
more evolved set of senses, and a sixth one to boot. And they had nerve:
they were willing to put money where their theory was. Three weeks after
the 1987 crash, when the markets calmed down, they cashed out of the
Treasury bonds with a profit of $50 million. All in all, the bets they placed
in the teeth of one of the greatest panics Wall Street had ever seen eventually made them more money than any bets they had ever made, perhaps
$150 million altogether. By comparison, all of Merrill Lynch generated
$391 million in profits that year. The lesson in this was not lost on the
young professors: panic was good for business. The stupid things people
did with money when they were frightened was an opportunity for more
reasonable people to exploit. The young professors knew that in theory
already; now they knew it in practice. It was a lesson they would regret
during the next big panic, far bigger and more mysterious than the Crash
of October 1987—the panic of August 1998. They would still be working
together, but at Long-Term Capital Management.

I was a tad uneasy about meeting these people again. All those pregnant
pauses! All those explanations! Even more than 10 years later, I can recall
the dreadful minutes after I had asked them to walk me through one of
their trades, when my brain felt like a beaten cornerback watching the
receiver dancing into the end zone. On top of it all was their Spock-like
analytical detachment, which still hung heavy in the air in Greenwich and
overshadowed any larger consideration, like shrewd management of the
press. "If everything had gone well," one of the young professors said not

long after I stepped off the elevator, "we wouldn't be talking to you." But everything did not go well, and they had decided to explain themselves to someone they had practice explaining things to.

When I heard that Long-Term Capital had collapsed, my initial reaction was a sneaky relief: Hans Hufschmid was no longer worth $50 million. Anyone who has quit one life for another will understand the importance of insuring that none of the people you leave behind do so well for themselves as to suggest that you have made a truly colossal mistake. Since I left Salomon Brothers in 1988 to make a living as a writer, I had remained curious about how rich I would have become if I had stayed on Wall Street. There were several people whose fortunes I considered fair proxies for my own, and whom I tagged for further observation, like wolves released in a wildlife experiment.

Hans was one of them. Back in 1986, Hans and I left the same New York training program for the same London trading floor, where we were ultimately supervised by John Meriwether. Although neither of us was a young professor, we had gone into the same arcane line of work. We both spent half of our time flying around Europe trying to coax innocent investors into complicated new American-born financial instruments and the other half seeking out speculations for those who needed no coaxing. But those were just our surface similarities. Deep down, Hans and I shared a dirty little secret: we couldn't keep up with the young professors. We belonged to a new semi-informed breed who could "pass" as experts on the new financial complexity without possessing true understanding.

In any case, Hans was one of those people I might have become had I remained on Wall Street. And so, at the end of 1993, after I heard that Salomon Brothers had paid Hans a bonus of $28 million, I spent at least three hours wondering why I hadn't done so. Twenty-eight million dollars was just the original insult. At the end of 1994, Hans left Salomon to become a partner in Long-Term Capital's London office. It gives you an idea just how desirable it was to work for John Meriwether that to do so people quit jobs at the finest Wall Street firms, which paid them bonuses of $28 million. Word came that Hans had sunk not merely his $28 million bonus into the fund but also $15 million he had borrowed from some bank.

The fund rose by 43 percent in 1995, by 41 percent in 1996 and by 17 percent in 1997. At the end of each year, Hans reinvested his profits in the fund. That was another odd thing about the people at Long-Term Capital. They did not define themselves in the usual Wall Street way, by their material possessions. Their hundreds of millions of dollars didn't lead inexorably to private jets and new life styles. (They would be better off now if that had been the case.) Their favorite form of conspicuous consumption was to buy more and more of their own investment genius. As a result, before their demise, Long-Term Capital's 16 partners had invested roughly $1.9 billion of their own money in their fund. Making some fairly conservative assumptions about Hans and his effective tax rate, $50 million of that pile belonged to him. This, to my way of thinking, made it a bit more expensive than it should have been not to be Hans Hufschmid.

And then . . . poof . . . it was not so very expensive at all. Not being Hans was positively joyous. By the end of September 1998, the same friends from Salomon Brothers who had informed me how rich Hans was becoming in late 1997 were telling me that he and all his partners were wiped out. As Hans himself had borrowed to invest in himself, it was at least conceivable that he was worth less than zero.

That did it for me: I demanded no further reparations. I was once again satisfied to be paid by the word. But it turned out that I was alone in this sentiment. A lot of people wanted not only Hans's money but also his hide, along with the hides of Larry Hilibrand, Victor Haghani, Eric Rosenfeld, Greg Hawkins and John Meriwether. Plus those of Robert Merton and Myron Scholes, Nobel Prize–winning economists who had joined Meriwether. (They won the 1997 Nobel Prize for their work on risk management of options.) Hans and his partners were accused by all sorts of people of behaving recklessly, succumbing to hubris and jeopardizing the economic health of the West.

One number that kept popping up in the papers was the "$1.2 trillion" that Hans and the young professors had supposedly wagered. The $1.2 trillion represented what are known as the open trading positions of the fund. Anyone who works on Wall Street knows that a firm's open trading positions contain all sorts of things that offset one another. At any given time, Goldman, Sachs or Shearson Lehman, which had only about twice as much capital available as Long-Term, might carry $7 trillion or $8 trillion in positions on their books. What was important was not the gross amount of the positions but the amount of risk in them.

That's where "leverage" came into the newspaper accounts. Leverage means borrowing to buy things you otherwise could not afford, and many of the public accounts invariably equated it with "risk." "At L.T.C.M.," wrote Carol J. Loomis in *Fortune*, "the best minds were destroyed by the oldest and most famously addictive drug in finance, leverage." Possibly there was once a time when leverage was a good measure of risk. But one consequence of the new complexity in financial markets has been to make any such simple calculation impossible. A portfolio might be leveraged 50 times and have almost no risk. A portfolio might be leveraged five times and be perfectly mad. Long-Term Capital had been in pretty much the same line of work as a Wall Street investment bank, and Wall Street investment banks were leveraged the same amounts, about 25 times (although a Wall Street investment bank can lay its hands on capital more quickly than a hedge fund can).

The important number in any portfolio is not its leverage but its volatility: how much do its net assets rise and fall each day? By that measure, to which no one paid much attention, Long-Term Capital was running a fund that looked to all of Wall Street a bit less risky than if it had taken its capital and simply invested all of it, unleveraged, in a diversified portfolio of U.S. stocks.

Then there was the inevitable search for True Character. One of the stories I had told in 1989 about Meriwether had been twisted beyond recognition into evidence that he was indeed a madman. The story ran as follows: John Gutfreund, who routinely dropped tens of thousands of dollars to the young professors playing liar's poker, a game of both chance and skill using the serial numbers on dollar bills, challenged Meriwether to one hand for $1 million. ("One hand, $1 million, no tears" was what he supposedly said.) Meriwether replied that he would play only for $10 million. Gutfreund walked away. End of story. All sorts of people, Gutfreund included, later denied that the incident ever occurred, but in any case the point of the episode was just the opposite of the interpretation now placed on it. The point of the story was that in a world where you weren't supposed to flinch from financial risk, Meriwether had found a clever way to avoid what was clearly an act of lunacy.

But even without knowing much about what Meriwether did, or how he did it, or what sort of man he was, you could see that the public accounts of the collapse of Long-Term Capital were, at the very least, incomplete. From the mid–80's right up until last summer, the young professors had been the most widely imitated men on Wall Street. If they were so wildly irresponsible, why had every big Wall Street firm copied them? Even after Long-Term's collapse, a lot of smart people were sniffing acquisitively around their portfolio. If that portfolio was so recklessly speculative, why was Warren Buffett, among others, trying to buy it?

Between the lines of the stories were hints of a more complicated one. The most remarkable gurgling noises from last summer's panic came from the inner sanctums of finance. Treasury Secretary Robert Rubin said then that "the world is now experiencing its worst financial crisis in 50 years." That was something coming from a man who specialized in soothing investors and who had been on a trading desk at Goldman, Sachs during the Crash of 1987. Alan Greenspan, the Federal Reserve Chairman, said that he had never seen anything in his lifetime that compared to the terror of August 1998. From one end of Wall Street to the other, firms were announcing record bond-trading losses. Goldman, Sachs, which worked harder than any other firm to copy Meriwether's success, explained its own disaster by saying that "our risk model did not take into account enough the copycat problem." That statement was true but inadequate. It failed to mention the name of the original cat.

If you didn't know who John Meriwether was, you wouldn't have the slightest curiosity about him. He has small, even features, a shock of cowlicky brown hair that droops boyishly down over his forehead and a blank expression that could mean nothing or everything. His movements are quick, however, and so is his talk. He speaks in fragments and moves rapidly from one idea to the next, leaving behind a trail of untidy thoughts. He shapes other people more completely than he does himself. His discomfort with the first person occasionally makes him difficult to follow, especially when he is supposed to be talking about himself. When he says, "If anyone wants to focus on anybody and wants to take them apart, he can," he means, "I believe that people set out to destroy me, and succeeded."

When I arrived, he was hunched over at his desk on the trading floor, but by the time I got to him he was in his office. It was a token office, big and empty and conspicuously unused. It had a nice view of some trees, which I'm sure no one had glanced at in months. A tall stack of books and a large basket of shiny apples crowded the area beside his desk. Meriwether offered me one of each.

The book was *Miracle on the 17th Green*, a fantasy for adults about a regular middle-aged man who one day is blessed with the talent of a golf champion. "Extraordinary things happen to ordinary people," said the back of the dust jacket. It was soon clear that this reflects Meriwether's own sense of himself and his current situation. About the first thing he said after we sat down across from his coffee table was, "I don't want this story to be about me."

To insure that it was not, he would not allow me to quote him much. And for good measure, he insisted that Richard Leahy, who hired me onto the Salomon trading floor and who is Meriwether's oldest business partner, sit in on our conversation.

My own guess is that Meriwether would rather people think him a bit weird than know the real reason he avoids publicity, which is that he is deeply uncomfortable with the attention. He has a phobia about public speaking, for instance. When you passed him on the Salomon trading floor, you could see him force himself to meet your eye. In conversations in which he might be expected to take control—say over drinks with a couple of new employees—he would shrink from the responsibility. He was one of those people whose desire in conversation was for everyone to be "equal." Oddly, the adjective he often chooses to describe the people he most admires is "shy." He means this as a compliment, as in "shy and polite." Shy and polite was a bizarre combination in the testosterone tank of the Salomon trading floor. It was a handicap, at least for someone seeking power in its usual corporate form, through control over large numbers of people. Meriwether sought power in a different form, through the markets.

In the five years after the 1987 crash, Meriwether and the young professors made billions for Salomon and tens of millions for themselves. They started out as oddballs but became the heart of the firm. From the mid-80's through the early 90's the rest of Wall Street, and Goldman, Sachs in particular, poached bond-trading talent from every major bond department at Salomon—corporates, governments, mortgages. Jon Corzine, who was co-C.E.O. of Goldman, Sachs until a shake-up earlier this month, rose in the firm in part by buying the right people off the Salomon trading floor.

The single exception to this diaspora was John Meriwether's group: it wasn't for sale. In the end, it was broken up by force. A government-bond trader at Salomon Brothers named Paul Mozer, who replaced Craig Coats in 1988 and who reported to Meriwether, tried to corner the U.S. Treasury-bond market. In 1990 and 1991, he submitted phony bids at the Treasury's quarterly auctions that enabled him to buy more than his legal share. Meriwether found out, and went to his superiors, including Gutfreund, and Gutfreund agreed that the Treasury should be informed. For whatever reason, Gutfreund failed to follow up immediately, and it was several months before Salomon informed the Government.

The fate of the firm hung in the balance until Warren Buffett, Salomon's biggest shareholder, stepped in and cut a deal with the Treasury. Salomon would survive if Buffett would oversee the reform of its culture, and Gutfreund was encouraged to resign. And though everyone including Buffett acknowledged that Meriwether had done nothing wrong, Meriwether was encouraged to resign, too. He quit and created a new firm.

In many ways, Long-Term Capital was better designed for the young professors than Salomon Brothers was. There was only one noticeable disadvantage. Other Wall Street firms might have sensed how well Salomon's young professors and their strategy was paying off and sought to mimic their subtle workings. But they could not actually see these workings. When the young professors left Salomon Brothers, they opened themselves and their bets up for inspection by Wall Street. In exchange for lending Long-Term Capital the money to make its trades, the big firms—Morgan Stanley, Merrill Lynch, Goldman, Sachs—demanded to know what it was up to. This in turn led to higher-fidelity imitation.

"Everyone else started catching up to us," Eric Rosenfeld says. "We'd go to put on a trade, but when we started to nibble the opportunity would vanish." Every time they took action, others noticed and copied them, and eliminated whatever slight irrationality had crept into the markets.

At some point, Meriwether lost control of his esoteric markets. In our conversation, I asked him how that experience had changed his ideas about making money. He replied that his old ideas, which worked so well for 15 years, have been in some sense consumed, and that he needs to find new ones. Then he proceeded to explain why.

In its broad outlines, the Long-Term Capital story could be described by a couple of pie charts. The first pie chart would lay out its losses. Of the $4.4 billion lost, $1.9 belonged to the partners personally, $700 million to Union Bank of Switzerland and $1.8 billion to other investors, half of them European banks. But as original investments had long ago been paid back to most of the banks, the losses came mainly out of their profits. The second and more interesting pie chart would describe how the money was lost. The public accounts have suggested that it was lost in all manner of exotic speculations that the young professors had irresponsibly digressed into. The speculations were exotic enough, but they were hardly digressions. When I paged through their trades, the only thing I hadn't expected to find was a taste for betting on corporate takeovers. One hundred fifty million dollars vanished from Long-Term Capital when a company called Tellabs failed to complete its acquisition of a company called Ciena, and the price of Ciena stock, which Long-Term owned, dropped from 56 to 31 1/4. ("This trade was by far the most controversial in our partnership," Rosenfeld says. "A lot of people felt we shouldn't be in the risk arb business because it is so information sensitive and we weren't trying to trade in an information-sensitive way.") Of course, Long-Term had some complicated notion of its advantage in risk arbitrage, but that notion now looked silly. Still, even taking account of the $150 million loss in Ciena shares, its stock-market trading was profitable.

The big losses that destroyed Long-Term Capital occurred in the areas the young professors had for years been masters of. The killer blows—a good $3 billion of the $4.4 billion—came from two bets that Meriwether and his team had been making for at least a decade: interest-rate swaps and long-term options in the stock market. Now there is no reason anyone should feel obliged to understand interest-rate-swap arbitrage. The important point about it is the degree of risk it typically involves.

Like most of Long-Term Capital's trades, these bets required the strategists to buy one thing and sell short another, so that they maintained a Swiss-like neutrality in the market. Like most of their trades, the thing they bought was similar to the thing they sold. (Their gift was for mathematical metaphor: they noticed similarities where others saw nothing but differences.) But like only some of their trades, the thing they bought became—or was supposed to become, after a period of time, and under certain conditions—identical to the thing they sold.

One way to understand this, and to see how bizarre was the panic of August 1998, is to imagine a world with two kinds of dollars, blue dollars and red dollars. The blue dollar and the red dollar are both worth a dollar, but you can't spend them for five years. In five years, you can turn them both in for green dollars. But for all sorts of reasons—a mania for blue, a nasty article about red—the blue dollar becomes more expensive than the red dollar. The blue dollar is selling for $1.05 and the red dollar is selling for 95 cents.

If you are an ordinary sane person who holds blue dollars, you simply trade them in for more red dollars. If you are Long-Term Capital, or any large Wall Street firm for that matter, and are able to borrow money cheaply, you borrow against your capital and buy a lot of red dollars and sell the same number of blue dollars. The effect is to force the price of red dollars and blue dollars back together again. In any case, you wait for blue dollars and red dollars to converge to their ultimate value of a dollar apiece.

At best, the odd passions that drove the red and the blue dollar apart subside quickly, and you reap your profits now. At worst, you must wait five years to collect your profits. The "model" tells you that you will one day make at least a nickel for every red dollar you buy for 95 cents and another nickel for every blue dollar you sell at $1.05. But as Ayman Hindy, a Long-Term Capital strategist, puts it: "The models tell you where things will be in five years. But they don't tell you what happens before you get to the moment of certainty."

Which brings us to the case of Long-Term Capital in August 1998, when the red dollar and the blue dollar were driven apart in value to ridiculous extremes. Actually, when you look at the young professors' books, you can see that the first sign of trouble came earlier, on July 17, when Salomon Brothers announced that it was liquidating all of its red dollar-blue dollar trades, which turned out to be the same trades Long-Term Capital had made. For the rest of that month, the fund dropped about 10 percent because Salomon Brothers was selling all the things that Long-Term owned.

Then, on Aug. 17, Russia defaulted on its debt. At that moment the heads of the other big financial firms recanted their beliefs about red dollars and blue dollars. Their fear overruled their reason. Once enough people gave into their fear, fear became reasonable. Fairly rapidly the other big financial firms unwound their own trades, which, having been made in the spirit of Long-Term Capital, were virtually identical to the trades of Long-Term Capital. The red dollar was suddenly worth 25 cents and the blue dollar $3. The history of red dollars and blue dollars made the statistical probability of that happening 1 in 50 million.

"What we did is rely on experience," Victor Haghani says. "And all science is based on experience. And if you're not willing to draw any conclusions from experience, you might as well sit on your hands and do nothing."

Aug. 21, 1998, was the worst day in the young history of scientific finance. On that day alone, Long-Term Capital lost $550 million.

The young professors' attachment to higher reason was a great advantage only as long as there was a limit to the market's unreason. Suddenly there was no limit. Alan Greenspan and Robert Rubin said they had never seen such a crisis, and neither had anyone else. It was one thing for the average stock-market investor to panic. It was another for the world's biggest financial firms to panic. The world's financial institutions created a bank run on a huge, global scale. "We put very little emphasis on what other leveraged players were doing," Haghani says, "because I think we thought they would behave very similarly to ourselves."

Long-Term Capital had worked on the assumption that there was a pool of professional money around that would see that red dollars and blue dollars were both dollars and therefore should maintain some reasonable relation to each other. But in the crisis, the young professors were the only ones who clung to such reasoning.

By the end of August, Long-Term Capital had run through $2 billion of its $4.8 billion in capital. Even so, the fund might well have survived and prospered. But what started as a run on the markets, at least from Long-Term Capital's point of view, turned into a run on Long-Term Capital. "It was as if there was someone out there with our exact portfolio," Haghani says, "only it was three times as large as ours, and they were liquidating all at once."

For nearly 15 years, Meriwether and the young professors had been engaged in an experiment to determine how far human reason alone could take them. They failed to appreciate that their fabulous success had made them, quite unreasonably, part of the experiment. No longer were they the creatures of higher reason who could remain detached and aloof. They were the lab rats lost in the maze.

Inside Long-Term Capital, the collapse is understood as a two-stage affair. First came the market panic by big Wall Street firms that made many of the same bets as Long-Term Capital. Then came a kind of social panic. Word spread that Long-Term was weakened. That weakness, Meriwether and the others say, very quickly became an opportunity for others to prey upon.

"The few things we had on that the market didn't know about came back quickly," Meriwether says. "It was the trades that the market knew we had on that caused us trouble." Richard Leahy, the Long-Term partner, says: "It ceased to feel like people were liquidating positions similar to ours. All of a sudden they were liquidating our positions."

It was this second stage of his demise that clearly ate at Meriwether. As our conversation drifted toward the subject his unease turned to bitterness and his phrasing became so tortured as to be as useless to me as he hoped it would be.

By the end of August, Long-Term Capital badly needed $1.5 billion. The trades that the strategists had made lost money, but they would recover their losses if they could obtain the capital to finance them. If Long-Term Capital could ride out the panic, Meriwether figured, it would make more money than ever. "We dreamed of the day when we'd have opportunities like this," Eric Rosenfeld says.

Meriwether called people rich enough to pony up the entire sum Long-Term Capital needed, among them one of America's richest men, Warren Buffett. Buffett was interested in the portfolio but not in Meriwether. "Buffett cares about one thing," one of the fund's partners says. "His reputation. Because of the Salomon scandal he couldn't be seen to be in business with J.M."

Meriwether also called Jon Corzine at Goldman, Sachs. Goldman, Sachs agreed to find the capital but in exchange wanted more than a fee. It wanted to own half of Long-Term Capital. Meriwether and Corzine had been aware of each other's existence since the late 60's, when they studied together at the University of Chicago. For 15 years, Corzine had done his best to figure out what Meriwether was up to. This was his chance to know for all time.

What neither man realized was that the game of saving Long-Term Capital was over before it began. First came the rumors. Traders at other firms began to use "Long-Term" the way weathermen used El Niño—to justify whatever they needed to justify. Lou Dobbs appeared on CNN to explain that certain stocks were falling because Long-Term Capital was selling them. The young professors, who had not been selling stocks or anything else, watched in wonder. International Financing Review, the most widely read trade sheet in the bond markets, wrote that Long-Term Capital was sitting on $10 billion of floating rate notes. The young professors say they owned no such things.

The rumors that contained some truth were more damaging, of course, and now the truth was out there, available to Goldman, Sachs and others. Every day someone would publish something about them that left them more exposed than ever to those who might prey on them. "Every rumor about the size of our positions was always double the truth," Richard Leahy says. "Except the rumor about our position in Danish mortgages. That was 10 times what we actually had."

Banks that called up to bid on Long-Term Capital's positions would say things like, "We can't buy all of what we've heard you've got, but we'd like a piece." They would then ask to buy twice what Long-Term actually owned. According to the young professors, Wall Street firms began to get out in front of the fund's positions: if a trader elsewhere knew Long-Term Capital owned a lot of interest-rate swap, for instance, he sold interest-rate swaps, and further weakened Long-Term's hand. The idea was that if you put enough pressure on Long-Term Capital, Long-Term Capital would be forced to sell in a panic and you would reap the profits. And even if Long-Term didn't break, the mere rumor that it had problems might lead to a windfall for you. A Goldman, Sachs partner had been heard to brag that the firm had made a fortune in this manner. A spokesman for Goldman, Sachs said that the idea that the firm had made money from Long-Term Capital's distress was "absurd" in light of how much Goldman, Sachs had lost making exactly the same bets.

When one player in any market is sufficiently big and weak, its size and weakness are reason enough for the market to destroy it. The rumors about Long-Term Capital led to further losses, which in turn led to more rumors. The losses mounted, but strangely. The losses in August were part of a market rout. The losses that continued into September were part of a rout of Long-Term Capital.

The trouble led the New York Federal Reserve to help bring together a consortium of Wall Street banks and brokerage houses to come to the rescue. Goldman, Sachs, a consortium member, was dissatisfied to find itself one of many. It had hoped to control Long-Term, and to acquire the wisdom of the young professors. And so before the consortium finalized its plans, Goldman, Sachs turned up with Warren Buffett and about $4 billion in an attempt to buy the firm.

Long-Term Capital was caught in a squeeze—for that's what it's called, and that's what it felt like to Meriwether and the young professors. On the very day, Sept. 21, that Warren Buffett and Goldman, Sachs turned up, Long-Term Capital, for the second time in its history, lost more than $500 million in one day. Half of that was lost in its second disastrous trade, a short position in five-year equity options. Essentially, it had sold insurance against violent movement in the stock market. The price it received for the insurance was so high that the bet would almost certainly be hugely profitable—in the long run. But on Sept. 21, the short run took over, in a new and more venal fashion. Meriwether received phone calls from J. P. Morgan and Union Bank of Switzerland telling him that the options he had sold short were rocketing up in thin markets thanks to bids from American International Group, the U.S. insurance company. The brokers were outraged on Meriwether's behalf, as they assumed that A.I.G. was trying to profit from Long-Term's weakness. A spokesman for A.I.G. declined to comment.

But what the people who called Meriwether did not know was that at just that moment, A.I.G. was, along with Warren Buffett and Goldman, Sachs, negotiating to purchase Long-Term Capital's portfolio. But one consequence of A.I.G.'s activities was to pressure Meriwether to sell his company and its portfolio cheaply. Meriwether is convinced that A.I.G. was trying to put him out of business, a contention A.I.G. would also not comment on.

It is interesting to look over the clippings and see the role played by the media in this stage of Long-Term Capital's demise. After the firm entered negotiations to sell its portfolio through Goldman, Sachs, rumors about its holdings trickled out in the financial press, exposing Long-Term Capital's trading positions to outside attack. After negotiations among the fund and Goldman, Sachs and Warren Buffett broke down, a new wave of articles appeared. Carol Loomis wrote in *Fortune*, "Warren Buffett is a longtime friend of this writer," and then went on to tell the following tale—that Long-Term Capital had refused his bid because John Meriwether didn't like his terms. The story played down the fact that William McDonough, president of the New York Fed, came to the same conclusions as Meriwether—different from Buffett's—that the fund could not legally sell without consulting its investors, which Buffett had given them less than an hour to do. Buffett declined to comment.

The *Fortune* story and others like it, the Long-Term strategists maintain, created even more pressure on Meriwether to sell the next time someone made a low bid. Meriwether also says that the A.I.G. trade was "minor compared to some of the things we saw." But he declined to say what these things were, and no wonder. On Sept. 23, a consortium of 14 Wall Street banks and brokerage houses gave Long-Term $3.6 billion, in exchange for 90 percent of the firm. Some of the things Meriwether "saw" could well have been perpetrated by some of the very Wall Street firms that now own his firm, and that he now works for.

Meriwether did say this about his treatment at the hands of the big Wall Street firms: "I like the way Victor"—Haghani, one of the young professors—"put it: The hurricane is not more or less likely to hit because more hurricane insurance has been written. In the financial markets this is not true. The more people write financial insurance, the more likely it is that a disaster will happen, because the people who know you have sold the insurance can make it happen. So you have to monitor what other people are doing."

In October 1987, the markets took power from people who traded with their intuition and bestowed it upon people who traded with their formulas. In August 1998, the markets took power away from people with formulas who hoped to remain detached from the marketplace and bestowed it upon the large Wall Street firms that oversee the marketplace. These firms will do pretty much exactly the same complicated trading as Long-Term Capital, perhaps in a slightly watered down form, once the whiff of scandal vanishes from the activity. Indeed, the global economy now expects it of them. Without it, risk would be poorly priced and capital poorly distributed. And in any case, Long-

Term Capital's portfolio has already turned around, rising almost 10 percent by year's end.

The events of August and September 1998 have left Meriwether and the young professors exactly where they did not want to be, working for the large Wall Street firms. Back is the messy company politics they thought they had left behind. In place of the hundreds of millions they made each year for themselves they are now paid salaries of $250,000, or the wage of a beginning bond trader without a bonus. In the best-case scenario, their portfolio will make the fortune they predicted for it, they will convince the money culture that they are still worth having around and they will find other rich people to replace their current owners. In the worst and more likely case, they are finished as a group.

It is interesting to see how people respond when the assumptions that get them out of bed in the morning are declared ridiculous by the wider world. There is obviously now a very great social pressure on the young professors to abandon the thing they cherish most, their hyperrational view of the world. In the coming months, they could very well be hauled before some Congressional committee to explain their role in jeopardizing the free world. Oddly, the question that occupies them is not whether to push on with their models of financial behavior but how to improve the models in light of what has happened to them. "The solution," Robert Merton says, "is not to go back to the old, simple methods. That never works. You can't go back. The world has changed. And the solution is greater complexity."

"It's like there are two businesses here," Eric Rosenfeld says, "the old business, which works fine under normal conditions, and this stand-by business, when the world goes mad. And for that, you either need to buy insurance or have a pool of stand-by capital to take advantage of these opportunities."

The money culture has never been very good at distinguishing bad character from bad judgment and bad judgment from bad luck, and in the complex case of Long-Term Capital it has been worse than usual. Reputations are ruined, fortunes lost and precious ideas simultaneously ridiculed and stolen. So maybe the most interesting thing to happen since Long-Term got itself into trouble is what has not happened. There have been none of the venal self-preservatory acts that often accompany great financial collapse. No one has pointed a finger at his partners. Already several partners have declined offers to work for other fund managers or big Wall Street firms.

Yet for the first time in 15 years, John Meriwether and his young professors cannot steer toward some moment of certainty in the distant future. What they hope will happen next is no longer the same as what they think will happen next. Which is to say that they are, for the first time in 15 years, just like everyone else.

10 Years After the Asian Crisis, We're Not Out of the Woods Yet

JOSEPH STIGLITZ

Project Syndicate, July 2007

This July marks the 10th anniversary of East Asia's financial crisis. In July 1997, the Thai baht plummeted. Soon after, financial panic spread to Indonesia and Korea, then to Malaysia. In a little more than a year, the Asian financial crisis became a global financial crisis, with the crash of Russia's ruble and Brazil's real.

In the midst of a crisis, no one knows how far an economy will drop or for how long. But capitalism, since its beginning, has been marked by crises; each time, the economy recovers, but each crisis carries its own lessons. So a decade after Asia's crisis, it is natural to ask: What were the lessons, and has the world learned them? Could such a crisis recur? Is another crisis imminent? Some similarities exist between the situation then and today: Before the 1997 crisis, there had been rapid increases in capital flows from developed to developing countries—a six-fold increase in six years. Afterward, capital flows to developing countries stagnated.

Before the crisis, some thought risk premiums for developing countries were irrationally low. These observers proved right: The crisis was marked by soaring risk premiums. Today, the global surfeit of liquidity has once again resulted in comparably low risk premiums and a resurgence of capital flows, despite a broad consensus that the world faces enormous risks (including the risks posed by a return of risk premiums to more normal levels).

In 1997, the International Monetary Fund and the United States Treasury blamed the crisis on a lack of transparency in financial markets. But when developing countries pointed their fingers at secret bank accounts and hedge funds, IMF and US enthusiasm for greater transparency diminished. Since then, hedge funds have grown in importance, and secret bank accounts have flourished. But there are some big differences between then and now. Most developing countries have accumulated massive foreign currency reserves. They learned the hard way what happens to countries otherwise, as the IMF and US Treasury marched in, took away economic sovereignty and demanded policies intended to enhance repayment to Western creditors, which plunged their economies into deep recessions and depressions.

Reserves are costly, for the money could have been spent on development projects that would enhance growth. Nevertheless, the benefits in reducing the likelihood of another crisis and another loss of economic independence far outweigh the costs. This growth in reserves, while providing insurance to developing countries, created a new source of global volatility. Especially as the dollar lost its sacred place as a store of value under the Bush administration, rebalancing these multi-trillion dollar portfolios entails selling off dollar holdings, contributing to the dollar's weakening.

Developing countries have also increasingly borrowed in their own currencies during the last few years, thus reducing their foreign exchange exposure. For those developing countries that remain heavily indebted abroad, an increase in risk premiums would almost certainly bring economic turmoil, if not crisis. But the fact that so many countries hold large reserves means that the likelihood of the problem spreading into a global financial crisis is greatly reduced.

In the midst of the 1997 crisis, a consensus developed that there was a need for a change in the global financial architecture: The world needed to do better in preventing crises and dealing with them when they occurred.

But the US Treasury and the IMF realized that the likely reforms, as desirable as they were for the world, were not in their interest.

They did what they could to ensure that no meaningful reforms occurred during the crisis, with the knowledge that after the crisis, momentum for reform would dissipate. They were more right than they knew. Who, after all, could have anticipated that President Bill Clinton would be followed in office by someone committed to undermining the multilateral system in all its manifestations? For example, when the IMF correctly suggested, after Argentina's crisis, that there needed to be a better way of restructuring debt (an international bankruptcy procedure), the US vetoed the initiative. When the Organization for Economic Cooperation and Development proposed an agreement to restrict bank secrecy, the Bush administration vetoed that initiative, too.

Indeed, the two most important lessons of the crisis have not been absorbed. The first is that capital market liberalization—opening up developing countries' financial markets to surges in short-term "hot" money—is dangerous. It was not an accident that the only two major developing countries to be spared a crisis were India and China. Both had resisted capital market liberalization. Yet today, both are under pressure to liberalize.

The second lesson is that in a highly integrated world, there is a need for a credible international financial institution to design the rules of the road in ways that enhance global stability and promote economic growth in developing countries. With the IMF so dominated by the US (it is the only country with a veto) and Europe (which, by custom, appoints its head), it has long been seen as representing the interests of international creditors. Its failures in the 1997 crisis further undermined its credibility, and its failure to do anything about the massive global financial imbalances that represent the main threat to global financial stability today have underscored its limitations.

Reforms are still needed—including an overhaul of the global reserve system. We may not be facing a repeat of the global financial crisis of 1997, but make no mistake, imperfections in the global financial system can still be costly, both in terms of global prosperity and stability.

Asia's Long Road to Recovery

KEITH BRADSHER

The New York Times, *June 28, 2007*

A s the founder of a petrochemicals business empire that aggressively expanded in refining, plastics, steel and cement, Prachai Leophairatana once ranked among Asia's wealthiest men.

But when Thailand devalued its currency a decade ago, on July 2, 1997—causing a financial crisis that engulfed nearly the entire region—Mr. Prachai's company was unable to keep up with payments on nearly $3 billion in debt, much of it denominated in dollars. Today, he has recovered somewhat, but he controls only the cement division and has not built a new factory in the last 10 years.

His experience speaks volumes about what has happened here since the Asian financial crisis, which raised alarms around the world and was probably the most damaging detour along the road to economic globalization of the post–cold war era. In the last decade, the crisis-affected Asian countries have steadied themselves but never regained the dazzling growth of the mid-1990s.

Looking back, an Asian Development Bank review of the five countries most affected—Thailand, Indonesia, Malaysia, South Korea and the

Philippines—found that incomes per person had all recovered to at least their levels before 1997. Trade balances, foreign currency reserves, corporate governance, depth of financial markets and quality of government regulation, as well as various indicators of public health: all these are now stronger than before.

Yet in all five countries a sense of loss persists, a sense of no longer being the darlings of foreign investors, a sense that the best times may lie in the past, not in the future. The economies of all five countries grew more slowly from 2000 to 2006 than they did from 1990 to 1996, with annual growth rates an average of 2.5 percent below the previous period.

"The losses we have suffered are really in that sense permanent," said Rajat M. Nag, the Asian Development Bank's managing director general, attributing slower growth to greater business and government caution about investments.

Many here and elsewhere in the region have been caught up in the aftermath of the crash as well. Sirivat Voravetvuthikun borrowed $8 million in 1995 to build two condominium towers outside Bangkok, but he went broke during the crisis and started a small business selling sandwiches on the streets of the capital. He predicted in early 1999 that his sandwich company would sell shares on the stock exchange within two years.

He is still predicting that a stock listing is just two years away. But he has expanded only to two coffee shops, two kiosks and 30 sidewalk vendors because he is scared to borrow money. "I am afraid that I will fail again," he said. "I'm 58 years old—I want this to be a long-lasting business for my children."

Political instability and a lingering problem of nonperforming bank loans have also held back growth in several countries. A military coup in Thailand last year and political violence in the south have hurt investment here. The Philippines faces a Communist insurgency. Indonesia has not entirely recovered from the rioting and toppling of the Suharto government that accompanied the financial crisis there and from the Bali bombings in 2002.

Finance Minister Chalongphob Sussangkarn of Thailand said in an interview that his country had dealt with its nonperforming loan problem and that the economy would do better after elections, late this year. "The likelihood of going to another financial crisis is now low," he said.

But he cautioned that middle-income countries like Thailand still face challenges in coping with large flows of money sloshing through global capital markets. He suggested that the double-digit growth rates of the mid-1990s were not sustainable for Thailand or any other country over the long term. Even the Chinese economy will slow at some point, he predicted, as its exports begin to saturate world markets.

Optimism about resilience to another financial crisis is now widespread in the region, even if slower growth may be the price of greater caution.

"Korea's economic policy has become more consistent during the last 10 years," said Lee Jang Yung, the assistant governor at the South Korean government's Financial Supervisory Service. "Its financial system has become stronger and sound."

To be sure, recent economic growth of 4 to 7 percent a year in the five most crisis-affected countries remains better than the performances of many developing countries.

But all five countries lag behind the growth rates of 9 to 11 percent in Asia's three current stars: China, India and Vietnam. Those countries offer greater political and economic stability and now attract much of the foreign investment that once flooded Southeast Asia.

Vietnam, which once rivaled Laos and Papua New Guinea as an economic basket case that could barely feed its people, has now surpassed Thailand in annual cement consumption, a key indicator of investment spending.

China is now the world's leading steel producer. India has become a global leader in computer software development and other outsourcing, and is now recording double-digit growth in manufacturing as well.

The Asian financial crisis prompted considerable discussion at the time about whether many countries in the region, acting partly on the advice of the International Monetary Fund, had gone too far in opening their financial markets to international investors.

Hedge funds, banks, multinational corporations and local companies all began selling local currencies and buying dollars in a mad rush to lock in profits or repay dollar-denominated debts in 1997. The result was a plunge in their currencies' value that made it even harder for many companies, like Mr. Prachai's empire, to repay money they had borrowed in dollars. Some in the region are still bitter, blaming Wall Street and Western investors.

"The financial people from New York came to attack Thailand; they acted like terrorists," Mr. Prachai said.

More recent economic analyses have suggested, however, that hedge funds and banks were less responsible for the downturn than a spate of sudden selling of Asian currencies by local companies as well as by international businesses like Dell and mutual funds like the T. Rowe Price New Asia Fund, which sought to limit their potential losses.

Malaysia weathered the crisis better than many countries in the region by imposing restrictions on the movement of large sums of money out of the country. That success has called into question the international economic orthodoxy that countries should keep their markets as open as possible at all times. But it has not reversed the trend toward freer trade and investment.

China, India and Vietnam all had severe limits on the entry and exit of short-term foreign investments in place long before the Asian financial crisis. All three weathered it relatively well, although the Chinese economy weakened temporarily as exports flagged.

The three are now moving to lighten their restrictions on money flows, but are moving at a very gradual pace that sometimes frustrates trade and finance negotiators from the United States and Europe.

"We have focused on building in safeguards to be able to pull the reins, if a crisis were to develop," Kamal Nath, India's minister of commerce and industry, wrote in an e-mail reply to questions.

The country most battered by sudden capital flows in recent months is once again Thailand. Faced with an incoming flood of stock and bond investments last December that threatened to push up the value of the country's currency and undermine the competitiveness of Thai exports in foreign markets, the government imposed a requirement that effectively taxed short-term foreign investments.

But when the Thai stock market plunged 15 percent in a day, the government promptly lifted the restriction for investments in equities.

In a less noticed move, however, the Thai government has made a series of adjustments over the last few months that have had the effect of keeping limits on foreign investors who bring large sums into the country for the purchase of fixed-income securities.

These investors are required to buy three-month forward currency contracts on the open market when they bring money into the country, thereby locking in the exchange rate at which they can take money out of Thailand.

The rule has prompted some grumbling among international investors that it limits the opportunity to profit from currency fluctuations. But the Thai baht has been one of the region's less volatile currencies in recent months.

"There are complaints it creates some costs, but basically it turns out to be an instrument to stabilize our currency," Mr. Chalongphob, the finance minister, said.

Aside from financial disruptions, another lingering worry for the five Asian crisis countries is that even as their exports to China have increased, they still remain deeply connected to American consumers.

Many Asian countries used to ship electronics and other goods directly to the United States. Today they tend to ship components to China, where they are assembled and shipped to American ports.

"Asia will need to prepare for a future in which it relies more on the strength of growth at home rather than on the strength of growth in the rest of the world," said Timothy F. Geithner, the president of the Federal Reserve Bank of New York.

Some executives are trying to do just that, including Mr. Sirivat. He even makes a point now of buying in Thailand all of the tuna for the sandwiches he serves as well as the rice for his premade sushi rolls and the bottled fruit juice he sells—a strategy that insulates him from any future fluctuations in the value of the baht. "I don't borrow money, I don't have to pay interest so I slowly save money," he said, while adding, "My business did not grow as fast as I expected."

Tracking an Online Trend, and a Route to Suicide

CHOE SANG-HUN

The New York Times, *May 23, 2007*

From their nondescript sixth-floor office, Kim Hee-joo and five other social workers troll the Internet to combat a disturbing trend in South Korea: people using the Web to trade tips about suicide and, in some cases, to form suicide pacts.

"There are so many of them," said Mr. Kim, secretary general of the Korea Association for Suicide Prevention, a private counseling group working to decrease the number of suicides, which nearly doubled from 6,440 in 2000 to 12,047 in 2005, the last year for which government figures are available.

One of the recent Internet suicide pacts involved two women who died of carbon monoxide poisoning in a one-room apartment south of Seoul.

In another, five young men and women who made a pact over the Internet and had failed in two previous suicide attempts drove to a seaside motel to discuss more effective methods. There, one member of the group had a change of heart and slipped out to call the police.

Figures released by the Organization for Economic Cooperation and

Development show that South Korea's suicide rate stood at 18.7 per 100,000 people in 2002—up from 10.2 in 1985. In 2002, Japan's rate was the same as South Korea's, but the rate in the United States was 10.2 per 100,000.

Experts attribute the increase to the stresses of rapid modernization and the degradation of rural life, but they are also concerned that the Internet is contributing to the jump. South Korea has one of the world's highest rates of broadband access and, as in Japan in recent years, the Internet has become a lethally efficient means of bringing together people with suicide on their minds.

In hardly more than a generation, South Korea has transformed itself from an agrarian society into an extremely competitive, technologically advanced economy where the pressure to succeed at school and work is intense.

Meanwhile, the traditional support base, the family, is under pressure: divorce rates are at a record high. And guarantees of lifetime employment evaporated with the Asian financial crisis in the 1990s.

In 2005, in the first rally of its kind, hundreds of high school students demonstrated in central Seoul, shouting, "We aren't study machines!" They gathered to mourn 15 students from around the country who had killed themselves, apparently because of the intense pressure to succeed.

The government does not compile figures on how many suicides may have been inspired or aided by the Internet. But in an analysis of 191 group suicides reported in the news media from June 1998 to May 2006, Kim Jung-jin, a sociologist at Korea Nazarene University, found that nearly a third of the cases involved people who had formed suicide pacts through Internet chat sites.

In Korea, the Internet has been implicated not only for helping people get together to die, but also for widely sharing individuals' suicidal thoughts.

One well-known actress, Jeong Da-bin, 27, posted her thoughts on her Web site a day before killing herself on Feb. 10.

Under the title "The End," she wrote: "For no reason at all, I am going crazy with anger. Then, as if lightning had struck, all becomes quiet.

"Then the Lord comes to me. The Lord says I will be O.K. YES, I WILL BE O.K."

Counseling centers in Seoul said calls for help jumped in the days after her death.

Notes like Ms. Jeong's—or ones that call for help in dying—are not difficult to find on Internet bulletin boards in Korea.

"I really want to kill myself," said a Yahoo Korea Web posting in April by an anonymous teenager who complained of bullying at school and his parents' pressure to improve his grades. "I only have 30,000 won," or about $32, he wrote, adding: "Can anyone sell me a suicide drug? I don't want a painful death like jumping from a high place."

In March a 28-year-old man who ran a suicide-related blog called "Trip to Heaven" was arrested on a charge of selling potassium cyanide to a 15-year-old boy he met via the Internet. The boy used the poison to kill himself.

Since 2005, Web portals, acting under pressure from civic groups, have banned words like suicide and death from the names of blogs. If a user keys in "suicide," search engines display links to counseling centers at the top of their search results.

Also in 2005, the Korea Internet Safety Commission, a government watchdog on cyberspace, ordered the removal of 566 blogs, chat groups and Web postings that encouraged suicide, up sharply from 93 cases a year earlier. The figure declined to 147 in 2006 and rose again to 161 in the first four months of this year.

The government is taking or discussing other measures to impede suicide as well. Since nearly 40 percent of South Koreans who kill themselves do so by drinking pesticides or jumping, the government is considering making pesticides less toxic and is installing more barriers on rooftops and bridges.

The Seoul subway system began erecting glass walls on platforms after 95 people, some wearing black plastic bags over their heads, threw themselves in front of subway trains in 2003, according to transit officials. Doors in the glass wall open only when trains pull into the station.

Kim Hee-joo's counseling group discovers an average of 100 suicide-related Web sites each month and asks portals to delete them. A few are serious enough that the staff alerts the police to possible violations of laws against assisting suicide or trading in hazardous substances.

"People used to use blog names like 'Let's Die Together,' " said Mr. Kim. "Now they're more careful. Once they've met each other they shut down the site and switch to e-mail and cellphones. You need a lot of searching and hunches and luck to track down these people."

Recently Mr. Kim's team discovered a blog called "Life Is Tough," described by its creator as a meeting place for people contemplating suicide. The site attracted several people who left their cellphone numbers and e-mail addresses to link up with others who wanted to "take the trip together."

The police are now searching for the blog's creator, who could face charges of aiding suicide, a crime punishable by up to 10 years in prison on conviction.

"People are social animals," said Jason Lee, director of the Metropolitan Mental Health Center in Seoul. "Some apparently want a companion even when committing suicide."

PART III

THE NEW NEW PANIC

The literature about booms and busts tends to be written in a tone of Olympian detachment by some presumably omniscient narrator with a gift for rendering the folly of man. The writer of these histories is usually amused, wryly; his reader, he assumes, shares his knowingness, understands that markets were ever thus, there is nothing new under the Wall Street sun, etc. Everything, in retrospect, is obvious. But if everything were obvious, authors of histories of financial folly would be rich. They'd spare themselves the trouble of making their living by writing books and articles about the financial folly and open hedge funds.

It's never entirely obvious what is going on inside some boom. Not only does financial history seldom repeat itself; it seldom even rhymes. Financial markets work in free verse, and no matter how much you've studied them—no matter how many times you've read Charles MacKay's *Extraordinary Popular Delusions and the Madness of Crowds*—you remain at risk of being sucked into the passions of the moment. The Internet boom and bust is an excellent case in point. In retrospect, it seems obvious that money-losing companies created by twenty-six-year-olds should never have been worth billions. But at the time, these companies appeared to have at least a shot at playing extremely important roles in wildly compelling versions of the future. That future never happened, in many cases. But who knew that then? Who could say which of these new things was Google or Microsoft—and which the next Pets.com?

The euphoria that preceded the panic began—as this section begins—on August 9, 1995, with the share offering of a company few had ever heard of called Netscape Communications. I'm not sure how many people on

Wall Street even knew what an Internet browser did, but the Netscape share offering taught them one of its critical functions: it made people rich. Overnight, Netscape founder Jim Clark became rich in a way that inspired awe even on Wall Street. The run up to the Internet panic—which can also be dated precisely—was so delicious that I've included a bit more of that here than in the other sections. (I wrote one of them, about Jim Clark's next act, after Netscape, in the world he'd done so much to create.) The Internet boom was unusual for many reasons but one of them was the sheer volume of writing it spawned; it was outdone in this only by the bust. On March 10, 2000—as John Cassidy recounts in his book *Dot.con*, excerpted here—the Nasdaq index of technology stock peaked. Ten days later the world changed.

Another strange thing about the Internet boom was the role played by journalists, many of whom were trying to get rich in their own Internet start-ups. After the fact, the Wall Street analysts who plugged Internet stocks were identified and strung up—see the excellent piece here by Erick Schonfeld on analysts' conflicts of interest, reprinted from *Fortune* magazine—but the truth is that in many cases they were more cautious in their assessments than journalists. If there is one rule in life it is: don't depend on the loyalty of journalists. And it was a journalist who kicked off the panic. His name was Jack Willoughby and his article appeared in *Barron's* on March 20, 2000. "Burning Up," he called it, and proceeded to point out, with some cold-blooded research and analysis, that a quarter of these supposedly futuristic companies were going to run through their cash in the next year, and it didn't look as if they'd be able to raise more. It was the equivalent on Wall Street of the release in Washington of an escort services client list: all sorts of important people scoured it to make sure their name wasn't on it, because everyone on it was assumed to be finished.

That was the moment when the Internet became synonymous with folly. The stocks of technology companies collapsed, and it was suddenly obvious to everyone at once that all these people involved in the creation and promotion of them were either fools or crooks. Once the stocks began their free fall, and panic ensued, the people who had created them and promoted them and invested in them on behalf of others fell all over themselves to apologize (sort of) for getting carried away. An age of sweaty materialism gave way to what turned out to be a brief spasm of anti-materialism. By October the enterprising Jerry Useem of *Fortune* was gathering up truckloads of mea culpas and insta-wisdom, some of which I've reprinted here. Word for word the best value in these came from Jim Cramer, then a hedge fund manager with what appeared to be a failed dot-com on his hands. "What's next for me?" Cramer asked himself. "Oh, this unbelievable project. It's called 'Coaching Fifth-Grade Soccer.' There I can accomplish everything I want in life. I can make everybody happy at home and have something to show for it in the end. I'm done with the material stuff." The cure, mercifully, was temporary. Jim Cramer recovered and went on to create the most materialistic show on cable television, CNBC's *Mad Money*.

I'll resist the urge to defend the Internet mania here because I haven't resisted the urge to include the defense I wrote during the panic for the *New York Times Magazine*—which ends this section. But I do think that what helped to disguise the manic events of the moment were the sentiments fueling it—not just greed but also idealism. Ten years later the same impulses would be directed into the presidential campaign of Barack Obama. A lot of people, most of them young, really thought they could change the world. Call them silly, or foolish, or callow. But they were charming, too. And they did, in the end, change the world. They just didn't profit from the experience quite as they might have hoped to.

Bigger Netscape Offering

The New York Times, *August 8, 1995*

The Netscape Communications Corporation has raised the size of its initial stock sale to the public to five million shares and the stock's indicated price to as high as $24. The company is scheduled to sell shares on Wednesday to raise about $120 million. It originally planned to sell 3.5 million shares at $13, but the new indicated price is $21 to $24 a share.

Underwriters Raise Offer Price for Netscape Communication

The New York Times, *August 9, 1995*

F aced with surprisingly strong demand for an initial public offering of the Netscape Communications Corporation, the underwriters yesterday raised the offering price to $28, more than double the original price.

The underwriters, led by Morgan Stanley & Company, also raised the number of shares to be sold to 5 million from 3.5 million.

Netscape makes browser software used to navigate the Internet. The company has yet to prove it can make money off of its software, and indeed has been giving away its browser software, Netscape Navigator, to increase its market share. Navigator is used on about 75 percent of computers linked to the Internet.

But cyberspace apparently has a special draw for many investors.

On Monday, the underwriters priced the offering at $21 to $24 a share, up from the target price of $12 to $14 a share when the offering prospectus was first issued July 17.

"Wall Street has a fascination with the Internet," said Peter Krasilovsky, marketing analyst at Arlen Communications, which tracks the Internet.

The problem is that investors "are trying to pick a winner two years out," he said.

Netscape reported a six-month loss of $4.31 million, and analysts said the company was unlikely to show a profit for at least two years. Netscape, based in Mountain View, Calif., plans to make money selling its server software and the service contracts that go with installing it. The software helps companies set up electronic addresses on the Internet and lets them exchange information between computers.

Still, interest is expected to be high when Netscape shares begin Nasdaq trading today. The ticker symbol is NSCP.

With Internet Cachet, Not Profit, a New Stock Is Wall St.'s Darling

LAURENCE ZUCKERMAN

The New York Times, *August 10, 1995*

A 15-month-old company that has never made a dime of profit had one of the most stunning debuts in Wall Street history yesterday as investors rushed to pour their money into cyberspace.

The Netscape Communications Corporation became the latest—and hottest—company in the Internet business to list shares on the nation's stock exchanges. Shares of Netscape, which had been priced at $28 before trading began at 11 A.M., opened far higher—at $71. The shares soon surged to as high as $74.75. By noon, money managers at big mutual funds and other institutional investors fortunate enough to be in on the ground floor could have cashed in at a profit of more than 150 percent and gone to lunch.

But that left plenty of action for other investors, some of whom racked up losses, during an afternoon of frantic buying and selling. Indeed, many of the 5.75 million available shares—13 percent of the total number of outstanding shares—traded hands more than once yesterday. The volume of trading of the stock on the Nasdaq market reached 13.88 million shares by the time the closing bell rang. The price of Netscape shares ended at $58.25 apiece, up $30.25 from the offering price.

The company's co-founder and chairman, who holds 9.7 million shares, ended up holding a stake valued at a half-billion dollars.

It was the best opening day for a stock in Wall Street history for an issue of its size. The overall dollar value of the one-day gain in the stock was $173.9 million. And the total market value of Netscape, including the shares held previously by management and venture capital firms, grew to $2.2 billion. That makes Netscape instantly bigger than some well-established software companies like Broderbund Software Inc.

But even more significantly, the surge was a sign of how the rush to commercialize the global computing web known as the Internet has created an investor frenzy not seen in the technology industry since the early days of the personal computer more than a decade ago.

"There is a mania under way," said Michael Murphy, the editor of *The Overpriced Stock Service*, a newsletter in Half Moon Bay, Calif.

Netscape, founded in April 1994, produces a popular software program that allows users of personal computers and modems to pilot their way through the Internet's World Wide Web. The company had revenue of $16.6 million for the first six months of the year, but reported a loss of $4.31 million for the period.

The company's debut is the latest in a recent run of successful stock offerings of Internet-related companies that have not yet turned a profit. The most noteworthy include Spyglass Inc., which competes directly with Netscape. Spyglass issued two million shares at $17 apiece in June, and yesterday the stock closed at $43.25, down $6, in Nasdaq trading. Uunet Technologies Inc., a company that provides Internet access to large companies and institutions, went public in May at $14 a share and closed yesterday at $43, down $3.25 in Nasdaq trading.

Typically, companies show a pattern of profitability over two or more quarters before an underwriter would try to take them public, but the Internet, as with some other promising technologies, is apparently different.

"For someone who looks at the fundamentals, this really represents a dangerous sign of overspeculation," said Robert S. Natale, an analyst with the Standard & Poor's Corporation in New York who follows new stock issues.

Indeed, so many investors were clamoring for shares of Netscape, that the two underwriters, Morgan Stanley and Hambrecht & Quist, increased the size of the offering and more than doubled the price.

Most initial public offerings are priced so that they will end the first day of trading with a small profit for investors. Occasionally, if the offering price is set too high, the shares will end the day lower, which is considered a failure for the underwriter. Only rarely is there such demand for a new issue that even a doubling of its offering price is a serious underestimate of the market's reaction, as was the case at Netscape's opening yesterday.

As a result of the phenomenal demand, some people are riding the Internet wave to phenomenal wealth—on paper at least. At the company's current valuation, James H. Clark, the company's 50-year-old chairman and largest shareholder, holds a stake worth $566 million. As the founder of Silicon Graphics Inc., a leading maker of computer work stations, Mr. Clark was already a millionaire many times over.

Making his first fortune yesterday was Marc L. Andreessen, Netscape's 24-year-old vice president of technology and an inventor of its prize software. Based on yesterday's closing price, his interest in Netscape is worth more than $58 million.

Behind the investment frenzy in Internet companies is an overall bull market for technology stocks, led by companies like the Intel Corporation and the Microsoft Corporation.

But the success of the personal computer industry is already an old story. The next revolution to sweep computing, goes the conventional wisdom, will be the Internet, which links millions of formerly isolated computers into a global information and entertainment bazaar.

"The commercialization of the Internet is analogous to the early days of the personal computer," said Michael K. Parekh, an on-line and Internet services analyst with Goldman, Sachs & Company.

And with the fortunes made as a result of the previous booms in personal computers, cellular phones and other technological wonders clearly in mind, investors are eager to get in on the ground floor of a company that some believe will become the next Microsoft.

Of all the Internet-related stocks, Netscape, based in Mountain View, Calif., has been seen as the top pick by investors because its Netscape Navigator software holds an estimated 75 percent of the market for Web browsers.

By giving away its Netscape Navigator for free to individual users, but charging companies who use the software to set up and operate Web sites, Netscape has moved aggressively to establish itself as the industry standard. If it succeeds, investors hope that some day it will be able to command near-monopoly profits, much as Microsoft dominates the market for operating software.

In addition, Mr. Clark, the chairman, is seen as a solid manager, based on his record at Silicon Graphics. And Mr. Andreessen, who helped write the first browser software as a student at the University of Illinois, is seen as a Wunderkind in the same mold as William H. Gates.

Still, Netscape's future is by no means assured. Many hot new issues have soared only to come crashing down to earth. The Internet is still considered to be in its infancy and there are many wealthy and powerful competitors.

Microsoft, for example, has licensed a rival browser from Spyglass and plans to distribute it along with the Microsoft Windows 95 software later this year. And publicly listed Internet access providers like Uunet also face competition from giants like AT&T and MCI Communications.

How Net Fever Sent Shares of a
Firm on 3-Day Joy Ride

CARRICK MOLLENKAMP AND
KAREN LUNDEGAARD

The Wall Street Journal, *December 9, 1998*

A t a little before 10 o'clock on the Wednesday morning before Thanksgiving, an unremarkable bit of news hit online chat rooms: Books-A-Million was launching an improved site on the World Wide Web.

Never mind that the Birmingham book retailer, which had posted lackluster financial results for the past year, already had been operating a Web site, booksamillion.com, for two years. Investors nonetheless started buying, pushing the stock up a dizzying 973% to $47 in just three days of trading. The reason: "dot.com frenzy," says Kate Delhagen, an online retail analyst at Forrester Research, a Cambridge, Mass., research firm. "It's absurd."

The frenzy has since subsided, as the stock settled back to more reasonable—but still too high, according to some analysts—levels in the $15 range. Left in the wake are some longtime shareholders kicking themselves for selling too early, stunned analysts whose advice was ignored and company executives who rushed to sell as the stock soared to four times what analysts said it was worth.

This is the story of that rise and fall—of chat rooms and boardrooms, of windfalls and short-lived euphoria.

Friday, November 20

After two years with a site that its Web designer Craig Hansen considered "a pilot," Books-A-Million quietly releases a glitzier one to the public. It is essentially the same as the original, with more color and better search capabilities. The most noticeable difference: cheaper prices.

The new Web page, says Mr. Hansen, whose Nashville company, Net-Central Inc.,˙ also designed the old site, is "competitive with everything that's out there."

It will need to be. Books-A-Million, which declined to return phone calls seeking comment for this article, doesn't release the number of visitors to its Web site. But according to one tracker of online activity, New York–based Media Metrix, it isn't many: Books-A-Million's page didn't crack the top 8,000 or so Web sites visited in October. Amazon.com of Seattle and Barnes & Noble of New York were among the top Web sites that month, with 8.2 million and 7.4 million visitors, respectively.

Tuesday, November 24

2:01 P.M.: Visitors to the Yahoo! online chat room dedicated to Books-A-Million's stock, apparently unaware of the company's new Web site, aren't very enthused about the stock. "FAT F——— CHANCE STOCK WILL BREAK IPO PRICE," one investor writes. "JUNK."

With 174 stores, the nation's No. 3 publicly traded book retailer, after Barnes & Noble and Borders Group of Ann Arbor, Mich., reported Nov. 19 that sales at stores opened at least a year fell 3.3% in the third quarter from a year earlier. Its stock has traded at the $5 range for the past year; it went public in 1992 with a price of $13 a share.

Some analysts have even given up, dropping coverage of the company in the past year. Says one, David Toung with Argus Research in New York: "They didn't look like they were going anywhere."

Wednesday, Nov. 25

9:57 A.M.: Books-A-Million's stock is up 38 cents at $5 a share.

9:58 A.M.: The company breaks the quiet of pre-Thanksgiving trading with a media release headlined, "Books-A-Million Announces Enhanced Website." The notice promises the site "offers some of the best prices on the Internet for books."

Even though the company already had a Web site, the stock begins to rise, propelled by the news and excited talk in online chat rooms.

10:30 A.M.: Fund manager Dirk Van Dijk glances at his trading terminal and does a double take: BAMM, Books-A-Million's symbol on the Nasdaq Stock Market, is at $9. Mr. Van Dijk, who works for Dean Investment Associates in Dayton, Ohio, at first thinks it's a bad quote. But before he can recheck it, Mr. Van Dijk must attend a staff meeting. His small-capitalization stock portfolio, which bought 121,600 shares in the second and third quarters, will have to sit on the shares for now.

10:51 A.M.: On Yahoo!'s message board, investors gleefully watch the stock and count their profits.

"Damn, I love this stock," writes one investor. "Bought 1500 shares at $5.25. Less than an hour later, sold all 1500 at $7.75."

12:40 P.M.: Another investor chimes in, "If you've missed out on all the other Internet high-flyers, here's your chance. BAMM will hit $100 by Christmas . . . Buy Buy Buy!!!"

1:11 P.M.: David Magee, one of three analysts who still cover the company, hustles together a report from his home. The analyst for Robinson-Humphrey in Atlanta notes: "There appears to be no fundamental reason for the strength of BAMM shares today other than the modest enhancement of the already existing web site. However, the web has not been, nor is it expected to be a meaningful part of BAMM's business, over the next year."

Mr. Magee downgrades the stock to a long-term "hold" from "buy." The stock is at $11.50, pushing Books-A-Million's market capitalization to $200 million from the $76.2 million level it traded at a day earlier. Mr. Magee's report hits the wire at 1:47.

2 P.M.: Mr. Van Dijk returns from his meeting and rechecks the stock. It's now at $12. He does a quick back-of-the-envelope calculation on its price-earnings and price-to-book ratios. The stock, he concludes, is highly

overvalued. "This thing should be an $8, $9, maybe even a $10 stock," he says later. "To announce that they've developed a Web site—everybody's got a Web site. . . . Give me a break."

Nervous about the stock's volatility, the fund manager tells his trader, Joe Gudorf, to sell all their Books-A-Million shares.

Mr. Van Dijk, who had watched the stock flounder at $5 for months, recalls telling himself: "Well, at least I've got something to give thanks for over turkey."

3:58 P.M.: Two minutes before trading ends, the online chat rooms are still abuzz. "Bamm it and slam dunk it . . . Look for $30 on this wonder."

4 P.M.: Books-A-Million closes at $12.938, nearly triple the opening price. Volume hits 33 million shares.

Thanksgiving Day, Nov. 26

3:44 P.M.: The chat rooms don't break for the holiday. The stock has room to rise further, some online gamblers figure. "BAMM should certainly be higher based on their recent understanding of the [new Web site enhancements]. We'll see!"

7–9 P.M.: Peter Verdu feels queasy, and it's not the turkey he ate with his family. A manager at Birmingham-based AmSouth's family of mutual funds, Mr. Verdu is sitting on 190,000 Books-A-Million shares and needs to decide what to do with them when the bell rings the next day.

He's already reached an unnerving conclusion from the previous day's jump: "It was clear that [the price] was out of the hands" of the large institutional dealers. "It clearly had gone into the hands of the Internet traders."

Internet traders, and their brethren, "day traders," usually never hold a position in a stock for more than day, and sometimes for no more than a few minutes.

At his computer in his home office, Mr. Verdu peruses the chat rooms, where some comments "blew my mind," he recalls. "A stock running up 300% in one day because you have an enhanced Internet site doesn't make a lot of sense."

Next he checks out the new Web site, which he likes. "The graphics are better than the Amazon site," he notes. But he's concerned that Amazon

.com could match the price cuts. And that, he says, means a price war that squeezes profits.

"The risk was on Monday, it would be back at $6," he says. He decides to sell, but hasn't determined how much and when.

Friday, Nov. 27

9:23 A.M.: The chat rooms are buzzing with anticipation about Books-A-Million. "I look for a run to $20 or $21 then a huge sell-off into the $9 or $10 range where it will close," one investor predicts.

9:30 A.M.: The market opens. Jimmy O'Neill, head of Robinson-Humphrey's capital markets division and trading unit, has added a trader to help handle Books-A-Million. The firm, the top market maker in the stock, is responsible for maintaining a systematic buy-and-flow of the shares—a task made more difficult because of the frenzied day trading.

9:42 A.M.: The stock spikes up $6.31 to $19.25 on trading of 283,000 shares.

10:26 A.M.: One day trader in Atlanta, Francis Chadwick, notes a mention of Books-A-Million's stock on CNBC and checks the ticker on his computer. Normally Mr. Chadwick shies away from Internet stocks. "It's kind of scary," he says.

He also has only a vague idea of what the company does in the book business. But that doesn't stop Mr. Chadwick from placing a buy order for 500 shares of Books-A-Million at $23.875. The minutes tick by. On his screen, he can see the stock surging up.

10:39 A.M.: Mr. Chadwick has had enough. He places a sell order, exiting at $29.75. "I was just too nervous," he says.

In 13 minutes, he made $3,000 after the stock rose $6. He exhales. "I just made six points," he tells someone later. "I can't remember the name of the stock."

Noon: In Birmingham, Mr. Verdu, the AmSouth fund manager, has been itching to sell. He and his trader, Al Wallace, dump 90,000 shares. Demand is high with an hour to go until the market closes for the shortened holiday session.

Meanwhile, insiders began registering to unload the stock, although it won't become clear exactly how much for days. According to Rockville, Md.-based CDA/Investnet, Chief Executive Clyde Anderson, whose grandfather founded the company, filed to sell 258,000 shares worth $7.74 million. His uncle, Joel, filed to sell 171,000 shares valued at $5.13 million. Chief Financial Officer Sandra Cochran filed to sell 110,900 shares worth $3.6 million; and Vice President Terrance Finley, 32,400 shares worth $1.13 million. Three other Anderson family members and a dozen family trusts filed to sell another 182,000 shares.

1 P.M.: Books-A-Million's stock is up $26, closing at $38.9375—an astounding $33 higher than where the stock had opened just a trading day earlier. Some 33 million shares traded, making it the most heavily traded stock on the Nasdaq.

Monday, Nov. 30

9:47 A.M.: In the first 17 minutes of trading, Books-A-Million's stock rises $7 to $46. Then, just as suddenly as it started climbing, the stock begins to free fall.

11:33 A.M.: The stock is trading at $30.25. Mr. Magee, the Robinson-Humphrey analyst, issues another report: "We do not believe BAMM shares are presently worth more than $7."

Noon: With the stock at $35, Mr. Verdu is exiting altogether. The AmSouth manager has told his trader, Mr. Wallace, to sell his final 100,000 shares.

Books-A-Million executives continue to make plans to sell: Chairman Charles Anderson, 397,047 shares valued at $11.9 million; his son, Clyde, 184,300 worth $5.53 million; brother, Joel, 181,100 worth $5.43 million. Other family members, foundations, trusts and executives filed to sell a total of 304,951 shares worth $9.5 million. The two-day total: 42 transactions of 1.82 million shares worth $55.5 million.

4 P.M.: Books-A-Million's stock closes at $29.50, down 24% on the day. Over the next several days, the stock settles back to the $15 range, its heady run over. Day traders search for the next play.

But others begin to look for an explanation. Mr. Magee, the analyst, remains slightly dazed. He offers a concession on his downgrade on the first day of the frenzy, a move that in general can sink a stock. "My comments really haven't been that relevant," he says. "You probably had two or three analysts downgrade the stock. I don't think people paid attention."

He admits he was caught off-guard by the impact of the chat rooms. "I've been surprised by the power of that," he says.

He, like other analysts, see limited potential for the cause of all the excitement, Books-A-Million's Web site.

"All the best shelf space on the Internet is taken," says Forrester Research's Ms. Delhagen, noting that Amazon.com and Barnes & Noble have signed exclusive deals with online providers and Internet search engines.

Meanwhile, some traders reminisce about what could have been. Mr. Van Dijk, the fund manager who sold the day before Thanksgiving, admits, "It would be nice to have gotten out at $35 instead of $12." But he'll take his profits.

That's more than some can say.

New New Money

MICHAEL LEWIS

from The New New Thing

One summer afternoon, after a meeting with the venture capitalists about Healtheon's future, Clark hopped into one of his sports cars and launched himself in the direction of San Francisco. With the top down and the speedometer's needle nudging past 100 he had to holler to make himself heard. "I'm starting to feel poor!" he shouted.

He intended it as both a joke and a complaint. He felt poor, and he realized that it was funny, or at least odd, that he felt poor. After all, his Netscape holdings were still worth nearly $600 million. Even if Microsoft succeeded in driving Netscape out of business (which Clark believed it would do), he thought he would soon be much richer than he now was. Despite all appearances he felt certain Healtheon would be an embarrassingly big success. Indeed, one of his purposes at the meeting that morning was to increase his stake in the company. No, he was less concerned about Healtheon than about the new new thing, whatever *that* might be. Whatever it was, it had to be even bigger and more dramatic than Healtheon. That was Clark's one rule about his new new things:

each one bigger than the last. "The idea so far is that I've put all my wood behind a single arrow," he explained. 'The risk now is that the next time the arrow gets so huge that the whole world is looking at it. And it's not an arrow anymore, it's an ICBM. 'Well, Jim Clark failed.' That'll be the story. And it'll be a *big* story."

The story began a month later, when a group of Wall Street investment bankers visited Healtheon. In 1986 when Clark had wanted Wall Street bankers to sell Silicon Graphics to the public, he flew to New York City, hat in hand. Many of the bankers treated him poorly. The CEO of Salomon Brothers, John Gutfreund, stood him up—left him sitting like some hick in the lobby of Salomon Brothers. These days, the investment bankers came to Silicon Valley. This was only one of many recent changes along the capitalist food chain. Wall Street had gone from being the celebrities of the money culture to being its lackeys. They crammed their lightly starched selves into a small conference room. What ensued was a wonderfully elaborate money ballet.

It took an hour or so for the dance to begin: when billions of dollars are on the line, you can't simply talk about money. It's too important. Healtheon CEO Mike Long took the seat at the head of the conference table. The investment bankers took seats along the table. A few Healtheon employees sat in chairs back against the wall. Clark took a chair by the door, which to the consternation of the bankers, he opened a crack. They didn't understand that nothing of true importance happened behind closed doors. The room stayed too stuffy for his tastes anyway, and all through the meeting he kept getting up and wandering around outside in the halls. Long introduced the Healtheon employees and then turned to the one man in the room who needed no introduction. "Jim Clark," he said, "why don't you tell us about your original vision here."

Jim Clark obliged. "Just after Netscape I was interested in a vertical market," he began, deploying the usual Internet lingo. A vertical market was a market for a single good or service, like books or travel. A horizontal market was a market that cut across many different goods and services, like a Web browser. Netscape was a horizontal market; Healtheon was in a vertical market. "I always thought that the biggest opportunity on the Internet was the vertical markets," Clark continued. "I didn't know anything about health care, but I was looking for something worth doing and . . ."

He went on for a few minutes about why turning the $1.5 trillion health care market on its head was "worth doing." Then he leaned his chair back on two legs against the wall and as much as handed the floor back to Mike Long. "The Internet changes everything," said Long. "Everyone can get connected on the Internet. And thank you, Jim, for that."

The bankers chuckled appreciatively. By their tone and their manner they conveyed the general idea that everyone who mattered in this new world was in this one little room. They felt safe here. The playing field was now Silicon Valley. Of course, an investment banker in Silicon Valley wasn't exactly a player. He was more of a waterboy. But at least he was *in* Silicon Valley. His colleagues back in New York were relegated to the bleacher seats of capitalism—and it nearly killed them. After all, what possibly could be the point of being an investment banker if you didn't make more money than everyone else?

Still, Wall Street bankers were higher up on the capitalist food chain than Swiss bankers. They participated directly in the miracle of Jim Clark, or thought they did. True, they'd been shoved a rung or two down the chain by entrepreneurs like Clark and venture capitalists like John Doerr. True, when Morgan Stanley and Goldman Sachs called Mike Long and said in their puffed-up way that they would take Healtheon public only if they were given sole possession of the deal, Long had only to say in a stern voice "put that in writing" before they caved and said they would do whatever he said, when he said it. But they'd made hundreds of millions of dollars off the Internet boom. They could plausibly claim, at least at that moment, to be the perpetrators rather than the victims of change. To take a company like Healtheon public they charged 7 percent of all monies raised, plus expenses. If a company raised $50 million, the investment bank would net $3.5 million for a few weeks of work. That fee was usually just a kind of down payment. Once the stock price of one of these Internet companies took off, it could be used to acquire other companies with lower stock prices. The Wall Street bankers acted as agents for these acquisitions. Their fees did not make them as rich as Clark or the people who worked for Clark or the people who worked for the people who worked for Clark or even the people who worked for the people who worked for the people who worked for Clark. But they were richer than Swiss bankers.

The meeting with the Wall Street bankers lasted four hours, from two until six, with one long break for coffee and phone calls. Long introduced the company with the new Healtheon diagram. The new diagram was even more impressive than the Magic Diamond, which it had replaced. It looked like this:

Informally known as the Chart of Many Bubbles, eleven to be exact, it still showed Healtheon in the center. But now the little company, which still had fewer than two hundred employees, sat in the middle of many obviously complicated things. The Chart of Many Bubbles proved that Mike Long, before he took over the health care industry, had at least bothered to learn the names of its component parts. The Morgan Stanley people took only a polite interest in the Chart of Many Bubbles, however. The opening of the meeting was pure ritual, a sprinkling of holy water over the sheep before it was slaughtered. You could tell how serious they were about it from their attitude toward the black box on the conference table. One of their colleagues, a woman who had stayed home sick, listened by speaker phone. From time to time a squeak or a gurgle emanated from the box at the center of the conference table. A baby! The woman from Morgan Stanley was holding a baby, and the baby was refusing to keep quiet. Each time it mewled, the room used it as an excuse to depart from the Chart of Many Bubbles and share a hearty laugh.

"If you're going to play the health care game," Mike Long said, "you've got to have a large percentage of your staff that can talk the talk."

"Gibagibagibagiba" went the baby.

"Ho, ho, ho," went all the people in the room.

But the Chart of Many Bubbles suggested one obvious question, and the investment bankers raised it: How would all the companies in the little bubbles feel about a Silicon Valley upstart organizing them into a Chart of Many Bubbles and moving into the middle? Long had a long and happy answer: Healtheon could slide in and eliminate $250 billion in waste without causing the people who made their living wastefully to raise hell, and it would do this by forming partnerships with the stronger companies. The stronger companies in each sector would use Healtheon services to kill the weaker ones. By the time the stronger companies figured out that Healtheon didn't need them either, it would be too late. The way Long said all this was perfectly soothing. He was not describing a ferocious upheaval in which hundreds of billions of capital would be redirected and hundreds of thousands of people would need to find new jobs. He was describing a friendly bake-off.

This was the Easy Listening version of Clark's original intention. Clark had seen the health care system as he saw much of the world, in black and white. To his way of thinking there were health care professionals who clearly served a purpose. They were called doctors. And there were people who clearly needed health care. They were called patients. Everyone else in between—the hundreds of billions in paperwork and bullshit—could go. All Mike Long's soothing talk about "partnering" and "win-win relationships with other health care firms" was a smoke screen for what Clark was up to when he created Healtheon. "We want to empower the doctors and the patients and get all the other assholes out of the way," Clark had once told me, then laughed. "Except for us. One asshole in the middle."

Long didn't mention the part about the one asshole in the middle. Instead, he handed the Chart of Many Bubbles to the doctors and other health care authorities in the room, mercenaries in a new civil war. Each man in turn explained how he planned to worm his way into his particular bubble and make it his own. First the drug companies (the drug company SmithKline had a seat on the Healtheon board), then the insurers (the insurance company United Health Care also had a board seat), PPOs,

HMOs, hospitals, doctors, patients, and so on. Each bubble represented a gargantuan market all its own. Over the past nine months Mike Long had talked one large entity in each bubble into becoming a guinea pig for Healtheon's software. In essence, the Healtheon employees were explaining to the Wall Street bankers how they planned to build, simultaneously, eleven separate multibillion-dollar businesses.

"So what have you been doing for the last year?" asked one of the bankers, when they'd finished. Everyone laughed. The baby cried. Everyone laughed some more.

"Pavan Nigam will now explain why all of this is going to work," said Mike Long.

Pavan—Healtheon's Chief Technology Officer—had been sitting quietly to one side pretending to be interested. Now he rose and stood in front of a giant screen, and I wondered if this is what he imagined when he put down the copy of *USA Today* in the Delhi hotel and decided to become an Internet entrepreneur. "Three years ago this would have been impossible to pull off," he began and then launched into a perfectly baffling presentation on the inner workings of Healtheon's software. Abstraction followed abstraction in the manner of contemporary art criticism. The Morgan Stanley people did not have much to say to this. How could they? They didn't understand it any better than you or I could. If they could write software, they wouldn't be schlepping companies for a living. But at the end of it one of them, perhaps hoping to dispel the impression that the reason investment bankers are investment bankers is that they don't have the brains to be software engineers, asked, "Is there any major piece of the platform that has not been built?" *Platform.*

"Not really," said Pavan.

The investment bankers just nodded knowingly. No one dared dig further. The baby squalled. Everyone laughed.

Through it all Clark had remained silent. At one point, when the bankers were asking about Healtheon's possibilities, he said, "This could be as big as Microsoft, and quicker too." Otherwise he sat back and watched the proceedings with the detachment of a small boy who has rolled a rock down a hill and watched it become an avalanche. His chief contribution to the meeting was to be there. He was attached to the business in the same way that Jack Nicholson was attached to a film script—thus increasing the likelihood that the script will become a movie. Simply by floating around and taking an interest, he makes all involved feel as if they engaged in something very special.

"What about competitors?" asked one of the bankers. "IBM has something called Health Data Networks."

Clark came alive, briefly. "They've got nothing on us," he said. "As soon as we hire a PR person, we're going to flatten them."

All talk of competition ended right there. The conversation turned to finances. The bankers asked several perfunctory questions: How much money did Mike Long think the company required? ($40 million) How fast could it grow? (How fast did they want it to grow?) How much was at stake? (The future of the single biggest market.) "The benefits of first-mover advantage in this space are so huge," said Long. "That's why we have this land-grab strategy." The bankers agreed mightily with this statement. One of them said, "That's true in every Internet space. Amazon. com is doing $87 million a quarter. Barnes and Noble is only doing $9 million. And Barnes and Noble has been as good as it gets in responding to the Internet threat."

"That's why we are in a mad panic to go out and *get lives on the system*," said Long, calmly. "Lives" was what health care business people called their customers. Mike Long was the sort of man who could claim to be in "a mad panic," while giving the impression of being in such complete control that there was no point in further discussion.

"The investor base is becoming a lot more creative in evaluating these deals," said the woman in the box on the table. The investment bankers had all these wonderfully soothing phrases that implied the world outside the room was climate controlled. The investor base! What she was referring to was a seeming peristaltic mass of junkies high on the giddiest boom the U.S. stock market had ever seen.

"No traditional Graham and Dodd investor invested in AOL," said a banker at the table. "They shorted it. And got fucked. They're learning the new model."

Mike Long said, "The main point is that *nobody* has driven a growth strategy in health care."

"That's why this is such an exciting opportunity," said one of the bankers. "It's like AOL in the beginning. Or Yahoo."

They'd arrived at the true purpose of their meeting. The true purpose of the meeting was *not* to determine whether Healtheon was worthy of Wall

Street's attention. It was to determine just how enthusiastic the bankers were prepared to sound about Healtheon. Their money was cheap: there was so much money pouring into the Valley that Mike Long had about twelve different ways he could get his hands on what he needed. The Valley was a little experiment of capitalism with too much capital. For a brief but shining moment capital lost its purchase on its own process. The process took on a momentum all its own, and the old-fashioned capitalist just came along for the ride. All he could offer was his ability to influence the minds of investors who had not figured out what had happened. The investment bankers were no longer selling money; they were selling talk.

The people from Wall Street now fell over each other praising the future of Healtheon. One said, "The opportunity really is huge." Another said, "The only problem is finding a way to explain it." A third said, "It's like AOL all over again." For the first time Clark became truly interested. "The market opportunity here is bigger then all of those guys put together—bigger than Netscape, than Amazon, than AOL, than Yahoo, than *all* of them," he said. "That's why when I look at your revenue projections they seem laughably small."

What *was* Healtheon worth? How did a sane person value a company that had never made a profit? The old formulas of old Graham and Dodd investors like Warren Buffett no longer applied. By those formulas Healtheon was worth zero. The company's balance sheet was filled with negative numbers. It showed losses running out as far as the eye could see. Like other Internet companies, it said to the stock market: our future will look nothing like our present; ergo, you cannot determine our value by looking at the present. You must close your eyes and imagine a new world. Look to the future! The future is bright! The belief was partly self-fulfilling: belief often is. Once the stock price took off, the company was halfway home. The competition would fall away or, more likely, offer itself for sale to Healtheon. Mike Long spoke of "an M&A strategy for growth." What he meant by that was that as soon as he was able to buy potential competitors with Healtheon stock he would do so.

The Internet formula for success turned traditional capitalism on its head. Traditionally a company persuaded people to invest in it by making profits. Now it persuaded people to invest in it first, and hoped the profits would follow.

Clark had understood the ass-backward nature of the enterprise from the start. The ass-backward nature of the enterprise is what gave him his tactical advantage. The trick was for Healtheon to get itself designated by the financial markets of the Official Health Care Sponsor of the Miracle Economy. That in turn depended on Healtheon's being viewed not as a health care company but as an Internet company. And that, in turn, depended on shrewd public relations. And public relations was driven in part by what the bankers said about the company. But since the bankers desperately wanted the fees that came from running the deal, they would say whatever they had to say to please Jim Clark and Mike Long, within reason. They did this with clear consciences. If they succeeded in persuading the capital markets that Healtheon belonged at the heart of the Chart of Many Bubbles, Healtheon might very well wind up at the heart of the Chart of Many Bubbles. In this new world skepticism was not a sign of intelligence. It was a sin.

When you sat back and looked at it, you saw that a single assumption underpinned the entire boom: the future would be better than the past. Healtheon existed in a state of pure possibility. It was the golden boy in his senior year headed toward some undefinable great height. The stock market would be asked to imagine the most breathtaking possibilities for it. It would be asked to devalue the past, to cease its usual talk about "track records," and to invest everything in an idea of how the future might turn out.

In other words, the stock market was being asked to adopt Jim Clark's value system. And the amazing thing is, it did.

The meeting lasted two hours more, and in those hours the baby found its way right up into the speaker phone. It cooed, it giggled, it spoke these adorable baby words. No one flinched or even smiled. I doubt anyone even heard it this time. From the moment the conversation had turned to the dollar value that might be placed on Healtheon, the baby had been priced out of the meeting.

A few days later Healtheon selected Morgan Stanley to lead its public offering. A few days after that the stock markets crashed. The bad news that ostensibly caused the collapse had nothing to do with the U.S. stock market. On Friday, July 22, 1998, a rumor passed along trading desks that Russia intended to default on its foreign debt. The rumor caused a panic, and the panic forced Russia to default. One large foreign country reneging on its debts caused investors to suspect that others would follow. This in turn led to the fear of all kinds of financial risk. Investors pulled their money out of corporate stocks and bonds and put it into cash or U.S. government bonds. Between July 1 and October 1 the Dow Jones industrial average fell 2000 points, or 25 percent. The riskier Nasdaq composite—the best measure of Silicon Valley's fortunes—fell from 2900 to 1450, or 50 percent. Netscape fell from 41 to 16. Clark went from being worth $640 million to being worth $248 million, give or take $50 million.

This period tested Clark's resolve. Some part of him feared that the game was over. The truth was, *he* thought most Internet stocks were ridiculously overpriced. He thought that Microsoft would wind up controlling the lion's share of Internet profits, and that most of the golden children of the miracle economy were doomed. "Fucking Yahoo is not worth thirty billion dollars," he'd say. "Once Microsoft controls the browser market, they'll take over Yahoo's market too." The trouble was he could not say publicly what he thought about Microsoft without hurting Healtheon. He thought that one day soon Microsoft would begin to take over the vertical markets on the Internet. "They're already into travel," he said. "They'll get into everything else."

Still, Clark did not sell his Netscape stock and buy U.S. Treasury bonds or, more logically, Microsoft stock. It was as if he had decided that the first in must also be the last out. I think he almost would prefer to be poor again than buy shares in Microsoft. Almost.

The stock market crash screwed up Clark's immediate plans for Healtheon. It caused Morgan Stanley—and every other Wall Street banker—to become cautious. Wall Street had taken 370 companies public in the year up to August; between August and October they had taken only one public. The IPOs of five new Internet companies (Earthweb, Theglobe.com, Interworld, Multex, Netgrocer) were postponed until further notice. Morgan Stanley canceled all but two of its IPOs scheduled for the fall. One of the two it did not cancel was Healtheon.

In retrospect it's odd that they went ahead. On the first of October 1998, in what was widely viewed as the worst market for IPOs since the early 1970s, they set out to sell a company, and restore the vigor to Jim Clark's bank account.

Cooling It: Wall Street Firms Try to Keep Internet Mania from Ending Badly

REBECCA BUCKMAN AND AARON LUCCHETTI

The Wall Street Journal, *February 24, 1999*

A dorning the office of Susanne Lyons, a senior Charles Schwab Corp. executive in San Francisco, is a gift recently sent by some Florida employees: a gale-warning flag. It refers to a huge effort Schwab has been making, in staffing and technology, to cope with the crush of trading in Internet stocks, a campaign Schwab calls "Market Storm."

That term resonates with Wall Street executives these days, with a different meaning. A growing number of them are concerned that the financial world's equivalent of a typhoon—with a menacing "dot.com" at the eye—could be hurtling the market's way. The signs are all there: wild price swings, valuations that seem from another world, rapid-fire trading by people completely new to the game.

So now, brokerage firms and industry regulators are battening down the hatches, to protect both themselves and their customers in case it happens. So fretful are firms that, in a few cases, they are even turning away business, the Wall Street equivalent of a bartender shooing away a patron who has had enough. "In the case of Internet stocks," marvels

L. Keith Mullins, a managing director and head of growth-stock research at Salomon Smith Barney, "there's enough concern to overcome Wall Street greed."

U.S. Federal Reserve Chairman Alan Greenspan, in his usual circumspect way, expressed concern Tuesday about the level of stock prices, noting that stock-market bubbles are sometimes not identified until after they've popped.

One hopeful sign, though, is that some of the froth in individual Internet stocks has drained off gradually in recent weeks, suggesting that even if highfliers are overvalued, they can avoid a blowup. But here is Wall Street's worst fear: that the volatile mixture of high-priced Internet stocks, novice investors and buying on margin is so combustible that a shock could spread quickly through the rest of the market, ruining some investors and jeopardizing the health of some smaller firms. With Wall Street helping to power the buoyant U.S. economy, a shock there could send ripples throughout struggling economies and markets world-wide.

So the barricades go up, even as Wall Street executives concede there's only so much they can do to head off trouble:

- The Nasdaq Stock Market, which boasts in its marketing that it rarely stops investors from buying and selling, is considering authorizing trading halts under certain circumstances.
- Schwab, Salomon Smith Barney, Waterhouse Securities Inc. and other firms are making it harder for customers to buy Internet stocks with borrowed funds. In some cases, they are barring clients from ordering shares of hot initial public offerings without setting a maximum price.
- Several online brokerage firms, including Schwab and E*Trade Group Inc., are scrambling to upgrade computer systems, which have sometimes faltered under the weight of heavy trading. Schwab, realizing that such breakdowns amid a plunging market could be catastrophic, has rigged its computer systems to run on two mainframes instead of one, buying time until it can make more permanent upgrades.

Why the sudden fuss? After all, for much of last year, Internet stocks rose robustly and online-stock trading was heralded as the next revolutionizing force on Wall Street. But unsettling swings in several little-known issues in late November jolted regulators and securities firms into action.

Around that time, tiny IPOs like Theglobe.com Inc. and Ticketmaster Online CitySearch Inc. skyrocketed in their opening minutes of trading, then plummeted, touching off investor complaints. Obscure companies like Books-A-Million Inc. tripled after announcing Web upgrades. Many investors got hurt in these swings, having placed orders when stocks were at one price but had them filled when prices were very different.

Amid this turbulence, Frank Zarb, chairman of the National Association of Securities Dealers, which runs Nasdaq, hastily called a teleconference with NASD executives. "This is not business as usual," he told his lieutenants, calling the volatility in Internet stocks "serious." Mr. Zarb, a former brokerage executive, told his regulatory staff to look at such drastic moves as expanding authority for the NASD to halt trading in some stocks. The NASD board is scheduled to consider the idea next month.

Mary Schapiro, president of NASD Regulation Inc., and her staff started calling online brokerage firms to grill them about their clients' exposure to the stocks of companies doing business on the Internet. How many customers held the stocks? How much were they borrowing to hold them? Later, regulators sent a memo to 5,500 brokerage firms listing steps they could take, including explaining the risks to investors and limiting their ability to buy with borrowed money.

These ideas weren't easy to swallow. Patrick Campbell, Nasdaq's enthusiastic chief operating officer, long opposed any notion of trading halts except in the rarest of circumstances. But he changed his view after noticing that some stocks were soaring simply because investors were mistaking their symbols for those of Internet companies.

This was a sure sign of trigger-happy investing. "We have an orderly market to run," says Mr. Campbell, choosing his words carefully. Glancing at a monitor on his desk, he sees that a hot computer stock has just dropped 7% in heavy trading. "These are extraordinary times," he concludes.

So extraordinary that Mr. Zarb phoned his chief competitor, New York Stock Exchange Chairman Richard Grasso, about a month ago to discuss whether Internet stocks should carry a higher margin-maintenance requirement, the amount of overall cash and equity customers need if they have bought stocks using borrowed funds. Mr. Grasso told him this would be "overkill," and Mr. Zarb ultimately dropped the idea.

Some firms haven't waited for industry regulators to move. At Salomon Smith Barney, Horace Derrick, a senior vice president who handles margin accounts, called in two risk analysts and asked what would happen if highfliers like Amazon.com Inc. and Yahoo! Inc. dropped 30% or more, given that the firm's customers had a huge $13 billion in margin loans.

One of the risk analysts ran a test. The results discouraged him: Hundreds of customers, having put up money for only part of the price of a stock and borrowed the rest from Salomon Smith Barney, could see their accounts wiped out by a big fall. It was "a very risky situation," the analyst, Colin Carney, told his boss. Mr. Derrick agreed, and persuaded the firm to raise margin requirements on 18 Internet stocks, and later on 85 in all.

Blake Darcy, chief executive of DLJdirect, the online-trading unit of Donaldson, Lufkin & Jenrette Inc., grew concerned about the Internet frenzy as he prepared to board a flight to Japan in late November. From a club lounge at Newark airport, he called the firm's head of compliance, Tony Festa, on a cell phone. "How are we doing?" Mr. Darcy asked, most worried about customers with heavy margin debt. Fine so far, Mr. Festa replied. But he was worried, too, and had a plan of action, a series of steps that mostly involved monitoring potentially troublesome stocks more closely and better scrutinizing each morning's queue of trade orders. The two also hastily identified about 15 stocks to add to their list of issues with tighter margin requirements.

Mr. Festa's parting words were, "Don't worry about it, Blake. We got it." But Mr. Darcy didn't stop worrying. In December, DLJdirect deepened its already-intense monitoring of "concentrated" accounts to look at short positions, in which clients sell borrowed shares in hopes of profiting from a decline. Because the client is obligated to replace those shares even if the stock soars, "with a short position, there's no limit to the amount of money you could lose," Mr. Darcy says.

DLJdirect is no stranger to risk. It and a few other firms have long sent form letters to customers who do rapid-fire or high-risk trading, warning them of the dangers and asking them to acknowledge receipt of the warning. But the stiffened margin rules "are a really clear signal" that the industry is concerned about the volatility, says James J. Angel, an associate finance professor at Georgetown University. That's because the rules limit trading, and "brokerage firms have a natural tendency not to want to slay the goose that's laying the golden eggs."

One concern is how many unseasoned traders the Internet stocks and online trading have attracted. At Schwab, the largest online broker, 50% of new customers are considered inexperienced.

At Ameritrade Holding Corp., a graduate student from Indianapolis named Lael Desmond opened a margin account in late 1997 even though he didn't know what a margin account was. Mr. Desmond, 27, had simply heard from his sister that "you can make a lot more money quickly" that way. He concedes he didn't read the fine print on the margin agreement.

He took notice in August, though, when his fully leveraged, $100,000 account took a dive after stocks such as Amazon, Excite Inc., Dell and Yahoo! stumbled. His margin calls, the added money Ameritrade required him to put up, exceeded the equity left in his account. Mr. Desmond wound up borrowing about $12,000 on four credit cards, though he also filed an arbitration complaint challenging the way Ameritrade handled the situation. Ameritrade says it hasn't yet received a copy of the complaint and thus can't comment.

"I will never trade on margin again," declares Mr. Desmond, who says he thought margin loans were like bank loans, requiring regular payments. He has since taken out a loan against his house to pay off the credit-card balances.

The same volatility and heavy trading by individuals convinced a market veteran, Bernard L. Madoff, that his trading firm should stop making a market in four wild Web stocks. "You're literally seeing hundreds of thousands of orders in these stocks," Mr. Madoff says. "That puts a strain on everybody's systems. And on the way down, it's always more extreme."

Throughout late 1998, Mr. Madoff, at his trading desk in Manhattan, watched tiny orders scroll across his monitor for stocks like Amazon, Yahoo, Infoseek Inc. and Egghead.com Inc. Then, he saw IPOs skyrocketing. But what did it for him was the action in Amazon in mid-December. An analyst from CIBC Oppenheimer Corp., Henry Blodget, issued what seemed an outlandish price "target" of $400, which equals $133 today after a 3-for-1 split. The stock leapt 19% in one day. Then Merrill Lynch & Co.'s better-known Jonathan Cohen struck back with a price target of only $50, or $17 after the split. The stock whipsawed back down.

To Mr. Madoff, "it was insanity. This thing was getting out of control." In January, his New York firm, which bears his name, dropped Amazon, Yahoo!, Infoseek and Egghead, even though trading them had been very profitable. Interestingly, shares of Amazon now trade at a bit over $115 a share—or, presplit, very close to Mr. Blodget's forecast. Mr. Cohen has since left Merrill. Mr. Blodget is now expected to take his job.

But Mr. Madoff lived through the October 1987 crash in stock prices—as Nasdaq's chairman. "I had to field all the unhappy phone calls when people felt the Nasdaq market had pretty much shut down," he says. "My attitude was, I do not want to relive that event." And now, even more of the trading is done by individuals.

Further complicating matters is the rapid rise of online trading, to an estimated 13% of stock transactions. On heavy days, they have jammed computer systems. E*Trade, Waterhouse and Ameritrade have all suffered embarrassing technology glitches that locked investors out of their systems and away from their money. So a question concerning some Wall Street executives is what would happen in a panicky market. To be ready for any rush of trades, Schwab persuaded a vendor in December to deliver a new server computer via chartered jet, a month ahead of schedule.

At a recent "town hall" meeting at a hotel near Disney World, Schwab staffers nevertheless were restless, peppering Ms. Lyons with questions about technological readiness. In an interview, she says that "virtually every project that's long term has been tabled so we can devote every resource to build up capacity."

But brokers remain on guard. On a recent day, investors who use the phone rather than a computer were pelting Schwab broker Amy Hommas in Orlando with requests: How much can I get for my shares of Global DataTel Inc.? How can I unload CyberGuard Corp. now that it has been delisted from Nasdaq? What's the market for options in Cisco Systems? Ms. Hommas handled the requests smoothly, telling the man who was trying to dump the thinly traded CyberGuard that "I can't guarantee you execution while we're on the phone."

Nearly all the calls came from investors in Internet stocks. During a one-hour stretch, Ms. Hommas handled exactly one call from a customer trading a traditional blue chip, and even it was far from staid—Lucent Technologies Inc. Ms. Hommas, concerned about clients being overexposed to Web stocks, says she tries her best to guide them, gently asking if they are diversified beyond Internet shares.

In all this, brokers are limited in the precautions they can take. They don't know how likely they are to face a market storm, and even if they do, they can't fully prepare. Says DLJdirect's Mr. Darcy: "You can never predict perfectly the scenario that's going to occur and how quickly it's going to occur. . . . All the planning we have will probably not have prepared us for a 40% correction."

Burning Up

JACK WILLOUGHBY

Barron's, *March 20, 2000*

Warning: Internet companies are running out of cash—fast

Fire Alarm

Here's when the 51 'Net companies below are likely to run out of cash, according to year-end 1999 data. Some can raise more funds through stock and bond offerings. Others will be forced to merge or go out of business. It's Darwinian capitalism at work.

2000	
MAR	Pilot Ntwk Services
	CDNow
APR	Secure Computing
MAY	Peapod
	VerticalNet
	MarketWatch.com
JUN	drkoop.com
	Infonautics
	Medscape
	Intelligent Life
	Digital Island
	Splitrock Services
	VitaminShoppe.com
JUL	Intraware
	Interliant
	MyPoints.com
	Egghead.com
	MotherNature.com
	ImageX.com
	BigStar Entmt
	Mail.com

AUG	Cybercash
	Applied Theory
	WorldTalk Corp
	Primix Solutions
	Newsedge
SEP	FTD.com
	ShopNow.com
	Beyond.com
	Healtheon
OCT	E Loan
	Interactive Pictures
	Ask Jeeves
	LoisLaw.com
	PlanetRx.com
NOV	LifeMinders.com
	SmarterKids.com
	drugstore.com
	Ashford.com
	NorthPoint Comm.
DEC	EarthWeb
	NetObjects
	Tickets.com
2001	
JAN	Salon.com
	Amazon.com
	PurchasePro.com
FEB	Cobalt Group
	Multex.com
	eToys
	Kana Comms
	E-Stamp

Source: Pegasus Research International

When will the Internet Bubble burst? For scores of 'Net upstarts, that unpleasant popping sound is likely to be heard before the end of this year. Starved for cash, many of these companies will try to raise fresh funds by issuing more stock or bonds. But a lot of them won't succeed. As a result, they will be forced to sell out to stronger rivals or go out of business altogether. Already, many cash-strapped Internet firms are scrambling to find financing.

An exclusive study conducted for Barron's by the Internet stock evaluation firm Pegasus Research International indicates that at least 51 'Net firms will burn through their cash within the next 12 months. This amounts to a quarter of the 207 companies included in our study. Among the outfits likely to run out of funds soon are CDNow, Secure Computing, drkoop.com, Medscape, Infonautics, Intraware and Peapod.

To assess the Internet sector's financial position, Pegasus assumed that the firms in the study would continue booking revenues and expenses at the same rate they did in last year's fourth quarter. While this method cannot predict the future precisely, it helps answer a question that has been nagging many stock-market analysts: When will the crowded Internet industry begin to be winnowed?

The ramifications are far-reaching. To begin with, America's 371 publicly traded Internet companies have grown to the point that they are collectively valued at $1.3 trillion, which amounts to about 8% of the entire U.S. stock market. Any financial problems at these Internet firms would affect the myriad companies that supply them with equipment, including such giants as Cisco Systems and Intel. Another consideration is that a collapse in highflying Internet stocks could have a depressing effect on the overall market and on consumer confidence, too. This, in turn, could make Americans feel less wealthy and cause them to spend less money on everything from cars to clothing to houses.

It's no secret that most Internet companies continue to be money-burners. Of the companies in the Pegasus survey, 74% had negative cash flows. For many, there seems to be little realistic hope of profits in the near term. And it's not just the small fry who are running out of cash. Perhaps one of the best-known companies on our list, Amazon.com, showed up with only 10 months' worth of cash left in the till.

Pegasus was working with the latest public financial data, from December 31, so the table doesn't reflect the fact that Amazon early this year managed to raise $690 million by issuing convertible bonds. But that money will last the firm only 21 months. Moreover, raising fresh funds will be more difficult if Amazon's operating losses continue to mount and its stock price continues to flag.

"What's critical is the stock price," says Scott Sipprelle, cofounder of Midtown Research in New York. "It's only when the stock price comes unglued that the burn rate means anything."

Several signs suggest that the era of "unglued" stock prices is fast approaching. Amazon.com, for example, is trading at about 65, down from its all-time high of $113. Then there's Internet Capital Group, trading at a recent 117, down from a high of 212. Many other 'Net fledglings are in far worse shape. E-Loan's shares have plummeted to about 10, from a high of 74. The broad picture isn't much better. The Dow Jones Internet Commerce Index had fallen 25% from the all-time high achieved last April.

Little wonder that so many 'Net firms are following Amazon's lead and looking for new funding. "The hunt for cash will become more desperate as the reserves deplete," says Greg Kyle, founder of New York-based Pegasus Research International.

Take for instance the firm at the top of our list, Pilot Network Services. It was just at the bottom of its cash hoard when it managed to get a $15 million investment from Primus Telecommunications. To obtain the funds, Pilot had to give Primus a 6% ownership stake. At the current burn rate, the cash infusion should last Pilot about 10 months.

VerticalNet, which helps businesses transact on the Internet, had to turn to Microsoft to replenish its dwindling cash supply. In exchange for a $100 million investment, Microsoft is getting a 2% stake in VerticalNet and requiring the Internet upstart to use Microsoft's technology.

Medscape, No. 9 on our list, apparently solved its cash problems by agreeing a few weeks ago to be bought by MedicalLogic Inc. for $733 million in stock.

Not all 'Net firms have been so lucky. Peapod, the fourth company on our list, unveiled crushing news last week. Peapod Chairman Bill Malloy intends to step down for health reasons from the online vendor of groceries. As a result, investors who had agreed to pony up $120 million in financing are backing out of the deal. Peapod has hired Wasserstein Perella to seek out new investors, but with only $3 million of cash on hand, Peapod's coffers could be empty within a month. That's even sooner than indicated by the financial data that Pegasus used to create its burnout rankings.

Another 'Net company in disarray is the online music retailer CDNow, No. 2 on our list. CDNow executives thought their problems were solved when they agreed to a takeover offer of more than $300 million from Columbia House, the mail-order record seller that's jointly owned by

Time Warner and Sony. One problem: It turned out Columbia House did not itself generate enough cash to make the merger work. Nancy Peretsman, a managing director at the investment bank Allen & Co., has been hired by CDNow to assess strategic options. Her job may not be easy. CDNow has enough cash to last less than one month, and its shares are trading at 64, down 80% from their all-time high.

THE BIG BOYS

The largest 'Net companies, generally speaking, have ample cash on hand and fairly easy access to the capital markets to raise more. Amazon.com has already replenished its coffers with proceeds from a convertible bond offering, insuring itself at least a year of life. VerticalNet recently solved its cash problem by selling stock to Microsoft for $100 million. But even big 'Net firms could find it difficult to get fresh funds if their operating losses widen sharply or if Wall Street sentiment turns cold. Keep an eye on Healtheon.

Company	Market Value* (billions)	Burnout Rank
Ariba	$24.3	143
Exodus Comm	24.1	181
Akamai Tech	23.6	117
Amazon.com	23.4	45
Inktomi	14.8	186
Commerce One	14.6	122
Vignette	13.5	202
InterNAP Ntwk Svs	13.0	130
Vitria Technology	11.6	163
Phone.com	9.0	195
Priceline.com	8.1	139
Healtheon	8.0	30
DoubleClick	8.0	203
VerticalNet	7.6	5
Ventro	7.3	79
Digital Island	7.0	11

E*Trade	6.0	158
E.piphany	6.0	135
HomeStore.com	5.1	69
China.com	5.0	141

*as of 2/29
Source: Pegasus Research International

As noted above, a depressed share price limits a company's ability to raise fresh funds. Let's face it, with lots of investors looking at losses on a stock investment, selling more shares into the market can be difficult, at best. A good example is eToys, a toy retailer that came public at $20 and surged to well over $80 amid great public enthusiasm. The concept was easy to understand and promised great riches. But the competition, in the form of Toys R Us, did not roll over and play dead. Toys R Us launched its own Website, and ardor cooled for eToys. Today shares of eToys repose at 114. All those people who bought in at prices ranging from $20 to $80 are none too eager to buy more shares, even at $12. EToys has enough cash on hand to last only 11 more months, so stay tuned.

Even a celebrity like Dr. Everett Koop is not immune. His Website, drkoop.com, came public at $9 a share, surged to over $40, and has since fallen back to $9. Drkoop.com ranks seventh on our list, with three months' cash left.

Another easy-to-understand e-play that has disappointed investors is FTD.com, the flower retailer. Its shares have wilted to a recent 3 5/8, from an all-time high of 12 1/2. FTD.com has about six months of cash remaining.

"That's the problem with these IPO run-ups. They introduce so much hype and emotion, when what's really needed is stability," says William Hambrecht, founder of Hambrecht & Quist, owner of W. R. Hambrecht, a pioneer in offering IPOs to investors via the Internet. "A volatile price on a new stock kills your ability to finance in the future. It's very destructive."

'Net companies are also finding it more difficult to raise funds by issuing convertible bonds. One reason: investors in these instruments are attracted to the possibility that the issuer's stock price will rise, enabling bondholders to reap a nice profit when they convert their bonds into stock at some future date. "Slowly the door's beginning to shut on the pure Internet plays in the convertible market," says Ravi Suria, chief of convertibles research at Lehman Brothers in New York. Indeed, E*Trade, Amazon.com and Ameritrade have had to offer unusually generous interest rates and conversion terms to sell their latest offerings of convertibles. With so many Internet stocks well off their highs, the promise of converting bonds into stocks at a huge profit seems more remote, making such deals a lot less alluring.

Egghead.com, with an estimated 4.4 months' worth of cash on hand, recently solved its hunt for capital, but its success may prove pyrrhic. Although a Bahamian outfit called Acqua Wellington agreed to invest $100 million in Egghead.com, Acqua plans to make its investment over a nine-month period, buying up stock at an unstated discount to the current market. "It's a curious situation, to be sure," says Pegasus' Kyle. And it's yet another sign that cash is getting more difficult for 'Net firms to come by.

Investors' distaste for 'Net stocks is especially prevalent when the business plans of the companies in question depend solely on selling goods to consumers. "The business models are coming under intense scrutiny for companies in the business-to-consumer sector, because both investors and venture capitalists are skeptical about the potential for profitability," says Jon A. Flint, founder of Boston-based Polaris Venture Partners, an initial backer of the successful Internet company Akamai Technologies.

BURN VICTIMS

Below are the 207 Internet companies we reviewed. They are ranked by how quickly they are likely to burn through their cash. Burnout rates are calculated as of March 1, 2000. An asterisk after a company name indicates that insiders have sold 25% or more of the shares made available in recent secondary offerings. Not a good sign.

			Results for Calendar 4th Qtr '99				Months
			Market Value		Operating	Operating	Till
Rank	Company	Symbol	2/29	Revenues	Expenses	Losses	Burnout
1	Pilot Ntwk Services	PILT	$557.60	$8.47	$3.83	-4.62	-0.14
2	CDNow	CDNW	239.00	53.11	44.34	-34.69	0.37
3	Secure Computing	SCUR	367.40	6.90	11.43	-7.60	1.51
4	Peapod	PPOD	147.50	21.56	14.55	-9.07	2.01
5	VerticalNet	VERT	7,688.80	10.09	17.10	-10.18	2.20
6	MarketWatch.com	MKTW	595.70	10.00	28.70	-22.46	2.52
7	drkoop.com	KOOP	229.20	5.10	25.73	-20.63	3.34

Rank	Company	Symbol	Market Value 2/29	Revenues	Operating Expenses	Operating Losses	Months Till Burnout
8	Infonautics	INFO	114.90	5.85	7.93	-2.07	3.41
9	Medscape	MSCP	512.90	4.02	27.99	-23.97	3.42
10	Intelligent Life	ILIF	66.00	3.75	17.04	-13.29	3.51
11	Digital Island	ISLD	7,029.90	7.60	32.27	-24.67	3.54
12	Splitrock Services	SPLT	2,656.80	89.56	168.01	-78.45	3.75
13	VitaminShoppe.com	VSHP	119.60	5.59	21.42	-19.21	3.94
14	Intraware	ITRA	1,853.70	24.77	13.39	-6.66	4.21
15	Interfiant	INIT	1,872.60	19.00	24.25	-16.89	4.37
16	MyPoints.com*	MYPT	1,188.90	13.25	22.05	-12.05	4.41
17	Egghead.com	EGGS	338.40	146.14	97.95	-91.93	4.44
18	MotherNature.com	MTHR	82.00	3.18	20.61	-20.46	4.47
19	ImageX.com	IMGX	414.00	4.87	9.72	-8.43	4.50
20	BigStar Entertainment	BGST	43.80	5.23	9.36	-8.01	4.52
21	Mail.com	MAIL	672.90	6.12	22.02	-21.96	4.83
22	Cybercash	CYCH	228.10	6.16	13.04	-10.35	5.57
23	Applied Theory	ATHY	604.20	11.91	10.62	-6.99	5.58
24	WorldTalk	WTLK	126.60	2.15	5.04	-3.42	5.79
25	Primix Solutions	PMIX	175.10	3.80	3.13	-2.25	5.85
26	Newsedge	NEWZ	114.20	19.72	27.42	-7.70	5.90
27	FTD.com	EFTD	183.30	23.59	18.45	-11.82	6.45
28	ShopNow.com	SPNW	491.60	13.42	37.63	-32.05	6.45
29	Beyond.com	BYND	186.90	35.26	38.84	-34.06	6.87
30	Healtheon	HLTH	8,080.50	102.15	305.05	-291.48	6.88
31	E Loan	EELN	372.80	7.71	34.94	-27.23	7.35
32	Interactive Pictures	IPIX	1,493.10	5.32	26.93	-24.73	7.53
33	Ask Jeeves	ASKJ	2,137.70	10.90	29.55	-24.42	7.75
34	LoisLaw.com	LOIS	468.60	2.32	8.17	-5.86	7.88
35	PlanetRx.com	PLRX	612.00	5.10	53.01	-52.17	7.99
36	LifeMinders.com	LFMN	1,041.70	8.04	25.11	-17.56	8.02
37	SmarterKids.com	SKDS	105.30	4.31	22.14	-21.04	8.40
38	drugstore.com	DSCM	824.00	18.49	45.16	-45.50	8.57
39	Ashford.com	ASFD	290.30	20.10	23.79	-20.16	8.60
40	NorthPoint Comm.	NPNT	2,870.40	11.62	53.08	-66.53	8.70
41	EarthWeb	EWBX	263.00	11.47	17.57	-9.93	9.36
42	NetObjects	NETO	1,005.00	7.91	10.77	-6.04	9.82
43	Tickets.com	TIXX	748.40	12.83	30.10	-26.10	9.93
44	Salon.com	SALN	80.50	3.02	9.82	-6.80	10.06
45	Amazon.com	AMZN	23,423.80	676.04	361.63	-273.78	10.08
46	PurchasePro.com*	PPRO	3,412.20	2.67	60.79	-58.39	10.25
47	Cobalt Group	CBLT	201.10	8.38	11.72	-5.02	11.07
48	Multex.com	MLTX	784.10	13.47	18.71	-8.83	11.29
49	eToys	ETYS	1,691.60	106.75	96.64	-76.36	11.36
50	Kana Comms	KANA	4,109.80	6.46	93.85	-90.60	11.68
51	E-Stamp	ESTM	371.40	0.96	28.73	-29.43	11.82
52	Streamline.com	SLNE	137.90	5.14	12.57	-7.43	12.16
53	uBid	UBID	378.10	69.90	18.70	-12.08	12.20
54	Theglobe.com	TGLO	206.30	6.42	21.18	-18.10	12.41
55	Quokka Sports	QKKA	544.50	6.66	14.01	-15.72	12.46
56	Prodigy	PRGY	1,778.00	67.12	65.09	-28.47	12.55
57	eCollege.com	ECLG	131.30	1.74	5.74	-9.51	12.61
58	Online Resources	ORCC	190.90	2.67	4.23	-4.28	13.06
59	AutoWeb.com	AWEB	153.40	11.61	19.29	-8.84	13.11

Rank	Company	Symbol	Market Value 2/29	Results for Calendar 4th Qtr '99			Months Till Burnout
				Revenues	Operating Expenses	Operating Losses	
60	Rhythms Net Connect	RTHM	2,733.70	5.47	86.19	-80.72	13.83
61	LookSmart	LOOK	3,689.30	18.51	38.08	-22.26	14.00
62	Barnes & Noble.com	BNBN	1,135.70	82.13	62.99	-46.34	14.02
63	Juno Online Svs	JWEB	805.40	18.01	24.42	-17.11	14.04
64	NetRadio	NETR	47.50	0.67	5.85	-5.43	14.35
65	Cylink	CYLK	581.60	17.47	18.15	-6.80	14.46
66	iVillage	IVIL	557.50	19.26	44.09	-31.68	14.62
67	Critical Path	CPTH	3,702.00	8.19	59.37	-58.88	14.67
68	Concentric Ntwk	CNCX	2,232.40	45.89	68.58	-22.69	14.78
69	HomeStore.com*	HOMS	5,105.50	27.37	50.45	-31.10	14.99
70	eGain Comms	EGAN	1,605.60	2.38	13.80	-14.52	15.33
71	Fogdog	FOGD	329.90	4.45	15.41	-14.79	15.34
72	Talk City	TCTY	262.10	3.33	12.87	-10.44	15.49
73	ZipLink	ZIPL	235.60	3.52	7.71	-4.19	15.58
74	TicketMaster-CitySearch	TMCS	2,867.40	36.39	59.26	-49.31	15.65
75	SilverStream Software*	SSSW	1,501.60	9.03	13.25	-8.34	15.86
76	Egreetings.com	EGRT	194.80	1.63	16.28	-14.65	16.31
77	TriZetto Group	TZIX	1,612.60	11.19	6.86	-5.39	16.43
78	Audible	ADBL	328.40	0.42	5.98	-5.93	16.65
79	Ventro	VNTR	7,377.80	19.28	17.75	-16.78	17.05
80	garden.com	GDEN	122.50	3.61	8.98	-8.00	17.13
81	VocalTec	VOCL	524.40	7.67	10.65	-5.26	17.20
82	Worldgate Comm.	WGAT	749.10	2.68	14.49	-11.82	17.21
83	NBCI	NBCI	2,676.90	15.68	81.09	-71.64	17.62
84	Quotesmith.com	QUOT	134.60	3.00	10.51	-7.51	17.83
85	Exactis.com	XACT	314.60	3.72	11.85	-8.63	17.93
86	Retek	RETK	2,752.80	11.40	20.72	-16.58	17.95
87	NetZero	NZRO	2,443.90	12.24	23.61	-26.51	18.24
88	MessageMedia	MESG	696.20	4.91	22.12	-19.01	18.43
89	Log On America	LOAX	127.80	1.66	5.20	-3.54	18.69
90	iGO	IGOC	174.20	8.00	9.82	-8.09	19.27
91	JFax.com	JFAX	168.40	2.63	6.42	-5.03	19.35
92	SportsLine	SPLN	1,079.30	21.04	22.95	-15.49	19.54
93	V-ONE	VONE	98.60	1.01	2.15	-1.29	19.71
94	VoxWare	VOXW	51.90	1.01	2.15	-1.29	19.71
95	USinterNetworking*	USIX	4,061.00	14.66	33.18	-32.72	19.75
96	DSL.net	DSLN	1,608.60	0.81	11.74	-10.93	19.81
97	Persistence Software	PRSW	321.46	4.71	7.82	-4.03	20.08
98	HealthCentral.com	HCEN	113.40	0.70	15.01	-14.31	20.32
99	Student Advantage	STAD	545.80	9.32	15.29	-5.97	20.35
100	CNET	CNET	4,895.30	38.31	62.88	-39.22	20.48
101	Lionbridge Tech.	LIOX	295.20	13.04	6.39	-2.57	20.97
102	Launch Media	LAUN	230.10	6.62	21.27	-15.71	21.16
103	Netcentives	NCNT	1,455.60	2.82	22.76	-19.94	22.88
104	OnDisplay	ONDS	1,771.00	11.10	23.75	-16.91	22.90
105	WatchGuard Tech*	WGRD	1,145.00	6.52	11.08	-6.96	23.54
106	yesmail.com	YESM	646.60	8.17	8.03	-4.91	23.90
107	InsWeb	INSW	524.40	2.02	12.29	-10.27	24.22
108	El Sitio	LCTO	870.30	5.34	21.41	-20.96	25.19
109	Ramp Ntwks	RAMP	360.10	4.81	6.40	-4.48	25.73
110	TheStreet.com	TSCM	285.10	5.12	16.11	-14.19	27.55
111	Viador	VIAD	432.00	4.20	8.08	-4.86	27.81

| | | | | Results for Calendar 4th Qtr '99 | | | Months |
| | | | Market Value | | Operating | Operating | Till |
Rank	Company	Symbol	2/29	Revenues	Expenses	Losses	Burnout
112	HealthExtras	HLEX	184.60	2.73	7.29	-4.71	27.93
113	Digital River	DRIV	754.50	27.46	13.00	-7.66	28.46
114	MedicaLogic	MDLI	1,131.40	6.62	17.58	-13.58	28.68
115	NextCard	NXCD	1,134.50	13.89	38.65	-24.75	28.69
116	Tumbleweed Comms	TMWD	1,559.80	2.39	7.65	-6.09	29.11
117	Akamai Tech	AKAM	23,609.20	2.70	30.82	-28.12	29.42
118	StarMedia Ntwk	STRM	3,040.50	9.00	39.87	-30.87	29.43
119	OneSource Info. Svs	ONES	86.40	10.31	7.60	-1.29	29.57
120	iXL Enterprises	IIXL	2,452.00	75.70	57.65	-24.38	29.73
121	Gric Communications	GRIC	1,222.90	4.18	11.61	-7.43	29.83
122	Commerce One	CMRC	14,698.90	16.89	22.04	-11.69	29.99
123	Stamps.com	STMP	1,143.40	0.36	32.72	-34.80	30.31
124	EDGAR Online	EDGR	140.00	2.05	3.82	-2.28	30.69
125	Onemain.com	ONEM	301.90	32.75	24.28	-37.19	30.78
126	OpenMarket	OMKT	2,212.10	25.27	24.69	-8.03	31.22
127	Calico Commerce	CLIC	1,448.50	8.72	11.92	-6.73	32.33
128	Mcafee	MCAF	1,425.90	8.40	12.00	-6.53	32.46
129	NetSpeak	NSPK	278.50	3.09	5.85	-2.92	33.21
130	InterNAP Ntwk Svs	INAP	13,059.90	5.50	14.92	-20.50	33.77
131	Silknet Software	SILK	3,710.00	7.86	10.17	-4.50	33.92
132	HearMe.co	HEAR	478.40	6.03	14.31	-9.75	34.08
133	NetPerceptions	NETP	1,077.50	6.31	8.34	-3.34	34.19
134	ZapMe!	IZAP	289.80	2.10	14.03	-11.93	34.44
135	E.piphany*	EPNY	6,049.10	8.71	12.15	-7.26	34.60
136	Mortgage.com	MDCM	166.60	13.92	11.07	-12.17	34.89
137	Interwoven*	IWOV	3,477.70	7.55	10.07	-5.59	35.44
138	GoTo.com	GOTO	2,840.10	13.30	20.25	-8.92	35.96
139	Priceline.com	PCLN	8,108.40	169.21	947.56	-923.83	36.52
140	Be Free	BFRE	2,359.60	2.62	7.78	-5.56	36.69
141	China.com*	CHINA	5,071.00	10.88	19.73	-16.05	37.06
142	FreeShop.com	FSHP	492.00	4.06	7.83	-4.17	39.00
143	Ariba	ARBA	24,332.10	23.48	32.36	-12.32	40.17
144	Web Street	WEBS	166.50	8.31	6.18	-2.77	40.43
145	autobytel.com	ABTL	198.10	12.44	18.66	-6.22	41.08
146	Bluestone Software*	BLSW	1,440.60	5.05	8.07	-4.59	42.09
147	ITXC	ITXC	2,929.20	11.11	18.25	-7.14	42.81
148	CommTouch Software	CTCH	698.00	2.24	9.04	-8.37	42.82
149	Knot	KNOT	90.80	2.49	5.38	-3.43	42.84
150	InterTrust Tech	ITRU	3,336.50	0.69	10.34	-10.20	43.35
151	Primus Knowledge	PKSI	1,709.30	8.61	11.52	-4.95	44.42
152	Mediaplex	MPLX	2,667.70	12.46	12.89	-9.90	44.89
153	Breakaway Solutions	BWAY	2,185.80	10.61	9.68	-3.85	45.80
154	About.com	BOUT	1,173.20	13.00	19.54	-11.18	49.66
155	Tut Systems	TUTS	491.40	10.64	9.32	-4.64	49.74
156	iBasis	IBAS	2,404.90	7.60	7.60	-8.19	50.40
157	SI Corporation	SONE	3,830.20	40.42	136.17	-117.69	51.73
158	E*Trade	EGRP	6,095.60	246.01	199.18	-60.23	52.90
159	Preview Travel	PTVL	637.70	1.22	7.19	-5.97	53.76
160	CyberSource	CYDS	696.40	5.02	8.62	-7.61	54.40
161	Broadbase Software*	BBSW	2,955.40	4.14	9.71	-7.03	54.49
162	GetThere.com	GTHR	797.20	5.49	16.61	-14.94	54.69
163	Vitria Technology*	VITR	11,640.40	12.20	14.58	-4.61	54.99

Rank	Company	Symbol	Market Value 2/29	Revenues	Operating Expenses	Operating Losses	Months Till Burnout
164	AltiGen Comm	ATGN	267.70	2.49	3.45	-2.13	55.97
165	Webvan Group	WBVN	599.10	9.07	57.35	-55.66	56.64
166	Quintus	QNTS	1,261.50	13.51	18.38	-9.07	56.65
167	Liquid Audio	LQID	547.50	1.35	9.98	-9.20	57.12
168	Hoover's	HOOV	134.60	5.47	6.89	-3.37	57.21
169	Digital Impact	DIGI	662.30	4.01	8.91	-6.84	58.23
170	Women.com	WOMN	453.70	13.36	23.89	-10.53	60.80
171	Earthlink	ELNK	827.20	199.15	266.78	-67.64	60.85
172	Telemate.Net Software	TMNT	73.80	4.06	4.98	-1.91	65.19
173	Active Software	ASWX	2,523.40	11.61	11.05	-1.77	73.88
174	Media Metrix	MMXI	688.10	7.57	20.55	-16.47	73.99
175	Keynote Systems*	KEYN	3,824.70	4.80	7.59	-2.80	74.61
176	HotJobs.com	HOTJ	775.10	8.60	13.20	-5.90	74.83
177	@plan.inc	APLN	110.70	2.38	3.66	-1.28	79.88
178	U.S. Interactive	USIT	881.70	11.60	15.48	-3.87	88.13
179	pcOrder.com	PCOR	441.30	14.39	9.76	-2.94	91.25
180	Data Return	DRTN	2,269.90	3.41	8.26	-4.85	91.69
181	Exodus Comm.	EXDS	24,111.00	101.39	62.87	-39.88	96.37
182	BackWeb Tech.	BWEB	1,344.70	7.87	9.30	-3.02	96.53
183	Internet.com*	INTM	1,038.00	7.49	8.27	-4.21	99.76
184	USWeb/CKS	USWB	3,249.80	186.94	123.64	-79.92	105.83
185	MP3.com	MPPP	1,186.40	15.27	25.47	-16.71	118.86
186	Inktomi	INKT	14,863.00	36.13	46.36	-10.23	129.79
187	Ameritrade	AMTD	3,250.70	110.85	144.54	-33.70	130.11
188	Jupiter Comm	JPTR	463.50	11.05	8.73	-2.20	130.24
189	eBenX	EBNX	838.00	5.78	8.50	-2.72	144.38
190	Accrue Software	ACRU	1,174.50	4.62	5.72	-1.79	145.21
191	Art Tech Group	ARTG	4,722.80	13.28	12.37	-2.81	153.26
192	Wit Capital Group	WITC	1,170.70	21.04	28.62	-7.58	160.79
193	Software.com	SWCM	3,958.00	15.51	16.03	-4.65	180.66
194	Spyglass	SPYG	1,049.30	8.21	6.67	-2.06	185.63
195	Phone.com	PHCM	9,021.20	12.78	31.88	-23.26	187.55
196	NetRatings	NTRT	1,167.00	1.55	7.05	-8.15	192.34
197	Scient*	SCNT	4,974.90	42.68	47.55	-4.87	196.96
198	Agile Software	AGIL	3,262.70	8.56	22.17	-15.68	207.02
199	Pivotal	PVTL	1,008.60	11.54	10.04	-0.72	218.25
200	Marimba	MRBA	1,505.80	10.07	10.34	-1.40	227.69
201	Andover.Net	ANDN	598.10	2.06	5.35	-3.77	239.88
202	Vignette	VIGN	13,504.00	40.94	33.36	-7.31	271.13
203	DoubleClick	DCLK	8,000.30	93.69	96.08	-43.97	271.16
204	PSINet	PSIX	3,034.90	185.40	354.70	-169.30	309.61
205	Allaire	ALLR	1,694.00	18.33	16.61	-1.18	401.49
206	C-Bridge Internet	CBIS	910.60	8.83	10.88	-2.05	427.37
207	Radware*	RDWR	952.90	5.01	4.40	-0.20	1,024.07

Notes: 1. Universe includes only companies that went public prior to December 31, 1999
2. Operating expenses and losses include non-cash charges 3. Based on earnings releases (not adjusted for follow-ons, acquisitions, etc.) 4. Months till Burnout adjusted for two-month lag (December 31, 1999 to March 1, 2000) 5. Burnout excludes non-cash charges
All monetary figures are millions
Source: Pegasus Research International

Could the depression felt in consumer-oriented 'Net companies spread to the business-to-business sector? Right now the sector is so beloved that it hardly seems possible. For instance, a purchasing site for businesses, PurchasePro, has a mere 10.2 months of cash remaining, yet the stock market totally sloughs it off. Recently, PurchasePro shares touched a spectacular 175, up 2,000% from the firm's $8 offering price (adjusted for a split) last September.

Still, don't be surprised if at some point such popular business-to-business stocks go the way of the consumer offerings such as eToys, FTD .com, or drkoop.com. "Many of these B2B companies have strategies that depend upon continuous access to capital," says Kyle. "If any of these firms were not able to raise their cash, the implosion would certainly affect stockholder confidence. We know that B2B stocks have to eventually come down, the question is when: five months or five years from now?"

Don't bet on the latter.

Part of the problem is that the 'Net companies' founders and early backers are eager to sell their shares while they still can. So far this year, 38 publicly traded Internet companies have tapped the markets for $16 billion in capital through secondary offerings. This represents a fivefold increase in the number of secondary offerings compared with the same period last year. Another key difference is that this year a far larger number of second-round deals involved insiders unloading their shares on the public. This hurts the companies in question because the cash raised by selling shareholders goes right into the pockets of those shareholders, and not into the companies' coffers.

Sure, venture capitalists and other early-stage investors are in the business of selling out at a profit eventually, but large sales of insider stock while a company is still reporting losses can choke off that company's access to fresh capital, thereby diminishing the chances for survival. In the investment world, this is akin to men on a sinking ocean liner pushing women and children aside to commandeer the lifeboats.

"The IPO market used to be available only to seasoned companies where the insiders' exit strategy didn't matter," says Hambrecht. "When you take a company public that still needs capital to continue as a going concern, you are taking a huge risk. Insider selling only makes it harder to raise money."

Venture capitalists, quite rightly, become incensed when their integrity gets impugned. After all, they were behind more than half of last year's 501 initial public offerings. For them, selling down positions to cover startup costs happens to be a business strategy.

The conflict of interest between venture capitalists and the public is well illustrated by the case of MyPoints.com, an Internet direct-marketing firm. With four months' cash left, MyPoints filed to raise $185 million by selling as many as four million shares to the public. At first blush, the offering would appear to refill MyPoints.com's coffers quite nicely. But a closer look reveals that 40% of the shares on offer are being sold by insiders. Thus, money seemingly destined for the company gets diverted to insiders.

Another notable insider selloff occurred at the Internet real-estate seller HomeStore.com, which at yearend 1999 had enough cash remaining to last a little over a year. The stock came public at 20 in August, rose to a high of 138, and has since slipped to 50. In January, Home-Store announced a $900 million secondary offering, in which the insiders reaped more than half the gross proceeds.

More often than not, venture capitalists sell when retail investors are eager to buy. As noted above, shares of PurchasePro.com recently touched $175. With 10.2 months' cash left, it should be no surprise that PurchasePro recently sold three million shares, one-third of which are owned by insiders.

The evidence shows the race for the exits is especially pronounced among Internet companies. So far this year, in two-thirds of the secondary stock offerings by Internet companies, 25% or more of the shares were sold by insiders, according to CommScan. In non-Internet deals, only about one-quarter of the deals involved insider selling of 25% or more.

The Internet investing game has been kept alive in large part by a massive flow of money out of Old Economy stocks and into New Economy stocks. Last week's steep slide in the Nasdaq and the sharp recovery of the Dow Jones Industrial Average may mark a reversal of this trend. As illustrated last week, once psychology changes, cash-poor Internet issues tend to fall farthest, fastest.

FIND YOUR 'NET STOCK

Below, sorted alphabetically, are the 207 Internet stocks we reviewed and their rankings. Remember, No. I is likely to burn through its cash first, No. 207, last.

Rank	Company	Rank	Company	Rank	Company
177	@plan.inc	160	CyberSource	168	Hoover's
154	About.com	65	Cylink	176	HotJobs.com
190	Accrue Software	180	Data Return	156	iBasis
173	Active Software	169	Digital Impact	90	iGo
198	Agile Software	11	Digital Island	19	ImageX.com
117	Akamai Tech	113	Digital River	8	Infonautics
205	Allaire	203	DoubleClick	186	Inktomi
164	AltiGen Comm	7	drkoop.com	107	InsWeb
45	Amazon.com	38	drugstore.com	10	Intelligent Life
187	Ameritrade	96	DSL.net	32	Interactive Pictures
201	Andover.Net	31	E Loan	15	Interliant
23	Applied Theory	158	E*Trade	130	InterNAP Ntwk Svs
143	Ariba	135	E.piphany	183	Internet.com
191	Art Tech Group	171	Earthlink	150	InterTrust Tech
39	Ashford.com	41	EarthWeb	137	Interwoven
33	Ask Jeeves	189	eBenX	14	Intraware
78	Audible	57	eCollege.com	147	ITXC
145	autobytel.com	124	EDGAR Online	66	iVillage
59	AutoWeb.com	70	eGain Comms	120	iXL Enterprises
182	BackWeb Tech.	17	Egghead.com	91	JFax.com
62	Barnes & Noble.com	76	Egreetings.com	63	Juno Online Svs
140	Be Free	108	El Sitio	188	Jupiter Comm
29	Beyond.com	51	E-Stamp	50	Kana Comms
20	BigStar Entertainment	49	eToys	175	Keynote Systems
146	Bluestone Software	85	Exactis.com	149	Knot
153	Breakaway Solutions	181	Exodus Comm	102	Launch Media
161	Broadbase Software	71	Fogdog	36	LifeMinders.com
127	Calico Commerce	142	FreeShop.com	101	Lionbridge Tech
206	C-Bridge Internet	27	FTD.com	167	Liquid Audio
2	CDNow	80	garden.com	89	Log On America
141	China.com	162	GetThere.com	34	LoisLaw.com
100	CNET	138	GoTo.com	61	LookSmart
47	Cobalt Group	121	Gric Communications	21	Mail.com
122	Commerce One	98	HealthCentral.com	200	Marimba
148	CommTouch Software	30	Healtheon	6	MarketWatch.com
68	Concentric Ntwk	112	HealthExtras	128	Mcafee
67	Critical Path	132	HearMe co	174	Media Metrix
22	Cybercash	69	HomeStore.com	152	Mediaplex

Rank	Company	Rank	Company	Rank	Company
114	MedicaLogic	159	Preview Travel	172	Telemate.Net Software
9	Medscape	139	Priceline.com	54	Theglobe.com
88	MessageMedia	25	Primix Solutions	110	TheStreet.com
136	Mortgage.com	151	Primus Knowledge	74	TicketMstr-CitySearch
18	MotherNature.com	56	Prodigy	43	Tickets.com
185	MP3.com	204	PSINet	77	TriZetto Group
48	Multex.com	46	PurchasePro.com	116	Tumbleweed Comms
16	MyPoints.com	166	Quintus	155	Tut Systems
83	NBCi	55	Quokka Sports	178	U.S. Interactive
103	Netcentives	84	Quotesmith.com	53	uBid
42	NetObjects	207	Radware	95	USinterNetworking
133	NetPerceptions	109	Ramp Ntwks	184	USWeb/CKS
64	NetRadio	86	Retek	79	Ventro
196	NetRatings	60	Rhythms Net Connect	5	VerticalNet
129	NetSpeak	157	SI Corporation	111	Viador
87	NetZero	44	Salon.com	202	Vignette
26	Newsedge	197	Scient	13	VitaminShoppe.com
115	NextCard	3	Secure Computing	163	Vitria Technology
40	NorthPoint Comm	28	ShopNow.com	81	VocalTec
104	OnDisplay	131	Silknet Software	93	V-ONE
125	Onemain.com	75	SilverStream Software	94	VoxWare
119	OneSource Info Svs	37	SmarterKids.com	105	WatchGuard Tech
58	Online Resources	193	Software.com	144	Web Street
126	OpenMarket	12	Splitrock Services	165	Webvan Group
179	pcOrder.com	92	SportsLine	192	Wit Capital Group
4	Peapod	194	Spyglass	170	Women.com
97	Persistence Software	123	Stamps.com	82	Worldgate Comm.
195	Phone.com	118	StarMedia Ntwk	24	WorldTalk Corp
1	Pilot Ntwk Services	52	Streamline.com	106	yesmail.com
199	Pivotal	99	Student Advantage	134	ZapMe!
35	PlanetRx.com	72	Talk City	73	ZipLink

Source: Pegasus Research International

From *Dot.con:*
The Greatest Story Ever Sold

JOHN CASSIDY

Over the long run—years and decades—the stock market rises and falls in line with economic growth and corporate profits. But in the short run—days and weeks—the market bounces up and down randomly, like a cork in a stream. Once the Fed embarked on a policy of raising interest rates, it was eminently predictable that technology and Internet stocks would fall, but it was impossible to know when, though there were hints that the moment of reckoning might not be far away. Outside of the technology sector, much of the market was already in a bear market: during the past year, more than 80 percent of the stocks in the S&P 500 index had fallen by 20 percent or more. The market was becoming much more volatile. Between 1988 and 1995, the Nasdaq moved up or down by more than 3 percent in a day just ten times. Since the start of 2000, there had already been twelve such days, six up and nine down. Even some longtime bulls were getting worried. On March 10, 2000, when the Nasdaq closed above 5,000, Jeremy Siegel, the Wharton economist who had previously argued that buying stocks was a good strategy regardless of their price, told CNN, "a big decline is very possible."

On Monday, March 13, the volatility resumed. In three days, the Nasdaq fell by almost 500 points before recovering somewhat later in the week. There were signs that the technology wave might be cresting. In two days, March 15 and March 16, the Dow, which had dipped back below 10,000, shot up 819 points as investors rediscovered Old Economy stocks like Ford Motor, Dow Chemical, and Home Depot. At the end of the week, the Dow stood at 10,595.20, up almost 7 percent on the week. The Nasdaq finished the week at 4,798.13, down about 5 percent, and the Dow Jones Internet Composite Index closed the week at 466.5, down about 8 percent. In this confused environment, on Saturday, March 18, *Barron's* published a long article about Internet stocks under the headline "Burning Up." Written by reporter Jack Willoughby, the piece asked:

> When will the Internet Bubble burst? For scores of 'Net upstarts, that unpleasant popping sound is likely to be heard before the end of this year. Starved for cash, many of these companies will try to raise fresh funds by issuing more stock or bonds. But a lot of them won't succeed. As a result, they will be forced to sell out stronger rivals or go out of business altogether. Already, many cash-strapped Internet firms are scrambling to find financing.

With the help of a research firm, Pegasus Research International, Willoughby had examined the financial statements of more than two hundred Internet companies. For each firm, he calculated the rate at which it was spending money and compared this to the cash and marketable securities on its balance sheet. His conclusion: within twelve months at least fifty Internet firms would have no money left, and some of them would run out of cash a lot sooner than that. Among the companies facing immediate problems were CDNOW, whose takeover by Time Warner and Sony had recently fallen through; Peapod, the online grocery, and drkoop.com, the medical Web site set up by Dr. C. Everett Koop, a former U.S. surgeon general. The situation facing many other firms was only slightly less dire. MotherNature.com would run out of money in four and a half months. Drugstore.com and PlanetRx.com had enough cash to last nine months; eToys would be out of money in eleven months.

The *Barron's* piece was the most damaging piece of journalism that the Internet boom had produced, but most devastating of all was its timing. Investors had been tacitly assuming that Internet companies, whatever their losses, would always be able to raise more cash. For a long time, this had been a reasonable assumption, but given the set-backs already suffered by a number of Internet stocks it no longer was. The *Barron's* article pointed out what would happen if the cash spigot got turned off permanently, and Internet companies were left to fend for themselves.

On Monday, March 20, many of the stocks on *Barron's* list fell sharply; it was another bad day for technology stocks generally. The Nasdaq fell 188 points, nearly 4 percent, to 4,610. During the next few days, there was a predictable attempt to discredit the *Barron's* piece. "I didn't set my performance record, which is about the best in the business, with any help from *Barron's*," Albert Vilar, head of the $700 million Amer-indo Technology Fund, declared. Investors who avoided Internet stocks during the next five or ten years would miss "the biggest explosion of profits and growth ever seen," Vilar continued. Many of the firms men-tioned by *Barron's* insisted that their burn rates had been overestimated. In some cases, this was true. The magazine's figures only went up to the end of 1999, since when some Internet firms had raised more money. Amazon.com and Digital Island, for example, had both issued hundreds of millions of dollars' worth of convertible bonds. But even if some of the figures quoted in the piece were out of date, the overall thrust of its argu-ment was incontrovertible.

Some internet companies were already facing a cash crunch. Firms like CDNOW and Peapod had seen their stocks collapse, and they didn't have the option to issue more shares. Theoretically, they could have tried to sell some bonds, but given the state of the market, that would have been a formidable challenge. Even market leaders like Amazon.com and E*Trade were being forced to pay higher yields on their loans because of the growing nervousness among investors. For struggling firms, the only real hope was to find another company either to invest in them or to buy them outright, but that was no easy matter. Potential buyers had an incentive to let the troubled business go bankrupt and then buy its assets on the cheap. Given this environment, the only option for the most cash-strapped Internet companies was to cut costs and hope for the best.

On Tuesday, April 11, the Nasdaq fell by 132.30 points, to 4,055.90, and the Dow Jones Internet Composite Index slid another 7.1 percent, to 313.83. Again there was remorseless selling of previous favorites: Oracle fell 5 1/8, to 77 3/8; Yahoo! fell 8 ½, to 133 ½. At the close of trading, for the first time since the start of February, the Nasdaq was in negative territory for 2000. The only good news was that it hadn't fallen through the 4,000 mark. At one point during the day, it had come close, but it had bounced back, raising hopes for a more sustained rally.

When the market reopened the next morning, Wednesday, April 12, these hopes were disappointed. Rick Sherlund, a respected analyst at Goldman Sachs, had lowered his revenue expectations for Microsoft, citing lower than expected sales in March, thereby shattering the illusion that the Fed's effort to restrain the economy wouldn't have any impact on technology companies. Microsoft's stock slipped 4 1/2, to 79 3/8. IBM and Hewlett-Packard both fell sharply, too, and they helped drag down the Dow, which closed at 11,125.13, off 161.95 points. Losers on the Nasdaq included Sun Microsystems, which dropped another 7 7/8, to $80, and Cisco Systems, which fell $5, to $65. The Nasdaq index closed at 3,769.63, down 286.27 points, or 7 percent. The decline in Internet stocks was exacerbated by Forrester Research, which, defying its usual optimism, issued a report predicting the ultimate demise of many online retailers. Said an analyst at the firm: "It's time to face facts: online retail's honeymoon is over." Amazon.com slumped by $7, to 56 3/8, but selling wasn't restricted to online retailers. America Online fell $3, to 62 1/2; eBay fell 12 7/8, to 142 3/8; Inktomi slipped 12 1/16, to $123. The Dow Jones Internet Composite Index fell by another 10 percent, to 283.33. The index was now 44 percent below its March 9 peak, and the Nasdaq was 25 percent below its March 10 peak, which meant that both were now in a bear market. (A fall of 20 percent or more is usually considered a bear market.)

The same self-reinforcing process that had propelled stock prices into the stratosphere was now operating in reverse, sending stocks hurtling back to earth. The herd mentality was as strong as ever, but investors were now copying each other selling. The technology that had made it so easy to buy stocks made it just as easy to sell them: all it took was a simple phone call or a few clicks of a mouse. As people shifted their savings out of technology funds and aggressive growth funds, mutual fund managers were forced to sell stocks that were already slumping, causing them to fall even further. The deep falls in many stocks prompted more margin calls, some of which couldn't be met, which, in turn, prompted further selling by the brokerage houses in order to raise cash. The falling market was feeding on itself, just as the rising market had fed on itself.

On the morning of Friday, April 14, 2000, investors tuned in to CNBC and CNNfn with trepidation, especially those with a historical bent. Eighty-eight years before, to the day, the *Titanic* had sunk. Now, new inflation figures showed prices rising faster than at any point in the last five years. This development, combined with another strong report on retail sales, meant that further interest rate hikes were virtually inevitable. Some analysts were predicting that the FOMC would raise rates by half a point at its next meeting. Shortly after 11 A.M. CNNfn's Terry Keenan reported: "We are seeing waves of selling hitting the Nasdaq right now. Yahoo! is down seven, Oracle down five, Amazon.com down five, Cisco is down two. And the carnage continues—an incredible sell-off. We are now down in percentage terms more than during the week of the October 1987 stock market crash." Unlike on Black Monday, when the stock ticker fell hopelessly behind and many brokers refused to answer their phones, there was no outright panic. The trading systems had been improved since 1987, which made it easier to track the market's fall. At 12:45 P.M., the Dow was down 320.56 points, almost 3 percent, and Nasdaq was down 245.21 points, or 6.7 percent. Losers were beating gainers by seven to one on the Nasdaq and by four to one on the New York Stock Exchange.

If investors were pinning their hopes on an afternoon recovery of the type that had taken place ten days earlier, they were disappointed. At 2 P.M., another wave of margin calls added to the selling pressure, which wasn't alleviated by Alan Greenspan, who had been making a lunchtime appearance at the American Enterprise Institute in Washington, the scene of his "irrational exuberance" speech in 1996. This time, Greenspan didn't mention the stock market or interest rates. At 2:45 P.M., the Dow was off more than 500 points, and the Nasdaq was off more than 300 points. The selling continued during the last hour of trading, reversing only slightly in the final few minutes, when a few bargain hunters stepped in. When the closing bell rang on the New York Stock Exchange, the Dow was at 10,305.66, down 617.58 points, its biggest ever points drop. The Nasdaq was at 3,321.29, down 355.49 points. This was not only the biggest points drop ever recorded by the index; it was also the second biggest percentage fall, bested only by October 19, 1987, Black Monday. Taking the week as a whole, the Nasdaq had suffered its worst week in history. After falling for five days in a row, it was down 1,125.14 points, or 25.3 percent, easily surpassing its 19.3 percent fall in the week of Black Monday. The Dow's slide had been less historic, but it was down 7.3 percent on the week.

The selling on Black Friday, as it came to be known, was across the board. Banks, airlines, and consumer companies got marked down alongside New Economy stocks: Citigroup fell 9 9/16; American Airlines fell $5; Procter & Gamble fell 6 5/8. In the technology sector, the big names all got hit: Cisco Systems fell 4 1/8, to $57; Microsoft fell 5 1/8, to 74 1/8; Intel fell 10 5/8, to 110 1/2. Internet stocks, already battered, were pummeled once more: Yahoo! dropped to 20 1/8, to $116; America Online dropped $4.25, to $55; and Amazon.com dropped 1 1/8, to 46 7/8. (Surprisingly, eBay managed to eke out a gain of 3/4, to 139 9/16.) Many smaller Internet stocks were crushed, a fact reflected in the Dow Jones Composite Internet Index, which dropped 31.24 points, or 12 percent, to 236.72. For the week, the index was off 37.1 percent.

After the market closed the Treasury Secretary, Lawrence Summers, appeared on CNN and issued an appeal for calm: "We are watching the developments in the markets, as we always do, but our focus continues to be on what is most important—the fundamentals of the American economy and their contribution to our economic expansion. And I'm confident that the economy will continue to grow over the next while, with fluctuations from quarter to quarter as always, but our fundamentals are sound."* Summers's words had a familiar ring to them. On October 25, 1929, the day after Black Thursday, President Herbert Hoover said: 'The fundamental business of the country—that is, the production and distribution of commodities—is on a very sound and prosperous basis."

Try as they might, Wall Street's bulls were unable to write off what had happened as a "healthy correction" or a "flight to quality." A five-week-long slump had climaxed in a panic. It had been an unusually long crash, but a crash all the same. Since peaking on March 10, the Nasdaq had dropped 1,727.33 points, or 34.2 percent. The Dow Jones Composite Internet Index was down 53.6 percent from its March 9 high. In just one week, $2 trillion of stock market wealth had been eviscerated. Microsoft alone had shed $240 billion in market capitalization since its peak. As for the Internet bubble, it had well and truly burst, as Table 1, which shows the performance of twenty leading Internet stocks during the five-week period from March 10 to April 14, demonstrates:

TABLE 1: **Internet Stock Prices (March–April 2000)**

	3/10/00	4/14/00	% Fall
Akamai Technologies	296	64 7/8	78.1
Amazon.com	66 7/8	46 7/8	29.9
America Online	58 5/8	55	6.2
Ariba	305 3/8	62 1/4	79.6
CMGI	136 7/16	52 1/16	61.8
Commerce One	257 9/16	66	74.4
DoubleClick	117 5/8	60 9/16	48.5
eBay	193 1/4	139 5/16	27.9
Excite/At Home	28 9/16	21 3/4	23.9
Healtheon/WebMD	41	18 5/16	55.3
Inktomi	169 5/16	100 13/16	40.5
Internet Capital Group	143 9/16	40	72.1
iVillage	23 7/8	10 5/16	55.8
Priceline.com	94 1/2	58 9/16	38.0
Razorfish	36	15 5/8	56.6
TheGlobe.com	8	3	62.5
TheStreet.com	12 9/16	5 3/4	54.3
VeriSign	239 15/16	97 13/16	59.2
Webvan	11 13/16	7 1/2	36.5
Yahoo!	178 1/16	116	34.8

The bullish psychology, upon which everything depended, had been shattered. Even Henry Blodget, the ultimate optimist, conceded that there was little chance of putting it together again, at least for now. "We're going to see the weaker companies come under more pressure," Blodget told *The Washington Post*. "There's no reason everything should suddenly recover in the near term." In a report issued by Morgan Stanley to its clients, Mary Meeker and her colleagues urged investors to concentrate their holdings in the market leaders like Amazon.com, eBay, and Yahoo! and hang on: "Perhaps we haven't seen a bottom yet, but for the leaders we certainly should be closer to the bottom than the top." For investors who were still shareholders in Meeker's other stock picks—Ariba, Veri-Sign, Healtheon/WebMD, Priceline.com, Women.com, Tickets.com, and the rest—such words offered little consolation.

Even James Cramer, perhaps the loudest and most vociferous voice of the bull market, admitted to Matt Lauer on the *Today* show that the bubble had burst. "And I can tell you," he said, "that it's a sobering and humbling experience. I feel I went from being, you know, top of the game to pretty humiliated." Stock in Cramer's company, TheStreet.com, had slipped further during the crash and was presently trading at $5. Asked whether the era of entrepreneurs raising millions of dollars on the basis of an idea had come to an end, he replied, "Yeah, it's over. The Gold Rush is over."

The High Price of Research:
Caveat Investor:
Stock and Research Analysts
Covering Dot-Coms Aren't as
Independent as You Think

ERICK SCHONFELD

Fortune, *March 20, 2000*

Objectivity should be the analyst's stock in trade. In the best of all worlds, analysts on Wall Street and at tech-industry research firms would spend their time giving unbiased, educated opinions about companies, markets, and trends. But in this world, filled as it is with dot-com money blowing every which way, objectivity seems a luxury few can afford. Analysts of all stripes—from Morgan Stanley's Mary Meeker on down to lowly researchers at the likes of the Aberdeen Group—increasingly derive a portion of their compensation, directly or indirectly, from the companies they cover. That helps put pressure on the quality of their work and encourages them to become more like cheerleaders than independent observers.

Let's be honest. It has always been hard to know how objective analysts really are. Consider who butters their bread. Wall Street investment banks compete to provide corporate finance services to many of the companies their analysts report on; firms such as Meta Group and Jupiter Communications sell consulting services and research to many of the companies that their analysts cover. Such basic conflicts have existed for years.

Internet mania exacerbates the problem. With scores of companies going public each year—many of which may be dogs—investors are hungry for guidance. Yet the sheer volume makes it harder for analysts to become truly expert on any one. Marvels a Net marketing executive: "It is amazing to see some of the folks that are quoted as experts, even in your publication." Star analysts with solid reputations such as Meeker, Merrill Lynch's Henry Blodget, or DLJ's Jamie Kiggen must contend with the overload too. Each of them "covers" 35 stocks or more. They do so with much help from their research "teams"—like 17th-century Dutch Masters, the works that bear their signature are often not entirely of their own hand. "It is the same way any management situation would work," explains Blodget. "There are ten companies I am closely involved with, but I am responsible for everything."

Besides the overload issue, the reason the objective value of the research is under siege is that it is no longer clear exactly whom Wall Street analysts are trying to serve. Traditionally, their primary audience has been large institutional investors that demanded unbiased, high-quality advice. But now analysts are increasingly answering to another master: corporate banking. With the competition to handle the ever-increasing number of Net IPOs, analysts have become increasingly important in landing those lucrative deals. Bill Burnham, an ex-Internet analyst at Credit Suisse First Boston and now a venture capitalist at Softbank, puts it bluntly: "In the technology world, there is no banking relationship without the analyst." The analyst is judge, jury, and executioner when it comes to deciding whether to pursue a company as a banking client, and it is the analyst who has the closest relationship with the company after the deal is done.

"This can collapse into a situation where the analyst becomes a spokesperson for the firm he is analyzing," warns Mathew Hayward, a professor at the London Business School. His research shows that companies get higher ratings from analysts they bank with than from analysts they don't. One example: Soon after Bank of America Securities underwrote a follow-on offering for theglobe.com, its analyst at the time, Alan Braverman, initiated coverage of the stock with a buy rating. The stock now trades below its initial offering price.

Trying to determine the validity of such reports is easier if you're an institutional investor who has been trained to read between the lines or who can simply pick up the phone and ask for the straight dope. But what about the investing public, which may have access to these same reports (thanks to the Internet) but doesn't have access to the analysts? It's not as though they can get a special Cap'n Crunch decoder ring to help them figure out what an analyst really means.

Keith Benjamin, another ex-Internet analyst turned venture capitalist, sympathizes. "The retail audience is groping for any information on this unprecedented number of new stocks," he explains. "The analyst has now grown in stature from providing advice to institutions to being a beacon for *Fortune* or CNBC. It's dangerous because it's impossible to give the same amount of detail in context or tone to retail investors."

So much for Wall Street. According to many Net execs, getting unbiased market research presents an even more difficult challenge. Analysts at many info-tech research firms are compensated according to how much "consulting" work they can generate. A fed-up Internet CEO reports, "If you pay them $10,000 to $30,000, it seems to me you have nice things said about you. It's a little like doing business in a foreign country." Stuart Read, until recently VP of marketing at Palm software company AvantGo, says, "Some companies are great about paying the money and getting covered. Call me jaded, but that is the way I understand it works."

With more and more revenues coming from consulting, analysts are under pressure to meet with and write about companies that are clients. As a result, "You have to take every piece of research with a grain of salt," says Paul Johnson, a former analyst at International Data Corp. who is now director of market research at CMGI. Harry Fenik, head of Zona Research, points out an even more disturbing trend. "The Internet has created a new monster," he says, "not as controllable or visible—analysts own stock in many of the companies they cover." This can make the analyst "overexuberant" about a company. Fenik tries to avoid this conflict as much as possible at Zona, but he cannot completely squelch the practice, because if he did, "we would not have anyone working here," he says (a boilerplate disclosure is printed on every piece of Zona research alerting the careful reader that such a conflict may exist). For the record, Fenick says this practice is much more rampant at other, bigger shops. How reassuring.

Fumble.com: Internet Companies Threw Millions into the Air at the Super Bowl. They're Still Pretending They Scored a Touchdown

KATHARINE MIESZKOWSKI

Salon, *May 3, 2000*

J ust suppose you blew a cool $3.5 million in a mere 90 seconds on three television ads starring yourself and hyping your little-known dot-com. What's impressive isn't just how much you spent to launch your company and see your own smiling face during the Super Bowl. It's how much of your total capital went into those three fleeting bathroom breaks.

Having started with just $5.8 million in seed financing, you squandered more than half of your capital in less time than it takes to soft-boil an egg. Congratulations! That fancy caper puts your little start-up in the running for the hotly contested title of Fastest Dot-Com to Piss Away the Greatest Percentage of Its Funding. And now it's time to—what else?— dust off your pitch and raise more money! How excruciating it must be to meet with potential investors, when the one thing your company is known for—if it's known for anything at all—is having the genius (or stupidity) to spend money at the rate of just under $38,889 a second.

Or not. Computer.com, a hand-holding help site for novice computer users, did actually run through 60 percent of its funding in 90 Super Bowl

seconds. But Michael J. Ford, the co-founder and president of the Maynard, Mass., company, is still sporting that smile. I quizzed him about the
red-faced reactions he must surely get from investors as he seeks more
funding. Doesn't cartoon steam shoot out of the ears of the blustering
moneybags as they roar: "Kid, you just spent $3.5 million in less than two
minutes. Why should I give you, of all people, any of my money!?"

Ford assured me that he's met with no such open indignation: "They
probably wouldn't say it to my face," he says.

Besides, Computer.com is hardly alone in this. It's the morning after
for the 17 dot-coms, both early stage start-ups and publicly traded companies, that shot their multimillion-dollar wads at the Super Bowl last
quarter—driving the price of a 30-second spot up to a record $2.2 mil-
lion. Just three months later, with the NASDAQ seesawing wildly, the
public markets' once-rabid desire for anything dot-com has chilled, and
even the public dot-coms that snuck their calling cards into investors'
psyches during that great haze of beer, snack food and a St. Louis Rams
victory are now trading below their late January price. Few of the sites
have enjoyed a demonstrable growth in traffic, or can point to any big
deals that were nudged into the end zone by Super Bowl advertising.

It can't be pretty for the big spenders who've got to justify their Super
Bowl blowouts to shareholders and investors. They're certainly not getting
a warm reception from the likes of Donna Novitsky, a partner at Mohr,
Davidow Ventures in Silicon Valley: "Advertising in the Super Bowl was
kind of a ludicrous thing to begin with," she says dismissively. "It's a very
untargeted way of reaching consumers." So, why did this horde of mostly
fledgling and unprofitable dot-coms do it? Novitsky's theory: "I think it's
an ego thing. . . . It was really a sign of excess."

January's Super Bowl strut left Neil Weintraut of 21st Century Internet Venture Partners similarly unimpressed. "This year, advertising on
the Super Bowl amounted to keeping up with the Joneses," he says. He
fantasizes about all the more "heretical" things a company could have
done to squeeze more buzz out of the same budget, like give away 100
Volkswagen Bugs. "The key thing is to do something that someone hasn't
done before. The key thing you want to say to consumers when you're
launching a company is, 'I'm an innovator,' and you're not going to do
that with the Super Bowl."

In 1999, only three dot-coms advertised nationally in the Super Bowl—

and got tons of media attention for doing so. But this year Net companies packed the game like sardines: AutoTrader.com, Britannica.com,
Computer.com, Epidemic.com, E-Trade.com, Hotjobs.com, kforce
.com, LastMinuteTravel.com, LifeMinders.com, Monster.com, Netpliance
.com, OnMoney.com, Oxygen.com, OurBeginning.com, Pets.com,
Webex.com and WebMD.com. Even ad aficionados would have trouble
remembering all the companies that warred for extravagantly priced air
time.

Mitch Davis, senior vice president of marketing for Britannica.com,
is amazed by the "irrational marketing" expenditures exhibited by the
wet-behind-the-ears dot-coms. "In two or three years, we're going to look
back and wonder how the hell did a company with $6 million in capital
spend half of it in less than two minutes," he says. But when he admits,
"I have the luxury of saying that because we have a brand"—implying
that Britannica is justified in spending millions on ads just because it has
a long history of doing so—he sounds just as delusional as the unknown
start-up founders who continue to argue that the Super Bowl was a fabulous investment.

So, what exactly did those dot-commers get for the money? It may be
all Monday-morning quarterbacking, but in retrospect, the bottom line
looks like a bit of gawking press coverage and a temporary uptick in site
traffic, but nothing so lasting that it could be called "brand building,"
and nothing so irrefutably valuable—except for maybe that priceless ego-
gratification—that it could possibly justify the huge expense for a whole
batch of unprofitable companies.

"They would have been better off had they taken the money that they
spent on Super Bowl advertising and gone to Vegas," says David Stewart,
professor of marketing at the University of Southern California's business school. "I think the odds of a positive outcome of spending those
dollars would have been higher in Vegas than in a one-time ad on the
Super Bowl."

For those gamblers who prefer the stock market to Las Vegas, a good
Super Bowl tip would have been to short all the publicly traded dot-
coms who advertised on it. None of the dot-coms that advertised in the
big bowl are trading at or above their game-day price, and many are
down by as much as 60 percent. Ego-gratifying Super Bowl ads are one
thing if you're a privately held company and your investors—for whatever

reason—will let you get away with it, but the shareholders of these publicly traded stocks seem to have cause to wonder what exactly these companies thought they were doing with investors' nest eggs.

At the close of trading Tuesday, Hotjobs stock was down 60 percent from its Jan. 31 trading price (the first trading day after the Super
Bowl)—from almost $28 to just above $11. Netpliance was down 65 percent from the $22 it commanded three months ago, to less than $8; and
its Internet appliance product, the I-Opener, is selling at a remarkable
discount—"Now only $99 (regular price $199)" chirps the Web site. And
Healtheon/WebMD was feeling the pain, down 69 percent from $65 to
$20. Not even a $220 million shot in the company's arm at the beginning
of April from the company's founder, Silicon Valley pioneer Jim Clark,
and famed venture capitalist John Doerr could give the stock more than
a few days' bounce.

But the saddest whimpering stock of the bunch is Pets.com, which
was down 73 percent from $11 on Jan. 31 to $3 after the dot-crash. The
wags on the company's Yahoo message board last week drubbed the company in messages with subject lines like "THIS DEAD PET."

Though Pets.com's big ad spending has done little to pump up the
company's stock, it has made that irrepressible sock puppet something
of a household image. So Pets.com is now pursuing a new strategy to
recoup some of the $20 million it has reportedly spent on ads starring the
floppy-eared mascot, a puppet which may prove to be its most valuable
asset. Last week, Pets.com announced its intention to sell merchandise
featuring the sock puppet in brick-and-mortar stores. Perhaps selling its
mascot's image offline will be more immediately profitable than its core
business of hawking Meow Mix over the Net. Maybe all that "brand
building" will pay off yet! As if to defend this important revenue stream
for the company, Pets.com is suing a former writer from *Late Night with
Conan O'Brien*, for defamation and trade libel of its "spokespuppet."

The recent trading history of the public dot-coms that joined the Super
Bowl binge might give pause to a company like WebEx, the online meeting company that brought a hyper-glam RuPaul before millions of beer-
swilling Super Bowl viewers, spending $1.2 million to secure a 30-second
spot just in major markets. In December, the company announced it had
closed a $25 million round of financing and had "committed a majority
of the new funds to marketing efforts." In April WebEx filed to go public,

so it shouldn't be too long before we see just how much market buzz $25 million and a celebrity drag queen can buy you.

We know stock prices can be fickle, especially lately. "That's just the market talking, not our customers," the dot-coms exclaim. But the only other quantifiable index of a site's branding success is traffic. And, excepting a temporary bounce in the days following the game, all that money spent on the Super Bowl has shown few signs of broadening these companies' audience.

Take the case of OurBeginning.com, an online stationery store in Orlando, Fla., with essentially no name recognition before the game. According to Media Metrix (whose numbers remain the industry standard, despite their apparent flaws), the site had 362,000 unique visitors in January; 547,000 in February; and "no reportable traffic" in March, meaning that by Media Metrix's count, fewer than 250,000 individuals visited the site.

Still, Michael Budowski, CEO of OurBeginning.com, defends his decision to run the ad, which featured cheesy brides viciously cat-fighting over stationery: "The Super Bowl bought our company credibility," he says, deadly serious. He says the ad gets the company in the door with some big corporate clients—"Oh, yes. You guys did the Super Bowl."—and has helped reel in at least one $3 million customer. He thinks they'll do another ad next year.

For sites like E-Trade, Monster.com or Pets.com, which have done extensive ad campaigns, the effect of the Super Bowl traffic is harder to measure. But Monster.com's attempt to use Robert Frost's "The Road Not Taken" poem to induce job-seekers to check out their classified-ad job site hasn't been evidently persuasive. While PC Data Online, which tracks Web usage statistics, reported that the site got an immediate 80 percent increase in traffic from the ad on the day of the game, there was no apparent longer term benefit—Media Metrix clocked the site's traffic at 3.6 million unique visitors in January, 3.5 million in February and 3.4 million in March.

So, if a Super Bowl ad didn't intrigue investors enough to drive up your stock price and didn't excite consumers enough to drive sustainable traffic to your site, what exactly was the point of the big outlay? Just a wacky once-a-year stunt?

Certainly, blasting more than 100 million consumers with your brand name is a weird way to win corporate clients. Stewart of USC dryly says: "The typical business manager doesn't watch the Super Bowl for purposes of finding his next vendor." So what were companies like WebEx and Healtheon/WebMD doing there in the first place? Perhaps trying to get their name out in front of investors (read: day traders) and well, yes, customers.

David Thompson, vice president of marketing for WebEx, says the venue made sense for the company's "hyper-branding" initiative since WebEx is a "B2E" play. (Um, "business-to-employee," I'm told.) "The Web turns old advertising rules on its head," he enthuses. (Wait, isn't this TV advertising?) "The best way to reach that man or woman may be through a Super Bowl ad. They're human beings first and customers second. Hit them where they live!"

Ford of Computer.com calculates media coverage his company got for doing the ad was worth $10 million, not the $3.5 million paid. Surely, the value of Diane Sawyer on ABC's *Good Morning America* cooing "I liked the Computer.com ads" cannot be quantified in mere digits. And Ford reminds me that I, too, am contributing to the return on his investment in the Super Bowl by writing about it: "I don't know if you're aware, but you're doing a story, so you're a part of it!" he says triumphantly.

As far as the highest goal of such advertising, the ever-elusive building of brand, it's not clear that those ads really "hit" anyone. The people who care about this stuff for a living, like the ad execs at D'Arcy Masius Benton & Bowles (DMBB) in St. Louis, which handles clients like Coca-Cola, Milky Way and TWA, were left scratching their heads about all those dot-com ads the day after the Super Bowl.

"We got together to look at all the Super Bowl advertising. We watched it as a group the next day, and we were pretty much unimpressed," says Mike Flynn, a senior account planner.

A month after the game, DMBB St. Louis surveyed 1,000 adults, and found 357 who'd watched at least three-quarters of the Super Bowl. Only 17 percent of those could name a single dot-com that had advertised during the game without any prompting. Not a single person remembered seeing ads from AutoTrader.com, Britannica.com, Computer.com, DowJones.com, Epidemic.com, kforce.com, LifeMinders, Netpliance, OnMoney.com, OurBeginning.com or Healtheon/WebMD without prompting.

Some of the companies that had done a lot of commercials before the game, like Pets.com, Monster.com and E-Trade, fared better. A whopping 6 percent of those surveyed remembered seeing an E-Trade ad. That was the big winner. Even with prompting, only 4 percent could recall Epidemic.com's creepy ad, which employed a sickening germ metaphor to invite viewers to send spam to friends.

The problem may not have been entirely with the somewhat loopy creativity in the ads themselves, which have been endlessly critiqued, rated and dissected.

Nigel Carr, the general manager of Kirshenbaum Bond & Partners West, an ad agency, says that in this year's Super Bowl the flood of dot-coms basically succeeded in drowning out each other. "Like everything in advertising, someone does something differently, and it works incredibly well because no one else is doing it, and then everyone rushes to copy it, and it stops working because everyone is doing it. That's basically the history of advertising in a nutshell."

USC's Stewart says that the dot-com ad rush—Net companies spent $3.1 billion on offline advertising last year alone, according to Competitive Media Reporting—parallels what happened historically in other "overcapitalized industries" like railroads, the telegraph, radio and TV, where new innovations caused a surge of money, and then of promotion to flood the markets with competing messages. "It's not really a unique phenomenon," he says. "It just happens to be the one that's happening today."

Mantra Number One: Cut Through the Clutter

Still, the companies most of us had never heard of before, and may never hear from again, defend the Super Bowl as just the thing for them. "It's probably the only event where people turn on the game, not just to see the game but to see the advertising. We knew that we could rise above a lot of the clutter out there," says David Miranda, CEO of LastMinute Travel.com.

Jim Blumenfeld, the CEO of OnMoney.com, a site designed to help you manage your money, says the same thing: "We feel we've broken through a lot of the clutter."

And the gyrations in the market don't phase any of these fearless entrepreneurs either. "There are a lot of companies that are probably thinking about it, if they haven't already pulled out of their marketing spends," says a pleased Blumenfeld. "It reduces the clutter out there and it could ultimately be a huge opportunity for us."

Mantra Number Two: Look Under the Hood

Budowski of OurBeginning.com is equally enthusiastic about the market drop. "It actually helps us," says Budowski, who plans to have a public offering by the end of this year. "People are going to become more selective and start looking under the hood and saying—'Hey, what's in there?' We think we have a real company."

The funny thing is that so does everyone else—about their own company, that is. Ford of Computer.com says: "There are a lot of quasi-business models, marketing plans masquerading as companies out there, and we're scaling up to be a long-term company." This, from a site that is a computer news and shopping site for newbies.

Miranda of LastMinuteTravel.com, who also plans on an IPO before year's end, says that a shakeout is inevitable, and "I'm happy to see it happen. What's happening in the dot-com world, if you look under the hood of some of these companies, what you see are some business models that are very suspect. You can't just put a dot-com on the end of everything. You have to separate the good ideas from the hype."

Did someone gives these guys a script with the words "under the hood" in it? Maybe it also had stage directions sending them all to advertise in the Super Bowl. Hmm, will it be picked up by entrepreneurs next year—giving us cause to rename Super Bowl XXXV as SuperBowl.com? "That's anybody's guess. Look at the stock market—you don't know how many dot-coms are going to be around next year," says Flynn of DMBB.

Such talk certainly doesn't rankle this year's Super Bowl cast. Ever the unflappable entrepreneur, Computer.com's Ford forges down the IPO road with no regrets about the one-day multimillion-dollar ad orgy. Though he has nothing to show for his flash of cash, except the free press (yes, including this article!)—he says: "We were very pleased with the results. The Super Bowl was a huge success for us. No one had heard of us before. Now, we have not only a national brand, but an international brand."

Media Metrix be damned. Maybe tens of millions of football fanatics the world over do have that generic URL, Computer.com, inextricably commingled with their misty memories of Super Bowl XXXIV.

They'd better. Ford, who's busily raising his next pile of dough, admits that he won't be doing a "huge marketing campaign" anytime soon. "Based on what happened with the stock market in the last couple of weeks, we're looking to do more targeted marketing."

Meet the Dumbest Dot-Com
in the World

MARK GIMEIN

Fortune, *July 10, 2000*

ere's a Silicon Valley recipe gone horribly awry. Take two newly minted Stanford Business School grads. Throw in a CEO who has run enough companies to think of himself as "adult supervision." Add annoying buzzwords like "infomediary" and an Amway-style marketing plan, and you get AllAdvantage, of Hayward, Calif.

Amid a heap of horrible dot-com business plans, this company has one of the worst: It pays people to surf the Web. When members sign up on the AllAdvantage site, they download an advertising bar that stays on their screens as they surf. For every hour they browse with the bar on their screen, they get 53 cents. If they refer another member to AllAdvantage, they get a 10-cent bonus for each hour the new member surfs. Members with a big "downline"—i.e., lots of referrals—have made several thousand dollars a month.

AllAdvantage expected 30,000 members after four months but got millions. At the end of the first quarter of 2000, its two million active members cost an average of $6.49 a month in payments and referral fees. It paid $40 million to members in that quarter alone.

The results have been devastating. AllAdvantage has burned through most of its $135 million investment, and it lost $66 million just in the first quarter. The situation can only worsen. Unlike other dot-coms, which can cut down on marketing costs and cancel big ad campaigns, AllAdvantage's model gets more precarious every day as word of mouth brings more and more people who sign up and demand to be paid.

This idea of an "infomediary"—a company that collects and aggregates information from a lot of users—has long been popular among Net gurus. AllAdvantage was supposed to finance the whole deal by selling advertisers information about its members' surfing habits. But that hasn't happened. It took in a meager $9 million in the first quarter of 2000. The prospect of "highly targeted" banner ads is still hypothetical; the information is all there, stored in AllAdvantage's data banks, but only a tiny fraction of it is currently useful to advertisers.

The company seems aware of its tenuous state. In late winter it started selling ads that appear on users' screens even when they're not actively surfing the Web. Then, last month, it began stretching member payments over a longer time period. But those are stop-gap solutions. Members still have to be paid, regardless of whether they get money every 30 or 45 days. And Web advertisers aren't lining up to reach people as they work on Excel spreadsheets.

AllAdvantage wouldn't discuss its plans, citing SEC rules that prevent companies in IPO registration from talking to the press. But David Pidwell, a venture capitalist who was AllAdvantage's first outside investor—he knew the founders from classes he had taught at Stanford on entrepreneurship, and he sits on the board—insists that the financiers know what they're doing. Pidwell says that in February, investors (including Softbank Capital Partners, which put in $70 million) valued the company at $700 million. "Are they stupid," he asks, "or are you stupid?" Good question—though hardly the most persuasive defense of the company.

AllAdvantage's hope was that $135 million would be enough to get it to the public market. That doesn't look likely. The company filed a public offering in February but put it on hold after the April Internet-stock crash. Now AllAdvantage is running out of time. Those close to the company say it has $50 million to $65 million, enough money to survive at least until the end of the year. That should give current investors—the likeliest source of additional cash—enough time to decide how much money they want to keep pouring down this sinkhole.

And that's the delicious irony of AllAdvantage's woes. This time the VCs are getting burned, while the site's members are profiting handsomely. Finally someone's getting revenge for investors who've been burned by dying dot-coms.

The Financial Page:
How Mountebanks Became Moguls

JAMES SUROWIECKI

The New Yorker, *November 13, 2000*

A decade from now, when we're all buying our power drills and our anniversary additions of *Tuesdays with Morrie* from Amazon and downloading our digital library of Jennifer Love Hewitt movies via the A.O.L.-Time Warner high-speed capable network, we may no longer remember the age of the story stock. But what an age it was, when businessmen perfected the art of turning blarney into billions, and companies whose main product wasn't servers or software but press releases acquired vast valuations. People nimble enough to get in and out at the right time became dynastically wealthy.

Today, we may have an easier time remembering that age, because it came to an end—let's say *offically*—just two weeks ago. The date was October 25th. Two things happened. First, after Nortel Networks announced that it had earned less than Wall Street had expected it to, the air started hissing out of the tech boom's last great bubble—the optical-networking sector. The folks in fibre no longer seemed invincible.

The other thing that happened was that C. Michael Armstrong, the head of A.T.&T., unveiled the company's scheme to "unlock shareholder value" by splitting into four separate stocks. It was the sort of yarn that the stock market had lapped up for much of the nineteen-nineties. But this time Wall Street shrugged, and A.T.&T.'s shares fell thirteen per cent. It was too late for tall tales. The nineties were over. Suddenly, investors have gone back to reading 10-Qs.

Now that value is supposedly back, it's easy to be dismissive of management by press release. But, when you think about it, the storytellers pulled off something remarkable. Instead of first building a business, then going public, they figured out that you could do it the other way around. They took the money, then set out to build the business. Of course, many companies realized that the first part of the process is a lot easier than the second. So, rather than bother with actually building a business, they merely propped up their stock price and attempted to use it to buy or bluff their way to the big time.

Hence the onslaught of road shows, CNBC appearances, and New Economy jive that sounded more like Arthur C. Clarke than Alfred Sloan. Take the idea of the I.P.O. as "branding event." Perhaps the credit for this one should go to Stephan Paternot and Todd Krizelman, the two silver-tongued young men who founded Theglobe.com, a Website that sought to "replicate society." When Theglobe went public, in November of 1998, it held down the price shares it sold. Because of this, the company raised less money than it could have. But what it got in exchange was a speculative mania in its shares, which rose six hundred per cent on the first day of trading. That, in turn, earned Theglobe's founding duo a ton of free press and put their company, which didn't really seem to do or earn much of anything, on the day traders' radar screen.

So far, so good. These two men—or their bankers—seemed to realize that their customers weren't customers but, rather, the people who buy and flip stock. Their ticker symbol was their brand. Nor was it just the startups who told fabulous tales. Blue-chip companies did, too. They wove elaborate narratives about the wireless revolution, or the rise of the networked world and the disappearance of the personal computer. They carefully guided Wall Street analysts so that their performance was always slightly better than expected.

In the long run, of course, this is no way to run a business, and those who didn't understand that eventually saw their precious stock prices fall apart. Theglobe turned out to be just another Japanese lantern: paper-thin and full of hot air. But the big talker—"the entrepreneurial C.E.O. with a thespian bent," as the venture capitalist Bill Gurley once put it—was onto something. In the right hands, a pumped-up stock could be a formidable business tool. Companies could use it to buy other companies, attract hotshot employees, and raise extra capital to expand their operations. As Michael Mauboussin, the chief investment strategist for Credit Suisse First Boston, points out, "Instead of the stock price just reflecting a company's fundamentals, it actually started *affecting* the fundamentals."

But it was a dangerous game. If you smoked your own supply—if you believed your own hype—the market eventually wised up and you were caught out. The winners were the ones who took advantage of their irrational valuations to grow their own businesses and acquire assets of genuine value. Take Paternot and Krizelman, the globe guys. They were probably doomed from the start, but imagine if they had used their high-flying stock to merge with a real company, like CNet. It's all in timing: you've got to know when to go legit, when to turn sizzle into steak—when to parlay that quack patent-medicine potion into a bona-fide beverage empire (have a Coke and a smile). You could argue that this is what A.O.L. did when it hooked up with Time Warner. And you have to admire the way Cisco used its stock, which was trading at mind-boggling multiples, to buy its way into a position of market dominance that has made those multiples halfway plausible. The savvy entrepreneurs converted fool's gold into the 24k kind. So who's the fool now?

Dot Coms: What Have We Learned?

JERRY USEEM

Fortune, *October 30, 2000*

ANNA ZORNOSA, age 41

> *Once a publishing executive, Zornosa has worked at four*
> *Internet startups so far: PointCast, SmartAge, Women.com,*
> *and now Topica, an e-mail company, where she is president.*

I went to Women.com specifically because I wanted to stay in the Internet but be in a place that was more mature, more stable than the early-stage startups I had worked in before. But I started noticing that I had excess energy. At the end of the day, I actually had cycles left. It was probably the first time in five years that I came home wishing that there was a mountain to tackle after I put my kids to bed and got to my computer. I woke up one morning and thought, "I'm ready for another early-stage startup." Nothing could have floored me more than if I had woken up and said, "I want to have a third child." Which I will never wake up and say.

So I joined Topica. In most ways, working at an early-stage Internet company today is no different than working at an early-stage Internet company in 1995. But this time, both me and my business partner have been involved in three Net companies; our CFO has been at two. With experience comes a sense of pacing yourself. When I started five years ago, every single decision felt so incredibly important. Today we have a larger sense of context.

I'll tell you one thing I've learned: If something seems stupid, it probably is stupid. If it seems stupid to spend $10 million in a quarter because your competitor is doing it, it probably is stupid. If it seems stupid to compete with your customers by doing an e-commerce play, it probably is stupid. Even if all the venture capitalists are telling you otherwise. The next time I see a phenomenon like this, I will definitely be the one going against the curve. I'll be saying, "If it seems stupid, it's stupid."

I've set a rule for myself to never lose the passion for upside, but to always temper it with specific answers to the question "What if it doesn't happen?" In my case, I'm happy as long as I've worked with a group of people that I like and respect, as long as I feel fairly compensated, and as long as I have learned something. When I'm recruiting, I try to build teams that are hungry for both financial upside and personal development. If the win is not in one place, then it's my promise to them that it will be in the other.

The thing is, I still owe it to this company to drive like crazy for the great big win. I wouldn't have signed on if I hadn't thought it was there. I'm looking for the great big win. I'm not counting on it.

DAVE MERRIWETHER, age 30

> *Serving as director of corporate development at Exchange-Wave, a B2B software company, is Stanford MBA Merriwether's second startup experience.*

I remember when I was working at a small software company, back in 1997. A buddy of mine who was a banker gave me the prospectus for Amazon. This was when it was all starting—Yahoo, all these companies. eBay didn't even exist. I looked at this thing, and I went, There's no way this will ever go anywhere. So it's—it's been an interesting road for me because I've seen some things happen that I never thought would happen. God, if I'd just been a part of that a long time ago, it would have been interesting. I kind of wish I had invested.

Then the AllAdvantage.com thing happened, and I went there as a summer intern from Stanford Business School. The mood at AllAdvantage was huge in the summer of 1999. We had a really dynamic CEO, and we knew that speed was important. We certainly didn't expect the number of people to sign up for the thing that did. So we were kind of in the midst of a storm trying to figure out, What's the best way to proceed here? The world was our oyster. The interns got an equity bonus for the summer, and a full-time offer to stay and quit school, which I actually considered. Would I have been a millionaire? Yeah, probably, if the company had filed. But the market collapsed.

The new company I'm at, ExchangeWave, is a little less interested in rapid or hyper growth and much more interested in strategic growth. You know, we look at our burn rate and how we're spending money. We're doing market research. If it goes really well, a liquidity event would be in the future. But that's not the end-all for us. The Internet is not quite the gold mine a lot of people think it is. It really is becoming more of a workplace than a let's-go-hang-out-and-do-weird-things-and-have-an-office-that-has-stuff-on-the-wall-and-conference-rooms-that-are-named-funny-things. It's becoming more of—more of a business.

Money Is Boring

DAVID WINER, age 45

> Winer is a Silicon Valley software veteran and founder of Userland Software, a Web publishing-tools company. He publishes his own Internet newsletter at Scripting.com.

From my point of view, we kind of skipped the dot-com mania. I've personally had a number of opportunities to, you know, be a CEO or a CTO of one of these shooting stars and make a lot of money and whatever. When it all shakes out, sure, I guess a lot of people are going to be very rich. But you know, I was lucky to get kind of rich myself a few years ago. So I have a sort of, I think a relatively mature appreciation for what value there is in having money. It's not the last thing you have to do in your life.

The frenzy last summer screwed things up, to be honest with you. The social scene in San Francisco was completely destroyed by it. Christmas parties for the last few years have been all about, you know, "Oh, we're about to do our IPO" or "Oh, the greatest thing is, we're pre-IPO." That's, like, wishful thinking. Maybe they've never heard of Murphy's law.

It's boring. Money is boring. And party conversation about money is even more boring. I want to know what people think, and I want to know what their passions are. I want to be inspired by them. I want them to do beautiful things that entertain me. I want my beautiful things to entertain them.

The Internet is a fantastic technology that helps me do these things. So what was last year like for me? It was frustrating as hell. I mean, to see everything turn to money is like kind of not that far from seeing everything turn to shit.

Soccer Coach

JAMES CRAMER, age 45

*New York hedge fund manager Cramer became a high-profile
Net dude when he co-founded TheStreet.com. The day the
company went public, its stock hit $60; at press time shares
were below $4.*

What I would say to you is that if TheStreet.com were a private company, and were a magazine, people would be astonished at our success. But we're a public company and we're a Website, so people think that we're idiots. I think what we've done is remarkable. But what we failed to do is tragic. And what's happened is, in all the confusion and hubbub, we look as if we don't know what we're doing.

In the very beginning when the company was set up, I wasn't allowed to run it. The government asked me not to. So it was my blueprint but not my execution. And that two-headed monster—me being a really visible guy associated with the site, but not really in charge—is a failure on my part. If I had been able to pick the right people from the beginning, this enterprise could have been hugely successful as opposed to just kind of successful.

I blame myself. I blame myself every single day. I should have realized that it was not possible to set up an enterprise and fund it when I could have no control over it. But that's what I did. And that's what I pay for every day.

Nobody really cares for the Internet—except for the newspapers and magazines that live off the advertising on it, and people who can't sleep and need something to do. It has created an undisciplined culture of slothfulness and foolishness that's now a culture of despair.

I'm sorry, I've got to call it like I see it. You know, there was a period where there was tremendous value to doing something different on the Web. But now all of it looks the same, equally tiresome. The technology has stalled, and the look and feel have stalled. It's just not that interesting. The Internet won't be embraced correctly until our children take over. I hope to live to see that.

The idea that you can develop something for the Net today and have it be commercially viable is crazy. AOL and Yahoo have taken 90% of the creativity and the capital and, at least when it comes to content, have made the Internet so that it's even more ossified and difficult to break into than TV. It happened in such a short period, it's astonishing to me. If I had something that I wanted to do to get people's attention, I would do it on TV, because it's easier, cheaper, and a lot more fun.

It's a shame, because the Internet was really fun for a while. It was fun for about three or four years. Oh, it was fun. It was cool. It was a really cool thing. Now it's just something I wish weren't in front of me, so I wouldn't have to look at it.

What's next for TheStreet.com? Excuse my language, but I don't have a fuckin' clue. It ain't up to me. It never was. I wish it were. But it wasn't. And that's the tragedy of the enterprise.

What's next for me? Oh, this unbelievable project. It's called "Coaching Fifth-Grade Soccer." There I can accomplish everything I want in life. I can make everybody happy at home and have something to show for it in the end. I'm done with the material stuff. The shocking riches-to-rags story that I've become because of my TheStreet.com hobby has made me realize that I'm a darn good hedge fund manager and a real good dad. I want nothing to do with the rest of it.

In Defense of the Boom

MICHAEL LEWIS

The New York Times Magazine, *October 27, 2002*

Wall Street Didn't Do It

A few weeks ago, on *Moneyline*, a guest who didn't fully understand just how much times have changed invoked some corporation's ability to beat Wall Street's forecasts for its quarterly earnings. Before you could say "market manipulation," the program's host, Lou Dobbs, said, "Do you really think anybody's paying attention to that silly expectation stuff anymore?" He dismissed forecasts as "the game of the late '90s." And he had a point. For many years, Wall Street analysts have lowballed their earnings estimates so that their corporate customers could announce to the press that they had "beaten" those estimates. This particular game was exposed beginning in the late 1990s by fledgling Web sites, which routinely published more accurate earnings forecasts than the Wall Street pros. By the middle of 1998 the stock market began to trade off the Web estimates rather than the Street estimates—which tells you how fully understood this quarterly forecast game had become even before the boom reached its turn-of-the-century heights.

But so long as the stock market rose, Lou Dobbs was happy to listen to Wall Street and corporate big shots blather on about how they had beaten their earnings forecasts. He didn't scorn them; like every other serious reporter, he treated them as useful informants (when he wasn't distracted by his bid to make his Internet fortune in a doomed start-up called Space.com). And yet now, somehow, Lou Dobbs, like every other serious reporter, knows enough to raise his eyebrows and harshen his tone when anyone mentions earnings estimates. As wide-eyed as he was three years ago, he is narrow-eyed now. You can't put one over on Lou Dobbs!

And that, in a way, is the point. If you can't put one over on Lou Dobbs, whom can you put one over on?

The markets, having tasted skepticism, are beginning to overdose. The bust likes to think of itself as a radical departure from the boom, but it has in common with it one big thing: a mob mentality. When the markets were rising and everyone was getting rich, it was rare to hear a word against the system—or the people making lots of money from it. Now that the markets are falling and everyone is feeling poor, or, at any rate, less rich, it is rare to hear a word on behalf of either the system or the rich. The same herd instinct that fueled the boom fuels the bust. And the bust has created market distortions as bizarre as—and maybe more harmful than—anything associated with the boom.

The recent wave of outrage about Wall Street's behavior began, you may recall, when New York State Attorney General Eliot Spitzer deployed an obscure state law to shoehorn out of Merrill Lynch every e-mail message Merrill employees had ever sent relating to the Internet boom. It was easy to see why Spitzer chose Merrill Lynch as his target. He has political ambitions (he wants to be governor of New York, at least), and unlike Goldman, Sachs or Morgan Stanley or one of the other big investment banks more central to the Internet bubble, Merrill actually serviced lots of small customers. It's a firm that voters can relate to.

What I didn't understand was Spitzer's hunger for Merrill's old e-mail. If the New York attorney general wanted to prove that the firm's analysts had been wildly optimistic about the Internet, and that their optimism helped the firm's investment bankers attract Internet business, and that there was, therefore, a deep conflict of interest on Wall Street, all he needed was an Internet search engine.

If you go back and read the public record, you can see clearly what people on Wall Street did between April 1995, when Netscape invented the Internet Initial Public Offering, or IPO, and the spring of 2000, when Internet stocks crashed. The story was never hidden, because Wall Street never tried to hide it. Indeed, you can pinpoint the very moment when Merrill Lynch signed on to the boom, and in what spirit they joined the party.

Until late in 1998, which was three years or so into the boom, Merrill and its brokers actually fought a rearguard action against Internet stocks. The Internet looked as if it would all but eliminate the commissions investors paid to buy and sell stocks and gut the already weakened core business of Merrill Lynch. The head of Merrill's stockbrokers, John Steffens, actually said that the Internet was "a serious threat to Americans' financial lives." Partly as a result of this self-serving truculence, Merrill had lagged badly behind Goldman, Sachs and Morgan Stanley and the other up-market firms in its ability to rake in fees from Internet stock offerings. At the same time, Merrill Lynch was also—and this is the key point—becoming ridiculous to the nearly five million account holders who kept their money at Merrill Lynch. You couldn't be running ads on TV saying you were "bullish on America" and at the same time be telling your customers they should be ignoring or dumping the hottest sector the U.S. stock market had ever seen.

On December 16, 1998, the contradiction finally became too much for Merrill Lynch to bear. On that day, the share price of Amazon .com touched $242. Merrill Lynch's Internet analyst, Jonathan Cohen, announced that the shares were worth at best $50 and that it was time to sell. Across town, Henry Blodget, a 32-year-old freelance-magazine-writer-turned-Internet-analyst for an obscure, second-tier firm called CIBC Oppenheimer, was saying that Amazon's stock would reach $400 a share. Sure enough, Amazon promptly rose to a split-adjusted high of $678. Cohen was wrong, and Blodget was right, and Merrill Lynch was the laughingstock of the market. And so Merrill fired Cohen, hired Blodget and, in effect, bought into Amazon.com at four hundred bucks a share.

It occurred to no one at the time that Merrill Lynch was conspiring to drive up Internet stocks. They were simply giving their brokerage customers what they wanted. Internet stocks had been rising too fast for too long for Merrill Lynch to be saying anything other than that Internet stocks would continue to rise. Merrill's investment bankers, theretofore incidental victims of their Internet analyst's bearish views, became incidental beneficiaries of the firm's new bullishness. They were quite open about this. They were happy to tell reporters, on the record, precisely what Eliot Spitzer would later claim he had uncovered as he pored over old e-mail. For instance, on April 13, 1999, Scott Ryles, the head of Merrill's technology banking division, explained his new success to Bloomberg News. "It's difficult to take companies public when your analyst has a less-than-constructive view on some of the biggest companies out there," Ryles said. Having Blodget on board was great, he said, because Blodget "has been unabashedly bullish and has been proved right. . . . It's clear the Internet stocks have been some of the best-performing stocks, and retail investors as well as institutional investors want that product."

The old e-mail was unnecessary to expose the absence of fire walls between bankers and analysts on Wall Street. Their overlapping interests were hidden in plain sight. Spitzer's investigation did not expose a clearer picture of the inner workings of Wall Street during the boom. What it did give investors, who had no problem at all with banker-analyst conflicts of interest as stocks soared, were villains to blame after stocks tanked. And Spitzer also used this e-mail to suggest to an angry investing public that he had discovered some previously unknown dark truth: *Henry Blodget hadn't believed a word he had said.*

But to anyone who had followed Henry Blodget in real time, this was obviously not quite right. Go back and read what Blodget said and when he said it. From the start of his astonishing Wall Street career, he had a very specific conviction about the future of the Internet. He thought that Internet companies would displace their real-world counterparts. He saw that businesses with high fixed costs were at extreme peril. He looked at Barnes & Noble, for instance, and saw that it would go out of business if an online competitor stole even 20 percent of its revenues.

Even back when he first expressed these views, in early 1997, they weren't earth-shatteringly original. All sorts of respectable people thought the Internet would transform American commerce much faster than it ultimately did. And in the context of this sensational belief, Blodget behaved almost prudently. Many times he declined opportunities to pump stocks even higher than they were. Many times he cautioned investors against being too optimistic about e-commerce revenue forecasts.

Many times he acknowledged that what he did for a living was largely guesswork. Around the time of his name-making, correct prediction that Amazon's stock would rise to $400 a share, a radio interviewer asked him what he thought of Merrill Lynch's more pessimistic view. "We are all looking into the future," he said. "We all have the same information, and we're just making different conclusions about what the future will hold." But what investor wanted to hear any of this? By the time Henry Blodget went to work for Merrill Lynch, the market was actually running ahead of Henry Blodget. By the end of the boom, he had gone from leading the market to trying to keep pace with it.

The most embarrassing thing about Henry Blodget was not that he was lying but that he was speaking his mind. He actually believed Amazon .com was a good long-term buy at $400 a share. He actually believed the Internet would be an engine for corporate profits.

No matter. The supply of scandal on Wall Street always rises to meet the demand, and Spitzer found what he was looking for. From the tens of thousands of Merrill Lynch e-mail messages, he culled one of Henry Blodget's written toward the end of 2000, which, when released to the media, did the job he—Spitzer—needed it to do. In it Blodget responds to e-mail from a Merrill Lynch banker who wanted him to express greater optimism about some Internet company. He writes:

> The more I read of these, the less willing I am to cut companies any slack, regardless of the predictable temper tantrums, threats and/ or relationship damage that are likely to follow. If there is no new e-mail forthcoming from [Merrill management] on how the instructions below should be applied to sensitive banking clients/situations, we are going to just start calling the stocks . . . like we see them, no matter what the ancillary business consequences are.

Out of context, during a crash, that sounds pretty damning. It sounds as if Henry Blodget never called a stock as he saw it. But in context, at the end of a boom that has made Henry Blodget a little god, who knows? It's hardly uncommon on Wall Street for analysts to play head games with their firm's bankers and brokers. To me, knowing Blodget's record, it sounds as if the young analyst is simply flexing his muscles. He's saying: if you mess with my turf, I'll mess with yours. It's hard to say. And that's the point: motives in any company, let alone a Wall Street one, are far too messy to be honestly discerned from a handful of carefully selected e-mail messages. The notion that they're more revealing of Blodget's true feelings than the public record is risible.

The Spitzer investigation is a curious exercise. It doesn't clarify history so much as distort it. It portrays the financial losses of countless madly greedy, very knowledgeable speculators as a kind of theft by a handful of people who acted in bad faith. Just enough of the texture of the financial 1990s has been (conveniently) forgotten to allow for this new, bizarre interpretation of the boom. At any rate, to judge from both the newspapers and the court filings, a lot of people have come to believe this story, and it's not hard to see why. It pays. It pays Eliot Spitzer, who gets credit for cleaning up Wall Street—which neither he nor anyone else will ever do. (Just wait till the next boom.) It pays investors who lost money, along with their ambulance-chasing attorneys, who now have fresh ammo in their lawsuits against Merrill Lynch. And, oddly enough, it pays Merrill Lynch. By forcing Merrill Lynch to agree that its advice was corrupt, Eliot Spitzer helped the firm avoid saying something much more damning and much more true: that its advice on the direction of stock prices is useless. Always. By leading the firm to the conclusion that it had misled the American investor, Spitzer helped it to avoid the much more embarrassing conclusion that the American investor had misled Merrill Lynch.

The whole of the muckraking machinery is designed to facilitate this simple inversion: the culprits of the 1990s, reckless speculators, are being recast as the victims. What the various investigations appear to be doing is cleaning up the markets and making it safe for sober investors. What they are actually doing is warping the immediate past and preserving investors' dignity along with their capacity to behave madly with their money the next time the opportunity presents itself. The rewriters of the boom are able to do this as well as they have because, for both legal and political reasons, all sorts of people who might resist the distortions are discouraged from speaking out. Certainly no one on Wall Street can defend himself without the risk of incurring legal bills far greater than he already has. Certainly, no public figure of any sort is going to stand up and take the position that the rich guys who have gotten themselves exposed and pawed over by the New York attorney general should be left alone. And so the attorney general, in effect, has the stage to himself.

At this very moment, Merrill Lynch is behaving just as it behaved during the boom: scrambling to get out in front of the mob. It has coughed up the $100 million it was fined by Eliot Spitzer, has run huge ads apologizing to American investors for its behavior, has publicly humiliated Henry Blodget and has said it will never again promote stocks it doesn't truly believe in. It's a pity Merrill didn't try a bit harder to defend itself. There is a lot to say, if not exactly on behalf of Wall Street, then at least on behalf of the recent boom Wall Street helped to fuel.

Silicon Valley Was Not a Bubble

The first good thing to say about the boom is what it did to the value system of the ordinary business schlep. It turned him from a person who complained about the company he worked for to a person who wondered, albeit for one brief moment, if maybe he didn't have his own better idea of how to do things. If he did, he went to Silicon Valley. What distinguished Silicon Valley from everyplace else on the planet was a) it had lots of start-up capital and b) the people who controlled that capital understood that, if you wanted to win big, you had to be willing to fail. Failure on Wall Street has always been construed as a crime. Failure in the valley was more honestly and bravely understood as the first cousin of success.

It's odd that their quest for justice has led the various regulators and prosecutors to big Wall Street firms. The striking fact about the boom, as it happened, was the insignificance of big Wall Street firms. The big Wall Street firms would never have had the nerve. The people who drove the stock market in the 1990s did not work on Wall Street. They worked as venture capitalists; they created companies. If in 1998 you told a venture capitalist that Henry Blodget—or any Wall Street analyst—would ultimately be held responsible for anything, he would have wondered what you had been smoking. You might as well blame the waiter for the size of the restaurant: the Wall Street people were the help. It might have been one of the most delightful aspects of the boom—the way it inverted the old financial status structure. All sorts of unlikely characters—seemingly half the population of India, for instance—now had a shot at fame and fortune.

Enron. WorldCom. Global Crossing. Adelphia Communications. Tyco. Bad things happened inside these places, no doubt about it, but these places were afterthoughts: the boom could have just as easily happened without them. The emblematic character of the boom was not Kenneth Lay or Bernie Ebbers or Dennis Kozlowski. The emblematic character was Jeff Bezos. Bezos was the original big-time Internet entrepreneur. He famously quit his job on Wall Street, threw his chattels in his car and drove across country to Seattle, with a view to transforming the book business. He thought it would take him 10 years. It took him 3, in large part because a Silicon Valley venture capitalist named John Doerr made sure Bezos had the capital to do it.

Three years ago Bezos was a hero and Doerr was the most vocal, eloquent champion of the Internet entrepreneur. By 1999 people in Silicon Valley actually wore campaign buttons that said "Gore and Doerr in 2004." Today Doerr has vanished from the public stage—"could not be reached for comment," they usually write, of a man who was just a few years ago impossible not to reach. Bezos has become something like an antihero, one of those Internet hypesters who was given a lot more capital than he deserved to create an Internet business that still—a full eight years later—has made only very small profits.

Many investors are trying to forget that they ever sank money into Amazon, and why. Various editors are trying to forget that they made Bezos their Person of the Year or their Most Influential Man of the Internet. Anyone on Wall Street who plugged Amazon.com is now a defendant, alongside Bezos and Doerr, in lawsuits brought by small shareholders who lost money on Amazon stock. There's now even a stage play, off Broadway, called *21 Dog Years*, in which a former Amazon employee named Mike Daisey takes full advantage of other people's willingness to believe the stupidest clichés about the Internet boom. "Daisey fears that he lost his soul when he was blinded by talk of stock options and strike prices and started to believe the myth of uncountable riches for all as soon as the options mature," reads an ad for the show. "He wonders if he, too, stopped being about something real." (It is convenient how people seem to discover the need to be "about something real" only after the money dries up.)

There are two things to say about all of this. More than two things, probably, but I'll control myself. The first is: look what Jeff Bezos did. That a Princeton graduate with a bright future on Wall Street would quit his lucrative, prestigious but socially pointless job to create a company—

well, that was a kind of miracle. That his company would actually realize its original ambition: how could that happen? But it did. Nearly $2.5 billion worth of books a year are now sold over the Internet, and some huge percentage of those are sold by Amazon. And even skeptics understand that those numbers are merely the beginning of a powerful trend. But who in 1996 had ever heard of Amazon.com? It was a silly name on a plaque of a small house in a bad neighborhood in Seattle. The very best a reasonable person might have hoped for in 1996 was that the oddly named Amazon.com would be acquired by Barnes & Noble and then ruined, to prevent Barnes & Noble from having to compete with it. Instead Amazon .com has lowered book prices, made it far easier for readers to buy books and thus increased the chances that an author will make a living. Is that a bad thing? (Nobody suggests that Barnes & Noble is unsound. But whose future would you rather have, Barnes & Noble's or Amazon.com's? Whose name?)

The other thing to say about the excessive ambition of Amazon.com is: was it so completely unreasonable for Jeff Bezos—or, for that matter, any other Internet entrepreneur—to behave as he did? It's easy to say so in retrospect but, really, at the time, what should he have done differently? He expanded as fast as he could because a) the market threw capital at him and b) he believed, rightly, that if he didn't he would be swallowed up by the competition. The job of the entrepreneur isn't to act prudently, to err on the side of caution. It's to err on the side of reckless ambition. It is to take the risk that the market allows him to take. What distinguishes a robust market economy like ours from a less robust one like, say, France's, is that it encourages energetic, ambitious people to take a flier—and that they respond to that encouragement. It encourages nerve, and that is a beautiful thing. As the business writer George Anders puts it, "The personality that allows you to be Jeff Bezos in the first place does not have a shutoff valve." If it did, Amazon.com wouldn't exist.

On June 3, 2002, Merrill Lynch published its first new, improved research report about the Internet. It was, as you might expect, designed to debunk all of the stuff Merrill Lynch was saying about the Internet two years before. In addition to the usual disclaimers, this one came with a little box on the cover that said, "Investors should assume that Merrill Lynch is seeking or will seek investment banking or other business

relationships with the companies in this report." The report, which promised to poke holes "in various Internet myths," focused on the academic
work of Dr. Andrew Odlyzko, formerly of AT&T Labs Research and currently the director of the Digital Technology Center at the University
of Minnesota. It quoted, derisively, both *BusinessWeek* and the former
chairman of the Federal Communications Commission, Reed Hundt,
for saying that (in *BusinessWeek*'s words) "Internet traffic is doubling every
three months." The problem with all that was said and written about the
Internet, according to Dr. Odlyzko, was that "there wasn't any hard data
behind it." The doubling of traffic every three months? "In every single
instance that I tried to investigate, I always ended up with statements by
people from WorldCom's UUNet unit. . . . I did not hear anybody else
make authoritative statements that their traffic was growing at this rate.
My management at AT&T would often talk about such growth rates, but
they were always careful to say Internet traffic, not our Internet traffic."

The point was: all sorts of seemingly reliable sources were assuming
that Internet traffic was growing at a rate that amounted to 1,000 percent
or more a year, when it was actually growing at somewhere between 70
and 150 percent a year. (It still is.) This is the assumption that underpinned Amazon's mad expansion, and, for that matter, the entire Internet
boom. Many Internet businesses that failed would certainly have succeeded if more customers were online. Internet businesses that succeeded
would have done better, more quickly. If Internet usage had grown the
way people were saying it was growing, back in 1996, all that unused pipe
laid by Global Crossing and WorldCom would look inadequate to meet
the demand. If that many more people had come online that quickly,
Amazon might indeed have put Barnes & Noble out of business in those
first few years.

And so Dr. Odlyzko makes an interesting point. But in doing it he
makes another, even more interesting one, albeit without meaning to,
that helps to explain the exuberance of the late 1990s. That feeling of
fantastic possibility everyone seemed to have by early 1997 wasn't just
manufactured out of whole cloth. Between December 1994 and December 1996 Internet traffic had grown at an unthinkably rapid rate. "During
those two years," says Dr. Odlyzko, "the annual growth rate was about
1,000 percent per year, doubling about every 100 days. . . . That really

was a period of manic growth." It wasn't until the end of 1997 that traffic-growth rates began to slow, and no one noticed.

In short, the financial climate the manic adoption of the Internet had given rise to persisted for several years after the manic growth slowed. In retrospect, this is hardly surprising, as by 1997 all manner of social and financial interests had aligned themselves with the growth rates of the previous two years. And, really, what happened technologically in this country between 1994 and 1996 was a kind of miracle. At the time who could honestly foresee what was going to happen next? Everyone was guessing; and if even Alan Greenspan couldn't exactly figure out what was going on, you and I can be forgiven our lack of prescience. It wasn't a question of whether this technology was going to transform many aspects of American business. It was only a question of how quickly it was going to do it.

A year or so ago a reporter who covers Silicon Valley for *The Wall Street Journal* sat in on a new technology company's conference call. Back when success was fashionable, they used to do this a lot, to get the feel of the thing, to write a "color" piece that served as a kind of invitation to investors interested in the IPO. *The Journal's* reporter had given the impression to the company's founders that she was sincerely interested in the company, but only on the condition that one of its investors, Jim Clark, the founder of Silicon Graphics, Netscape and Healtheon/WebMD, join the discussion. (Disclosure: My book *The New New Thing* was about Clark.) The reporter was shrewd. Had she called Clark directly, he would have no doubt avoided her. Like everyone else in Silicon Valley, Clark seems to have figured out that the media were happy to hold everyone but themselves accountable for the Internet frenzy, and so the best thing to do in these dark times is to hide in some well-stocked cellar. And sure enough, the minute Clark came on the line, the *Journal* reporter turned the conversation from the matter at hand into a grilling about Clark's behavior during the 1990s.

Of course, this very same journalist was, just a few years ago, a great fan of Internet companies. Like every other newspaper, *The Journal* was once interested mainly in fantastic success and added its share of fuel to the Internet boom. Now, like every other newspaper, *The Journal* is interested mainly in failure. Failure, even in Silicon Valley, is suddenly a form of corruption. And that's a pity. Because the other, earlier attitude actually produced some real, measurable returns.

Throwing Out the Boom with the Bath Water

If your measure of social progress is corporate profits, it is easy to take a dim view of the boom. It is more difficult to do so if you step back a bit and survey the bigger economic picture.

An obvious point about stock market downturns always seems to get lost right after one of them occurs. Stock market losses are not losses to society. They are transfers from one person to another. For instance, at the end of 1999, I sank a bunch of money into an Internet company called Exodus Communications. I was a greedy fool to have done it, but I had been to a Merrill Lynch conference (them again!) that featured Exodus Communications, and the story Henry Blodget and a few other people told was so good that I figured that even if Exodus Communications didn't wind up being a big success, enough people would believe in the thing to drive the stock price even higher and allow me to get out with a quick profit. Everyone else was getting rich without working; why not me? I should have sensed that the moment I finally decided Internet stocks were a buy is precisely when they became a sell. Instead, I jumped into Exodus Communications at $160 a share and watched it run up a few points—and then collapse.

What happened to my money? It didn't simply vanish. It was pocketed by the person who sold me the shares. The suspects, in order of likelihood: a) some Exodus employee; b) a well-connected mutual fund that got in early at the IPO price; or c) a day trader who bought it at $150.

About the trillions that have been shaved off the stock market in the past two and a half years, the more general question is: from whom did it come and to whom did it go? A coming book, *In the Company of Owners*, written by the sociologist Joseph Blasi and the economist Douglas Kruse with the *BusinessWeek* reporter Aaron Bernstein, ingeniously answers this second question. The professors combed through the record of stock-option sales by ordinary employees of the 100 biggest New Economy-type companies. And they found that, while the executives of these companies made off with great wads of cash, the ordinary employees, as a group, did far better. Through the boom, investors forked over $78 billion to the regular employees of 100 start-ups. The grunts of the bankrupt Excite@Home, for instance, made off with an estimated $660 million before their company went under.

The astonishing thing, to the authors, was the egalitarian structure of boom companies. "No other industry," they write, "has ever attempted, much less achieved, the depth, breadth and extent of wealth-sharing found among these firms." Of course, the recriminations of the bust imply that the "wealth sharing" was mainly a giant con game. But to anyone who thinks about it for even a moment, this obviously was not true. The people who worked for these companies, in the main, believed in what they were doing and proved it by holding on to many outstanding shares until the bitter end. Employees of Exodus Communications held some huge numbers of Exodus Communications shares at its moment of doom.

Back in 1984, an economist named Martin Weitzman wrote what should have been a world-changing book called *The Share Economy*. In it he described, as a kind of economic utopia, what would come to be the innovative corporate structure of the 1990s. Weitzman pointed out that recessions may be inevitable, but that their most tragic consequence, unemployment, didn't have to be. The layoffs that came with recessions occurred because wages tended to be "sticky," i.e., companies couldn't persuade their workers to accept lower wages in bad times. Unable to trim payrolls, companies instead laid off workers.

In bad times, in effect, labor overpriced its services. The solution Weitzman proposed was breathtakingly simple: make some part of what workers are paid a function of the company's fortunes. Give them stock instead of cash. In good times the stock would have more value and be the equivalent of a raise. In bad times the stock would lose value and be the equivalent of a pay cut.

For more than a decade Weitzman's idea was hailed as brilliant by his profession and went ignored by the wider world. Then, in spectacular fashion, it took hold. Suddenly a more rational structure—in which workers had a stake in their enterprise—gained popular acceptance. And now, just as suddenly, it is thought to be discredited. Why?

I don't imagine that stock market trauma is ever, in and of itself, a good thing for an economy. But this most recent one was not nearly so bad, economically or even morally, as advertised. The most forward-looking companies in America experimented with a corporate structure based on worker ownership. It made a lot more sense than the old-fashioned corporate structure. People like me who played craps with some hot stock received an expensive lesson about playing craps in the stock market. Our punishment was swift and just. It was the rewards of the boom that seemed, in retrospect, wacky and arbitrary.

But were they? Compare the boom, as many amateur historians now seem to want to do, to the early-17th-century tulip craze in Holland. If speculators drive up the price of tulip bulbs to ridiculous heights, a result is a lot of rotting tulip bulbs. But if speculators drive up the price of tech stocks to ridiculous heights, a result is vast numbers of young people with technical training and a lust for entrepreneurship, a higher social status for the entrepreneur and, uncoincidentally, many interesting business ideas that are at the moment ahead of their time but one day may well be right of it. A result is also, in this case, hundreds of thousands of miles of surplus optical fiber, which is a bit wasteful—we don't need it yet—but not a total waste: we will need it one day soon. Another result, finally, is a lot of formerly sleepy big companies that had the living hell scared out of them by upstarts—and scrambled to make themselves more efficient. Say what you will about the boom: it kept people on their toes.

The massive transfer of greenbacks into the engineering department of American society had some useful side effects. Or, if you want to argue that it hasn't, you have some explaining to do. You need to explain, for instance, the continuing rapid growth of a great many of the companies created during the boom. "From the end of 1999 to the end of 2001," write the authors of *In the Company of Owners*, employment in the top 100 boom-era companies climbed 26 percent. That's 177,000 jobs. These companies have real customers and real sales, which have continued to grow after the high-tech bust and the demise of the dot-coms. As of July of this year, just 8 of the 100 have failed. Only 3 more beyond these experienced falling revenues. According to the authors, the rest are growing and have accounted for an increase of $59 billion in combined sales in the past three full years.

And what is to be made of the robust productivity numbers that began to roll in 1995 and continue to roll in to this day? "Productivity," which is the measure of output per worker hour, is by far the best measure of the health of the economy. It is the closest that economic statistics come to capturing the wealth of the nation. A coming paper written by Prof. William Nordhaus of Yale, to be published by the Brookings Institution, shows that, beginning in 1995, there was a mysterious surge in worker productivity. Mysterious because ultimately no one can say precisely where it or any other surge in productivity comes from, or why. But ultimately, Nordhaus would argue, "it comes from technological change. People find better ways to do the same things."

What were the late 1990s all about if not about using new tools to find new, better ways to do the same things? Indeed one way of viewing this entire financial period is as an attempt by the market to pay people for innovation rather than for profits, on the assumption that innovation, in the long run, would lead inevitably to greater profits.

The disjuncture between corporate profits and economic productivity suggests a couple of intriguing questions. The first is: Are corporate profits overrated? Not long ago Professor Nordhaus (who is, I should say, more of a New Economy agnostic than an apologist) asked a similar question: Do industries with high rates of productivity growth also enjoy high rates of growth in corporate profits? No. Just the opposite. That is, the industries of the future, the fast-growing ones, the ones in which people are most rapidly becoming more productive, are among the least profitable. American economic life tends always to conform to the interests of investors, but that doesn't mean that it always should. The Internet-Telecom boom is one of many examples of an extremely useful technology bursting upon the scene that failed to make corporate profits. There are huge, immeasurable social and economic benefits to improving the speed and availability of information; and yet companies have had, to put it mildly, some trouble making money by speeding up information or making it more widely available.

But the same charge might be made against a lot of other new technologies, starting with, say, the airplane. Warren Buffett, who got himself badly singed by US Airways stock, is fond of introducing air travel as an example of a technology that has regularly failed to make investors a penny. But what's bad for Warren Buffett isn't bad for America. We're not better off economically without air travel. Investors are simply better off steering clear of companies that sell it. The sad truth, for investors, seems to be that most of the benefits of new technologies are passed right through to consumers free of charge. (Microsoft, thanks to its monopoly powers, is the main exception.)

For this reason, sane, cautious investors like Warren Buffett make a point of avoiding high technology investments. For this reason, too, a sane, rational stock market channels less than the socially optimal amounts of capital into innovation. Good new technologies are a bit like good new roads: their social benefits far exceed what any one person or company can get paid for creating them. Even the laissez-faire wing of the economics professions has long agreed that government might profitably subsidize innovation by, for instance, financing university engineering departments. Government has obviously done this, albeit in a haphazard fashion. Still, there remains a huge gap between the optimum investment in technical progress and the amount we usually invest to achieve it. In this respect, the late 1990s were an exception.

That suggests another interesting question. Not: Were the late 1990s a great disaster for the U.S. economy? But: As a social policy, might we try to re-create the late 1990s?

The Old Old Thing Is Back

A few months ago there was a vivid illustration of the price we pay, not for the boom, but for the irrational reaction against it. It had to do with a money manager named Bill Gross. For the past 30 years Gross has run a very conservative bond fund in Southern California called Pimco; more recently he has also written a monthly online investment column. The column is an outlet for Gross's literary ambition. His articles are nicely written and fun to read. They were also generally ignored, until recently. That changed when a) Pimco, the closest place in the financial markets to that space beneath your mattress, swelled from $230 billion in assets to $301 billion and replaced Fidelity's Magellan Fund as the world's biggest mutual fund, and b) Gross decided he wanted to write about the integrity of American commerce.

Casting about for material for his March column, his eye fell upon an item in the "Credit Markets" column buried in the back of Section 3 of *The Wall Street Journal*. A woman at GE Capital was quoted saying that GE had decided to sell $11 billion in bonds because "absolute yield levels are at historic lows . . . so we think now is the right time to be doing an offering like this." That struck Gross as an outrageous lie.

Now at this point in the story any ordinary person might wonder, "He got upset by *that*?" Yes, he did. "Historic lows?" Gross thundered in his column. Then he proceeded to talk bond talk. "Maybe three months and 100 basis points ago, but not now, I'm afraid." He then went on to explain to his readers what GE was actually doing: shoring up its balance sheet on the sly. During the boom GE had taken advantage of low short-term interest rates and investor lassitude to borrow a lot of money short term, and less money long term. It was like the owner of a house who had opted for the 30-day floating-rate instead of the 30-year fixed-rate mortgage: it was exposed to rising interest rates. At any moment, investors might change their minds about the company and cease to lend it money; if they weren't going to do it on their own, Gross was going to help them. "GE Capital," wrote Gross, "has been allowed to accumulate $50 billion of unbacked commercial paper"—short-term loans—"because of the lack of market discipline. By issuing $11 billion in debt, GE was sensing its vulnerability." Gross concluded by charging GE with dishonesty, and saying that "Pimco will own no GE commercial paper in the foreseeable future."

A few hours after Gross hit "send" and posted his column, GE's stock began what would be a quick 10 percent drop, GE's financial officers were on the phone to Gross making hysterical sounds and reporters on GE-owned CNBC were accusing Gross of talking down GE bonds so that he might snap them up cheaply for himself. By the time Gross finished explaining himself in late April, GE had lost a quarter of its market value, and the company was holding hastily thrown together conference calls to reassure investors. In the end, GE announced that it would restructure its operations. Gross had written his thousand words or so to slake his literary vanity and chosen, pretty much arbitrarily, GE for his material. He himself could not quite believe how much trouble he was able to cause. "My point was a· general one about corporate honesty," he says, more than a little sheepishly, "and I wound up hitting GE. And I really didn't give a darn about GE."

It's hard not to take pleasure in the misfortune of others, especially when those others are rich and powerful. Who does not squeal with delight when he sees yet another article about Jack Welch's divorce? But still: this is absurd. The country's biggest company, sensing its balance sheet is out of whack, goes and tries to do something about it and, for its troubles, gets swatted around by a bond guy in need of material for his column.

At any rate, when a bond guy can terrorize GE, it isn't GE who suffers. Not really. Raise the cost of capital to GE, and GE can live with it. GE doesn't like it, but GE can live with it. The person who really suffers from terror in the financial markets is the person who needs capital and who is on the brink of not getting it. The capital markets are a game of crack the whip: the gentle curve experienced by the big guy at the front is felt by the little guy in the rear as a back-snapping hairpin turn. When GE can be terrorized by a single mutual fund is when the venture capitalists of Silicon Valley start giving back the $100 billion of capital to its original owners, rather than invest it in start-ups.

That's the odd thing about the present moment: it is widely understood as a populist uprising against business elites. It's closer to an elitist uprising against popular capitalism. It's a backlash against the excessive opportunity afforded the masses. (No more free capital!)

The big issue in capitalism is who gets capital, and on what terms. And when the little guy does not get capital, the big guy usually benefits. Look around. Who is winning the bust? The old guard. Corporate authority of the ancient, hoary kind, bond traders, leveraged-buyout firms, regulated utilities. There's no more talk of the need to break up Microsoft. Instead there's new talk about letting AT&T get back together again. Even the big Wall Street firms, beleaguered as they might seem, have probably actually improved their positions relative to online brokers.

The Virtues of Vice

There's plenty to criticize about American financial life, but the problems are less with rule-breaking than with the game itself. Even in the most fastidious of times it is boorishly single-minded. It elevates the desire to make money over other, nobler desires. It's more than a little nuts for a man who has a billion dollars to devote his life to making another billion, but that's what some of our most exalted citizens do, over and over again. That's who we are; that's how we seem to like to spend our time. Americans are incapable of hating the rich; certainly they will always prefer them to the poor. The boom and everything that went with it—the hype, the hope, the mad scramble for a piece of the action, the ever escalating definition of "rich," the grotesque ratcheting up of executive pay—is much closer to our hearts than the bust and everything that goes with it. People who view us from a distance understand this. That's why when they want to attack us, they blow up the World Trade Center and not the Securities and Exchange Commission. Why don't we understand this about ourselves?

It is deplorable that some executives fiddled their books and stole from their companies. But their behavior was, in the grand scheme of things, trivial. Less than trivial: expected. A boom without crooks is like a dog without fleas. It doesn't happen. Why is that? Why do periods of great prosperity always wind up being periods of great scandal? It's not that it happens occasionally. It happens every time. The railroad boom makes the Internet boom look clean. The Wall Street boom of the 1980s, the conglomerate boom of the 1960s, when they came to an end, had their evil villains and were followed by regulatory zeal that appears to have had exactly zero effect the next time the stock market went up.

Is it possible that scandal is somehow an essential ingredient in capitalism? That a healthy free-market economy must tempt a certain number of people to behave corruptly, and that a certain number of these will do so? That the crooks are not a sign that something is rotten but that something is working more or less as it was meant to work? After all, a market economy is premised on a system of incentives designed to encourage an ignoble human trait: self-interest. Is it all that shocking that, when this system undergoes an exciting positive transformation, self-interest spins out of control?

Of course, it is good that the crooks are rounded up. We can all move on feeling as if justice was done, and perhaps the next time around fewer people will succumb to temptation. But in the meantime it's worth asking: how did the crooks get away with it in the first place? Where were the bold regulators and the fire-breathing journalists five years ago, when it actually would have been a little brave, possibly even a little useful, to inveigh against the excesses of the boom? Where in the stock market of five years ago was Eliot Spitzer? (Fully invested with Jim Cramer, who wrote the book about how to use the media to juice one's own portfolio.)

Where was the press? Egging on the very people they now seek to humili-ate. The very people who are now baying so loudly for blood were in most cases creating the climate that rewarded corrupt practices.

Around the time the Enron scandal broke last October, there was a good example of just how effortlessly the celebration of the 1990s became the retribution of the 2000s. As gleefully reported by *Forbes* magazine, *Fortune* magazine was about to go to press with a cover article for its November 26 issue about the post-9/11 economy in which "the smartest people we know" were consulted. As it happened, one of those people was Kenneth Lay, the chairman and chief executive of Enron Corpora-tion. The issue was laid out, with Lay's picture right there on the cover when the Enron scandal broke. You might think that would pose a big problem for *Fortune* magazine, but if it did, the magazine didn't show it. Using a nifty 1990s piece of photo-editing software, the editors were able to erase Ken Lay. *Fortune* published on schedule and, ignoring all the flattery it had lavished on Enron over the past few years, piled right onto the scandal. It took only a few months before two of *Fortune*'s writers had sold their Enron book for $1.4 million.

Good for them, I say. We all have to earn a living. But the next time some editor, or regulator, or politician seeking re-election, begins to shriek about the iniquities of the boom, someone needs to turn to him and ask: where were you when it was happening? And if the answer happens to be, "Making the boom work for me," the best thing you can do is forgive him for it. Really, it wasn't such a bad way to spend your time.

PART IV

THE PEOPLE'S PANIC

One difference between the previous financial panics and the real estate and subprime-mortgage collapse is the sheer number of people involved. "No money down" was an invitation for people far away from Wall Street to take Wall Street-like risks. Just about everyone in America could afford no money down. It wasn't a financial market that panicked, it was the larger society; and the list of people and ideas that could plausibly be blamed for the mess was long: ratings agencies, mortgage brokers, mortgage originators, Bill Clinton. Gretchen Morgenson at the *New York Times* blamed Wall Street, for exploiting the middle class. Wall Street people—who lost a lot more money than the poor—blamed their CEOs. The brokers at Merrill Lynch blamed Stan O'Neal, and bankers at Bear Stearns blamed Jimmy Cayne. I wrote a satirical piece—included here—blaming poor people. Seen from the point of view of a rich hedge fund trader, the subprime-mortgage mess looked like a gigantic con perpetrated upon rich people, such as himself, by the poor, who had the hedge fund manager-like audacity to take whatever money was offered to them. Few saw the satire. Some readers were upset by the callousness of hedge fund traders. Many agreed with me, and hoped I'd run for president and teach the poor a lesson.

The 1987 stock market crash was blamed on program trading; the Asian currency crisis was blamed on some combination of hedge funds and IMF-induced policies; the Internet bubble was blamed on Wall Street analysts. The subprime-mortgage panic has yet to find its one big culprit, and I'm not sure it ever will. I've tried hard to include a glimpse of all the putative villains, but the task has proved impossible. I've failed to locate, for instance, anything really interesting written about several of the Wall

Street CEOs who led their firms to oblivion. On the other hand, a lot of great stuff has been written and said about this mess. This section opens with Dave Barry's very funny book excerpt that, almost inadvertently, gets to the bottom of the panic: the long-standing and hard-sold American belief that the way to get rich is to buy a house. There's a brief piece by Jim Surowiecki about the role of the mortgage lenders and a superb piece from the *Wall Street Journal* chronicling the collapse of Bear Stearns. John Cassidy is back again, with a reported essay from *The New Yorker* in which (in 2002!) he not only predicted the crash but blamed Alan Greenspan for it. Anyone who wonders how long prices can continue to rise after they have reached the point where, to some intelligent outside observer, they appear insane now has one answer: four years.

Just now there's a feeling in the air that the American financial system has reached some kind of terminus. In an interesting column, included here, Paul Krugman makes the distinction between liquidity and solvency. It's one thing to need money to tide you over until the next payday. It's another to need money because there are no more paydays. In this crisis, unlike the previous three, our problem is not liquidity but solvency. We can't afford to run our financial system in this manner. Another difference between this panic and the others is the sheer amount of destruction it's caused inside big Wall Street firms. As of this writing one big firm has collapsed, five CEOs have been fired, 50,000 Wall Street jobs have been lost, and Wall Street shareholders have lost more than a trillion dollars. It's unlikely that markets will allow the big firms to indulge in the same leverage as they have, or to use complexity to hide the risk being taken. It's going to be hard for them to get into this much trouble again any time soon.

But that doesn't mean that the game is over. Since the crash of 1987, when the government set out explicitly to prevent this sort of thing from happening again, the cycles of euphoria and panic have become more and more thrilling: whoever has been seeking to minimize drama in the financial markets has been doing a poor job of it. Step back from it and you can't help but wonder if anyone is really trying. If perhaps this is the nature of global capitalism—ever more complex, ever more opaque, ever faster booms and busts—and it's not the markets that need to change but our reaction to them. How many times does the end of the world as we know it need to arrive before we realize that it's not the end of the world as we know it?

At the bottom of the modern financial markets are the incentives that people who manage money have been allowed to create for themselves by investors who continue to place far too much faith in their wisdom. Our allocators of capital, when they make huge sums of money, are allowed to keep a huge chunk of the winnings; if they lose a huge sum of money, they walk away debt-free—and create another hedge fund. (See Matthew Lynn's piece on hedge funds, below, and note the losses of John Meriwether's new fund.) Before the subprime collapse, the big Wall Street firms had turned themselves into giant hedge funds, with their profits, increasingly, coming from their trading. It's easy to imagine this changing, and these firms becoming less risky and less profitable businesses, and the people inside them making a lot less money. It's harder to imagine the people who are taking home tens of millions of dollars a year for themselves by making big bets with other people's money becoming glorified bank tellers. More likely, the subprime-mortgage panic will accelerate the trend of the action moving out of these bigger firms into smaller hedge funds.

The critical document from this drama—the takeaway—may be Gregory Zuckerman's riveting *Wall Street Journal* piece, part of Zuckerman's forthcoming book, that introduced the world to John Paulson. A hedge fund manager no one had ever heard of, Paulson took home $3.7 billion for himself shorting subprime mortgages. That is more money than anyone has ever made on Wall Street in a year; and you can bet his example has not been lost on others. Just the other day an item flitted across the news wires: Josh Birnbaum, one of the traders at Goldman Sachs who shorted the subprime-mortgage market, made the firm $4 billion, and helped it to avoid the same fate as other Wall Street firms, announced his resignation. He planned to raise a billion dollars and start his own hedge fund to invest in mortgage securities. To get whatever he wanted, everyone seemed to agree, he needed only to snap his fingers.

How to Get Rich in Real Estate

DAVE BARRY

from Dave Barry's Money Secrets

t's easy to get rich in real estate. You don't have to take any risk, or work hard, or even have a central nervous system. That's how profitable real estate is! How do we know this? The same way we know everything: television. Turn on your TV pretty much any weekend and click through the channels, and soon you'll see an infomercial featuring a real estate genius sitting poolside at a swank vacation resort and explaining his simple system for getting rich, which he has decided, out of generosity, to share with everybody in the world:

REAL ESTATE GUY: Hi! I'm Bob Pronghandle, and I'm sitting poolside at this swank resort connoting success because I want to tell you about my incredible program, Get Rich by Becoming Wealthy Making Big Money in Real Estate. You know, as I was driving here today in one of my several Rolls-Royces that I own because I have so much money from real estate, I was thinking about some amazing facts I'd like to share with you:

- Did you know that more millionaires got rich through real estate than any other way?
- Did you know that you can buy real estate without having any money?
- Did you know that over the long run, real estate always goes up in value?
- Did you know that every night, giant flying lobsters from Mars play Scrabble on top of the Chrysler Building?

Well, my incredible program, Get Rich by Becoming Wealthy Making Big Money in Real Estate, can show you how to *harness the power* of this information to break out of your loser infomercial-watching existence and achieve the lifestyle and Rolls-Royce quotient you have always dreamed of. But don't take my word for it! Joining me here poolside are two regular people like you, Norm and Gladys Hingler. Norm and Gladys, welcome!

NORM: Thanks, Bob. Good to be poolside.

REAL ESTATE GUY: Tell us about your experience with my incredible program, Get Rich by Becoming Wealthy Making Big Money in Real Estate.

NORM: Bob, in my own unrehearsed words, it is a dream come true. Our lives have totally changed. Like, last night, Gladys ate the whole jar of cashews from the minibar, and I took a look at the price and it was $12.50, and for a minute there I was like, "ARE YOU OUT OF YOUR FRICKING *MIND*, GLADYS? TWELVE-FIFTY FOR LIKE SEVENTEEN FRICKING NUTS??" Then I remember, "Hey! We're rich now, from real estate!" Although if you ask me, swank resort or not, $12.50 is a ripoff.

GLADYS: They weren't even that fresh.

NORM: It's OK to say "fricking," right? They told me don't say "fu . . ."

REAL ESTATE GUY (*INTERRUPTING*): OK, getting back to my program, Get Rich by Becoming Wealthy Making Big Money in Real Estate: Can you tell us how you found out about it?

NORM: Well, Bob, things were bad. I'd been working most of my life in the field of roadside fireworks sales, but it wasn't steady work.

GLADYS: It was two weeks a year.

NORM: So anyway, a year ago, two days before the Fourth of July, which is the height of our busy season, I had an on-the-job injury, which I won't go into the details of here.

GLADYS: He shot himself in the scrotum with a bottle rocket.

REAL ESTATE GUY: Huh. Well, getting back to . . .

GLADYS: Is it OK to say scrotum?

NORM: It was a freak thing, Bob. It's a little demonstration I used to do where I launched the rocket from my pants. I called it the "Fart of Doom." It's a great sales booster—kids love it—and I did it a thousand times with no trouble, but this one time, I don't know what the hell happened—bad fuse, probably—but next thing I know I'm an unemployed man with a third-degree burn on the old nutsack that would *not* heal. Gladys was changing those bandages ten times a day. Is it OK that I said "fart"?

GLADYS: Do you have any idea how much pus a burned scrotum can produce?

REAL ESTATE GUY: No.

GLADYS: Most people don't.

NORM: So we were hurting for cash, I tell you. We have five children under the age of three, and it got to the point where we had to choose between buying food for them, or cigarettes. *No* parent should have to make that choice, Bob.

REAL ESTATE GUY: No.

NORM: So there we were: Our kids were starving, and our rent was past due. They even repossessed my Bowflex machine.

GLADYS: Like you ever used it.

NORM: It was the *humiliation,* goddammit, pardon my French.

REAL ESTATE GUY: So things were bad.

NORM: They were terrible. We didn't have two nickels to rub together. Gladys was thinking about turning tricks.

REAL ESTATE GUY: That's awful!

GLADYS: Not really, I saw something about it once on *The Maury Show,* "Hooker Housewives." You can make good money, set your own hours. And it's not like I was getting a lot of loving from Mister Scrotum Wound, here. He still can't get his . . .

REAL ESTATE GUY (*INTERRUPTING*): So you were desperate for money . . .

NORM: Right, we were desperate, and just when I thought we had hit bottom, we discovered a money-making concept that changed our lives.

REAL ESTATE GUY: My incredible program, Get Rich by Becoming Wealthy Making Big Money in Real Estate?

NORM: No, robbing convenience stores. Not with a gun, of course; we're both religious people. We had this fake bomb we made with duct tape.

GLADYS: Inside it was Tampax.

NORM: I'd say, "Give her the money, or I set off this bomb!" It worked the first two times, but the third time, the guy says, "OK, OK! Here's your money!" But instead of cash, he pulls out a fricking *shotgun*. You can't trust anybody, Bob.

GLADYS: When Norm saw the shotgun, he jumped behind me and yelled, "Don't shoot me! It's *her* Tampax!"

NORM: I was thinking of the kids. They need a father.

REAL ESTATE GUY: So getting back to . . .

NORM: We ended up in prison, five to ten, and that's where I saw your infomercial, Bob.

REAL ESTATE GUY: You mean for my incredible program, Get Rich by Becoming Wealthy Making Big Money in Real Estate?

NORM: No, this was back when you were selling that kidney dialysis-by-mail program. Boy, *that* was a stinker, huh? I heard there were a *lot* of lawsu . . .

REAL ESTATE GUY: I don't think we need to . . .

NORM: But the thing was, I liked your style, Bob. First time I saw you, I said to Skag—Skag was my best friend in prison . . .

GLADYS: "Best friend," he calls it.

NORM (*IGNORING HER*): . . . I said, "Skag, this guy has something. When I watch this infomercial, I say to myself, now *that* is an infomercial."

REAL ESTATE GUY: Thank you.

NORM: So I started following your work, and when I made parole, first thing I did was get your tape, Get Rich by Getting Rich in whaddycallit.

REAL ESTATE GUY: Real estate.

NORM: Right. And Bob, in my own words, it is a dream come fricking true.

REAL ESTATE GUY: So you've made money?

NORM: Out the wazoo, Bob. If I can say "wazoo."

REAL ESTATE GUY: By applying the principles described in my program?

NORM: The what?

REAL ESTATE GUY: The principles of successful real estate investing.

NORM: Sure, whatever.

GLADYS: How come he made you get that tattoo, if he's your "best friend"?

NORM: Don't you make air quotes at me, bitch.

GLADYS: Oh, right, *I'm* the bitch.

REAL ESTATE GUY (*TO CAMERA*): There you have it: One couple's true story of how they achieved financial independence through my program, Get Rich . . .

NORM: At least I'm not a whore.

REAL ESTATE GUY: . . . by Becoming Wealthy . . .

GLADYS: Tell that to your "best friend," Skag.

REAL ESTATE GUY: . . . Making Big Money . . .

NORM (*LUNGING TOWARD GLADYS, KNOCKING OVER THE CAMERA*): I SAID DON'T MAKE AIR QUOTES AT ME, BITCH!

VOICE OF REAL ESTATE GUY (*OVER SOUNDS OF STRUGGLE*): . . . in Real Estate!

VOICE OF GLADYS (*BEING CHOKED*): WHORE!!

(THE SCREEN GOES DARK AS THE CAMERA FALLS INTO THE POOL.)

I admit that the preceding is not a totally realistic depiction of a real estate infomercial. The real ones are even stupider. But the message is the same: *Anyone can make money in real estate!*

The only problem with this message is that it is, with all due respect, a tub of whale shit.* I say this because I personally have, on numerous occasions, failed to make money in real estate. I've owned a string of houses, in good real estate markets and bad, and no matter what, I have almost always managed to not make money.

What's my secret? Simple: I make certain fundamental mistakes, and I make them consistently. These are proven, time-tested mistakes, and I believe that anybody—even somebody who has no previous experience losing money in real estate—can apply them.

* Pardon my French.

Mistake Number One: Buy an Older House

The reason people usually give for buying an older house is that older houses have "character." What do we mean by "character"? We mean "dry rot."

The problem is that many, if not most, older houses were built in the past. Back then, people were stupider than they are today, and one result was that they built their houses largely out of wood. This was a mistake, because wood—and you can look this up if you don't believe me—comes from trees.

What's wrong with trees as a building material? Plenty. Go outside and examine a tree. From a distance, it appears to be a sturdy, permanent object, but when you examine it closely, you discover that it is a living organism, like a big hamster, except that virtually every part of the tree is constantly being eaten, bored into, nested on, or otherwise occupied by a vast teeming horde of ants, beetles, worms, termites, vines, toadstools, spiders, mosses, hornets, woodchucks, birds, chipmunks, squirrels, snakes, bats, and so on. A tree is nothing more than a giant hotel/buffet for critters. This is why the tree must keep committing acts of photosynthesis and growing new branches: If it didn't, in a matter of days it would be termite poop.

Cutting a tree down and calling it "lumber" does not change what it is: It's still a tree. Building a house out of "lumber" is really no different from building a house out of pepperoni or Cool Whip. *It's still edible.* Sooner or later, critters are going to resume eating it. The most deadly critter is the dry-rot fungus, an organism made up of tiny but voracious spores that, when magnified 127,000 times, look like this:

There are millions of these things munching away at the typical house. The older the house is, the more they've munched, until in time, what's holding the house up, structurally, is paint.

And that's not the only problem with the older house. It probably also has an antiquated electrical system, installed back in the days when electricity traveled at only 57 miles per hour and wires were fashioned from goat hair and beeswax. The plumbing system—consisting of pipes made from some material no longer considered safe, such as arsenic-coated lead—passes water about as smoothly as a ninety-one-year-old man with a prostate the size of a bowling ball. The windows, which cannot be opened, are as effective against drafts as a volleyball net. The heating system, although it has been modernized on several occasions (most recently 1928) was originally designed to burn some fuel that is no longer available, such as heretics. The air-conditioning system, if there is one, was apparently tacked onto the house in a single frenzied day by unskilled workers using only chainsaws. The current roof was put on during the administration of Warren G. Harding; the attic insulation consists primarily of spider corpses; and the basement is prone to flooding, as evidenced by the presence of a thriving coral reef.

In other words, an older home is a giant collection of costly defects held together by a few coats of grime and latex. But many people, when they look at an older home, don't see these problems: They see *character*. I know this because I am one of these people. More than once I have had my brain paralyzed by what psychiatrists call Old House Delusion Disease (OHDD).

My wife and I bought an old house that had every known old-house problem, including termites, not to mention a grand total of one closet, and *an entire room that had no electrical outlets*—a clear indication that the house was not built by or for people with a need for, say, lighting. Were we discouraged? No! We thought it was quaint!

Here's how delusional we were. We had plumbing problems (of course), and at one point, in an effort to fix a leak, some plumbing guys were crawling around under our house. They emerged holding some yellowed, crumbling, rolled-up newspapers, which they'd found wrapped around our pipes, apparently as insulation. We carefully unwrapped one of the newspapers and found that it was a *Miami Herald* from 1927. It had a story in it about Charles Lindbergh.

So consider our situation: There we were, confronted with stark evidence that our pipes, in addition to leaking, were very old. It's like being aboard a boat in the middle of the Pacific and discovering that not only were you sinking, but also that your hull was made entirely of Triscuits.

And how did we react to this horrible news? We were *thrilled!* Charles Lindbergh! It was so *charming!*

The plumbers were also very excited, but in their case it was because they knew we would be putting all their children through Harvard.

Old House Delusion Disease is very powerful. Usually, when you buy an old house, you hire professional house inspectors. These inspectors are very thorough: They spend a whole day crawling around the house, and then they give you a detailed, written report, which says *DO NOT BUY THIS HOUSE, YOU IDIOT.*

Not in so many words, of course. The report breaks the house down by major defects, which are further broken down into sub-defects, sometimes hundreds of them. The house, according to this report, consists entirely of defects. You *read* this report, but because you have OHDD, none of it actually penetrates into your brain. Your brain remains impervious, even when the inspector goes out of his way to warn you about serious problems:

INSPECTOR: OK, there's something I want to show you here in the living room . . .

YOU: Don't you *love* the living room? It has such character! The molding!

INSPECTOR: Right, about the molding, I wanted you to see this. (*The inspector takes a screwdriver and taps the tip gently against the molding. The molding disappears in a smokelike puff of wood particles, through which can be seen, in the gloom, an exposed wire that periodically emits a shower of sparks, illuminating a dripping pipe covered with green slime. A rat darts past, pursued by what appears to be a boa constrictor.*)

YOU: Ha ha! These quirky old houses! That can be repaired, right?

INSPECTOR: Well, yes, I suppose it could, if you're willing to completely . . .

YOU: I'm not worried about cosmetic problems, as long as the house is structurally sound. They knew how to build these babies in the old days. (*You stamp your foot on the floor to emphasize this point. Your foot goes through the floor.*)

INSPECTOR: Um, that's another thing I wanted to mention. Your floor joists have been almost entirely eaten away.

YOU (*RETRACTING YOUR FOOT*): Termites? No biggie! A lot of the old houses have termites! We can just have it treated by . . .

INSPECTOR: Actually, it's beavers.

YOU: Beavers?

INSPECTOR: They're building a dam in the basement.

YOU:

INSPECTOR: I've never seen that before.

YOU (*RECOVERING*): The kids have been wanting a pet!

At this point the inspector, who has dealt with OHDD before, gives up and edges out of the room, taking care not to put too much weight on any one part of the floor.

You, of course, go ahead and buy the house. As a true OHDD victim, you would buy this house if it was actively on fire. Since it is yours, you begin calling what will become a never-ending parade of skilled, highly paid craftsmen, who will spend so much time at your house that eventually they will become a part of your family and invite you to attend their children's graduations from Harvard.

To summarize what we have covered so far, the first proven technique guaranteed to lose you money in real estate is to buy an older house. This leads us to:

Mistake Number Two: Buy a New House

Unlike old houses, which fall apart over time, new houses start falling apart immediately. Often the last subcontractors on the job have to spring from the house as it begins to collapse around them, like Indiana Jones in the Temple of Doom.

There are several reasons for this. First, new houses are crap. No, wait, that's unfair to crap. In parts of rural Nepal, people make houses out of actual dung, and these houses are much sturdier than new American homes in subdivisions with names like Manor Oaks Estates Phase IV.

One problem is materials. We've established that a major flaw in older-home construction was that the houses were built out of wood, a material that not only rots and burns but also is viewed as lunch by large segments of the animal and fungus kingdoms. So today, new houses are built out of: wood.

Yes! We've learned nothing! Only now, thanks to modern manufacturing techniques, the wood we use is much flimsier. Take the "two-by-four." This was originally a sturdy piece of lumber that measured two inches by four inches, which is how it got its name.* But over the years, the lumber industry—whose executives live in homes constructed entirely of stainless steel—has been cutting costs by reducing lumber sizes, so that now a "two-by-four" is more along the lines of a Popsicle stick:

Modern "Two-by-Four"

(actual size)

Scientists in the lumber industry are working day and night to reduce the size of the "two-by-fours" even more. They dream of a day, in the not-so-distant future, when a "two-by-four" will be invisible to the naked human eye, and a single termite will be able to consume an entire home in forty-five minutes.

Another problem with new homes is the quality of the builders. Don't get me wrong: I'm not saying there are no good builders. There *are* good builders: Their names are Arnold and Herb Frinker, and they are honest, competent, reliable, and reasonably priced. They retired in 1987.

But the rest of the field is pretty bleak. In parts of the nation, all you need to do to become a professional house builder is take a brief course and pass an exam that is not overly demanding, as we see from these actual questions:

Professional House-Builder License Exam Questions

1. What type of vehicle should a professional house builder drive?
   a. A truck type of vehicle.
   (Correct Answer: a.)
2. You're building a house for a customer who is locked into a very

---

* Its name is Harold.

rigid move-in date. You have repeatedly assured this customer that the house will absolutely, positively, definitely, no question, count on it 110 percent, be finished in six months. Assume that the date is March 1. When will this house be finished?

    a. You mean, like, *completely* finished?

    b. Not this year, that's for sure.

    c. How the hell should I know?

(Correct Answer: These are all correct.)

3. A buyer has just moved into a house you built and is calling you repeatedly to complain that there is a toilet installed in the middle of the living room; that there is no floor in the kitchen; and that hot water is gushing from the electrical outlets. How do you respond to these problems?

    a. Get a new phone number.

    b. Explain that these are normal things caused by the house "settling."

    c. What problems?

(Correct answer: There is nothing wrong with any of these answers.)

To review what we have learned about real estate so far: It is a huge mistake to buy an older house, because it will fall apart and you will forever be repairing it. The same is true if you buy a new house. But you can't buy *any* kind of house unless you have money, which leads us to:

Mistake Number Three: Get a Mortgage

A mortgage is a great big wad of money that you borrow so you can buy a house that you cannot, by any sane standard, afford.

There are many different kinds of mortgages available, including fixed rate 30-year, fixed rate 15-year, variable rate 30-year, variable rate 10-year jumbo with balloon, variable fixed year 15-balloon jumbo rate, and 30 variably rated ballooning yearly jumbos, to name just a few.

Before applying for a mortgage, you should thoroughly familiarize yourself with the advantages and disadvantages of each type of mortgage. Then you should pick one at random, because they all work exactly the same way: Every month, you send a payment to your lender, and no matter how many times you do this, *you still owe the same total amount*. It's like the movie *Groundhog Day,* where no matter what Bill Murray did, he always ended up starting over in exactly the same place.

Fact: Inside the mortgage business, customers are commonly referred to as "Bill Murrays."

The difference is that *Groundhog Day* eventually ends, whereas a mortgage never does. To date, the Egyptians have made more than 55,000 monthly mortgage payments on the pyramids, and they still owe exactly as much on their mortgage—a 30-year variable jumbo balloon—as they did in 2600 B.C. (They're thinking about refinancing.) You should just accept the fact that you're going to have a giant mortgage balance until you die, possibly as a result of beaver bites.

Conclusion

As we have seen, real estate is an exciting field, offering many opportunities for a financial novice such as yourself to screw up. In this chapter, I have done my best to cover as much ground as possible without imparting a single shred of useful information. Now it's up to you to get out there and apply these techniques. Because as the late football coach Vince "Vince" Lombardi so often said: "If you don't get up off the bench and get into the game, you can never suffer a career-ending knee injury." Those words are still very true today, and although Coach Lombardi has passed away, I have no doubt whatsoever that somehow, somewhere, his mortgage lives on.

Shaky Foundation:
Rising Home Prices Cast
Appraisers in a Harsh Light

JOHN HECHINGER

The Wall Street Journal, *December 13, 2002*

Hotel worker Danny Ruiz was living with his wife and four children in a cramped New York apartment when he saw a television ad promising the family a way out. "Why rent when you can own your own home?" a Pennsylvania builder asked.

The company even offered to pay his rent for a year, while he saved for a down payment. So the Ruizes fled the city for the Pocono mountains, where they bought a three-bedroom Cape Cod in 1999 for $171,000. But when they tried to refinance less than two years later, the home was valued at just $125,000. "I flipped," says Mr. Ruiz. His wife, he says, "went nuts."

In a time of rising real-estate prices, how could their home have lost so much of its value? The Pennsylvania attorney general has a theory: an inflated appraisal. State officials have sued an appraiser and builder, saying they colluded to sell inflated Poconos property to 170 homeowners including the Ruiz family. The state has also launched a criminal investigation.

The case is part of a widening assault on appraisers, with consumer advocates, mortgage companies—and even many appraisers—questioning the integrity of the real-estate-valuation process. Federal prosecutors are focusing on inflated-appraisal schemes as part of an effort to root out mortgage fraud, which has risen sharply in recent years. Congress is revisiting regulation of appraisers for the first time since the savings-and-loan debacle of the 1980s. And more appraisers are finding themselves defendants in lawsuits arising from home loans that went bad.

To many in the real-estate business, unreliable appraisals expose the shaky foundations of today's hot housing market. Spurred by low interest rates, mortgages and refinancings are expected to rise 19% to a record $2.4 trillion this year. But with the economy stuck in low gear and sales slowing, many experts fear home prices could soon drop. If so, substantial blame may fall on the nation's 40,000 residential appraisers—much as Wall Street securities analysts are being criticized for hyping overpriced stocks before the Internet bubble burst.

Federal regulations require some form of appraisal for virtually every residential real-estate loan to protect lenders and homeowners against overextending themselves. Unlike loan brokers and real-estate agents, appraisers get paid whether the deal gets done or not, and the fee—typically $250 to $500—isn't a percentage of the price. A good appraisal requires hours of legwork, visiting a property to check its condition, and coming up with at least three comparable sales.

The profession first organized in the 1930s, when plunging Depression prices made valuing property more difficult. In 1989, when appraisers came under fire for valuations that supported shaky S&L loans, Congress passed a law establishing state licensing requirements for appraisers, including coursework and continuing education.

But Congress hadn't reckoned on a major shift in the lending industry: Few of the people involved in making mortgage loans these days have a long-term interest in them. Traditionally, bankers had made loans directly and held them, giving the lenders a strong incentive to find fair appraisals to protect their interests. Today, many appraisers are picked by independent mortgage brokers, who are paid per transaction and have little stake in the long-term health of the loans. Many lenders also have lost a long-term interest in their loans, because they sell them off to investors.

Appraisers increasingly fear that if they don't go along with higher valuations sought by brokers, their business will dry up, says Don Kelly, spokesman for the Appraisal Institute, the profession's main association. More than 7,000 appraisers have signed a petition saying they have been subjected to customer pressure and calling on regulators to forbid the practice.

P. E. Turner Jr., who has worked for 30 years as an appraiser in Richmond, Va., says the message is often subtle. If he doesn't agree that a property is worth enough to support a loan, a broker will just never call back with new business.

But three to five times a week, he says, brokers spell out what they want in black-and-white—as one did in a recent fax: "Please let me know first if we can get this value before charging customer," it says. "Do not do appraisal if less."

"The truly sad part about this is they are going to find some whore appraiser to do this when I tell them no," says Mr. Turner, who declined to identify the faxing broker.

In a suit filed in October in state court in Atlanta, the mortgage units of National City Corp. and two other banks accused developer Phillip E. Hill Sr. and two appraisers of duping them in a scheme that exposed them and other lenders to tens of millions of dollars in losses on more than 600 properties. The lenders claim that Mr. Hill relied on inflated appraisals and the appraisers received hundreds of dollars above customary fees for valuing the properties. Mr. Hill couldn't be reached for comment, and his attorney didn't return calls; the appraisers named in the suit, Fred Farmer, of Roswell, Ga., and Julian Perez, of Winston, Ga., also didn't return calls seeking comment, but in court papers Mr. Perez denied the allegations and asked for the suit against him to be dismissed. An attorney for Mr. Farmer, John G. Haubenreich, says: "Mr. Farmer's position is he did not participate in any fraud. All his work was done in a professional manner using appropriate properties for comparing values."

The Department of Justice says it has made fighting mortgage fraud a priority. In October, federal prosecutors won a conviction against a Washington, D.C., appraiser, James E. Golden Jr., who was sentenced to seven years in prison for performing inflated appraisals on 45 local properties so speculators could secure government-backed mortgages. Mr. Golden is appealing.

Prosecutors said Mr. Golden's co-conspirators bought distressed properties and then, using his inflated appraisals, sold them for a big profit.

The arrangement could net as much as $130,000 per deal. Twenty of the overpriced and poorly maintained homes ended up in foreclosure, costing taxpayers $1.5 million in repayment of the mortgage loans. The scheme would have been impossible without a "dirty appraiser," prosecutor Virginia Cheatham told a federal judge. To perform the appraisals, the government said Mr. Golden got up to $1,500 from others involved in the fraud—on top of his standard fee of $400.

The FBI says the amount of mortgage fraud reported by federally chartered banks and thrifts has nearly doubled over the last two years to $293 million. But John Gillies, chief of the FBI financial-institution fraud unit, says that vastly understates the total amount because half of all mortgage firms operate without a federal charter and don't report to the government.

The FBI doesn't track how much of the fraud involved appraisers. But the Mortgage Asset Research Institute, which follows fraud for the industry, says 21% of the cases it tracked in 2000, the latest year for which data are available, involved bogus appraisals, quadruple the percentage five years before, making appraisal-related schemes the fastest-growing form of mortgage fraud.

Alarmed by the trend, the U.S. Senate Banking Committee earlier this year asked the General Accounting Office to determine whether state and federal authorities are adequately overseeing the appraisal process. U.S. Rep. Jan Schakowsky, an Illinois Democrat, has sponsored a bill that would prohibit brokers from coercing or intimidating appraisers or tying payment for an appraisal to a desired property value.

In suddenly hot real-estate markets, especially those with new construction, properties can be especially difficult for buyers to value. Such conditions developed in the 1990s in the Poconos, a longtime resort destination for New Yorkers that was being transformed into a commuter community. Ninety minutes by car from New York city, the area offered homes far cheaper than closer-in towns.

Gene Percudani, a 51-year-old native of Queens, New York, built a thriving home-building business in this market, running folksy television ads offering New Yorkers new homes in Pennsylvania for as little as $1,000 down and $685 a month. Atop winding mountain roads, the developments featured gates and guards, tennis courts and swimming pools. Appearing in shirt sleeves, the telegenic, square-jawed Mr. Percudani sold a vision of country living, free of crime and crowds. "Remember," he would say, "All you have to lose is your landlord."

If they joined Mr. Percudani's program, called Why Rent, homeowners would find financing through another of his companies, Chapel Creek Mortgage, which brokered loans from J.P. Morgan Chase & Co.'s Chase Manhattan Mortgage unit.

For years, the Why Rent program appealed to police officers, teachers and others with modest salaries who had trouble saving enough money for a down payment. Before he moved to the Poconos, Eberht Rios, a truck driver for United Parcel Service, his wife, Elizabeth, and four children lived in an apartment in Jamaica, Queens, paying $710 a month in rent. In 1997, the couple bought a three-bedroom colonial in a development called Pocono Country Place, in Tobyhanna, Pa., for $140,608, with a mortgage of $126,450. "It sounded great," says Mr. Rios, 38 years old. "We couldn't get a house in New York for $140,000."

But in 1998, Mr. Rios was laid up with a back injury and was out on disability for four months, making it difficult to meet his mortgage payments. This year, when he tried to refinance, he was told the home was only valued at $100,000. "We came here to have a good life," says Mr. Rios, who emigrated from Ecuador at age 13. "We're struggling."

In the 1990s, one local appraiser, Dominick Stranieri, signed off on most of the Why Rent deals that state officials now say were overpriced, including the Rioses'. As a result, Mr. Stranieri now faces the attorney general's suit, filed in state court in Harrisburg. In an unrelated case, Mr. Stranieri paid a $10,000 fine in 2001 to settle state regulatory charges of inflating appraisals of three Poconos properties. He neither admitted nor denied the accusations.

In another lawsuit, filed in U.S. District Court in Harrisburg, Pa., Poconos homeowners claim that Mr. Stranieri overappraised their properties by 35% to 45%. The lawsuit, seeking unspecified damages and class-action status, accuses Messrs. Stranieri and Percudani of fraud and conspiracy.

James Sysko, senior deputy attorney general, says Mr. Stranieri told investigators Mr. Percudani's firm picked him because of his quick work and low fee of $250, instead of the typical $300 to $400. In exchange for a steady stream of work, Mr. Sysko says, Mr. Stranieri accepted without question valuations from Mr. Percudani's company. The lawsuit claims

Mr. Stranieri valued land at $20,000 to $27,000 per parcel that a Percudani family partnership had purchased for $1,250 to $12,000.

The homeowners and the attorney general in their separate suits argue that Mr. Percudani sought inflated appraisals to earn higher profits, and offset the cost of shouldering homeowners' rent payments—the critical element of his Why Rent plan. Under the program, before buying a house, customers would pay a monthly fee for a year toward a down payment on a home while Mr. Percudani's company paid the homeowners' rent.

The lawsuits also argue that Mr. Percudani misled homeowners into buying homes they couldn't afford. In addition, the attorney general argues that the program misled Chase Manhattan because it appeared that the borrowers had been able to save for a substantial down payment— often 10% of the purchase price—while making their rent payments. The state says Chase didn't know Mr. Percudani's company was actually paying homeowners' rent.

Freddie Mac, the government-sponsored buyer of mortgages, purchased many of the Why Rent loans from Chase. Worried about high default rates, Freddie Mac obtained new appraisals on 33 properties and found that they were each valued at tens of thousands of dollars less than Mr. Stranieri had said in his evaluations, according to an exhibit in the attorney general's lawsuit.

Messrs. Stranieri and Percudani deny any wrongdoing and say they operated independently. They say that any home that declined in value did so because of a weaker economy. "Mr. Stranieri believed then and he believes now that his appraisals accurately reflect the fair market value of the properties being appraised," says his attorney, Philip Lauer of Easton, Pa.

"It's like buying a stock," Mr. Percudani says in an interview. "The value goes up. The value goes down."

Mr. Percudani also says the rent payments reflected a legitimate sales concession common in the industry. He says the program was well known to Chase. Mr. Percudani has filed defamation suits against the local Pocono Record newspaper and its Web site, for articles it ran on his business and property values; the Record says it stands by the stories and is contesting the suit. Dow Jones & Co., which owns this newspaper, also owns the Record, through its Ottaway Newspapers subsidiary.

With many Why Rent homeowners falling behind on their payments, and some refusing to pay because of allegations of inflated appraisals, Chase Manhattan offered to forgive some of the principal amount owed on 258 loans valued at $35 million that it made through Mr. Percudani's Chapel Creek Mortgage. In all, 205 accepted the offer, reducing the amount outstanding by about $10 million. The Rios family's loan, originally $126,450, was reduced to $116,000. The mortgage held by the New York hotel worker, Mr. Ruiz, which was $153,900 to start, was cut to $105,000. Chase says it ended its relationship with Mr. Percudani's company in late 2000.

Chase, which declined to comment on either suit, says it cut the amount owed on the mortgages so that homeowners could remain in their houses.

Mr. Sysko, the deputy attorney general, says the state is now pursuing half a dozen fraud cases against Poconos builders he wouldn't name. Most involve allegations of inflated property valuations. State officials are alarmed by rising numbers of foreclosures, and fear more homeowners and lenders may face heavy losses. "It's like the value of these homes is built on shifting sands," Mr. Sysko says.

For his part, Mr. Percudani says he isn't surprised that later appraisals, or even different appraisals made at the same time, could result in different values. "Appraisals are opinions," he says. "Value, like beauty, is in the eye of the beholder."

The Next Crash

JOHN CASSIDY

The New Yorker, *November 11, 2002*

On July 8, 1949, the Long Island *Star Journal* published a full-page ad for a community of affordable homes that the developer Levitt & Sons was building on a tract of farmland near Farmingdale, about twenty miles east of Queens. The ad featured an eight-hundred-square-foot ranch house on a sixty-by-one-hundred-foot plot. "This is Levittown! All yours for $58!" a month, the ad read. "Practically everything you can think of is included in that price. Refrigerator, range, Bendix, Venetian blinds, General Electric oil burner, legal fees, appraisal charges—yes, sir, the whole works are in." Prospective buyers could choose from five slightly different models, which were all priced at $7,990. If they were former G.I.s, as most were, the government guaranteed them a mortgage, with no down payment.

As recently as the summer of 2000, there were houses for sale in Levittown for under two hundred thousand dollars. After the Nasdaq crash of April, 2000, prices fell for several months in a row, and Richard Dallow, the owner of the Dallow Agency, one of Levittown's leading real-estate agents, thought that the long-predicted property slump had arrived. He

283

had to reduce the price of one house from $199,000 to $189,000, and then to $179,999. It finally sold for $177,000. But in the fall of 2000 buyers returned to the market. To Dallow's surprise, prices kept rising right through the recession that began in March of last year, through the aftermath of 9/11, and through the first nine months of this year. "If we could buy that house for two hundred thousand dollars today, we'd grab it in an instant," he said. "Today, that same house would probably be in the two-hundred-and-seventy-five-thousand-dollar-to-three-hundred-thousand-dollar range, and it would go quickly."

Richard Dallow's family has been selling real estate in Levittown since 1951, when his father, Ted, moved there from Queens. Dallow has lived through several real-estate booms since joining the family business, in 1971, but the endurance of this one has stunned him. During the 1990–91 recession, house prices in Levittown fell by about a fifth, and they remained steady for several years. Dallow expected the current recession to cause a similar downward adjustment, but instead houses keep getting more expensive. "It has to impact at some point," he said. "But, then again, in the summer of 2000 I thought it was impacting, and then things came back."

By and large, the kinds of people buying houses in Levittown are the same as they have always been: cops, firefighters, janitors, retail workers, and others to whom fifty thousand dollars a year is a good salary. But now many of them have to apply for jumbo mortgages—loans of more than three hundred thousand dollars—which used to be reserved for the well-to-do. "Levittown has always been a low down-payment area," Dallow explained. "If the price is three hundred and thirty thousand and you put down five per cent, that's a mortgage of three hundred and thirteen thousand five hundred. You need a jumbo mortgage. For Levittown."

A few years ago, it became fashionable to deny what was, in retrospect, perfectly obvious: a speculative bubble had developed on Wall Street. Instead of warning investors to go easy, bullish analysts came up with increasingly outlandish justifications for stratospheric stock prices: the death of inflation; the rise of the Internet; a productivity "miracle"; the end of the business cycle; the aging of the baby boomers. Such rationalizations aren't heard much in connection with the stock market these days, but similar arguments are becoming prevalent in discussions of real estate. "The single-family housing market is not in a bubble, and I don't

think it is susceptible to a bubble," said Frank Nothaft, the chief economist at Freddie Mac, one of two government-sponsored companies—the
other is Fannie Mae—that provide mortgage financing to tens of millions
of American families. "The economic fundamentals help to explain a lot
of what we have seen with house prices in recent years." Nothaft ran
through a list of these fundamentals: the mildness of the recession; low
mortgage rates; the modest inventory of new homes; rising demand for
housing from immigrants and "echo boomers"—boomers' children who
are old enough to start families and buy a home. "We are not going to
see the price of single-family homes fall," he insisted. "It ain't going to
happen."

Many independent economists are also sanguine. Karl Case, a Wellesley
economics professor who specializes in the real-estate market, reminded
me that the average price of houses across the country has risen every
single year since the Second World War. Alan Greenspan, the chairman
of the Federal Reserve Board, has also dismissed comparisons between
the real-estate market and the stock market. Speaking on Capitol Hill in
July, he said that house prices reflected rising immigration and a shortage
of building land. Of course, Greenspan has a vested interest in keeping
the housing market humming. For the past eighteen months or so, he
has been relying on the stimulative effects of the housing boom to offset
a precipitate fall in business investment. If he succeeds in exploiting the
buoyant housing market to prevent a "double dip" recession, it will be
one of the great Houdini acts of economic policymaking.

Considering the way that Greenspan helped inflate the stock market
during the late nineteen-nineties, by keeping interest rates artificially low
and refusing to acknowledge the bubble, some homeowners might be
tempted to put their properties on the market while they still can. In Levittown and elsewhere, many of them are doing just that. "They are saying we are never going to see prices like this again, and it's time to sell,"
Richard Dallow said. In Manhattan, where the average price of a two-
bedroom apartment is now nine hundred and thirty-three thousand dollars, the number of properties for sale has risen sharply in the past couple
of months, but would-be sellers may have missed the peak. In March,
April, and May, the Corcoran Group, one of the city's largest real-estate
agencies, enjoyed the best three months in its history. Since then, the
volume of sales has fallen short of expectations, and prices have started

to slip. "Anecdotally, I can say that certain apartments are not getting the prices that they did in the spring," Pamela Liebman, the president and C.E.O. of the Corcoran Group, confirmed.

The market is softening in other affluent areas as well, including parts of San Jose and the Dallas suburbs. This may be what Wall Street analysts used to call a "healthy correction," which doesn't spread to places like Levittown, but it could also mark the beginning of something much more serious. "In a real-estate crash, the top end of the market usually cracks first," Christopher Wood, a financial analyst at C.L.S.A. Emerging Markets, a brokerage and investment bank, warned. "Then the bad news cascades down." In 1989, at the peak of the last real-estate boom, Wood advised his New York friends to sell their apartments and rent for a year. He is issuing the same advice again. "The American housing market is the last big bubble," he said. "When it bursts, it will be very ugly. In places like Manhattan and San Francisco, prices could easily drop forty or fifty per cent."

Even Nothaft concedes that prices can't keep on rising vertiginously. Over the next few years, he predicts, they will gradually revert to their historic rates of increase: between four and five per cent per annum. The many Americans who view their houses as their most important and enduring store of wealth will be hoping fervently that Nothaft is right. However, his optimistic prognosis inevitably brings to mind the declamations of stock-market analysts like Abby Joseph Cohen and James K. Glassman. While the Dow and the Nasdaq were on the ascent, these seers regularly predicted a reversion to more modest gains at some point, but they dismissed the prospect of a severe and lasting downturn.

Unfortunately, there is no reliable way to determine how much houses are worth. Many factors come into play, including location, size, condition, interest rates, and the overall state of the economy. In the end, the search for intrinsic value is doomed to failure: all assets are worth what somebody will pay for them. Twenty years ago, gold was worth seven hundred dollars an ounce; now its price is about three hundred dollars an ounce. In January, 2000, stock in Yahoo! was worth nearly five hundred dollars; now it is worth . . . well, no need to go into painful details.

Houses are less volatile than Internet stocks, but their prices vary greatly from time to time and place to place. Taking the United States as a whole, house prices have appreciated by almost forty per cent since

1997, which is the biggest jump in a five-year period since the late nineteen-seventies. Regionally, the pattern has been uneven. In San Francisco, house prices have risen by seventy-five per cent in the past five years; in Boston, they have virtually doubled; on Long Island, they have increased by about eighty per cent. Meanwhile, homeowners in other parts of the country, such as Mississippi, New Mexico, and West Virginia, have largely missed out.

If house prices are considered relative to income—a common method of assessing value—prices in the country as a whole are at their highest levels since the late nineteen-eighties. In San Francisco in 1989, for example, a typical house was selling for a price equal to three and a half times the average family income in the city. During the early nineteen-nineties, the ratio of house prices to income fell, to two and a half. Last year, it moved back above three. In Boston, New York, and Washington, the pattern is similar. Meanwhile, the ratio of house prices to rents has risen to an all-time high. "Valuation looks quite extreme, and not just at the top end," Ian Morris, the chief United States economist at HSBC Bank, said. "Even normal mom-and-pop homes are now very expensive relative to income."

Of course, most people who buy or sell a home don't look at valuation ratios. Potential sellers look at what other homes in the area have fetched; potential buyers work out whether they can afford the monthly payments. Low interest rates and ready access to credit are the main things propelling the market. Last month, the fixed rate on a thirty-year mortgage dropped below six per cent for the first time since 1965.

Richard Dallow ran through the financial arithmetic facing a young couple who buy a home in Levittown for three hundred and forty thousand dollars. Assuming they put five per cent down, their monthly mortgage payments come to about two thousand dollars. Including property taxes and utilities, Dallow estimated the couple's total monthly housing costs at about three thousand dollars. This may sound like a lot of money for a city cop earning less than fifty thousand dollars a year, but the government subsidizes house buyers with a generous tax break on interest, and in most families there are two wage earners. "When I first started in the business, people could afford a house on one income," he said. "Today, the husband and the wife both work, and the husband generally works two jobs, just to make ends meet."

Developments in the financial industry have also made it easier for middle-class families to get big loans. Many real-estate agents now have an in-house mortgage broker who can go online and arrange a loan from any one of dozens of financial institutions. "That is one of the things that has changed drastically," Dallow said. "We get people approved within a few hours. Some of them don't even need approval. They come pre-approved." Twenty years ago, lenders used to set a strict limit of twenty-eight per cent of gross income for mortgage repayments. Today, they rely on software programs, which also take into account the borrower's credit rating, rental history, and other factors, and some homebuyers end up getting loans with monthly payments that are close to forty per cent of their income. As a result, mortgage-interest payments are consuming a record share of household income.

During the past decade, the Clinton and Bush Administrations have pursued the goal of increased homeownership by encouraging Fannie Mae and Freddie Mac to expand their lending. "Owning something is freedom as far as I'm concerned," President Bush said recently. "It's part of a free society." Thanks to low interest rates and to Fannie and Freddie, sixty-eight out of every hundred American households now own their homes, but worthy policies can have unintended consequences. Cheap money and declining lending standards are often associated with specula-tive peaks, which invariably are followed by busts.

Whether they realize it or not, homeowners who burden themselves with hefty mortgages are taking a risk, especially if they might need to sell within the next few years. In the housing market, affordability is not the same thing as sustainable value. Current interest rates reflect the depressed state of the economy, and they can't last. In the next few months, the economy could improve, in which case the mortgage rate would rise considerably. Should it reach 8.5 per cent, which is where it was in the middle of 2000, the monthly payment on a mortgage of three hundred thousand dollars would rise by about five hundred dollars, and many potential buyers in places like Levittown would be priced out of the market. If, on the other hand, a double-dip recession materializes, mort-gage rates may drop to 5.5 per cent, but unemployment will increase and many homeowners will be forced to put their homes on the market. At the moment, the jobless rate is only 5.6 per cent, well below its average level over the past thirty years, and most people are either employed or confident of finding work. But if unemployment rises sharply, as it does during most recessions, potential buyers will be too worried about their future to take on a big mortgage, and house prices will fall dramatically.

Realtors like to boast that property is much safer than the stock market, but that isn't always true. "Ultimately, the weaknesses that infect the stock market almost always catch up with the property market," HSBC's Ian Morris warns. After the stock-market crash of October, 1987, house prices rose for three years, but then dropped at the end of 1990. In Tokyo, where the biggest property bubble of the twentieth century took place during the nineteen-eighties, the stock market peaked in December, 1989. Real estate kept going up for another year, whereupon it collapsed.

A homebuyer needs to ask not whether prices are rising currently but how much future buyers will be willing to pay when he or she wants to sell. Many people seem to have forgotten what happened after the property boom of the nineteen-eighties came to an end. Between 1989 and 1995, inflation-adjusted house prices in San Francisco and San Jose fell by almost forty per cent. In Honolulu, the downturn lasted a full decade: between the second quarter of 1991 and the first quarter of 2001, the real price of houses fell by almost a third. These cases are not atypical. In housing markets where speculative bubbles have developed, falls of thirty, forty, or fifty per cent are often needed to restore balance.

When inflation is running at five or ten per cent a year, housing can be made cheaper without prices having to fall much in absolute terms. Sellers keep their asking prices steady, and inflation gradually eats into them. This is what happened during the early nineties in many areas. Today, though, the option of invisible price cuts is no longer available, because inflation has virtually disappeared. (In September, the consumer price index was just 1.5 per cent above its September, 2001, level.) If house prices have to come down in order to restore sanity in the real-estate market, the falls will be out in the open, where everybody can see them.

If the housing market does crack, the ramifications for the rest of the economy are huge. Since the end of 2000, housing has been the biggest source of spending growth in the economy, both directly, through increased homebuilding, and indirectly, through the so-called wealth effect. (When a family sees the value of its home rising, it is less apt to save for the future, because it is getting better off anyway.)

As anybody who has tried to hire a carpenter or a builder recently already knows, the country is in the midst of a construction boom. Every month, a hundred and fifty thousand new homes are being built, and in some areas land is getting scarce. The "teardown," once considered a California curiosity, is now a familiar sight in other places, such as the Hamptons and the North Shore of Long Island. When new homes are built, and when existing homes get more expensive, the country's stock of wealth increases. In the past seven years, about $2.6 trillion of housing wealth has been created, which translates to about thirty-five thousand dollars for every homeowner. This isn't nearly as much as the eight trillion dollars of stock-market wealth that has been eviscerated since the Nasdaq crash, but houses are distributed more equitably than stocks, which tend to gather in the portfolios of the already wealthy. Consequently, changes in house prices tend to have a bigger effect on spending patterns than changes in the stock market.

Many families have offset their losses in the stock market by refinancing their mortgages and taking out home-equity loans. During the past two and a half years, homeowners have raised more than three hundred and fifty billion dollars in this way, of which they have already spent more than a hundred billion, on S.U.V.s, furniture, and other consumer goods. In the words of *Fortune*, "The American home has become a virtual ATM." Should house prices start to fall, the cash machine would run out of money. Homeowners who bought at or near the top of the market would see the value of their homes fall below the value of their mortgages, a condition known as "negative equity," and they would try to rebuild their savings. In Japan, Britain, and Scandinavia, this process has in the past led to collapses in consumer spending, and the same thing could easily happen here. Businesses have already severely curtailed their expenditures. Were corporations and consumers to retrench simultaneously, there would be little that Alan Greenspan, or anybody else, could do to prevent a full-blown slump.

Homeowners wouldn't be the only ones to suffer in a property crash. In the past, the biggest victims were often banks that had extended dubious loans to house buyers and real-estate developers. During the past decade, however, the mortgage industry has changed almost beyond recognition, and banks now play a much smaller role. Today, when Citibank or J. P. Morgan Chase gives one of its customers a mortgage, it is usually acting as a broker. Once a bank has issued a home loan, it bundles it with thousands of others and sells it to investors, a process known as securitization. The investors receive the homebuyer's monthly payments; and if the homeowner defaults they suffer the consequences.

By far the biggest purchasers of residential mortgages are Fannie Mae and Freddie Mac. The two quasi-governmental enterprises are now among the biggest financial institutions in the country, with almost four trillion dollars in assets between them. Their remarkable growth has helped millions of Americans to purchase their first home, but it has also concentrated a great deal of risk in two enterprises that maintain a smaller capital cushion than regular banks. Fannie and Freddie both buy mortgages on which the borrower has put down as little as three per cent of the purchase price, and they're giving an increasing number of loans to people with suspect credit histories. Inevitably, concerns have arisen about what would happen to them if the housing market crashed. "They look O.K., but they are big, they are powerful, and they have systemic risk," Karl Case commented. "And it's not the kind of risk you can diversify around. You can't hedge real-estate values."

Frank Nothaft, Freddie Mac's chief economist, repudiated concerns about its financial stability. He reminded me that Fannie and Freddie have their own regulator, the Office of Federal Housing Enterprise Oversight, which is about to subject them to quarterly "stress tests," in which it simulates a sharp rise in interest rates and mortgage delinquencies over a ten-year period, and then checks whether they have enough capital to survive. So far, Fannie and Freddie have passed all the dry-run tests. "For a calamity to happen to Freddie Mac or Fannie Mae, you are talking about some economic scenario that is probably as severe as, if not worse than, the Great Depression," Nothaft said.

Not everybody is convinced by this argument. William Poole, the president of the Federal Reserve Bank of St. Louis, recently warned that the sheer size of Fannie and Freddie could create a "massive problem in the credit markets." To pay for all the mortgages they buy, Fannie and Freddie issue bonds, which pay interest to their owners. What would happen, Poole asked, if the market value of these bonds fell sharply, because investors grew concerned about the financial soundness of Fannie and Freddie? "I do not know, and neither does anyone else," he said. Poole is hardly alone in expressing concern. A couple of months ago, Fannie's stock price sank after it announced that the recent wave of mortgage refi-nancings had adversely affected the balance it tries to maintain between its assets and its liabilities. (Fannie has since moved to restore the bal-ance, and its stock price has recovered some of its losses.)

If Fannie or Freddie did get into serious trouble, the repercussions would dwarf the problems at Long-Term Capital Management in 1998, when buyers and sellers withdrew from the credit markets and the finan-cial system almost seized up. That "liquidity crisis" prompted the Fed to organize a multibillion-dollar bailout, which a number of big Wall Street firms paid for. If Fannie and Freddie needed bailing out, taxpayers would probably end up paying for it. The federal government doesn't guarantee the survival of Fannie or Freddie, but it is unthinkable that it would let either of them fail. When it comes to housing, even the most ardent con-servatives in Congress tend to forget their free-market principles.

In Levittown, the prospect of a real-estate crash still seems remote. A few weeks back, I took a tour of some properties for sale with Bruce Golub, a Realtor in the Dallow Agency, who had just come from a clos-ing, at which a house sold for three hundred thousand dollars. Until a couple of years ago, Golub owned a bike shop in town, but a Target opened nearby, and he decided to go into the real-estate business. His first sale was for a hundred and sixty-three thousand dollars. Recently, he sold the same house again, this time for two hundred and seventy thousand dollars.

First, we visited an unmodernized Cape—something of a bargain at two hundred and fifty-nine thousand, but already under contract. Next, we saw a ranch that had been converted into a sprawling five-bedroom, with two separate wings. Its owners, who had moved to Florida, were asking three hundred and forty-nine thousand, and Golub was confident they would get it. Compared with the surrounding towns—Hicksville, Bethpage, Wantagh, East Meadow—Levittown is still relatively cheap. Compared with the North Shore of Long Island, where Golub lives, it is a bargain. "People are literally paying eight hundred thousand or a mil-lion for houses and tearing them down," he told me. "A small ranch sold on my block for eight hundred thousand. I'm driving down the street, I said, 'Where's it gone?' It wasn't there anymore. They are building a ten-thousand-square-foot home."

Like millions of Americans, the owners of that monstrosity are betting that bricks and mortar will continue to be the most secure and rewarding of all investments. If they turn the house into a home and live there for several decades, their gamble will probably pay off. But, if they are looking to make some quick and easy money, they may soon discover new meaning in the phrase "safe as houses."

As Bubble Speculation Rises, Industry Sees Little Fear

ROBERT JULAVITS

American Banker, *January 28, 2003*

For a year the public has been bombarded with newspaper and magazine articles exploring the possibility that the housing boom is a bubble about to burst.

"The Next Crash," screamed a November *New Yorker* article. "Is Housing the Next Bubble?" *Fortune* magazine asked in April—and then followed with a cover story on the issue in October. "The Bubble," a *Chicago Tribune* headline intoned that month.

But does a real estate bubble exist? And if so, how much pain would the mortgage industry feel if it burst in whole or in part?

"The more time that goes by, the less concerned I am about a housing bubble," said Doug W. Naidus, the chief executive officer of MortgageIT, a New York mortgage bank and the largest mortgage broker in the New York metropolitan area. "The fact that the prices have not been growing at an alarming rate in recent months suggests a softer landing."

Other players also say the market is sound. Though several mortgage executives acknowledged that a year ago they worried about a bubble, they said they aren't worried now.

Regional deflations are more likely, real estate and mortgage executives said. Trade group economists have repeatedly pointed out that never since the Great Depression have housing values dropped nationwide.

Brad Inman, who publishes the online real estate newsletter *Inman News*, predicted on CNBC in early January that local bubbles will deflate this year. The only question, he said, is whether they will burst or "let the air out slowly."

San Francisco, Boston, Atlanta, Dallas, and Seattle are singled out as markets likely to decline. Bay Area prices have already dropped, and real estate professionals in Boston, Atlanta, and Dallas say for-sale signs are multiplying there while the number of buyers shrinks.

But the national real estate and lending industries could easily weather downturns in a few regions, experts say.

Keith Gumbinger, vice president of HSH Associates, a Butler, N.J., mortgage research firm, said the issue gets a lot of play because many news organization are based in New York, Los Angeles, and other metro areas where prices have increased at lightning speed.

"If your perception is influenced by areas where prices are outrageous, you may fail to acknowledge that there are pieces of the world where prices have only increased a couple percent," Mr. Gumbinger said.

"Of course, they're out in the middle of a cornfield someplace," he quipped, "but normal appreciation is happening."

Some worry that warnings of a bubble could undermine consumer confidence.

"Sometimes it's a self-fulfilling prophecy," said Helen Garrity, the managing director of Nexstar Financial Corp., a St. Louis outsourcer for mortgage lenders. "If people talk about it so much or convince themselves that something is going to happen," it might.

Bill Campbell, a principal with the Campbell Lewis Communications public relations firm, agreed.

"Eventually there's going to be enough doubt cast on the marketplace that people are going to panic," he said. "And then suddenly real estate may fall, just as tech stocks did."

Many say luxury home prices have already softened.

Jonathan Miller is the founder and president of Miller Samuel Inc., which appraises New York residential real estate. Though prices have not dropped, he said, they have flattened; sales have slowed, and more properties are sitting on the market without buyer interest.

But business is still booming for homes worth less $1 million, Mr. Miller said, and the current climate is distinctly different from that of 15 years ago, he said.

"In the late '80s, when we went into the recession, we had a housing surplus that took seven years to absorb," Mr. Miller said, "but when we went into the recession of 2000 and 2001 we had a housing shortage."

Bill Griffin is the president and chief executive officer of Lender's Service Inc., a title, evaluation, and closing company in Coraopolis, Pa. He said he has seen no changes in lender behavior that would indicate serious concerns about a bubble.

Most lenders are focused on speeding up the mortgage process to reduce the mountain of refinancing and purchase applications at mortgage banks, Mr. Griffin said.

If lenders suspected that home prices were too high, he said, Lender's Service would see more requests for full appraisals. "We haven't seen a change in behavior patterns that would cause somebody to see a bubble on the horizon," Mr. Griffin said.

Still, nerves are fraying on the open-house circuit; many real estate agents say that in recent months more contracted buyers than ever before are pulling out of deals late in the process. One agent in Brooklyn said that after the *New Yorker* article in November, nobody showed up to walk through two open houses she hosted for co-ops in the $650,000 range.

Mr. Gumbinger of HSH said the increasingly public debate can unsettle new homeowners and those looking to buy. People who have owned a home for more than three years have less to worry about, because there is less chance that their appreciation would erode, he said. For those who bought in the last year—and paid an already "reasonably inflated" price for it—the specter of price declines would be much more troubling.

"Would a price correction of 10% to 20% be possible?" Mr. Gumbinger asked. "Yeah, that happens all the time in real estate."

Whatever happens, several observers said, lenders and developers are in much better shape than during the last realty disaster, when the savings and loan crisis led to the demise of many smaller financial institutions.

Housing was in massive oversupply in 1990; in contrast, supply was very lean when the recent recession began. Moreover, despite three years of economic downturn, demand for housing has barely blinked. The balance of supply and demand has kept sales brisk and prices climbing, experts say.

Because most lenders and third-party providers hand off loan risk to the secondary market, the biggest problems would come from plummeting business and revenue. Though some thrifts keep their home loans, the government-sponsored Fannie Mae and Freddie Mac buy most mortgages of less than $323,000.

Making up for lost income is easier than dealing with massive defaults. Moreover, experts say, a long, deep real estate downturn would escalate many recent trends, such as consolidation, outsourcing the mortgage process, and subprime lending.

Even in the secondary market, where most of the loan risk exists, the players are ready to withstand a major real estate recession, experts say.

Fannie Mae and Freddie Mac have enough capital to survive a prolonged economic disaster, their regulator said in late December. Armando Falcon Jr., the director of the Office of Federal Housing Enterprise Oversight, said they had passed a "significant milestone" in meeting that new test.

MortgageIT's Mr. Naidus said that the more distance the market puts between itself and the 2000-2001 recession without a major real estate meltdown, the less likely one becomes.

At the end of 2001 many industry observers predicted that interest rates would rise in 2002, undermining sales and the refi boom and pushing home prices down. With the economy struggling and unemployment rising because of troubled sectors such as technology, that would have been disastrous, they said.

But rates did not rise, and the mortgage and real estate markets remained torrid. As a result, many are much more confident. Mr. Naidus, for example, said the resilience of real estate suggests that the nation's economic troubles will spare home prices.

"The so-called bubble is not growing," he said. "It's becoming either static or slightly shrinking, and that lessens the likelihood of a burst."

But like everyone else contacted for this article, he acknowledged that no one really knows what this year will bring. After all, 2002 proved the experts wrong. Production probably topped 2001's record $2 trillion.

A cooling off now would be normal and healthy, experts said. In fact, Mr. Gumbinger said it has already started. The slump may feel especially sharp, he said, because the industry has been swimming in applications for three years. "You get so accustomed to running flat out that when you slow down to only the speed limit, it's going to feel like you came to a grinding halt."

But though "a shutdown would be very bad," Mr. Gumbinger said, "a slowdown is healthy."

This Is the Sound of a Bubble Bursting

PETER S. GOODMAN

The New York Times, *December 23, 2007*

Cape Coral, Fla.

Two years ago, when Eric Feichthaler was elected mayor of this palm-fringed, middle-class city, he figured on spending a lot of time at ribbon-cuttings. Tens of thousands of people had moved here in recent years, turning musty flatlands into a grid of ranch homes painted in vibrant Sun Belt hues: lime green, apricot and canary yellow.

Mr. Feichthaler was keen to build a new high school. He hoped to widen roads and extend the reach of the sewage system, limiting pollution from leaky septic tanks. He wanted to add parks.

Now, most of his visions have shrunk. The real estate frenzy that once filled public coffers with property taxes has over the last two years given way to a devastating bust. Rather than christening new facilities, the mayor finds himself picking through the wreckage of speculative excess and broken dreams.

Last month, the city eliminated 18 building inspector jobs and 20 other positions within its Department of Community Development.

They were no longer needed because construction has all but ceased. The city recently hired a landscaping company to cut overgrown lawns surrounding hundreds of abandoned homes.

"People are underwater on their houses, and they have just left," Mr. Feichthaler says. "That road widening may have to wait. It will be difficult to construct the high school. We know there are needs, but we are going to have to wait a little bit."

Waiting, scrimping, taking stock: This is the vernacular of the moment for a nation reckoning with the leftovers of a real estate boom gone sour. From the dense suburbs of northern Virginia to communities arrayed across former farmland in California, these are the days of pullback: with real estate values falling, local governments are cutting services, eliminating staff and shelving projects.

Families seemingly disconnected from real estate bust are finding themselves sucked into its orbit, as neighbors lose their homes and the economy absorbs the strains of so much paper wealth wiped out so swiftly.

Southwestern Florida is in the midst of this gathering storm. It was here that housing prices multiplied first and most exuberantly, and here that the deterioration has unfolded most rapidly. As troubles spill from real estate and construction into other areas of life, this region offers what may be a foretaste of the economic pain awaiting other parts of the country.

Cape Coral is in Lee County, across the Caloosahatchee River from Fort Myers. In the county, a tidal wave of foreclosures is turning some neighborhoods into veritable ghost towns. The county school district recently scrapped plans to build seven new schools over the next two years. Real estate agents and construction workers are scrambling for other lines of work, and abandoning the area. As houses are relinquished to red ink and the elements, break-ins are skyrocketing, yet law enforcement is resigned to making do with existing staff.

"We're all going to have to tighten the belt somehow," says Robert Petrovich, Cape Coral's chief of police.

Florida real estate has long been synonymous with boom and bust, but the recent cycle has packed an unusual intensity. The Internet made it possible for people ensconced in snowy Minnesota to type "cheap waterfront property" into search engines and scroll through hundreds of ads for properties here. Cape Coral beckoned speculators, retirees and snow-birds with thousands of lots, all beyond winter's reach.

Creative finance lubricated the developing boom, making it easy for buyers to take on more mortgage debt than they could otherwise handle, driving prices skyward. Each upward burst brought more investors—some from as far as California and Europe, real estate agents say.

Joe Carey was part of the speculative influx. An owner of rental property in Ohio, he visited Cape Coral in 2002 and found that he could buy undeveloped quarter-acre lots for as little as $10,000. Nearby, there were beaches, golf courses and access to the Caloosahatchee River, which empties into the Gulf of Mexico.

Builders were happy to arrange construction loans, then erect houses in as little as six months. Real estate agents promised to find buyers before the houses were even finished.

"All you needed was a pulse," Mr. Carey said. "The price of dirt was going up. We took that leap of faith and put down $10,000."

Backed by easily acquired construction loans, Mr. Carey's investment allowed him to buy three lots and top off each with a new home. He flipped them immediately for about $175,000 each, he recalls. Then he bought more lots, confident that Cape Coral and Fort Myers—the county seat across the river—would continue to blossom. From 2000 to 2003, the population of the Cape Coral–Fort Myers metropolitan area grew to nearly 500,000 from 444,000, according to Moody's Economy.com.

"Jobs were very plentiful," Mr. Carey said. "The construction trade was up, stores were opening up, and doctors were coming in. It kind of built its own economy."

In 2003, Mr. Carey became a real estate agent. The next year, he opened a title company. Then he teamed up with seven others to open a local office for Keller Williams Realty, the national realty chain. They hired 40 agents.

By 2004, the median house price in Cape Coral and Fort Myers had shot up to $192,100, according to the Florida Association of Realtors—a jump of 70 percent from $112,300 just four years earlier. In 2005, the median price climbed an additional 45 percent, to more than $278,000.

Lots that Mr. Carey once bought for $10,000 were now going for 10 times that. During the best times back in Ohio, he once earned about $100,000 in a year. At the height of the Florida boom, in 2005, he says he raked in $800,000. "If you just got up and went to work," he says, "pretty much anybody could become an overnight millionaire."

National home builders poured in, along with construction workers, roofers and electricians. But as a kingdom of real estate materialized, growth ultimately exceeded demand: investors were selling to one another, inflating prices. When the market figured this out in late 2005, it retreated with punishing speed.

"It was as if someone turned off the faucet," Mr. Carey said. "It just came to a screeching halt. When it stopped, people started dumping property."

By October this year, the median house price was down to $239,000, some 14 percent below the peak. That same month, he and his partners shuttered his real estate office. In November, he closed the title company. On a recent afternoon, he went to his old office in a now-quiet strip mall to take home the remaining furniture. He was preparing to move to the suburbs of Atlanta.

While speculators may find it easy enough to pack up and move on, they are leaving behind an empire of vacant houses that will not be easily sold. More than 19,000 single-family homes and condos are now listed on the market in Lee County. Fewer than 500 sold in November, meaning that at the current rate it would take three years for the market to absorb all the houses.

"Confusion abounds because nobody knows where the bottom is," says Gerard Marino, a commercial Realtor at the Re/Max Realty Group in Fort Myers.

Commercial builders are unloading properties at sharply reduced prices, sometimes even below construction costs, which further adds to the glut.

"It's our goal to clear out the inventory," James P. Dietz, the chief financial officer of WCI Communities, a Florida-based home builder, said in an interview two weeks ago. "We have to generate cash to make payroll." Last week, Mr. Dietz announced he would leave WCI at the end of this year to pursue a career in the vacation resort business.

At Pelican Preserve, a gated community set around a 27-hole golf course in Fort Myers, WCI has halted building, leaving some residents staring at mounds of earth where they expected to see manicured lawns. Half-built condos sit isolated in a patch of dirt, cut off from the road.

"It bugs the hell out of my wife," says Paul Bliss, 61, whose three-bedroom town house is next to a half-built home site. "She looks out and sees that concrete slab."

But the builder makes no apologies. "There was such a falloff in demand that it made no sense to build new units," says Mr. Dietz, adding that the pause in construction "doesn't in any way detract from the property."

Throughout Lee County, a sense of desperation has seized the market as speculators try to unload property or lure renters. On many lawns, a fierce battle is under way for the attention of passers-by, with "for rent" signs narrowly edging out "for sale."

In Cape Coral, foreclosure filings in the first 10 months of the year reached 4,874, more than a fourfold increase over the same period the previous year, according to RealtyTrac, an online provider of foreclosure information.

Elaine Pellegrino and her daughter, Charlene, see no way to avoid joining that list.

Seven years ago, Ms. Pellegrino and her husband bought their three-bedroom house in northwestern Cape Coral for $97,000, without having to make a down payment.

The land was mostly empty then. But as construction crews descended and a thicket of new homes took shape, values more than doubled. The Pellegrinos' mailbox brimmed with offers to convert that good fortune into cash by refinancing their mortgage. They bit, borrowing against the inflated value of their home to buy two businesses: an auto repair shop and a lawn service.

"We were thinking we were on the way up," Ms. Pellegrino says.

But last December, Ms. Pellegrino's husband died unexpectedly, leaving her with the two businesses, both deeply in debt, and $207,000 she owed against her home, which is now worth about $130,000, she says.

Disabled and 53 years old, Ms. Pellegrino does not work. She says she lives on a $1,259 monthly Social Security check. Her daughter, a college student, receives $325 a month for child support for one child. Charlene Pellegrino has been looking on the Web for office work for months, but with so many people being laid off, she has come up empty, she says. They have not paid their mortgage in four months.

"What can we do?" Charlene Pellegrino asks, as dusk nears and her driveway lights glow into a void. The rest of the block lies in shadows, with little light emanating from surrounding homes.

"We're probably going to lose the house," she says.

But not anytime soon. The Pellegrinos have joined a new cohort offered up by the real estate unraveling: they are among those waiting in their own homes for the seemingly inevitable. The courts are so stuffed with foreclosures that they assume they can stay for a while.

"We figure we have at least six months," Elaine Pellegrino says. "We haven't heard a thing from the bank for a long time."

As construction and real estate spiral downward, the unemployment rate in Lee County has jumped to 5.3 percent from 2.8 percent in the last year. With more than one-fourth of all homes vacant, residential burglaries throughout the county have surged by more than one-third.

"People that might not normally resort to crime see no other option," says Mike Scott, the county sheriff. "People have to have money to feed their families."

Darkened homes exert a magnetic pull. "When you have a house that's vacant, that's out in the middle of nowhere, that's a place where vagrants, transients, dopers break a back window and come in," the sheriff adds.

The county's Department of Human Services has seen a substantial increase in applications for a program that helps pay rent and utility bills for those in need. Half the applicants say they have lost jobs or seen their work hours reduced, said Kim Hustad, program manager.

At Grace United Methodist Church in Cape Coral, Pastor Jorge Acevedo normally starts aid drives this time of year for health clinics in places like India and Africa. This year, the church is buying Christmas presents for about 50 children in the congregation, many who are are in families suffering through job losses.

At Selling Paradise Realty, a sign seeks customers with a free list of properties facing foreclosure and "short sales," meaning the price is less than the owner owes the bank. Inside, Eileen Rodriguez, the receptionist, said the firm could no longer hand out the list. "We can't print it anymore," she says. "It's too long."

In late November, more than 2,600 of the 5,500 properties for sale in Cape Coral were short sales, says Bobby Mahan, the firm's owner and broker. Most people who bought in 2004 and 2005 owe more than they paid, he says. "Greed and speculation created the monster."

As much as anything, the short sales are responsible for the market logjam. To complete a deal, the lender holding the mortgage must be persuaded to share in the loss and write off some of what is due. "A short sale is a long and arduous process," Mr. Mahan says. "Battling the banks is horrendous."

Kevin Jarrett is stuck in that quagmire. In 1995, freshly arrived from Illinois, he put down $1,000 to buy a house in Lehigh Acres, in eastern Lee County.

Three years later, Mr. Jarrett left his mental health-counseling job and began selling real estate. He bought progressively nicer homes, keeping the older ones to rent, while borrowing against the rising value of one to finance the next.

Mr. Jarrett acquired a taste for $100 dinners. He bought a powerboat and a yellow Corvette convertible. (In a photograph on his business card, Mr. Jarrett sits behind the wheel, the top down, offering a friendly wave.) Last summer, he paid $730,000 for a 2,500-square-foot home in Cape Coral with a pool and picture windows looking out on a canal.

But Mr. Jarrett hasn't closed a deal in three months. He is on track to earn about $50,000 for the year, he said. Yet he needs $17,000 a month just to pay the mortgages, insurance, taxes and utility bills on his four properties—all worth less than half what he owes. Rental income brings in only about $3,500 a month.

Mr. Jarrett has not paid the mortgage on two of his properties in six months and is behind on the others as well, he says. His goal is to sell everything, move into a rental and start over.

He is supplementing his income by selling MonaVie, a nutritional juice that retails for $45 a bottle. He recently dropped health insurance for his family, saving about $680 a month. He is applying for a state-subsidized health plan that would cover his 9-year-old daughter. "I'm in survival mode," he says.

Many others are in similar straits, and the situation has had a ripple effect on the local economy. Scanlon Auto Group, a luxury car dealer, says it has seen its sales dip significantly—the first time that's happened in 25 years. Rumrunners, a popular Cape Coral restaurant with tables gazing out on a marina, says its business is down by a third, compared with last year.

Furniture dealers are folding. Hardware stores are suffering. At Taco

Ardiente in Lehigh Acres, business is down by more than three-fourths, complains the owner, Hugo Lopez. His tables were once full of the Hispanic immigrants who filled the ranks of the construction trade. The work is gone, and so are the workers.

At the state level, Florida's sales tax receipts have slipped by nearly one-tenth this year, and by 14 percent in Lee County. That is a clear sign of a broad economic slowdown, said Ray T. Kest, a business professor at Hodges University in Fort Myers.

"It started with housing, the loss of construction jobs, mortgage companies, title companies, but now it's spread through the entire economy," Mr. Kest says as he walks a strip of mostly empty condo towers on the riverside in downtown Fort Myers. "It now has permeated everything."

In recent years, Bishop Verot Catholic High School in Fort Myers had raised as much as $200,000 by selling goods at a dinner auction. Michael Pfaff, a Cape Coral mortgage broker, used to donate a weekend cruise on his 40-foot catamaran. But Mr. Pfaff's business has all but disappeared, and he recently sold the boat. This year, the school canceled the auction and is deferring building maintenance.

The county school district's decision to cancel construction of new public schools reflects a broader diminishing of resources. Developers have to pay so-called impact fees to the district to help fund new facilities. Two years ago, the district took in $56 million in such fees. Next year, it expects only $25 million.

New schools are no longer needed anyway, says the schools superintendent, James W. Browder. Many families connected to construction and real estate have moved away, so school enrollments are growing more slowly than expected. This could generate a snowball effect all its own: the new schools were to cost as much as $60 million each to build, so canceling them could mean further job cuts for the already reeling building industry.

Mr. Browder points out an upside of the housing downturn: Hiring people has become easy. In recent years, the school system struggled to find bus drivers, given the abundance of jobs at twice the pay driving dump trucks in home construction. "Now, we get 14 applicants for every job," he says.

The county government depends on property taxes for a third of its general funding. Since taxes are assessed based on the previous year's real estate values, it has yet to feel a dent. But agencies are under significant pressure to pare back in anticipation of a dip in next year's funds.

Tax-cutting advocates cheer this prospect. Governments have gotten fat on the boom, they say. A constitutional amendment facing Florida voters in January would expand tax caps for many residences statewide.

"All the local governments were drunk with money," says Mr. Kest, the finance professor. "Now, they're going to have to cut back and learn how to manage."

But local officials counter that they are already being forced to contemplate significant changes that could affect everyday life. The county's public safety division, which operates ambulance services, says it could be obliged to cut staff. The county's Natural Resources Department recently delayed a $2.1 million project to filter polluted runoff spilling into the Lakes Regional Park—a former quarry turned into a waterway dotted by islands and frequented by native waterfowl.

People who were priced out of the earlier boom here could wind up the winners. "We had an affordable-housing crisis," says Tammy Hall, a Lee County commissioner. "The people who were here for a fast buck are gone. You're going to see normal people go back into that housing."

When Andrea Drewyor, 24, moved to Cape Coral from Ohio this year to take a teaching job, she found a brand-new two-bedroom waterfront duplex in a gated community with a fitness center, a swimming pool and a Jacuzzi—all for $875 a month in rent.

At night, most of the units around her are dark. The developer can moan.

Not Ms. Drewyor.

"I like not having a lot of people living here," she said. "This place is awesome."

Opening Statement of Chairman Christopher Dodd—Hearing on "Mortgage Market Turmoil: Causes and Consequences"

CHRISTOPHER DODD

U.S. Senate Committee on Banking, Housing, and Urban Affairs, March 22, 2007

I want to welcome everyone to today's hearing, which we have entitled "Mortgage Market Turmoil: Causes and Consequences."

You cannot pick up a newspaper lately without seeing another story about the implosion of the subprime mortgage market.

The checks and balances that we are told exist in the marketplace, and the oversight that the regulators are suppose to exercise, have been absent until recently.

Our mortgage system appears to have been on steroids in recent years—giving everyone a false sense of invincibility. Our nation's financial regulators were supposed to be the cops on the beat, protecting hard-working Americans from unscrupulous financial actors. Yet, they were spectators far too long. Risky exotic and subprime mortgages—all characterized by high payment shocks—spread rapidly through the marketplace. Almost anyone, it seemed, could get a loan. As one analyst put it, underwriting standards became so lax that "if you could fog a mirror, you could get a loan."

Some of these loans have legitimate uses when made to sophisticated borrowers with higher incomes. But a sort of frenzy gripped the market over the past several years as many brokers and lenders started selling these complicated mortgages to lower-income borrowers, many with less than perfect credit, who they knew, or should have known, would not be able to afford to repay these loans when the higher payments kicked in.

I am going to take a few moments to lay out what I can only call a chronology of neglect:

Regulators tell us they first noticed credit standards deteriorating late in 2003. By then, Fitch Ratings had already placed one major subprime lender on "credit watch," citing concerns over their subprime business.

In fact, data collected by the Federal Reserve Board clearly indicated that lenders had started to ease their lending standards by early 2004.

Despite those warning signals, in February of 2004 the leadership of the Federal Reserve Board seemed to encourage the development and use of adjustable rate mortgages that, today, are defaulting and going into foreclosure at record rates. The then-Chairman of the Fed said, in a speech to the National Credit Union Administration:

"American consumers might benefit if lenders provided greater mortgage product alternatives to the traditional fixed-rate mortgage."

Shortly thereafter, the Fed went on a series of 17 interest rate hikes in a row, taking the fed funds rate from 1% to 5.25%.

So, in sum: By the Spring of 2004, the regulators had started to document the fact that lending standards were easing. At the same time, the Fed was encouraging lenders to develop and market alternative adjustable rate products, just as it was embarking on a long series of hikes in short term rates. In my view, these actions set the conditions for the perfect storm that is sweeping over millions of American homeowners today.

By May, 2005, the press was reporting that economists were warning about the risks of these new mortgages.

In June of that year, Chairman Greenspan was talking about "froth" in the mortgage market and testified before the Joint Economic Committee that he was troubled by the surge in exotic mortgages. Data indicated that nearly 25% of all mortgage loans made that year were interest-only.

Yet, in December, 2005, the regulators proposed guidelines to rein in some of the irresponsible lending. And we had to wait another seven months, until September, 2006, before that guidance was finalized.

Even then, even now, the regulators' response is incomplete. It was not until earlier this month—more than 3 years after recognizing the problem—that the regulators agreed to extend these protections to more vulnerable subprime borrowers. These are borrowers who are less likely to understand the complexities of the products being pushed on them, and who have fewer reserves on which to fall if trouble strikes. We still await final action on this guidance, which I urge the regulators to complete at the earliest possible moment.

Let me explain why these new rules are so important. The subprime mortgage has been dominated in recent years by hybrid ARMs, loans with fixed rates for 2 years that adjust upwards every 6 months thereafter. These adjustments are so steep that many borrowers cannot afford to make the payments and are forced to refinance, at great cost, sell the house, or default on the loan. No loan should force a borrower into this kind of devil's dilemma. These loans are made on the basis of the value of the property, not the ability of the borrower to repay. This is the fundamental definition of predatory lending.

Frankly, the fact that any reputable lender could make these kinds of loans so widely available to wage earners, to elderly families on fixed incomes, and to lower-income and unsophisticated borrowers, strikes me as unconscionable and deceptive.

And the fact that the country's financial regulators could allow these loans to be made for years after warning flags appeared is equally unconscionable.

We have invited the top five subprime lenders to testify today to explain these practices to us. Unfortunately, New Century declined to appear, even as they face a blizzard of loans going into early default. Their absence from this hearing is regrettable. New Century played a leading role in pushing unaffordable subprime loans and they should be here to explain their actions.

How many homeowners were sold loans they could not afford in the time that the regulators delayed? How many of these borrowers are still receiving these loans?

The people paying the price for the regulators' inaction are homeowners across America struggling to maintain their piece of the American Dream. Homeownership is supposed to be the ticket to the middle class. Predatory lending reverses the trip.

A study done by the Center for Responsible Lending estimates that up to 2.2 million families with subprime loans will lose their homes at a cost of $164 billion in lost home equity. In the words of the former Federal Reserve Board member Edward Gramlich, "We could have real carnage for low-income borrowers."

These are numbers. I hope we can stay focused on the human tragedies behind these numbers. We need to keep in mind Ms. Delores King, the elderly, retired woman who testified before us last month. Ms. King was advised by her mortgage broker to take out a new loan whose payments quickly shot up beyond her means, simply to pay off a $3,000 debt.

We need to keep in mind Amy Womble, our other witness, a small businesswoman and widow with two children, who was promised a mortgage at $927 per month and ended up with a mortgage costing her $2,100.

Both of these women are now struggling to keep their homes. We should not let them struggle alone. We need to let them know, and the American people know, that we intend to fight for them.

We will hear this morning from another victim, Ms. Jennie Haliburton, about these practices that cause so much hardship.

The challenges are clear. In my view, we need to take several steps.

First, we need to put a stop to abusive and unsustainable lending. The regulators must finalize the recent subprime guidance as quickly as possible.

Second, the Federal Reserve should exercise its authority under the Home Ownership and Equity Protection Act (HOEPA, pronounced HOPE-A) and the FTC Act to prohibit these abusive practices and products for all mortgage market participants, regardless of what kind of charter they have.

Third, I intend to work with my colleagues and all interested parties to introduce legislation to attack the problem of predatory lending. Passing such legislation will be tough—there are plenty of market players out there who stand to lose if we provide decent protections for consumers. But we must try to push forward.

Finally, we need to deal with the problem of the millions of homeowners who may face foreclosure after being hit with the payment shocks built into their mortgages. The solution to this problem may not be legislative. Instead, I intend to ask leaders from all the stakeholders—regulators, investors, lenders, GSEs, and FHA, and consumer advocates—to come together and try to work out an efficient process for providing relief to homeowners. I hope to have more to say on this in the next couple of weeks. One thing I know for sure—we cannot simply sit back and watch as up to 2.2 million families lose their homes and, with them, their financial futures.

Let me be clear, the purpose of this hearing is not to point fingers but to find solutions. We need to get to the bottom of this problem, understand thoroughly what went wrong, and then work to make sure we don't see a repeat of these problems.

Subprime Homesick Blues

JAMES SUROWIECKI

The New Yorker, *April 9, 2007*

Not long ago, New Century Financial—a mortgage lender specializing in loans to the subprime, or high-credit-risk, market—dubbed itself "a new shade of blue chip." Today, with its stock price down more than ninety per cent in the past six months and the company close to bankruptcy, it looks more like a new shade of Enron. And it is not alone. In the past year, more than two dozen subprime lenders have shut their doors. The percentage of their borrowers who are delinquent (meaning that they've missed at least one payment) has doubled, and predictions of more than a million foreclosures have become commonplace. As concerns grow that the subprime crisis could spread to the rest of the housing market, pundits and politicians looking for a culprit have seized on New Century and its ilk, charging them with causing the crisis with their "predatory lending" practices, duping tens of millions of homeowners into borrowing more money than was good for them.

The backlash against the subprime lenders is understandable, since their business practices were often reckless and deceptive. Instead of responding to the slowdown in the housing market by cutting back their lending, they pressed their bets—last year, six hundred billion dollars' worth of subprime loans were issued. Many of the lenders hid their troubles from investors, even as their executives were dumping stock; between August and February, for instance, New Century insiders sold more than twenty-five million dollars' worth of shares. And there's plenty of evidence that some lenders relied on what the Federal Reserve has called "fraud" and "abuse" to push loans on unwitting borrowers.

For all that, "predatory lending" is a woefully inadequate explanation of the subprime turmoil. If subprime lending consisted only of lenders exploiting borrowers, after all, it would be hard to understand why so many lenders are going bankrupt. (Subprime lenders appear to have been predators in the sense that Wile E. Coyote was.) Focusing on lenders' greed misses a fundamental part of the subprime dynamic: the overambition and overconfidence of borrowers.

The boom in subprime lending made huge amounts of credit available to people who previously had a very hard time getting any credit at all. Borrowers were not passive recipients of this money—instead, many of them used the lax lending standards to make calculated, if ill-advised, gambles. In 2006, for instance, the percentage of borrowers who failed to make the first monthly payment on their mortgages tripled, while in the past two years the percentage of people who missed a payment in their first ninety days quadrupled. Most of these people did not suddenly run into financial trouble; they were betting that they would be able to buy the house and quickly sell it. Similarly, last year almost forty per cent of subprime borrowers were able to get "liar loans"—mortgages that borrowers can get simply by stating their income, which the lender does not verify. These loans were ideal for speculative gambles: you could buy far more house than your income justified, and, if you could flip it quickly, you could reap outsized profits. Flat-out fraud also proliferated: consider the mortgage taken out by one "M. Mouse."

While some subprime borrowers were gaming the system, many just fell victim to well-known decision-making flaws. "Consumer myopia" led them to focus too much on things like low teaser rates and initial monthly payments rather than on the total amount of debt they were assuming. Then, there was the common tendency to overvalue present gains at the expense of future costs—which helps explain the popularity of so-called 2/28 loans (which come with a low, fixed-interest rate for the first two years and a much higher, adjustable rate thereafter). People were willing to trade the uncertainty of what might happen in the long run for the benefit of owning a house in the short run.

Another thing that led subprime borrowers astray was their expectation that housing prices were bound to keep going up, and therefore the value of their house would always exceed the size of their debt. This was a mistake, but one that many Americans have made in response to the real appreciation in housing prices over the past decade—how else could one justify spending two and a half million for a two-bedroom apartment in New York? Given the government's subsidizing and promotion of home-ownership, it's not surprising that borrowers leaped at the chance to buy a home even on onerous terms. The problem, of course, is that the cost of misplaced optimism is much higher for subprime borrowers.

The result of all this is that many subprime borrowers would have been better off if lenders had been more stringent and not granted them mort-gages in the first place; that's why there have been countless calls for the government to ban or heavily regulate "exotic" subprime loans like the 2/28s. But what's often missed in the current uproar is that while a substantial minority of subprime borrowers are struggling, almost ninety per cent are making their monthly payments and living in the houses they bought. And even if delinquencies rise when the higher rates of the 2/28s kick in, on the whole the subprime boom appears to have created more winners than losers. (The rise in homeownership rates since the mid-nineties is due in part to subprime credit.) We do need more regulatory vigilance, but banning subprime loans will protect the interests of some at the expense of limiting credit for subprime borrowers in general. And while the absence of a ban means that some borrowers will keep making bad bets, that may be better than their never having had the chance to make any bet at all.

Triple-A Failure

ROGER LOWENSTEIN

The New York Times, *April 27, 2008*

The Ratings Game

I n 1996, Thomas Friedman, the *New York Times* columnist, remarked on *The NewsHour with Jim Lehrer* "that there were two superpowers in the world—the United States and Moody's bond-rating service—and it was sometimes unclear which was more powerful. Moody's was then a private company that rated corporate bonds, but it was, already, spreading its wings into the exotic business of rating securities backed by pools of residential mortgages.

Obscure and dry-seeming as it was, this business offered a certain magic. The magic consisted of turning risky mortgages into investments that would be suitable for investors who would know nothing about the underlying loans. To get why this is impressive, you have to think about all that determines whether a mortgage is safe. Who owns the property? What is his or her income? Bundle hundreds of mortgages into a single security and the questions multiply; no investor could begin to answer them. But suppose the security had a rating. If it were rated triple-A by a firm like Moody's, then the investor could forget about the underlying mortgages. He wouldn't need to know what properties were in the pool, only that the pool was triple-A—it was just as safe, in theory, as other triple-A securities.

Over the last decade, Moody's and its two principal competitors, Standard & Poor's and Fitch, played this game to perfection—putting what amounted to gold seals on mortgage securities that investors swept up with increasing élan. For the rating agencies, this business was extremely lucrative. Their profits surged, Moody's in particular: it went public, saw its stock increase sixfold and its earnings grow by 900 percent.

By providing the mortgage industry with an entree to Wall Street, the agencies also transformed what had been among the sleepiest corners of finance. No longer did mortgage banks have to wait 10 or 20 or 30 years to get their money back from homeowners. Now they sold their loans into securitized pools and—their capital thus replenished—wrote new loans at a much quicker pace.

Mortgage volume surged; in 2006, it topped $2.5 trillion. Also, many more mortgages were issued to risky subprime borrowers. Almost all of those subprime loans ended up in securitized pools; indeed, the reason banks were willing to issue so many risky loans is that they could fob them off on Wall Street.

But who was evaluating these securities? Who was passing judgment on the quality of the mortgages, on the equity behind them and on myriad other investment considerations? Certainly not the investors. They relied on a credit rating.

Thus the agencies became the de facto watchdog over the mortgage industry. In a practical sense, it was Moody's and Standard & Poor's that set the credit standards that determined which loans Wall Street could repackage and, ultimately, which borrowers would qualify. Effectively, they did the job that was expected of banks and government regulators. And today, they are a central culprit in the mortgage bust, in which the total loss has been projected at $250 billion and possibly much more.

In the wake of the housing collapse, Congress is exploring why the industry failed and whether it should be revamped (hearings in the Senate Banking Committee were expected to begin April 22). Two key questions are whether the credit agencies—which benefit from a unique series of government charters—enjoy too much official protection and whether their judgment was tainted. Presumably to forestall criticism and possible legislation, Moody's and S.&P. have announced reforms. But they reject the notion that they should have been more vigilant. Instead, they lay the blame on the mortgage holders who turned out to be deadbeats, many of whom lied to obtain their loans.

Arthur Levitt, the former chairman of the Securities and Exchange Commission, charges that "the credit-rating agencies suffer from a conflict of interest—perceived and apparent—that may have distorted their judgment, especially when it came to complex structured financial products." Frank Partnoy, a professor at the University of San Diego School of Law who has written extensively about the credit-rating industry, says that the conflict is a serious problem. Thanks to the industry's close relationship with the banks whose securities it rates, Partnoy says, the agencies have behaved less like gatekeepers than gate openers. Last year, Moody's had to downgrade more than 5,000 mortgage securities—a tacit acknowledgment that the mortgage bubble was abetted by its overly generous ratings. Mortgage securities rated by Standard & Poor's and Fitch have suffered a similar wave of downgrades.

Presto! How 2,393 Subprime Loans Become a High-Grade Investment

The business of assigning a rating to a mortgage security is a complicated affair, and Moody's recently was willing to walk me through an actual mortgage-backed security step by step. I was led down a carpeted hallway to a well-appointed conference room to meet with three specialists in mortgage-backed paper. Moody's was fair-minded in choosing an example; the case they showed me, which they masked with the name "Subprime XYZ," was a pool of 2,393 mortgages with a total face value of $430 million.

Subprime XYZ typified the exuberance of the age. All the mortgages in the pool were subprime—that is, they had been extended to borrowers with checkered credit histories. In an earlier era, such people would have been restricted from borrowing more than 75 percent or so of the value of their homes, but during the great bubble, no such limits applied.

Moody's did not have access to the individual loan files, much less did it communicate with the borrowers or try to verify the information they provided in their loan applications. "We aren't loan officers," Claire Robinson, a 20-year veteran who is in charge of asset-backed finance for Moody's, told me. "Our expertise is as statisticians on an aggregate basis. We want to know, of 1,000 individuals, based on historical performance, what percent will pay their loans?"

The loans in Subprime XYZ were issued in early spring 2006—what would turn out to be the peak of the boom. They were originated by a West Coast company that Moody's identified as a "nonbank lender." Traditionally, people have gotten their mortgages from banks, but in recent years, new types of lenders peddling sexier products grabbed an increasing share of the market. This particular lender took the loans it made to a New York investment bank; the bank designed an investment vehicle and brought the package to Moody's.

Moody's assigned an analyst to evaluate the package, subject to review by a committee. The investment bank provided an enormous spreadsheet chock with data on the borrowers' credit histories and much else that might, at very least, have given Moody's pause. Three-quarters of the borrowers had adjustable-rate mortgages, or ARMs—"teaser" loans on which the interest rate could be raised in short order. Since subprime borrowers cannot afford higher rates, they would need to refinance soon. This is a classic sign of a bubble—lending on the belief, or the hope, that new money will bail out the old.

Moody's learned that almost half of these borrowers—43 percent—did not provide written verification of their incomes. The data also showed that 12 percent of the mortgages were for properties in Southern California, including a half-percent in a single ZIP code, in Riverside. That suggested a risky degree of concentration.

On the plus side, Moody's noted, 94 percent of those borrowers with adjustable-rate loans said their mortgages were for primary residences. "That was a comfort feeling," Robinson said. Historically, people have been slow to abandon their primary homes. When you get into a crunch, she added, "You'll give up your ski chalet first."

Another factor giving Moody's comfort was that all of the ARM loans in the pool were first mortgages (as distinct from, say, home-equity loans). Nearly half of the borrowers, however, took out a simultaneous second loan. Most often, their two loans added up to all of their property's presumed resale value, which meant the borrowers had not a cent of equity.

In the frenetic, deal-happy climate of 2006, the Moody's analyst had only a single day to process the credit data from the bank. The analyst wasn't evaluating the mortgages but, rather, the bonds issued by the investment vehicle created to house them. A so-called special-purpose vehicle—a ghost corporation with no people or furniture and no assets either until the deal was struck—would purchase the mortgages. Thereafter, monthly payments from the homeowners would go to the S.P.V. The S.P.V. would finance itself by selling bonds. The question for Moody's was whether the inflow of mortgage checks would cover the outgoing payments to bondholders. From the investment bank's point of view, the key to the deal was obtaining a triple-A rating—without which the deal wouldn't be profitable. That a vehicle backed by subprime mortgages could borrow at triple-A rates seems like a trick of finance. "People say, 'How can you create triple-A out of B-rated paper?' " notes Arturo Cifuentes, a former Moody's credit analyst who now designs credit instruments. It may seem like a scam, but it's not.

The secret sauce is that the S.P.V. would float 12 classes of bonds, from triple-A to a lowly Ba1. The highest-rated bonds would have first priority on the cash received from mortgage holders until they were fully paid, then the next tier of bonds, then the next and so on. The bonds at the bottom of the pile got the highest interest rate, but if homeowners defaulted, they would absorb the first losses.

It was this segregation of payments that protected the bonds at the top of the structure and enabled Moody's to classify them as triple-A. Imagine a seaside condo beset by flooding: just as the penthouse will not get wet until the lower floors are thoroughly soaked, so the triple-A bonds would not lose a dime unless the lower credits were wiped out.

Structured finance, of which this deal is typical, is both clever and useful; in the housing industry it has greatly expanded the pool of credit. But in extreme conditions, it can fail. The old-fashioned corner banker used his instincts, as well as his pencil, to apportion credit; modern finance is formulaic. However elegant its models, forecasting the behavior of 2,393 mortgage holders is an uncertain business. "Everyone assumed the credit agencies knew what they were doing," says Joseph Mason, a credit expert at Drexel University. "A structural engineer can predict what load a steel support will bear; in financial engineering we can't predict as well."

Mortgage-backed securities like those in Subprime XYZ were not the terminus of the great mortgage machine. They were, in fact, building blocks for even more esoteric vehicles known as collateralized debt obligations, or C.D.O.'s. C.D.O.'s were financed with similar ladders of bonds, from triple-A on down, and the credit-rating agencies' role was just as central. The difference is that XYZ was a first-order derivative—its assets included real mortgages owned by actual homeowners. C.D.O.'s were a step removed—instead of buying mortgages, they bought bonds that were *backed* by mortgages, like the bonds issued by Subprime XYZ. (It is painful to consider, but there were also third-order instruments, known as C.D.O.'s squared, which bought bonds issued by other C.D.O.'s.)

Miscalculations that were damaging at the level of Subprime XYZ were devastating at the C.D.O. level. Just as bad weather will cause more serious delays to travelers with multiple flights, so, if the underlying mortgage bonds were misrated, the trouble was compounded in the case of the C.D.O.'s that purchased them.

Moody's used statistical models to assess C.D.O.'s; it relied on historical patterns of default. This assumed that the past would remain relevant in an era in which the mortgage industry was morphing into a wildly speculative business. The complexity of C.D.O.'s undermined the process as well. Jamie Dimon, the chief executive of JPMorgan Chase, which recently scooped up the mortally wounded Bear Stearns, says, "There was a large failure of common sense" by rating agencies and also by banks like his. "Very complex securities shouldn't have been rated as if they were easy-to-value bonds."

The Accidental Watchdog

John Moody, a Wall Street analyst and former errand runner, hit on the idea of synthesizing all kinds of credit information into a single rating in 1909, when he published the manual "Moody's Analyses of Railroad Investments." The idea caught on with investors, who subscribed to his service, and by the mid-'20s, Moody's faced three competitors: Standard Statistics and Poor's Publishing (which later merged) and Fitch.

Then as now, Moody's graded bonds on a scale with 21 steps, from Aaa to C. (There are small differences in the agencies' nomenclatures, just as a grande latte at Starbucks becomes a "medium" at Peet's. At Moody's, ratings that start with the letter "A" carry minimal to low credit risk; those starting with "B" carry moderate to high risk; and "C" ratings denote bonds in poor standing or actual default.) The ratings are meant to be an estimate of probabilities, not a buy or sell recommendation. For instance, Ba bonds default far more often than triple-As. But Moody's, as it is wont to remind people, is not in the business of advising investors whether to buy Ba's; it merely publishes a rating.

Until the 1970s, its business grew slowly. But several trends coalesced to speed it up. The first was the collapse of Penn Central in 1970—a shattering event that the credit agencies failed to foresee. It so unnerved investors that they began to pay more attention to credit risk.

Government responded. The Securities and Exchange Commission, faced with the question of how to measure the capital of broker-dealers, decided to penalize brokers for holding bonds that were less than investment-grade (the term applies to Moody's 10 top grades). This prompted a question: investment grade according to whom? The S.E.C. opted to create a new category of officially designated rating agencies, and grandfathered the big three—S.&P., Moody's and Fitch. In effect, the government outsourced its regulatory function to three for-profit companies.

Bank regulators issued similar rules for banks. Pension funds, mutual funds, insurance regulators followed. Over the '80s and '90s, a lattice-work of such rules redefined credit markets. Many classes of investors were now forbidden to buy noninvestment-grade bonds at all.

Issuers thus were forced to seek credit ratings (or else their bonds would not be marketable). The agencies—realizing they had a hot product and, what's more, a captive market—started charging the very organizations whose bonds they were rating. This was an efficient way to do business, but it put the agencies in a conflicted position. As Partnoy says, rather than selling opinions to investors, the rating agencies were now selling "licenses" to borrowers. Indeed, whether their opinions were accurate no longer mattered so much. Just as a police officer stopping a motorist will want to see his license but not inquire how well he did on his road test, it was the rating—not its accuracy—that mattered to Wall Street.

The case of Enron is illustrative. Throughout the summer and fall of 2001, even though its credit was rapidly deteriorating, the rating agencies kept it at investment grade. This was not unusual; the agencies typically lag behind the news. On Nov. 28, 2001, S.&P. finally dropped Enron's bonds to subinvestment grade. Although its action merely validated the market consensus, it caused the stock to collapse. To investors, S.&P.'s action was a signal that Enron was locked out of credit markets; it had lost its "license" to borrow. Four days later it filed for bankruptcy.

Another trend that spurred the agencies' growth was that more companies began borrowing in bond markets instead of from banks. According to Chris Mahoney, a just-retired Moody's veteran of 22 years, "The agencies went from being obscure and unimportant players to central ones."

A Conflict of Interest?

Nothing sent the agencies into high gear as much as the development of structured finance. As Wall Street bankers designed ever more securitized products—using mortgages, credit-card debt, car loans, corporate debt, every type of paper imaginable—the agencies became truly powerful.

In structured-credit vehicles like Subprime XYZ, the agencies played a much more pivotal role than they had with (conventional) bonds. According to Lewis Ranieri, the Salomon Brothers banker who was a pioneer in mortgage bonds, "The whole creation of mortgage securities was involved with a rating."

What the bankers in these deals are really doing is buying a bunch of I.O.U.'s and repackaging them in a different form. Something has to make the package worth—or seem to be worth—more that the sum of its parts, otherwise there would be no point in packaging such securities, nor would there be any profits from which to pay the bankers' fees.

That something is the rating. Credit markets are not continuous; a bond that qualifies, though only by a hair, as investment grade is worth a lot more than one that just fails. As with a would-be immigrant traveling from Mexico, there is a huge incentive to get over the line.

The challenge to investment banks is to design securities that just meet the rating agencies' tests. Risky mortgages serve their purpose; since the interest rate on them is higher, more money comes into the pool and is available for paying bond interest. But if the mortgages are too risky, Moody's will object. Banks are adroit at working the system, and pools like Subprime XYZ are intentionally designed to include a layer of Baa bonds, or those just over the border. "Every agency has a model available to bankers that allows them to run the numbers until they get something they like and send it in for a rating," a former Moody's expert in securitization says. In other words, banks were gaming the system; according to Chris Flanagan, the subprime analyst at JPMorgan, "Gaming is the whole thing."

When a bank proposes a rating structure on a pool of debt, the rating agency will insist on a cushion of extra capital, known as an "enhancement." The bank inevitably lobbies for a thin cushion (the thinner the capitalization, the fatter the bank's profits). It's up to the agency to make sure that the cushion is big enough to safeguard the bonds. The process involves extended consultations between the agency and its client. In short, obtaining a rating is a collaborative process.

The evidence on whether rating agencies bend to the bankers' will is mixed. The agencies do not deny that a conflict exists, but they assert that they are keen to the dangers and minimize them. For instance, they do not reward analysts on the basis of whether they approve deals. No smoking gun, no conspiratorial e-mail message, has surfaced to suggest that they are lying. But in structured finance, the agencies face pressures that did not exist when John Moody was rating railroads. On the traditional side of the business, Moody's has thousands of clients (virtually every corporation and municipality that sells bonds). No one of them has much clout. But in structured finance, a handful of banks return again and again, paying much bigger fees. A deal the size of XYZ can bring Moody's $200,000 and more for complicated deals. And the banks pay only if Moody's delivers the desired rating. Tom McGuire, the Jesuit theologian who ran Moody's through the mid-'90s, says this arrangement is unhealthy. If Moody's and a client bank don't see eye to eye, the bank can either tweak the numbers or try its luck with a competitor like S.&P., a process known as "ratings shopping."

And it seems to have helped the banks get better ratings. Mason, of Drexel University, compared default rates for corporate bonds rated Baa with those of similarly rated collateralized debt obligations until 2005 (before the bubble burst). Mason found that the C.D.O.'s defaulted eight times as often. One interpretation of the data is that Moody's was far less discerning when the client was a Wall Street securitizer.

After Enron blew up, Congress ordered the S.E.C. to look at the rating industry and possibly reform it. The S.E.C. ducked. Congress looked again in 2006 and enacted a law making it easier for competing agencies to gain official recognition, but didn't change the industry's business model. By then, the mortgage boom was in high gear. From 2002 to 2006, Moody's profits nearly tripled, mostly thanks to the high margins the agencies charged in structured finance. In 2006, Moody's reported net income of $750 million. Raymond W. McDaniel Jr., its chief executive, gloated in the annual report for that year, "I firmly believe that Moody's business stands on the 'right side of history' in terms of the alignment of our role and function with advancements in global capital markets."

Using Weather in Antarctica to Forecast Conditions in Hawaii

Even as McDaniel was crowing, it was clear in some corners of Wall Street that the mortgage market was headed for trouble. The housing industry was cooling off fast. James Kragenbring, a money manager with Advantus Capital Management, complained to the agencies as early as 2005 that their ratings were too generous. A report from the hedge fund of John Paulson proclaimed astonishment at "the mispricing of these securities." He started betting that mortgage debt would crash.

Even Mark Zandi, the very visible economist at Moody's forecasting division (which is separate from the ratings side), was worried about the chilling crosswinds blowing in credit markets. In a report published in May 2006, he noted that consumer borrowing had soared, household debt was at a record and a fifth of such debt was classified as subprime. At the same time, loan officers were loosening underwriting standards and easing rates to offer still more loans. Zandi fretted about the "razor-thin" level of homeowners' equity, the avalanche of teaser mortgages and the $750 billion of mortgages he judged to be at risk. Zandi concluded, "The environment feels increasingly ripe for some type of financial event."

A month after Zandi's report, Moody's rated Subprime XYZ. The analyst on the deal also had concerns. Moody's was aware that mortgage standards had been deteriorating, and it had been demanding more of a cushion in such pools. Nonetheless, its credit-rating model continued to envision rising home values. Largely for that reason, the analyst forecast losses for XYZ at only 4.9 percent of the underlying mortgage pool. Since even the lowest-rated bonds in XYZ would be covered up to a loss level of 7.25 percent, the bonds seemed safe.

XYZ now became the responsibility of a Moody's team that monitors securities and changes the ratings if need be (the analyst moved on to rate a new deal). Almost immediately, the team noticed a problem. Usually, people who finance a home stay current on their payments for at least a while. But a sliver of folks in XYZ fell behind within 90 days of signing their papers. After six months, an alarming 6 percent of the mortgages were seriously delinquent. (Historically, it is rare for more than 1 percent of mortgages at that stage to be delinquent.)

Moody's monitors began to make inquiries with the lender and were shocked by what they heard. Some properties lacked sod or landscaping, and keys remained in the mailbox; the buyers had never moved in. The implication was that people had bought homes on spec: as the housing market turned, the buyers walked.

By the spring of 2007, 13 percent of Subprime XYZ was delinquent— and it was worsening by the month. XYZ was hardly atypical; the entire class of 2006 was performing terribly. (The class of 2007 would turn out to be even worse.)

In April 2007, Moody's announced it was revising the model it used to evaluate subprime mortgages. It noted that the model "was first introduced in 2002. Since then, the mortgage market has evolved considerably." This was a rather stunning admission; its model had been based on a world that no longer existed.

Poring over the data, Moody's discovered that the size of people's first mortgages was no longer a good predictor of whether they would default; rather, it was the size of their first and second loans—that is, their total debt—combined. This was rather intuitive; Moody's simply hadn't reckoned on it. Similarly, credit scores, long a mainstay of its analyses, had not proved to be a "strong predictor" of defaults this time. Translation: even people with good credit scores were defaulting. Amy Tobey, leader of the team that monitored XYZ, told me, "It seems there was a shift in mentality; people are treating homes as investment assets." Indeed. And homeowners without equity were making what economists call a rational choice; they were abandoning properties rather than make payments on them. Homeowners' equity had never been as high as believed because appraisals had been inflated.

Over the summer and fall of 2007, Moody's and the other agencies repeatedly tightened their methodology for rating mortgage securities, but it was too late. They had to downgrade tens of billions of dollars of securities. By early this year, when I met with Moody's, an astonishing 27 percent of the mortgage holders in Subprime XYZ were delinquent. Losses on the pool were now estimated at 14 percent to 16 percent—three times the original estimate. Seemingly high-quality bonds rated A3 by Moody's had been downgraded five notches to Ba2, as had the other bonds in the pool aside from its triple-A's.

The pain didn't stop there. Many of the lower-rated bonds issued by XYZ, and by mortgage pools like it, were purchased by C.D.O.'s, the second-order mortgage vehicles, which were eager to buy lower-rated mortgage paper because it paid a higher yield. As the agencies endowed C.D.O. securities with triple-A ratings, demand for them was red hot. Much of it was from global investors who knew nothing about the U.S. mortgage market. In 2006 and 2007, the banks created more than $200 billion of C.D.O.'s backed by lower-rated mortgage paper. Moody's assigned a different team to rate C.D.O.'s. This team knew far less about the underlying mortgages than did the committee that evaluated Subprime XYZ. In fact, Moody's rated C.D.O.'s without knowing which bonds the pool would buy.

A C.D.O. operates like a mutual fund; it can buy or sell mortgage bonds and frequently does so. Thus, the agencies rate pools with assets that are perpetually shifting. They base their ratings on an extensive set of guidelines or covenants that limit the C.D.O. manager's discretion.

Late in 2006, Moody's rated a C.D.O. with $750 million worth of securities. The covenants, which act as a template, restricted the C.D.O. to, at most, an 80 percent exposure to subprime assets, and many other such conditions. "We're structure experts," Yuri Yoshizawa, the head of Moody's' derivative group, explained. "We're not underlying-asset experts." They were checking the math, not the mortgages. But no C.D.O. can be better than its collateral.

Moody's rated three-quarters of this C.D.O.'s bonds triple-A. The ratings were derived using a mathematical construct known as a Monte Carlo simulation—as if each of the underlying bonds would perform like cards drawn at random from a deck of mortgage bonds in the past. There were two problems with this approach. First, the bonds weren't like those in the past; the mortgage market had changed. As Mark Adelson, a former managing director in Moody's structured-finance division, remarks, it was "like observing 100 years of weather in Antarctica to forecast the weather in Hawaii." And second, the bonds weren't random. Moody's had underestimated the extent to which underwriting standards had weakened everywhere. When one mortgage bond failed, the odds were that others would, too.

Moody's estimated that this C.D.O. could potentially incur losses of 2 percent. It has since revised its estimate to 27 percent. The bonds it rated have been decimated, their market value having plunged by half or more. A triple-A layer of bonds has been downgraded 16 notches, all the way to B. Hundreds of C.D.O.'s have suffered similar fates (most of Wall Street's losses have been on C.D.O.'s). For Moody's and the other rating agencies, it has been an extraordinary rout.

Whom Can We Rely On?

The agencies have blamed the large incidence of fraud, but then they could have demanded verification of the mortgage data or refused to rate securities where the data were not provided. That was, after all, their mandate. This is what they pledge for the future. Moody's, S.&P. and Fitch say that they are tightening procedures—they will demand more data and more verification and will subject their analysts to more outside checks. None of this, however, will remove the conflict of interest in the issuer-pays model. Though some have proposed requiring that agencies with official recognition charge investors, rather than issuers, a more practical reform may be for the government to stop certifying agencies altogether.

Then, if the Fed or other regulators wanted to restrict what sorts of bonds could be owned by banks, or by pension funds or by anyone else in need of protection, they would have to do it themselves—not farm the job out to Moody's. The ratings agencies would still exist, but stripped of their official imprimatur, their ratings would lose a little of their aura, and investors might trust in them a bit less. Moody's itself favors doing away with the official designation, and it, like S.&P., embraces the idea that investors should not "rely" on ratings for buy-and-sell decisions.

This leaves an awkward question, with respect to insanely complex structured securities: What can they rely on? The agencies seem utterly too involved to serve as a neutral arbiter, and the banks are sure to invent new and equally hard-to-assess vehicles in the future. Vickie Tillman, the executive vice president of S.&P., told Congress last fall that in addition to the housing slump, "ahistorical behavorial modes" by homeowners were to blame for the wave of downgrades. She cited S.&P.'s data going back to the 1970s, as if consumers were at fault for not living up to the past. The real problem is that the agencies' mathematical formulas look backward while life is lived forward. That is unlikely to change.

From "Rudolph the Red-Nosed Reindeer"

LARRY ROBERTS

Irvine Housing Blog, November 26, 2007

Asking Price: $1,249,000
Purchase Price: $1,157,00
Purchase Date: 1/6/2005

The property was purchased in January 2005 for $1,157,000. The combined first and second mortgages totaled $1,156,730 leaving a down payment of $270. Let's just call it 100% financing.

By April, the owners were unable to find refinancing through Countrywide with a $999,999 first mortgage. This mortgage was an Option ARM with a 1% teaser rate. The minimum payment would be $3,216 per month.

Also in April of 2005, they took out a simultaneous second mortgage for $215,000 pulling out their first $58,000.

So look at their situation: They are living in a million dollar plus home in Turtle Ridge making payments less than those renting, and they "made" $58,000 in their first four months of ownership.

Apparently, these owners liked how hard their house was working for them, so they opened a revolving line of credit (HELOC) in August 2005 for $293,000. Did they spend it all? I can't be sure, but the following certainly suggests they did.

In December of 2005, they extended their HELOC to $397,990.

In June of 2006, they extended their HELOC to $485,000.

In April of 2007, the well ran dry as they did their final HELOC of $491,000. I bet they were pissed when they couldn't get more money.

So by April 2007, they have a first mortgage (Option ARM with a 1% teaser rate) for $999,999, and a HELOC for $491,000. These owners pulled $333,000 in HELOC money to fuel consumer spending.

Assuming they spent the entire HELOC (does anyone think they didn't?), and assuming the negative amortization on the first mortgage has increased the loan balance, the total debt on the property exceeds $1,500,000. The asking price of $1,249,000 does not look like a rollback, but if the property actually sells at this price, the lender on the HELOC (Washington Mutual) will lose over $300,000.

These owners will probably just walk away. I doubt they have any assets. They never put any money into the deal, they pulled out $333,000 in cash, and they got to live in Turtle Ridge for 3 years. Not a bad deal—for them.

Bear CEO's Handling of Crisis Raises Issues

KATE KELLY

The Wall Street Journal, *November 1, 2007*

A crisis at Bear Stearns Cos. this summer came to a head in July. Two Bear hedge funds were hemorrhaging value. Investors were clamoring to get their money back. Lenders to the funds were demanding more collateral. Eventually, both funds collapsed.

During 10 critical days of this crisis—one of the worst in the securities firm's 84-year history—Bear's chief executive wasn't near his Wall Street office. James Cayne was playing in a bridge tournament in Nashville, Tenn., without a cellphone or an email device. In one closely watched competition, his team placed in the top third.

As Bear's fund meltdown was helping spark this year's mortgage-market and credit convulsions, Mr. Cayne at times missed key events. At a tense August conference call with investors, he left after a few opening words and listeners didn't know when he returned. In summer weeks, he typically left the office on Thursday afternoon and spent Friday at his New Jersey golf club, out of touch for stretches, according to associates and golf records. In the critical month of July, he spent 10 of the 21 workdays out of the office, either at the bridge event or golfing, according to golf, bridge and hotel records.

Mr. Cayne evidently didn't court business on the links, as some CEOs do. "The golf course for him was an escape," says John Angelo, a hedge-fund client and frequent golf partner. Another golf partner, talk-show host Maury Povich, says: "Believe it or not, many words are not exchanged about business." During the bridge event, at a time when Bear's executive committee in New York was meeting almost daily, Mr. Cayne took part by phone, then played bridge most of the afternoon.

In a short interview, Mr. Cayne declined to address his performance or his focus on Bear's summer crisis. Other Bear executives scoff at any notion that Mr. Cayne, 73 years old, isn't fully engaged. They say he reached out to clients this summer and has led by effectively delegating responsibilities to deputies.

"Anyone who thinks that Jimmy Cayne isn't fired up every day and ready to get to work hasn't been living in my world," says Alan Schwartz, Bear's president. He notes that over Labor Day weekend, Mr. Cayne flew to China to help seal a partnership with a Beijing investment bank.

Still, Mr. Cayne's actions amid the turmoil contrast with the hands-on roles of peers such as James Dimon of J.P. Morgan Chase & Co., Richard Fuld Jr. of Lehman Brothers Holdings Inc. and Lloyd Blankfein of Goldman Sachs Group Inc. In August, Messrs. Dimon and Fuld got personally involved in negotiations for new financing terms on the sale of a Home Depot Inc. unit that had lost value amid the squeeze. Mr. Blankfein canceled plans to spend the last two weeks of August at his beach house, missing a chance to spend time with his sons before they headed to college. Through the summer's market gyrations, Mr. Blankfein frequently visited Goldman mortgage desks

The fund trouble was a shock for Bear, which was known as one of the Street's savviest risk managers. For years the firm relied on a system of "ferrets," or managers who monitored trades, to spot problems. Potential issues were reviewed in weekly meetings, at which Alan "Ace" Greenberg, the 80-year-old executive-committee chairman who led Bear until 1993, was an active participant. Nowadays, say people with knowledge of the gatherings, the firm's risk-review meetings are held more than once a week, and after years of spotty attendance, Mr. Cayne is a more-regular participant.

The tough-talking Mr. Cayne personifies Bear's aggressiveness. A one-time scrap-iron salesman, he joined Bear in 1969 and rose quickly in the brokerage division, catering to wealthy individuals. He developed a rapport with Mr. Greenberg, who shared his love of bridge, and the two frequently played after hours at the Regency Whist Club in New York. In 1993, Mr. Cayne unseated Mr. Greenberg to become Bear's CEO. Mr. Greenberg referred questions to a Bear spokeswoman.

Over the next 14 years, Bear expanded and its stock price rose nearly 600%. Mr. Cayne made some progress in turning the firm, a trading powerhouse, into more of an investment bank that helps companies with financing and mergers. Colleagues say he has been good at developing young talent, such as Chinese-born Donald Tang, who eventually became a vice chairman and chief of Bear's Asian operations.

Mr. Cayne's management style at Bear headquarters in Manhattan is to strategize in small groups in his private sixth-floor office, often wielding a lit cigar. He often seeks consensus, after consulting associates. Mr. Cayne is "a great captain" who's made a "tremendous contribution to growing a very significant franchise" over many years, says David Winters, a former chief of mutual-fund firm Franklin Mutual Advisers LLC, long one of Bear's larger institutional shareholders.

For the year 2006, Mr. Cayne took home $34 million in pay and became the first Wall Street chief to own a company stake worth more than $1 billion. Although the value of his stake has since fallen, along with Bear's share price, he remains one of the firm's single biggest investors, according to public records.

He has resisted overtures to sell Bear. In 2002, when Mr. Dimon, then head of Bank One Corp., raised the possibility of buying Bear, Mr. Cayne didn't give the idea much consideration, according to people to whom he spoke. Mr. Cayne told members of Bear's executive committee he would do a deal only for a significant stock price premium, a big personal payout and the use of a private jet, say people familiar with the conversation. The takeover idea ultimately faded away.

Mr. Cayne revels in being a Wall Street maverick. He has described his disinclination to travel for business matters, saying privately he wouldn't meet with President Bush about economic issues unless the president came to Bear's New York offices.

He is blunt. Investment-firm chief Alexandra Lebenthal brought her

11-year-old son to visit Bear a few years back. She says she introduced him to Mr. Cayne, who pulled her aside and said, "That kid's got a rotten handshake. He's going nowhere in life." Ms. Lebenthal, chief of a unit of Israel Discount Bank of New York, says she instructed her son on the importance of a firmer handshake.

Mr. Cayne, who has also used bridge to help recruit clients, considers tournaments a welcome break, say people who've spent time with him at the events. He has played in at least three so far this year, staying from a few days to over a week at each.

Attendees say Mr. Cayne has sometimes smoked marijuana at the end of the day during bridge tournaments. He also has used pot in more private settings, according to people who say they witnessed him doing so or participated with him.

After a day of bridge at a Doubletree hotel in Memphis, in 2004, Mr. Cayne invited a fellow player and a woman to smoke pot with him, according to someone who was there, and led the two to a lobby men's room where he intended to light up. The other player declined, says the person who was there, but the woman followed Mr. Cayne inside and shared a joint, to the amusement of a passerby.

Mr. Cayne denied emphatically that such an incident occurred. "There is no chance that it happened," he said. "Zero chance."

Asked more generally whether he smoked pot during bridge tournaments or on other occasions, Mr. Cayne said he would respond only "to a specific allegation," not to general questions.

Bear's travails began early this year with signs of trouble in the mortgage market. Home prices were slipping, while delinquencies on loans to the weakest borrowers, called subprime loans, were up. Late February brought a swoon in an index that tracks packages of subprime loans that have been sliced up and resold to investors in the form of complex securities.

Two Bear Stearns hedge funds—investment partnerships for rich people and institutions—were heavily invested in such securities. The funds used leverage, or borrowed money, to amplify their bets, magnifying both gains and losses. Reflecting their holdings, one fund was called the Bear Stearns High-Grade Structured Credit Strategies Fund. The other had the same name plus the words "Enhanced Leverage." That one had $638 million in investor cash and at least $6 billion in borrowed capital. So for every dollar of investor money, it borrowed roughly $10.

Mr. Cayne showed little sign of concern about the mortgage market at a dinner with analysts in late March, according to one attendee. But soon that market took a turn for the worse. The values of some holdings in both hedge funds sank. The more leveraged fund told its investors in early June that it was down 23% for the year through April, prompting demands by many to get their money back.

To raise cash, both funds began selling billions of dollars of the assets they'd acquired with borrowed money. All this selling put still more pressure on the values of such securities.

About this time, Mr. Cayne began his summertime ritual of taking a helicopter from New York City to Deal, N.J., on Thursdays to make a late-afternoon golf game at the exclusive Hollywood Golf Club, associates say. (He pays for the 17-minute, $1,700 trips himself, one person says.) After spending the night in his vacation home nearby, associates add, Mr. Cayne generally hits the golf course again Friday morning for another 18 holes, followed by 8 A.M. tee-offs on Saturday and Sunday. Friends say that after his Saturday game, he often heads back to his local home for several hours of online poker and bridge and to play with his grandchildren.

Samuel Molinaro Jr., Bear's chief operating and financial officer, says, "I've never had a problem reaching him."

In the first week of June, the more leveraged fund told investors who wanted out that it couldn't immediately return their money. Wall Street creditors that had lent the fund money reacted sharply to this news, making margin calls, or requests for additional collateral. One creditor, Merrill Lynch & Co., which was owed $400 million, seized the assets that backed its loan on June 15. Mr. Cayne was on the golf course in New Jersey part of that day, a Friday, having left the office Thursday afternoon, according to a Web site that tracks individuals' golf scores.

Mr. Angelo says Mr. Cayne doesn't carry a cellphone or email device while golfing, in accordance with a policy at the Hollywood club. Mr. Povich says that on Fridays, Mr. Cayne would occasionally use a land line near the course's ninth hole to check in with the office. Associates of Mr. Cayne say top Bear executives often didn't try to contact him between 8 A.M. and 1 P.M. on Fridays, preferring to leave messages with his assistants at Bear to call the office when he was free.

Even when he wasn't there in person, Mr. Cayne was hands-on, say other associates. Mortgage-division head Tom Marano, who temporarily left his post over the summer to help stabilize the two flailing funds in the firm's asset-management division, says Mr. Cayne offered some helpful advice on handling irascible creditors during a critical period in July. Mr. Marano says the CEO told him in a phone call to "keep your Irish down," or cool his temper and try to negotiate calmly. (Mr. Marano is of Irish and Italian descent.)

Late in June, as the outcry from investors in Bear's hedge funds grew, Bear authorized an 11th-hour loan of up to $3.2 billion to the less-risky of the two beleaguered funds. The fund ultimately borrowed about half that amount from its parent company.

On July 12, chatting with visitors over lunch, Mr. Cayne seemed less interested in discussing the markets than in talking about a breakfast-cereal allergy and his stash of unlabeled Cuban cigars. On another occasion, he told a visitor he pays $140 apiece for the cigars, keeping them in a humidor under his desk.

Five days later managers of both funds informed investors their holdings were virtually worthless.

The next day, July 18, Mr. Cayne left for Nashville to play in the bridge tournament, accompanied by his wife, Patricia, who is a neuropsychologist and another avid bridge player. Mr. Cayne took part in a prestigious event called Spingold KO. He was in Nashville all or parts of 10 days, according to bridge and hotel records.

For most of that time, Warren Spector—then co-president of Bear and also a competitive bridge player—was in Nashville as well. Mr. Spector was in charge of asset management at Bear, along with all of its trading operations and its prime-brokerage unit, which handles trades for big clients such as hedge funds as well as lending them money.

Amid the hedge-fund crisis, Bear's five-member executive committee gathered almost daily. Mr. Cayne and Mr. Spector dialed in from Nashville in the hours before the afternoon games began.

On the calls, Mr. Cayne rarely dictated orders, participants say. When fingers were pointed, he urged others not to "worry about who got us here."

The funds reached an impasse on July 26. Fretting over a margin call that hadn't been met, Bear took the painful step of seizing most of the remaining collateral in the less-leveraged fund, to which Bear had extended $1.6 billion in credit. Although the fund had paid back $300 million of the loan, it couldn't come up with any more cash, essentially forcing its own parent company to shut it down. Days later, Mr. Marano, who had been unable to avert the seizure, initiated bankruptcy proceedings for both funds.

The following day, Mr. Cayne left Nashville to return to New York. By then, new troubles were brewing at Bear Stearns Asset Management, the umbrella division for the two troubled hedge funds. Another, unrelated fund was also facing investor demands for their money back.

Amid the turmoil, Mr. Cayne on Aug. 1 called in Mr. Spector, the co-president who had been with him at Nashville. Mr. Cayne was annoyed that Mr. Spector had been away from the office during the fund crisis, according to people familiar with his thinking. He told Mr. Spector he had lost Mr. Cayne's confidence and should resign, these people say. Mr. Spector left his boss's office without committing to do so.

On Friday, Aug. 3, with investors in Bear's stock worried about how solid its financing was, executives convened a conference call to reassure people. Mr. Cayne opened it by saying the firm was "taking the situation seriously" and addressing the market issues. He turned over the call to Mr. Molinaro, the CFO. Mr. Molinaro called the bond market's condition "about as bad as I've seen it" in a 22-year career.

An analyst asked Mr. Cayne a question, but there was silence. Mr. Cayne had left, say two people who were with him in a Bear conference room at the start of the call. One says Mr. Cayne had been summoned out by a lawyer advising him on the pending departure of Mr. Spector, who by then was planning to resign. Mr. Cayne later returned, but the hundreds of listeners weren't told this, leaving them with the impression that the CEO had left the call altogether.

As word spread about the call and Mr. Molinaro's grim assessment, the financial markets began to sink. The Dow Jones Industrial Average fell more than 300 points, before recovering slightly to end the day down 2%.

Later that day, WSJ.com reported the anticipated resignation of Mr. Spector. The co-president, a 49-year-old former mortgage trader, had been seen as a likely heir to Mr. Cayne. The move left Bear with no apparent succession plan, though in a recent interview Bear's lead director, Vincent Tese, said that "the front-runner is clearly Alan," meaning Mr. Schwartz.

The following day, a Saturday, Mr. Cayne scored a respectable 88 at the Hollywood golf course, according to the golf Web site. But for Bear, things seemed to be falling apart that weekend. Major clients of the firm's prime brokerage division were threatening to pull their business.

Bear executives scrambled to reassure them in phone calls Sunday, Aug. 5, saying that Bear's financing was secure and its risks contained. Yet Bear did lose some prime-brokerage business—from, among others, Brahman Capital Corp. and a fund connected to Mariner Investment Group, say people familiar with the matter.

Although Mr. Cayne didn't take part in the Aug. 5 calls to clients, according to people familiar with the calls, he spent a rare Sunday at the office leading a hastily called board meeting to accept Mr. Spector's resignation.

Late the Friday of Labor Day weekend, Mr. Cayne flew to Beijing with Mr. Tang, the Chinese-born executive, for a series of meetings that would culminate in a deal.

On Sept. 20, Bear reported earnings for its Aug. 31 quarter: a 61% year-over-year drop—reflecting an 88% fall in bond revenue and $200 million in costs linked to the closing of the two hedge funds. Bear shook up its mortgage unit, laying off more than 500 people. It has just laid off 300 more people throughout the firm, though the head count remains at about 15,000.

Bear faces reviews of the hedge-fund collapses by the Securities and Exchange Commission, the Justice Department and Massachusetts state regulators. Bear's board has retained attorney Robert Fiske Jr. to sort out what went wrong. On Oct. 22, Bear and Citic Securities Co., a Chinese investment bank, announced a deal in which each will invest about $1 billion in the other. In sealing that deal, Mr. Cayne's long-term relationship with the Chinese bank's officials "had gone a long way," says Mr. Tang. Bear's stock edged up on the news but remains down about 30% for the year, the worst performance of any major brokerage firm.

Bear's travails have of late taken a back seat to those of competitors like Merrill Lynch, where a write-down of $8.4 billion cost chief executive Stan O'Neal his job. Many of Bear's rivals continue to grapple with the fallout of the summer's credit crunch, and when conditions will improve remains unclear.

Friends of Mr. Cayne say he is troubled by the summer's events and concerned about his legacy. "It's one thing if you're 55," says Mr. Angelo, the hedge-fund manager and golf partner. "It's another if you're 73," he says, adding that amid turmoil such as this year's, it can take "periods of time to get your reputation back."

What Wall Street's CEOs
Don't Know Can Kill You

MICHAEL LEWIS

Bloomberg News, March 26, 2008

On March 14, a Friday, the market believed that Bear Stearns Cos. was worth $30 a share. Say what you will about Bear Stearns on that day, you can't say that it was flying below the radar. It was as intently scrutinized as a public corporation can be, by some of the shrewdest people on our planet, and perhaps some smarter people from distant planets, too. For nine months it had been in obvious distress; in just the previous three days its shares had fallen $30. A billionaire from outside the place—the sort of investor who has the power to know as much as it is possible for an investor to know about a Wall Street firm—was long the stock at $107 a share.

Three days earlier, on theStreet.com, Jim Cramer listed Bear Stearns common stock as a "buy" at $62. On his CNBC program that day, he showed his viewers a chart of Bear Stearns stock price and hollered, "Bear Stearns is fine! Do not take your money out of Bear." Over that weekend—days when the markets were closed and there was no material news about the company—Bear Stearns was believed to be worth $2 a share, so long as the Federal Reserve assumed the downside risk of almost $30 billion of its mortgage securities. JPMorgan Chase & Co. Chief Executive Officer Jamie Dimon obviously thought it was worth more than that, or he wouldn't have bought it. How much more is hard to say but the number now being floated, $10 a share, appears to sound about right even to the sellers.

Cramer's "Buy"

TheStreet.com quickly removed Cramer's March 11 "buy" recommendation from its page devoted to Bear Stearns. (The Cramer-obsessed Don Harrold's YouTube account of all this is priceless.) And Cramer went back on CNBC to explain that he never intended for anyone to go and actually BUY shares in Bear Stearns—only that, if they happen to bank with Bear Stearns, they shouldn't worry about losing their money (a public service to all those "Mad Money" viewers who use Bear Stearns as a bank).

All of this raises an obvious question: If the market got the value of Bear Stearns so wrong, how can it possibly believe it knows even the approximate value of any Wall Street firm? And if it doesn't, how can any responsible investor buy shares in a big Wall Street firm? At what point does the purchase of such shares cease to be intelligent investing, and become the crudest sort of gambling?

CEO Ignorance

There is, of course, a reason that the market doesn't understand Wall Street firms: The people who run Wall Street firms, and who convey news of their inner workings to the outside world, don't understand them either.

Jimmy Cayne plays bridge, and Stan O'Neal golfs while their firms collapse, not because they don't care their firms are collapsing, but because they don't know that their firms are collapsing.

Across Wall Street, CEOs have made this little leap of faith about the manner in which their traders are making money, because they don't fully understand what their traders are doing.

Late last November, in a superb account of the demise of Citigroup CEO Charles Prince, Carol Loomis of *Fortune* magazine revealed that Prince resigned after he was informed of the consequences of liquidity puts—options that allowed buyers of complex and presumably safe mortgage securities to hand them back to Citigroup at par if they became hard to finance.

Crappy Mortgages

Liquidity puts were about to make Citigroup the new owner of $25 billion of crappy mortgage securities at par, cost Prince his job, and put the company into the hands of Robert Rubin. Rubin is an extremely smart man with keen instincts of self-preservation, and he sat closer to Prince than anyone else at Citigroup.

Rubin said he had never heard of liquidity puts.

To both their investors and their bosses, Wall Street firms have become shockingly opaque. But the problem isn't new. It dates back at least to the early 1980s when one firm, Salomon Brothers, suddenly began to make more money than all the other firms combined. (Go look at the numbers: They're incredible.)

The profits came from financial innovation—mainly in mortgage securities and interest-rate arbitrage. But its CEO, John Gutfreund, had only a vague idea what the bright young things dreaming up clever new securities were doing. Some of it was very smart, some of it was not so smart, but all of it was beyond his capacity to understand.

Ever since then, when extremely smart people have found extremely complicated ways to make huge sums of money, the typical Wall Street boss has seldom bothered to fully understand the matter, to challenge and question and argue.

New New Thing

This isn't because Wall Street CEOs are lazy, or stupid. It's because they are trapped. The Wall Street CEO can't interfere with the new new thing on Wall Street because the new new thing is the profit center, and the people who create it are mobile. Anything he does to slow them down increases the risk that his most lucrative employees will quit and join another big firm, or start their own hedge fund. He isn't a boss in the conventional sense. He's a hostage of his cleverest employees.

At this point you have to at least wonder if Wall Street firms should be public companies. Their complexity renders them inherently opaque. Investors are right now waking up to this fact: They will demand to be paid for opacity, and also for volatility.

The firms have been revealed to be so treacherous in bad times that the only way they survive as public companies is to make outrageously huge sums in good times. That is, as public companies, to be economically viable they are likely to be socially problematic.

If they aren't about to go under, they are making so much money that everyone else hates them.

Something is about to give.

The Bear Flu: How It Spread

DAVID HENRY AND MATTHEW GOLDSTEIN

BusinessWeek, *December 31, 2007*

W hen the subprime mortgage market began to unravel late in 2006, global bond markets barely flinched. But when two Bear Stearns hedge funds collapsed in June, the event sparked a global credit crisis that has yet to ease. New evidence sheds light on how those hedge funds—and their managers—became star players in the subprime bust, the biggest financial disaster in decades. The revelations also show how other players in the mortgage market adopted the Bear funds' tactics, collectively building a financing structure with many of the hallmarks of a pyramid scheme.

The legal consequences are still unfolding. In recent weeks securities regulators and federal prosecutors have stepped up their investigations into the two funds, probing the fuzzy math used to value the underlying assets, the aggressive sales pitches that portrayed the funds as safe, and frequent trades with other Bear-managed portfolios. On Dec. 19, Barclays, which lent one Bear fund hundreds of millions, filed a lawsuit alleging fraud over misleading statements about the portfolio's health.

Says a Bear spokesman: "We believe that any such lawsuit is unjustified and without merit."

Investigators also are asking why Ralph R. Cioffi, the funds' top manager, moved $2 million of his own $6 million investment in the hedge funds into another fund in early 2007 while simultaneously raising cash for the funds, trying to sell them to Cerberus Capital Management, and telling investors they couldn't redeem their shares until the end of June. People familiar with the situation at Bear stress that Cioffi, who left the firm the week of Dec. 10, was simply investing in a different Bear fund with which he was involved. Cioffi's lawyers did not return e-mails or calls seeking comment.

It's too soon to tell whether authorities will find any wrongdoing. But a *BusinessWeek* analysis of confidential hedge fund reports and interviews with lawyers, investors, and securities experts reveals just how pivotal a role Cioffi's funds played in the mortgage market's dramatic rise, dizzying peak, and disastrous fall.

The analysis shows Cioffi and his team developed a novel investment product to attract money-market funds—a new class of investor—to the mortgage market. Their innovation, a particularly aggressive form of collateralized debt obligation, or CDO, became the building blocks of the industry's push to keep growing for longer than it otherwise would have. After the market turned, it became clear the Cioffi money machine contributed to much of the $10 billion-plus in writedowns that Citigroup and Bank of America revealed in November. Fresh evidence also suggests Cioffi's team may have engaged in self-dealing by using the new CDOs to buy assets from the funds, artificially boosting returns. Citi and Bank of America declined to comment.

At the center of it all was the new breed of CDO pioneered by Cioffi and his team to tap into the $2 trillion universe of money-market accounts in which individuals and corporations stash their spare cash. Cioffi's CDOs, initially branded "Klio Funding," were entities that sold commercial paper and other short-term debt to buy higher-yielding, longer-term securities. The Klios were a win-win proposition for money-market funds. They paid a higher interest rate than the usual short-term debt. And investors didn't need to worry about the risky assets the Klios owned because Citigroup had agreed to refund their initial stake plus interest, through what's known as a "liquidity put," if the market soured. Cioffi engineered three such deals in 2004 and 2005, raising $10 billion in all.

What did Citigroup get for guaranteeing the Klios? For one thing, fees. The Klios were also a ready buyer of Citi's own stash of mortgage-backed securities and other debt. Citi probably never imagined it would have to make good on those guarantees because the underlying assets had the highest credit ratings.

Cioffi used the money from each deal to purchase billions in mortgage-backed securities and pieces of other CDOs for his three Klios. He bought many of the assets directly from the two Bear hedge funds he managed. The move also supplied the hedge funds with cash.

A Longer Life Span

The Klios had another powerful feature: They allowed the Bear funds to lock in longer-term financing. Typically, hedge funds borrow for short periods of time, usually just days or weeks. Under the terms of the Klio deals, Cioffi could use the money for at least a year without having to worry that it would disappear overnight if the market got volatile. He discussed that advantage in an Apr. 25 call with hedge fund investors, boasting that the funding wasn't subject to market fluctuations.

The Klio structure spread rapidly as other hedge funds, CDO managers, and banks, including Barclays, Bank of America, and Société Générale, followed Cioffi's lead. From 2004 through 2007, Wall Street raised some $100 billion through these innovative CDOs, essentially creating a whole new way for the industry to finance risky subprime loans. That success, in turn, inspired copycat products such as structured investment vehicles, which also sold short-term debt. At their peak, in February, 2007, SIV assets hit $300 billion. Barclays declined to comment, but the company announced on Nov. 15 losses from CDO investments that it had been forced to take on its books. A Société Générale spokesman said it has transferred all of its risk to a large, global financial institution.

In hindsight, CDOs and SIVs served as a foundation for a pyramid-like structure that Yale University economist Robert J. Shiller says occasionally arises from bull markets. As new investors arrive to the party, they bid up prices, boosting returns for those who got in earlier. The big gains attract more investors, and the cycle continues—as long as the players don't try to take out their money en masse.

The mortgage-market system played out much the same way. The new type of CDO lured a different tier of investors: money-market funds. The flood of fresh money made it even cheaper and easier for buyers to get mortgages. That, in turn, drove up home prices, holding off defaults and foreclosures. The process enriched the people who bought earlier in the boom and triggered more speculation.

Lax Lending

The complexity of the Klios and their ilk only encouraged lax lending practices by putting too much distance between the borrowers and the ultimate holders of their debt. Since the Klios offered a refund policy, money-market managers didn't have to worry about whether home buyers would pay back their loans. Their investments were protected even if the owners eventually defaulted on their mortgages.

Indeed, as the bubble inflated, there was little incentive for the array of middlemen collecting fees—mortgage brokers, real estate appraisers, bankers, money managers, and others—to do the proper checks. The lack of oversight likely contributed to the rampant fraud on some underlying loans, says S. Kenneth Leech, chief investment officer of bond-investing firm Western Asset Management. "Nobody wanted to take the punch bowl away from the party," adds Charles Calomiris, a professor at Columbia Business School. "They were all making fees."

Now investigators are trying to determine whether Cioffi and his team crossed legal lines. The Klios provided the Bear hedge funds with a ready, in-house trading partner. Their financial reports, which were reviewed by *BusinessWeek*, show many months in which the Cioffi-managed Klios traded only with the Cioffi-managed Bear funds. For example, in April, 2006, one Klio CDO bought $114 million worth of securities from one of the Bear funds. Such trades, says Steven B. Caruso, an attorney who represents several Bear hedge fund investors, may be "indicative of an incestuous, self-serving relationship that appears to have been designed to establish a false marketplace."

If that's why the trades were made, the maneuvers could have falsely boosted the hedge funds' returns—and the fees Cioffi and his team collected. In an e-mail to Cioffi and co-manager Matthew Tannin cited in a legal filing, Raymond McGarrigal, another executive at the Bear funds, gushed about the Klio setup, writing that "one of the great things we've done is allow the Klio to buy assets from the hedge fund." Lawyers for Tannin and McGarrigal declined to comment.

Amid the market turmoil earlier this spring, Cioffi hoped the Klios would work their magic once again. In April, as losses at the funds began mounting, Cioffi set up another CDO, High Grade Structured Credit CDO 2007-1, which issued short-term paper and offered investors a money-back guarantee from Bank of America. Cioffi had raised nearly $4 billion by late May, making it the biggest CDO of the year, according to Thomson Financial.

Just as before, Cioffi used the money to buy assets from the hedge funds, perhaps to prop up the portfolios, which by then were on the brink of collapse. In an April conference call with the hedge funds' investors, Cioffi said the new CDO was part of his plan "to get the funds back on track to generate positive returns." It didn't work. Just weeks after the deal for the CDO closed, the Bear funds imploded, wiping out $1.6 billion of investors' money. (The fund into which Cioffi moved $2 million, Bear Stearns Structured Risk Partners, was up 6.5% as of Nov. 30.)

By autumn the practice of using CDOs to raise cash was dead. Money-market funds had stopped buying the short-term debt, and the credit markets were frozen. That forced Citigroup and Bank of America to make good on their guarantees to investors in Cioffi's CDOs, triggering big losses at the two banks.

The global markets are dealing with the consequences: The tab from the mortgage mess could run up to $500 billion, and central bankers are struggling to stave off recession. As investigators sort through the wreckage, the records of Bear Stearns' doomed hedge funds are turning out to be some of the most revealing in an era of financial folly.

A Wall Street Trader Draws Some Subprime Lessons

MICHAEL LEWIS

Bloomberg News, September 5, 2007

So right after the Bear Stearns funds blew up, I had a thought: This is what happens when you lend money to poor people. Don't get me wrong: I have nothing personally against the poor. To my knowledge, I have nothing personally to do with the poor at all. It's not personal when a guy cuts your grass: that's business. He does what you say, you pay him. But you don't pay him in advance: That would be finance. And finance is one thing you should never engage in with the poor. (By poor, I mean anyone who the SEC wouldn't allow to invest in my hedge fund.)

That's the biggest lesson I've learned from the subprime crisis. Along the way, as these people have torpedoed my portfolio, I had some other thoughts about the poor. I'll share them with you.

1) They're masters of public relations.

I had no idea how my open-handedness could be made to look, after the fact. At the time I bought the subprime portfolio I thought: This is sort of like my way of giving something back. I didn't expect a profile in *Philanthropy Today* or anything like that. I mean, I bought at a discount.

But I thought people would admire the Wall Street big shot who found a way to help the little guy. Sort of like a money doctor helping a sick person. Then the little guy wheels around and gives me this financial enema. And I'm the one who gets crap in the papers! Everyone feels sorry for the poor, and no one feels sorry for me. Even though it's my money! No good deed goes unpunished.

2) Poor people don't respect other people's money in the way money deserves to be respected.

Call me a romantic: I want everyone to have a shot at the American dream. Even people who haven't earned it. I did everything I could so that these schlubs could at least own their own place. The media is now making my generosity out to be some kind of scandal. Teaser rates weren't a scandal. Teaser rates were a sign of misplaced trust: I trusted these people to get their teams of lawyers to vet anything before they signed it. Turns out, if you're poor, you don't need to pay lawyers. You don't like the deal you just wave your hands in the air and moan about how poor you are. Then you default.

3) I've grown out of touch with "poor culture."

Hard to say when this happened; it might have been when I stopped flying commercial. Or maybe it was when I gave up the bleacher seats and got the suite. But the first rule in this business is to know the people you're in business with, and I broke it. People complain about the rich getting richer and the poor being left behind. Is it any wonder? Look at them! Did it ever occur to even one of them that they might pay me back by WORKING HARDER? I don't think so.

But as I say, it was my fault, for not studying the poor more closely before I lent them the money. When the only time you've ever seen a lion is in his cage in the zoo, you start thinking of him as a pet cat. You forget that he wants to eat you.

4) Our society is really, really hostile to success. At the same time it's shockingly indulgent of poor people.

A Republican president now wants to bail them out! I have a different solution. Debtors' prison is obviously a little too retro, and besides that it would just use more taxpayers' money. But the poor could work off their debts. All over Greenwich I see lawns to be mowed, houses to be painted, sports cars to be tuned up. Some of these poor people must have skills. The ones that don't could be trained to do some of the less skilled labor—

say, working as clowns at rich kids' birthday parties. They could even have an act: put them in clown suits and see how many can be stuffed into a Maybach. It'd be like the circus, only better.

Transporting entire neighborhoods of poor people to upper Manhattan and lower Connecticut might seem impractical. It's not: Mexico does this sort of thing routinely. And in the long run it might be for the good of poor people. If the consequences were more serious, maybe they wouldn't stay poor.

5) I think it's time we all become more realistic about letting the poor anywhere near Wall Street.

Lending money to poor countries was a bad idea: Does it make any more sense to lend money to poor people? They don't even have mineral rights!

There's a reason the rich aren't getting richer as fast as they should: they keep getting tangled up with the poor. It's unrealistic to say that Wall Street should cut itself off entirely from poor—or, if you will, "mainstream"—culture. As I say, I'll still do business with the masses. But I'll only engage in their finances if they can clump themselves together into a semblance of a rich person. I'll still accept pension fund money, for example. (Nothing under $50 million, please.) And I'm willing to finance the purchase of entire companies staffed basically with poor people. I did deals with Milken, before they broke him. I own some Blackstone. (Hang tough, Steve!)

But never again will I go one-on-one again with poor people. They're sharks.

After the Money's Gone

PAUL KRUGMAN

The New York Times, *December 14, 2007*

On Wednesday, the Federal Reserve announced plans to lend $40 billion to banks. By my count, it's the fourth high-profile attempt to rescue the financial system since things started falling apart about five months ago. Maybe this one will do the trick, but I wouldn't count on it.

In past financial crises—the stock market crash of 1987, the aftermath of Russia's default in 1998—the Fed has been able to wave its magic wand and make market turmoil disappear. But this time the magic isn't working.

Why not? Because the problem with the markets isn't just a lack of liquidity—there's also a fundamental problem of solvency.

Let me explain the difference with a hypothetical example.

Suppose that there's a nasty rumor about the First Bank of Pottersville: people say that the bank made a huge loan to the president's brother-in-law, who squandered the money on a failed business venture.

Even if the rumor is false, it can break the bank. If everyone, believing that the bank is about to go bust, demands their money out at the same time, the bank would have to raise cash by selling off assets at fire-sale prices—and it may indeed go bust even though it didn't really make that bum loan.

And because loss of confidence can be a self-fulfilling prophecy, even depositors who don't believe the rumor would join in the bank run, trying to get their money out while they can.

But the Fed can come to the rescue. If the rumor is false, the bank has enough assets to cover its debts; all it lacks is liquidity—the ability to raise cash on short notice. And the Fed can solve that problem by giving the bank a temporary loan, tiding it over until things calm down.

Matters are very different, however, if the rumor is true: the bank really did make a big bad loan. Then the problem isn't how to restore confidence; it's how to deal with the fact that the bank is really, truly insolvent, that is, busted.

My story about a basically sound bank beset by a crisis of confidence, which can be rescued with a temporary loan from the Fed, is more or less what happened to the financial system as a whole in 1998. Russia's default led to the collapse of the giant hedge fund Long-Term Capital Management, and for a few weeks there was panic in the markets.

But when all was said and done, not that much money had been lost; a temporary expansion of credit by the Fed gave everyone time to regain their nerve, and the crisis soon passed.

In August, the Fed tried again to do what it did in 1998, and at first it seemed to work. But then the crisis of confidence came back, worse than ever. And the reason is that this time the financial system—both banks and, probably even more important, nonbank financial institutions—made a lot of loans that are likely to go very, very bad.

It's easy to get lost in the details of subprime mortgages, resets, collateralized debt obligations, and so on. But there are two important facts that may give you a sense of just how big the problem is.

First, we had an enormous housing bubble in the middle of this decade. To restore a historically normal ratio of housing prices to rents or incomes, average home prices would have to fall about 30 percent from their current levels.

Second, there was a tremendous amount of borrowing into the bubble, as new home buyers purchased houses with little or no money down, and as people who already owned houses refinanced their mortgages as a way of converting rising home prices into cash.

As home prices come back down to earth, many of these borrowers will find themselves with negative equity—owing more than their houses are worth. Negative equity, in turn, often leads to foreclosures and big losses for lenders.

And the numbers are huge. The financial blog Calculated Risk, using data from First American CoreLogic, estimates that if home prices fall 20 percent there will be 13.7 million homeowners with negative equity. If prices fall 30 percent, that number would rise to more than 20 million.

That translates into a lot of losses, and explains why liquidity has dried up. What's going on in the markets isn't an irrational panic. It's a wholly rational panic, because there's a lot of bad debt out there, and you don't know how much of that bad debt is held by the guy who wants to borrow your money.

How will it all end? Markets won't start functioning normally until investors are reasonably sure that they know where the bodies—I mean, the bad debts—are buried. And that probably won't happen until house prices have finished falling and financial institutions have come clean about all their losses. All of this will probably take years.

Meanwhile, anyone who expects the Fed or anyone else to come up with a plan that makes this financial crisis just go away will be sorely disappointed.

Hedge Funds Come Unstuck
on Truth-Twisting, Lies

MATTHEW LYNN

Bloomberg News, April 9, 2008

H as the hedge-fund industry been built on a series of lies?

For the past decade, its explosive growth has been based on a simple claim: that skilled money managers, motivated by high performance fees, could outperform the market when it was going up— and sidestep the trouble when it was going down.

And yet the credit crunch has shown that to be a myth. Although a few hedge-fund managers have done brilliantly, far more have come unstuck.

Now it looks as if the industry might be based on a more systematic falsehood. Two recent academic studies suggest that hedge funds have been routinely dishonest, or at least economical with the truth.

If that's right, then it is worrying for alternative-asset managers. As the idea gets out that hedge funds can't deliver the kind of guaranteed returns they promised, a lot of money is heading for the door marked exit.

There is no questioning the gloom surrounding a once-booming industry. Almost every day brings news of another fund stumbling. More than a dozen big hedge funds have shut up shop, frozen redemptions or been forced to find outside capital this year as markets turned volatile.

Peloton Partners LLP liquidated its largest fund after making bets on mortgage securities that turned sour, while JWM Partners LLC, run by former Long-Term Capital Management LP chief John Meriwether, was hurt by swings in Japanese government bonds. Overall, hedge funds turned in their worse quarterly performance in six years, according to Chicago-based Hedge Fund Research.

Distorted Returns

Everyone knows that the markets go down as well as up. There isn't any investment that makes money every year. The hedge funds were bound to go through a bad patch. But what if the funds have been distorting the truth?

Veronika Krepely Pool, assistant professor of finance at Indiana University in Bloomington, Indiana, and Nicolas Bollen, associate professor of finance at Vanderbilt University in Nashville, Tennessee, examined how hedge funds reported to their investors over several years. Although the funds often scored a gain of 1 percent a month, they rarely reported a loss of the same amount.

"We estimate that approximately 10 percent of returns in the database we use are distorted," they concluded. "This suggests that misreporting returns is a widespread phenomenon."

Of course, you can understand why that might be happening. It's embarrassing to own up to losing money when you have promised investors you will make a profit. The difference between losing 0.1 percent and making 0.1 percent might not add up to much in money terms. Yet in terms of presentation it can be crucial. You might excuse that as a small lie. The trouble with small lies, however, is that they lead to bigger ones.

"Outright Con Artists"

A report from the Wharton School of the University of Pennsylvania suggests dishonesty on a greater scale. Statistics Professor Dean Foster and Brookings Institution Senior Fellow H. Peyton Young said it is easy for

hedge funds to start up and make money without having any real investment skills.

"It is very hard to set up an incentive structure that rewards skilled
hedge-fund managers without at the same time rewarding unskilled managers and outright con artists," they said in a paper called "The Hedge
Fund Game."

So how is it done? They say you can just replicate an investment strategy devised elsewhere, take big positions, and collect enormous performance fees until the whole thing blows up. By then, you will already have
pocketed plenty of money, and you won't have to pay any of it back if the
fund goes bust.

"It is extremely difficult to detect, from a fund's track record, whether
a manager is actually able to deliver excess returns, is merely lucky, or is
an outright con artist," they said.

Raw Deal

There is nothing about those conclusions that will surprise anyone who
has followed the hedge-fund industry. The deal was that in return for
high fees, which in effect gave the managers a stake in the fund, investors
would get above-average returns.

Yet, it appears many funds have just been relying on a rising market
and sitting back and collecting 20 percent—the typical performance fee
on a hedge fund—of the profits.

The conclusion? The promise on which the industry was built looks to
be largely a false one.

If investors start to question the hedge funds' ability to produce consistently superior returns, they will start to exit the industry in droves—
and rightly so.

The hedge funds need to start tightening up their reporting procedures. Massaging your results to make your performance look better isn't
acceptable.

More important, they need to re-examine their strategies to see if they
are genuinely beating the market—because if they aren't, they should
hand their money back to investors.

Trader Made Billions on Subprime

GREGORY ZUCKERMAN

The Wall Street Journal, *January 15, 2008*

On Wall Street, the losers in the collapse of the housing market are legion. The biggest winner looks to be John Paulson, a little-known hedge fund manager who smelled trouble two years ago.

Funds he runs were up $15 billion in 2007 on a spectacularly success-ful bet against the housing market. Mr. Paulson has reaped an estimated $3 billion to $4 billion for himself—believed to be the largest one-year payday in Wall Street history.

Now, in another twist in financial history, Mr. Paulson is retaining as an adviser a man some blame for helping feed the housing-market bubble by keeping interest rates so low: former Federal Reserve Chairman Alan Greenspan.

On the way to his big score, Mr. Paulson did battle with a Wall Street firm he accused of trying to manipulate the market. He faced skepticism from other big investors. At the same time, fearing imitators, he used software that blocked fund investors from forwarding his emails.

One thing he didn't count on: A friend in whom he had confided tried the strategy on his own—racking up huge gains himself, and straining their friendship.

Like many legendary market killings, from Warren Buffett's takeovers of small companies in the '70s to Wilbur Ross's steelmaker consolidation earlier this decade, Mr. Paulson's sprang from defying conventional wisdom. In early 2006, the wisdom was that while loose lending standards might be of some concern, deep trouble in the housing and mortgage markets was unlikely. A lot of big Wall Street players were in this camp, as seen by the giant mortgage-market losses they're disclosing.

"Most people told us house prices never go down on a national level, and that there had never been a default of an investment-grade-rated mortgage bond," Mr. Paulson says. "Mortgage experts were too caught up" in the housing boom.

In several interviews, Mr. Paulson made his first comments on how he made his historic coup. Merely holding a different opinion from the blundering herd wasn't enough to produce huge profits. He also had to think up a technical way to bet against the housing and mortgage markets, given that, as he notes, "you can't short houses."

Also key: Mr. Paulson didn't turn bearish too early. Some close students of the housing market did just that, investing for a downturn years ago—only to suffer such painful losses waiting for a collapse that they finally unwound their bearish bets. Mr. Paulson, whose investment specialty lay elsewhere, turned his attention to the housing market more recently, and got bearish at just about the right time.

Word of his success got around in the world of hedge funds—investment partnerships for institutions and rich individuals. George Soros invited Mr. Paulson to lunch, asking for details of how he laid his bets, with instruments that didn't exist a few years ago. Mr. Soros is famous for another big score, a 1992 bet against the British pound that earned $1 billion for his Quantum hedge fund. He declined to comment.

Mr. Paulson, who grew up in New York's Queens borough, began his career working for another legendary investor, Leon Levy of Odyssey Partners. Now 51 years old, Mr. Paulson benefited from an earlier housing slump 15 years ago, buying a New York apartment and a large home in the Hamptons on Long Island, both in foreclosure sales.

After Odyssey, Mr. Paulson—no relation to the Treasury secretary—became a mergers-and-acquisitions investment banker at Bear Stearns

Cos. Next he was a mergers arbitrager at Gruss & Co., often betting on bonds to fall in value.

In 1994 he started his own hedge fund, focusing on M&A. Starting with $2 million, he built it to $500 million by 2002 through a combination of its returns and new money from investors. After the post-tech-bubble economic slump, he bought up debt of struggling companies, and profited as the economy recovered. His funds, run out of Manhattan offices decorated with Alexander Calder sculptures, did well but not spectacularly.

Auto Suppliers

By 2005, Mr. Paulson, known as J.P., worried that U.S. economic strength would flag. He began selling short the bonds of companies such as auto suppliers, that is, betting on them to fall in value. Instead, they kept rising, even bonds of companies in bankruptcy proceedings.

"This is crazy," Mr. Paulson recalls telling an analyst at his firm. He urged his traders to find a way to protect his investments and profit if problems developed in the overall economy. The question he posed to them: "Where is the bubble we can short?"

They found it in housing. Upbeat mortgage specialists kept repeating that home prices never fall on a national basis or that the Fed could save the market by slashing interest rates.

One Wall Street specialty during the boom was repackaging mortgage securities into instruments called collateralized debt obligations, or CDOs, then selling slices of these with varying levels of risk.

For buyers of the slices who wanted to insure against the debt going bad, Wall Street offered another instrument, called credit-default swaps.

Naturally, the riskier the debt that such a swap "insured," the more the swap would cost. And this price would go up if default risk appeared to be increasing. This meant an investor of a bearish bent could buy the swaps as a way to bet on bad news happening.

During the boom, however, many were so blind to housing risk that this "default insurance" was priced very cheaply. Analyzing reams of data late at night in his office, Mr. Paulson became convinced investors were far underestimating the risk in the mortgage market. In betting on it to crumble, "I've never been involved in a trade that had such unlimited upside with a very limited downside," he says.

Paulo Pellegrini, a portfolio manager at Paulson & Co., began to implement complex debt trades that would pay off if mortgages lost value. One trade was to short risky CDO slices.

Another was to buy the credit-default swaps that complacent investors seemed to be pricing too low.

"We've got to take as much advantage of this as we can," Mr. Paulson recalls telling a colleague around the middle of 2005, when optimism about the housing market was at its peak.

His bets at first were losers. But lenders were getting less and less rigorous about making sure borrowers could pay their mortgages. Mr. Paulson's research told him home prices were flattening. Suspecting that rating agencies were too generous in assessing complex securities built out of mortgages, he had his team begin tracking tens of thousands of mortgages. They concluded it was getting harder for lenders to collect.

His confidence rose in January 2006. Ameriquest Mortgage Co., then the largest maker of "subprime" loans to buyers with spotty credit, settled a probe of improper lending practices by agreeing to a $325 million payment. The deal convinced Mr. Paulson that aggressive lending was widespread.

He decided to launch a hedge fund solely to bet against risky mortgages. Skeptical investors told him that others with more experience in the field remained upbeat and that he was straying from his area of expertise. Mr. Paulson raised about $150 million for the new fund, largely from European investors. It opened in mid-2006 with Mr. Pellegrini as co-manager.

Adding to the Bet

Housing remained strong, and the fund lost money. A concerned friend called, asking Mr. Paulson if he was going to cut his losses. No, "I'm adding" to the bet, he responded, according to the investor. He told his wife "it's just a matter of waiting," and eased his stress with five-mile runs in Central Park.

"Someone from more of a trading background would have blown the trade out and cut his losses," says Peter Soros, a George Soros relative who invests in the Paulson funds. But "if anything, the losses made him more determined."

Investors had recently gained a new way to bet for or against subprime mortgages. It was the ABX, an index that reflects the value of a basket of subprime mortgages made over six months. An index of those made in the first half of 2006 appeared in July 2006. The Paulson funds sold it short.

The index weakened in the second half. By year end, the new Paulson Credit Opportunities Fund was up about 20%. Mr. Paulson started a second such fund.

On Feb. 7, 2007, a trader ran into his office with a press release: New Century Financial Corp., another big subprime lender, projected a quarterly loss and was restating prior results.

Once-complacent investors now began to worry. The ABX, which had begun with a value of 100 in July 2006, fell into the 60s. The new Paulson funds rose more than 60% in February alone.

But as his gains piled up, Mr. Paulson fretted that his trades might yet go bad. Based on accounts of barroom talk and other chatter by a Bear Stearns trader, he became convinced that Bear Stearns and some other firms planned to try to prop the market for mortgage-backed securities by buying individual mortgages.

Adding to his suspicions, he heard that Bear Stearns had asked an industry group to codify the right of an underwriter to modify or buy out a faltering pool of loans on which a mortgage security was based. Mr. Paulson claimed this would "give cover to market manipulation." He hired former Securities and Exchange Commission Chairman Harvey Pitt to spread the word about this alleged threat.

In the end, Bear Stearns withdrew the proposal. It was merely about clarifying "our right to continue to service loans—whether that be modifying loans when people can't pay their mortgage or buying out loans when rep and warranty issues are involved in the underwriting process," says a Bear Stearns spokesman.

Events at Bear Stearns soon added to the worries: Two Bear Stearns hedge funds that invested in subprime mortgages collapsed in mid-2007. Suddenly, investors began to shun such mortgages.

As Mr. Paulson's funds racked up huge gains, some of his investors began telling others about the funds' tactics. Mr. Paulson was furious, worried that others would steal his thunder. He began using technology that prevented clients from forwarding his emails.

In the fall, the ABX subprime-mortgage index crashed into the 20s. The funds' bet against it paid off richly.

Credit-default swaps that the funds owned soared, as investors' perception of risk neared panic levels and they clamored for this insurance.

And the debt slices the funds had bet would lose value, indeed fell—to nearly worthless.

Debt Protection

One concern was that even if Mr. Paulson bet right, he would find it hard to cash out his bets because many were in markets with limited trading. This hasn't been a problem, however, thanks to the wrong bet of some big banks and Wall Street firms. To hedge their holdings of mortgage securities, they've scrambled to buy debt protection, which sometimes means buying what Mr. Paulson already held.

The upshot: The older Paulson credit funds rose 590% last year and the newer one 350%.

Mr. Paulson has tried to keep a low profile, saying he's reluctant to celebrate while housing causes others pain. He has told friends he'll increase his charitable giving. In October, he gave $15 million to the Center for Responsible Lending to fund legal assistance to families facing foreclosure. The center lobbies for a law that would let bankruptcy judges restructure some mortgages.

Helping Homeowners

"While we never made a subprime loan and are not predatory lenders, we think a lot of homeowners have been victimized," Mr. Paulson says. "Bankruptcy is the best way to keep homeowners in the home without costing the government any money."

The bill, besides helping borrowers, could help the Paulson funds' bearish mortgage bets. If the result was that judges lowered monthly payments on some mortgages, their market value could fall. Mr. Paulson says it's far from certain his funds would benefit. The center says that none of the $15 million will be used to lobby.

Mr. Paulson, who was already worth over $100 million before his windfall, isn't changing his routine much. He still gets to his Manhattan office early—wearing a dark suit and a tie, unlike many hedge-fund operators—and leaves around 6 P.M. for the short commute to his East Side townhouse.

One thing is different: It's easy to attract investors now. The firm began 2007 managing $7 billion. Investors have poured in $6 billion more in just the past year. That plus the 2007 investment gains have boosted the total his fund firm manages to $28 billion, making it one of the world's largest.

Mr. Paulson has taken profits on some, but not most, of his bets. He remains a bear on housing, predicting it will take years for home prices to recover. He's also betting against other parts of the economy, such as credit-card and auto loans. He tells investors "it's still not too late" to bet on economic troubles.

At the same time, he's looking to the next turn in the cycle. In a recent investor presentation, he said his firm would at some point "start preparing" for opportunities in troubled debt.

ACKNOWLEDGMENTS

When Dave Eggers and I first discussed the idea for this book, he offered up a creature I'd never met, known as "the *McSweeney's* Intern." This character lives a life alien to most human beings in the twenty-first century, though he is faintly reminiscent of the wandering scholar of the Middle Ages. He is well educated, but ill-paid. He bathes rarely, and haphazardly. He sleeps all day and works all night. He subsists mainly on water, the occasional slice of bread, and the love of literature. Even so, he is astonishingly effective.

All the proceeds from this anthology go to 826 National and a fund inside the Greater New Orleans Foundation dedicated to the rebuilding of that city. All the people who worked on it, including me, donated their time and energy, and so the book has no doubt left a lot of people—including me—yearning to be thanked. Naturally, I begin by thanking myself; but as I do I look around and see an army of *McSweeney's* interns and staff who deserve to be thanked even more. Five people in particular had a lot to do with how the book turned out, but don't have the pleasure of seeing their names in giant letters on the cover: Chris Benz, Darren

Franich, Chris Lindgren, Sharareh Lofti, and Nicole Pfaff. These people searched long and hard in archives for the material included here, and about ten times more of it that wound up on the cutting room floor. All five helped me to come to an understanding of financial chaos, and Benz went one step further, and did the lay reader the great favor of writing the glossary of financial terms at the back of the book. At *McSweeney's* Michelle Quint coordinated the gathering of rights. She was helped by David Aloi, Peter Mack, Michael Zelenko, M. Rebekah Otto, Candice Chan, and Claire Donato.

Finally, I would like to thank the writers who allowed us to include their work in this book. They can't be repaid but they deserve to be reread.

GLOSSARY

Chris Benz

2/28 Loans. Loans lasting 2 years at a low fixed rate and 28 years at an adjustable rate.

ABS. See *asset backed securities*.

ARM. See *adjustable rate mortgage*.

Adjustable Rate Mortgage (ARM). A loan at which the payments begin at a low "teaser rate" and then jump up later, usually after two years. See *2/28 loan*.

Appropriation Risk. Investing on the assumption that government policies will stay consistent—for example, that congress will not cut subsidies on solar power, so it is safe to invest in solar panels.

Arbitrage. The simultaneous trading of identical, or very similar, goods at different prices.

Asset. A tangible thing, worth money, that a person owns. For instance, a house.

Asset Backed Securities (ABS). Financial products backed by assets. Many mortgages were securitized into ABSs, then sold on the markets.

Bear. A falling market, or a person who predicts one.

Black-Scholes. A complex mathematical model that attempts to identify the correct pricing of options. It led to the idea of *portfolio insurance*. The model assumes many preconditions to be true, including that options have a correct price. It also assumes European options. Traders still use it to help make estimates. See *option*.

Bloomberg Terminal. A type of computer terminal that provides information about markets. Companies obtain them by subscription.

Blue-chip Stocks. Stocks of highly reputable, reliable, large corporations.

Borrow Short, Lend Long. A typical bank strategy. They borrow short-term from other banks, ideally at something near the *fed funds rate*. Then, they loan long-term to investors at a higher rate. The difference between these rates is called a margin. A typical margin is 4 percent. For example, a bank could borrow at 4 percent short and lend at 8 percent long. When the Fed purchases enough securities (creating money) to lower the fed funds rates, banks get higher profits. For example, they borrow at 3 percent and earn back 8 percent. The idea is that soon, someone cuts in and says he's willing to take a 4 percent margin and offers a 7 percent home loan. Competition lowers rates, encouraging entrepreneurs to purchase capital improvements and consumers to get home loans.

Brady Commission. A presidential commission set up to investigate the 1987 crash. It concluded that there were a lot reasons for the crash. One of these was portfolio insurance.

Bull. A strong market, or a person who believes in one.

Call. A type of options contract granting the right to buy shares of a stock at a certain price. To purchase a call is typically a hedge against a price jump. See *option*.

Capital. Wealth that improves the ability to produce more wealth: a new factory, or a forklift, is an investment in capital. Cash is capital. Low interest rates encourage entrepreneurs to borrow money, and, they hope, to invest in capital improvements. For example, low interest rates in the '00s may have enabled a building spree among competing colleges.

Capital Market Liberalization. A controversial aspect of globalization, capital market liberalization is the policy of opening up markets to rapid movement of foreign capital. It is a strategy advocated by market fundamentalists, notably the IMF. In Southeast Asia in 1997, capital market liberalization allowed speculative "hot capital" to enter countries and compound into a bubble. Speculators could also withdraw capital quickly.

CDO (Collateralized Debt Obligation). A CDO is a bundle of debt you can buy. In the sense of loans, it works like this: An underwriter, or investment bank, buys many loans, and pools together everyone's first few payments, then their next few payments, and calls these tranches. Each tranche is sliced up and sold as CDOs, and each tranche carries an increasing degree of risk. The highest quality rated tranches get the first dibs on payment from the loan pools. However, because they are less risky, the interest rates they earn are not as high as those for tranches that are later in line.

Think of it as one of those tiered chocolate fondue fountains that's shaped like upright, stacked satellite dishes. The top bowl has to overflow to fall into the next bowl. If the chocolate stops running (think default, early repayment), the first cup gets filled with what's still in the system, and maybe some of the second tier, but people at the bottom, who otherwise would have had the most chocolate, are instead stuck there holding their toothpicks and wishing they'd just ordered the cheesecake.

Commercial Paper. Short-term corporate debt. It helps corporations run operations from month to month, if a lot of money is tied up in capital.

Confirmer. A speculator who buys and then sells before her first mortgage payment.

Credit. The potential to receive loans; or, the faith of another.

Credit Crunch. When no one has good credit, lending standards increase and lenders hold onto their cash. They hope to increase their own liquidity instead of lending it out.

Default. To throw up your hands and say you can't or won't repay a bond. To default on a national debt is a rather destabilizing act for the world economy. Mexico defaulted on its debt in 1982, and in the aftermath, some Latin American dictatorships, like Pinochet's in Argentina, collapsed. Russia defaulted in 1997, some say due to speculative attacks on its currency.

Derivatives. Contracts that derive value from that of an underlying investment. The contracts may be traded. Options, Futures, and CDOs are examples of derivatives. In the 1987 crash, derivatives tied to the performance of the stock market fell rapidly, and media coverage focused on them as a potential explanation for the crash.

Downgrade. When a ratings agency lowers the rating of a bond.

Discount Window. Not a real window. The imaginary place where the Fed loans money to real banks as lender of last resort at a low rate. A loan at the discount window is considered an emergency move. When Northern Rock went to the British version of the discount window, media coverage (exacerbated by politicians looking for a poster-child for financial neglect) led people to make a run on the bank.

Equity. Ownership, more or less. A corporate stock is an equity. The amount of a house that you own is equity. When you pay a mortgage payment, your equity increases. When the price of the house increases, your equity increases. The formula for determining equity is this: value of asset – amount of money still owed on the asset = equity.

Equity Stripping. A common scam in which a scammer convinces a victim to sign over the title to her house, takes equity, or money that has already been paid, and then lets the house foreclose with the victim as a renter.

Exchange Controls. Restrictions on the exchange rate, such as pegging and restrictions on how much currency may be imported. See *tight money policy*.

Exchange Traded Fund (ETF). A fund, similar to a mutual fund, that tracks the performance of an index. The SPDR, for example, tracks the S&P 500. It was the first ETF, and appeared in 1993.

Fannie Mae and Freddie Mac. These lenders, operating with a government guarantee, focus exclusively on mortgage loans.

Fed Funds Rate. The rate at which banks lend to each other. The Fed's *target rate* hopes to set this.

Fiscal Policy. A government's spending and taxing, as opposed to *monetary policy*. The President and Congress determine fiscal policy. It can complement or conflict with the effects of monetary policy.

Floating Rate Notes. A type of bond with an interest rate that adjusts periodically.

Futures. A contract to trade a commodity at a set price on a set date—for example, to purchase 100 bushels of wheat from the September harvest at $10 a bushel on September 10, or to purchase 100 Eurodollars at 64 cents each on January 1. These contracts are then traded. Futures contracts allow hedging, so a baker drawing up a budget can hedge against a global oil shortage, lifting the price of wheat, for example.

Currency and even the performance of a market index can all be contractualized into futures.

Rather than pay for the goods at signing, futures contracts require a 5 to 15 percent "good faith deposit," or *margin*. This allows heavy *leverage*. During the 1987 panic on the Chicago Mercantile Exchange, this caused serious havoc, when leveraged investors, hoping to cut losses, rushed to sell futures contracts. A futures buyer is called the long; a seller is called the short. Futures are a *zero sum market*.

Globalization. The expansion of markets to encourage global trade. This topic deserves a small library of its own.

Greenspan Put. A "put" protects an asset in case of a crash. The Greenspan Put is the assumption, widely held, that if asset prices dive, the Fed will lower interest rates and prevent them from falling below a certain level.

Hedge Fund. An invitation-only fund that invests people's money for them and receives a performance fee. By being somewhat exclusive in choosing investors, hedge funds do not fall under existing classifications, so they are free to implement riskier investment strategies than mutual funds. Standard & Poor's estimated in 2005 that there were 8,000 hedge funds with combined portfolios of $1 trillion. At the same time, they estimated that there are between 7,000 and 8,000 open-ended mutual funds with a combined control over $8 trillion.

Index. Assets bound together by math magic so that they reflect the market as a whole.

Index Arbitrage. A type of arbitrage that exploits the price difference between index futures and the underlying stocks.

Index Futures. Futures contracts pegged to the value of market indexes, such as the S&P 500, the Dow Jones Industrial Average, or the Morgan Stanley Biotech Index. Traders use index futures to hedge their portfolios.

Individual Investors. Investors, rarely professionals, who invest independently. Individual investors, as opposed to institutional investors, tend to comprise a smaller segment of American market activity.

Inflation, Core. Inflation of the less volatile goods—not food or oil.

Inflation, Headline. Inflation of all goods.

Institutional Investors. Organizations (like mutual funds) that invest for themselves or for clients. Institutional investors tend to invest in high volume, and comprise the bulk of American market activity.

International Monetary Fund (IMF). An international organization meant to strengthen developing economies by offering policy advice ("technical assistance"), loans, and monitoring of a nation's economy. Its goal is especially to prevent "sudden, unpredictable" changes in exchange rates, in which countries harm one another. It regularly advises free exchange of currency, rather than *exchange controls*. The IMF's advice to developing countries in the 1997 Asian financial crisis, to maintain high interest rates and a minimum of market regulation, later drew criticism. It is not the *World Bank*.

The Invisible Hand. A metaphor first introduced by Adam Smith in his 1776 seminal economics text, *Wealth of Nations*. The invisible hand of the market is more or less the organizing force of individual desires. The idea is that markets manage themselves somewhat efficiently: If the price of tobacco is relatively high, more people will grow tobacco instead of wheat, thus increasing the supply of tobacco, thus lowering the scarcity of the product, thus lowering the price of tobacco. The invisible hand, like any concept, is used to justify all sorts of choices of which its creator would have never approved.

IMF. See *International Monetary Fund.*

Jumbo Mortgage. A mortgage that provides more money than standard limits set by Fannie and Freddie.

Junk Bond. A bond, or piece of debt for sale, with the lowest possible rating, "junk." Junk bonds tend to pay high yields to make up for the shaky likelihood that they will be repaid. In the 1980s, the arbitrage of junk bonds in high volume accounted for a great deal of profit, especially by Salomon Brothers and Drexel.

Leverage. The use of debt to finance a financial operation. JP Morgan, Lehman Brothers, and the like are leveraged corporations. Leverage amplifies both gains and losses.

Liar Loans. A loan made to a borrower who is encouraged to lie about his income, thus making it easier for the lender to justify his actions. See *ninja loan*.

LIBOR. See *London Interbank Offered Rate*.

Liquidity. Value that can transfer quickly—cash, for example. In seconds, a bank account can transfer its value to someone else. A house cannot.

London Interbank Offered Rate (LIBOR). Like the Fed funds rate, LIBOR is an interest rate charged by banks for short-term loans to each other. Many adjustable mortgages tie their rates to this.

Long Position. The position one is in if one owns a security. Also, buying a commodity through a futures contract. See *futures*.

Louvre Currency Accord. A February 1987 agreement by leaders of the G-7 industrialized nations to try to halt the declining value of the dollar.

Margin. The minimum downpayment a person must make to buy a security. A person trading on margin is essentially taking a loan and hoping that the stock will rise enough to pay the loan off. Such investors are said to be *leveraged*. Leverage is a risk-intensive way to amplify gains (and losses.) Hedge funds are notorious for heavy leverage. In any market panic, someone leveraged loses his shirt. See *futures*.

Margin Call. When an authority demands that people trading on the margin pay up. Also called margin maintenance, it doesn't mean they pay everything, just that they've paid the minimum required percentage. For example, futures contracts require a 10 percent deposit. As the value of the contract fluctuates, the contract holder's debt fluctuates. A margin call requires her to make sure she has paid 10 percent of her new debt.

Market Capitalization. A measure of the total value of a company or economy. Market capitalization is the price of all the shares of a company. Investors use this measure when gauging the size of a business in which they invest, as well as the strength of a particular economy. The math formula: number of shares in existence x price of share = market cap.

Market Specialists. The voice of the invisible hand, a market specialist has the power to change the bid-ask price of a specific stock to encourage a balance between buyers and sellers. Each specialist is responsible for one stock. This removes any *order imbalance*. The specialist must buy the excess inventory if an imbalance remains. In the 1987 crash, automated computer trading led to severe order imbalances, clearly a serious financial conflict for specialists. They were later accused of failing to discharge their duty as "buyers of last resort."

Monetary Policy. The trading of government securities to change the supply of money, as opposed to *fiscal policy*. The Fed determines monetary policy in America, the European Central Bank in Europe. When someone says "central bankers" they mean people who set monetary policy, like Alan Greenspan and Mervyn King of the Bank of England. Monetary policy can complement or conflict with fiscal policy. The central bank in the United States, which guides monetary policy independent of lawmakers, was established to control inflation.

Money Market. The market for short-term debt, like commercial paper, and some bonds. Money markets trade freely and often.

Money Market Fund. A mutual fund that law requires to invest in low-risk securities.

Moral Hazard. In context, usually: taking greater risks with money than you otherwise would because you assume, if things go wrong, the government will bail you out. Many people oppose government intervention in troubled markets because bailouts encourage moral hazard.

Mutual Fund. A fund that pools the money of many investors to create a diversified investment portfolio. An investor owns shares of a mutual fund, not shares of its stocks.

M-LEC (Master-Liquidity Enhancement Conduit). A $100 billion buyer of last resort for SIVs, set up by Citigroup, JPMorgan Chase, and Bank of America. The deal did not end up going through.

Negative Equity. Owing more money on a loan than a house would sell for. This happens to some people who bought at the height of the real estate boom. A person with negative equity is likely to default, having little incentive to continue to overpay for a house.

Nominal Interest Rates. Interest rates that do not account for inflation.

Ninja Loans. No income, no job, no assets, and getting a loan anyway.

Northern Rock. A bank in northern England with heavy subprime exposure that failed after a bank run. The Bank of England, after promising not to intervene (and encourage moral hazard), guaranteed Northern Rock's deposits. Northern Rock's troubles became very public after they got a loan from the lender of last resort. The British government ended up owning the joint.

Option. A contract giving the buyer the option to trade a stock at a set price before an expiration date. Options are often used to hedge against market failure: that is, if the stock falls, an investor can resell it at a high price to cut losses, or even hold a minor profit. A put is an option to sell. A call is an option to buy.

Options are derivatives. Investors can trade options, and do. "European Options" only allow the option to buy or sell on a set date, while "American Options" may be traded at any time before the expiration date.

Order Imbalance. When there are vastly more sell orders than buy orders for a certain security (or, hypothetically, vice versa). During an order imbalance, a market specialist may suspend trading for the security in question. Specialists are in charge of setting opening and closing prices to balance the number of buyers and sellers, and must buy the excess if they fail.

Perma-Bears. Those who believe that the U.S. economy as a whole is a bubble, supported by cheap credit and unsustainable risks.

Phillips Curve. The economic theory, now considered overly simplistic, that suggests an inverse relationship between inflation and unemployment: that is, low unemployment leads to high inflation, because labor is relatively cheap (being paid in less valuable money), while low inflation leads to high unemployment. The Phillips curve fails to describe the relationship accurately enough, as "stagflation" in the 1970s and low-inflation growth in the 1990s demonstrated.

Pit. The physical place on an exchange where traders trade.

Portfolio Insurance. An idea based on the Black-Scholes pricing model, which suggested that an investor could hedge against losses with the rapid short selling of index futures. However, when massive numbers of investors programmed computers to do exactly this, they all sold at once, helping to drive prices very low.

Price to Earnings Ratio. The ratio between the price of a stock and the yearly earnings it pays in dividends. If a stock pays for itself in ten years ($60 a share, $6 a share yearly dividend) its price to earnings ratio is 10. This is one of the main indicators investors look at when deciding whether to purchase a stock.

Put. A type of options contract granting the right to sell shares of a stock at a certain price. See *option*.

Quant. Quantitative analyst. A quant translates the intangible world into numbers, creating things like risk analysis models and mathematics-based investment strategies. Some institutional investors rely more heavily on quants than others, and some quants have proven more profitable than others.

Rationality. An assumption of economic theory. Economics assumes that people in a market will act in their own self-interest, rationally. Like all models, economics is an incomplete science.

Real Interest Rates. Interest rates that factor in the rate of inflation, as opposed to nominal interest rates.

Sarbanes-Oxley Act of 2002. Legislation that attempted to create more transparency and responsibility in corporate accounting. It is not entirely popular with bankers.

Security. 1. A debt that can be traded. U.S. national debt, for instance, is mostly in bonds (securities) that can trade on an open market. 2. A stock, or rights to ownership, like an option.

Shadow Market. The market in Chicago for index futures, which are futures contracts that promise cash deliveries based on the performance of market indexes. Many participants in the shadow market in 1987 were highly leveraged, and attempting to hedge their portfolios according the concept of "portfolio insurance." These highly leveraged investors had programmed the DOT computer system to automatically sell index futures short in case their portfolios fell. When the market crashed in 1987, the shadow market, understandably, crashed hard.

Short Position. Selling a commodity through a futures contract. See *futures*. Can also refer to the position one is in while shorting stock.

S&P. Standard & Poor's. A business that rates stocks and creates indexes.

S&P 500. An index of the 500 largest stocks in the market.

SIV. See *structured investment vehicle*.

Stock. A share of ownership in a business.

Subprime. Worse than prime. A prime borrower has credit to receive good "prime" rates. A subprime borrower has unreliable credit, and must get a "subprime loan" with very high interest rates.

Structured Investment Vehicle (SIV). An SIV is an entity that sells short-term commercial paper and medium-term notes to banks at a high yield. In other words, it makes very high-risk loans. Banks usually set up and manage SIVs, but do not have to mark it on their balance sheet, because SIVs have offshore balance sheets.

Target Rate. The rate established by the Federal Open Market Committee. The target rate is the Fed funds rate the FMOC would like to see. They control it through the supply of bonds that Fed branches trade. After the 2007 credit crunch, the Fed had a hard time getting banks to loan at the target rate.

Teaser Rate. The early rate of an adjustable rate mortgage, meant to convince someone to get the loan.

Tight Money Policy. A form of *monetary policy* in which a central bank raises interest rates to decrease the supply of money, reducing spending in an overheated economy. A tight money policy helps to raise the value of a currency in relation to other currencies.

Tranche. A section of a CDO, or of another syndicated asset or loan.

Underwriter. A person who accepts the risk for a venture in exchange for some of its profit. This term originated with sea voyages in the distant past.

Venture Capitalist. A type of investor who raises money, researches new business models, and invests the money in new enterprises, particularly Internet-related ones.

Wealth Effect. The propensity for people who feel like they have money to spend more. Owning a house, or part of one, makes people feel wealthy. Because more Americans own homes than stocks, a decrease in home prices causes a greater decrease in American spending than a decrease in the stock market.

World Bank. International Bank for Reconstruction and Development. The World Bank funds reconstruction in developing nations. It is not the *IMF*. Few people can tell the difference.

Write Down. Reducing the value of an asset on the books.

Zero Sum Market. A market in which any money made is money another person has lost.

CONTRIBUTORS' BIOGRAPHIES

Reed Abelson writes for the *New York Times* on health care and the economy.

The American Enterprise Institute for Public Policy Research is a private, nonpartisan, not-for-profit institution dedicated to research and education on issues of government, politics, economics, and social welfare. Founded in 1943, AEI is home to some of America's most accomplished public policy experts— from economics, law, political science, defense and foreign policy studies, ethics, theology, medicine, and other fields. The institute sponsors research and conferences and publishes books, monographs, and periodicals. AEI's purposes are to defend the principles and improve the institutions of American freedom and democratic capitalism—limited government, private enterprise, individual liberty and responsibility, vigilant and effective defense and foreign policies, political accountability, and open debate.

Dave Barry is an author and Pulitzer Prize–winning humorist whose column in the *Miami Herald* was nationally syndicated from 1983 to 1985. He is the author of many books, his latest being *Dave Barry's History of the Millennium (So Far)*.

Keith Bradsher was the Detroit bureau chief of the *New York Times* from 1996 to 2001. He won the George Polk Award and was a finalist for the Pulitzer Prize. A *Times* reporter since 1989, he is the paper's Hong Kong bureau chief.

Wayne Arnold is Singapore, Heather Timmons in New Delhi, and Choe Sang-Hun in Seoul contributed reporting to Bradsher's article.

Rebecca Buckman is a special writer in the San Francisco bureau of the *Wall Street Journal*, where she currently covers the venture-capital industry and area start-up companies. Prior to joining Dow Jones, she worked as a general assignment and education reporter for the *Indianapolis Star and News* from mid-1992 to April 1996.

John Cassidy is a staff writer at *The New Yorker* and a contributing editor at Condé Nast *Portfolio*. He is also the author of *Dot.con: The Greatest Story Ever Sold*.

Choe Sang-Hun joined the *International Herald Tribune* as its Korea correspondent in 2005 after working for the Associated Press for eleven years. Coauthor of two books, Choe is a member of the AP team that won the 2000 Pulitzer investigative journalism award. He lives in Seoul.

Sen. Christopher Dodd is a senior Democrat from Connecticut in the United States Senate and chairman of the Senate Banking Committee.

Franklin Edwards is a professor of finance and economics at the Graduate School of Business at Columbia University and holds the Arthur F. Burns Chair in Free and Competitive Enterprise at Columbia. He holds a PhD in economics from Harvard University and a JD from New York University Law School. He is the author of *The New Finance: Regulation and Financial Stability* (1996) and a textbook, *Futures and Options* (1992). In addition, he has authored more than a hundred professional articles dealing with financial institutions, hedge funds, corporate governance, derivatives markets, energy markets, and financial regulation.

Frontline began in 1983 as "the last best hope for broadcast documentaries." Confronting complex stories of the human experience in a comprehensive and captivating manner, *Frontline* reports on such varied subjects as Abu Ghraib and the O. J. Simpson trial.

CONTRIBUTORS' BIOGRAPHIES

Mark Gimein has written for *New York Magazine, BusinessWeek,* and the *New York Times* on subjects ranging from hedge funds to malpractice lawsuits to the advertising business. Before that, he was a senior writer at *Fortune,* where he did investigative stories and profiles of major public figures.

Matthew Goldstein is an associate editor with *BusinessWeek* who specializes in covering hedge funds and Wall Street investment banks. He was the Wall Street editor for TheStreet.com. His other journalism jobs include reporting positions with SmartMoney.com, *Crain's New York Business,* the *New York Law Journal,* and several daily newspapers in New Jersey. He also is a nonpracticing attorney. In 2006, Goldstein was a finalist for the Gerald Loeb financial journalism award.

Peter S. Goodman has been a national economic writer for the *New York Times* business section since October 2007. Previously, he was the Shanghai-based Asian economic correspondent for the *Washington Post,* where he spent a decade. Goodman graduated from Reed College in 1989 and later earned an MA in Asian Studies at the University of California, Berkeley. He began his journalism career as a freelance writer in Southeast Asia and served as a metro reporter at the *Anchorage Daily News* in Alaska. Goodman shared in the 2005 Jesse Laventhol Prize for deadline reporting conferred by the American Society of Newspaper Editors for the *Post's* coverage of the Indian Ocean tsunami. He received a Citation for Excellence from the Overseas Press Club for stories from China about the tensions generated by market-embracing reforms. He was awarded the Hugo Shong Prize for best coverage from Asia for the year from Boston University's School of Journalism for a 2004 series on China's growing appetite for energy. He lives in Prospect Heights, Brooklyn.

David Henry is a senior writer in the finance section of *BusinessWeek.* Henry came to *BusinessWeek* in 2001 from *USA Today,* where he was the Wall Street columnist. He has worked at *Newsday, Forbes,* the *Jackson Sun,* and the *Nashville Banner.* In 2002, Henry won a Gerald Loeb Award and a World Leadership Forum Business Journalist of the Year award for stories on corporate accounting. He holds a bachelor's degree in journalism from Northwestern University.

John Hechinger is a senior special writer covering education in the Boston bureau of the *Wall Street Journal.* He wrote the Heard in New England stock market column included in the New England edition of the *Journal.*

David Holley writes for the *Los Angeles Times.*

Robert Julavits has held the position of West Coast deputy markets editor for *American Banker* and is a spokesperson for CitiGroup.

Kate Kelly is a New York–based staff writer for the *Wall Street Journal's* Money & Investing section, where she covers the New York Stock Exchange, the Nasdaq Stock Market, the American Stock Exchange, and trading firms. Prior to joining the *Wall Street Journal* in January 2001, Kelly was a writer and reporter for *Time* magazine, where she covered business, society news, and politics, including the presidential vote recount. She also worked as a reporter for the *New York Observer* from 1997 to 2000.

Stephen Koepp became deputy managing editor of *Time* magazine in January 2001. He received his BA in journalism from the University of Wisconsin–Eau Claire before joining the staff of *Time*, where he wrote mainly for the business section. He cowrote a feature film, *The Paper*, with his brother David in 1994.

Paul Krugman joined the *New York Times* in 1999 as a columnist on the op-ed page and is professor of economics and international affairs at Princeton University. Krugman received his BA from Yale University in 1974 and his PhD from MIT in 1977. He has taught at Yale, MIT, and Stanford. At MIT he became the Ford International Professor of Economics. Krugman is the author or editor of 20 books and more than 200 papers in professional journals and edited volumes. His professional reputation rests largely on work in international trade and finance; he is one of the founders of the "new trade theory," a major rethinking of the theory of international trade.

Stephen Labaton is a *New York Times* correspondent in Washington. He received a master's degree in philosophy and a law degree from Duke University.

Roger Lowenstein reported for the *Wall Street Journal* for over a decade and has authored a number of books, including *Origins of the Crash: The Great Bubble and Its Undoing* and *Crashes, Booms, Panics, and Government Regulation*. He is also a director of Sequoia Fund.

Aaron Lucchetti reports on exchanges and trading issues in stocks, bonds, and derivatives. From 2003 to 2005, he was responsible for coverage of credit markets. From 1996 to 2003, he covered a variety of finance and Wall Street beats for the *Wall Street Journal* in New York and Chicago, including mutual funds, small stocks, and commodities.

Karen Lundegaard worked as a reporter for the *Wall Street Journal* for eight and a half years. She is employed by the *Star Tribune* in Minneapolis as an assistant business editor.

Matthew Lynn is a columnist for Bloomberg News.

Scott McMurray is a former senior writer for the *Wall Street Journal* who specializes in corporate histories as well as business, technology, and finance feature writing. He has contributed to several publications focusing on business, technology, and financial issues, including *Business 2.0*, *Institutional Investor*, *Chicago*, *U.S. News & World Report*, *Crain's Chicago Business* and the *Wall Street Journal Small Business Report*.

Richard Meislin is the editor of news surveys and election analysis for the *New York Times*. He has also written about technology and electronics for the publication.

Tim Metz is author of *Black Monday: The Catastrophe of October 19, 1987 . . . and Beyond*.

Katherine Mieszkowski is a senior writer for Salon.com, where she writes about technology, business, and the environment. Mieszkowski has also contributed to *Ms.*, *All Things Considered*, *Slate*, *Reader's Digest*, the *San Francisco Chronicle*, and the *Financial Times*.

Carrick Mollenkamp is a reporter in the Atlanta bureau of the *Wall Street Journal* covering financial institutions. Mollenkamp joined the *Journal* in November 1997. He has worked for the *Marietta Daily Journal* (Ga.), the *Triangle Business Journal* in Raleigh, N.C., the *Raleigh News & Observer* (N.C.), and Bloomberg News. He is coauthor of *The People v. Big Tobacco*, a book about tobacco litigation.

Larry Roberts contributes to the Irvine Housing Blog, focused on real estate topics pertaining to the city of Irvine, California.

Robert L. Rose was an editor and writer for the *Wall Street Journal* until 2004, when he left to write for the *Philadelphia Inquirer.*

Erick Schonfeld is the coeditor of TechCrunch. He previously served as contributing editor at *Fortune* and ran the Next Net blog for *Business 2.0*.

Robert J. Shiller is the Stanley B. Resor Professor of Economics, Department of Economics and Cowles Foundation for Research in Economics, Yale University, and Professor of Finance and Fellow at the International Center for Finance, Yale School of Management. He received his BA from the University of Michigan in 1967 and his PhD in economics from the Massachusetts Institute of Technology in 1972. He has written on financial markets, financial innovation, behavioral economics, macroeconomics, real estate, statistical methods, and on public attitudes, opinions, and moral judgments regarding markets. He has been a research associate at the National Bureau of Economic Research since 1980.

Joseph Stiglitz was a member of the Council of Economic Advisers from 1993 to 1995, during the Clinton administration, and served as CEA chairman from 1995 to 1997. He then became chief economist and senior vice president of the World Bank from 1997 to 2000. He founded one of the leading economics journals, *The Journal of Economic Perspectives*, and has published a number of books. He coauthored *The Three Trillion Dollar War: The True Cost of the Iraq Conflict* with Linda Bilmes of Harvard University.

James Surowiecki is a staff writer at *The New Yorker*, where he writes the business column "The Financial Page." His work has appeared in a wide range of publications, including the *New York Times*, the *Wall Street Journal*, *Artforum*, *Wired*, and *Slate*. He is the author *The Wisdom of Crowds*.

Terri Thompson became director of the Knight-Bagehot Fellowship in Economics and Business Journalism at Columbia Graduate School of Journalism in 1993. In her twenty years as a business journalist, she has reported, written and/or edited for the *Coralville* (Iowa) *Courier, Purchasing Magazine, BusinessWeek, Institutional Investor, U.S. News & World Report,* and *Lear's*. A graduate of New York University and Columbia Graduate School of Journalism, and a 1981 Bagehot Fellow at Columbia, she is the author of *Biz Kids' Guide to Success: Money-Making Ideas for Young Entrepreneurs* and editor of *Writing About Business: The New Columbia Knight-Bagehot Guide to Economics and Business Journalism*.

Lester C. Thurow has been a professor of management and economics at MIT since 1968. He was dean of the MIT Sloan School of Management from 1987 until 1993. A 1960 graduate of Williams College, Thurow received his MA in 1962 on a Rhodes Scholarship at Balliol College (Oxford) and his PhD in economics from Harvard University in 1964. A prolific writer, Thurow is the author of several books, three of them New York Times best sellers, aimed at a general audience.

In the past, Thurow has served on the editorial board of the *New York Times*, as a contributing editor for *Newsweek*, and as a member of *Time* magazine's Board of Economists. He is a fellow of the American Academy of Arts and Sciences and served as vice president of the American Economics Association in 1993.

Jerry Useem is a senior writer at *Fortune* magazine, where he writes about general management and corporate enterprise. His writing has also appeared in such publications as the *Boston Globe*, *Wired*, *The American Prospect*, and *Business 2.0*, while his commentaries have been heard on National Public Radio.

Eric J. Weiner is a freelance journalist and the author of *What Goes Up: The Uncensored History of Modern Wall Street as told by the Bankers, Brokers, CEOs and Scoundrels Who Made It Happen*, which was named one of the best books of 2005 by *Barron's* and *Kiplinger's* magazines. A former columnist and Wall Street reporter for Dow Jones, he has written for numerous publications, including the *Wall Street Journal*, the *Los Angeles Times*, the *Boston Globe*, the *New York Post*, and the *Village Voice*. He spent two years as a communications aide to former New Jersey Governor Jim Florio. He lives in Great Barrington, Massachusetts, with his wife, Paige, and their golden retriever, Annie.

Jack Willoughby is senior editor for *Barron's*, the Dow Jones financial weekly.

Gregory Zuckerman is a special writer at the *Wall Street Journal*. He writes about hedge funds and writes the Heard on the Street column. He also writes about other investing and Wall Street–related topics and has covered the bond market for the *Journal*. Zuckerman appears on CNBC-TV twice a week to discuss hedge funds and stocks. He is part of a team that was nominated for the 2008 Gerald Loeb Award for coverage of the mortgage crisis and was part of a team that won the 2007 Gerald Loeb Award for breaking news coverage of the collapse of the hedge fund Amaranth Advisors. He also was part of a team that won the 2003 Gerald Loeb Award for breaking news coverage of the demise of World-Com. He joined the paper in 1996 after writing about media companies for the *New York Post*. Previously, he was the managing editor of *Mergers & Acquisitions Report*, a newsletter published by Investment Dealers' Digest. He graduated from Brandeis University magna cum laude in 1988.

Laurence Zuckerman is a journalist who reports on aviation and aerospace, among other subjects, for the *New York Times*.

CREDITS